NORTHERN CALIFORNIA WINE COUNTRY ACCESS®

W9-CPV-446

Orientation

Many people, even some San Franciscans, don't realize how close the wine country is to the City by the Bay. The town of **Sonoma**, where California's wine-making history began in the mid-19th century, is only about an hour's drive away, and the entire county is close enough for an easy day trip. **St. Helena** and the heart of **Napa Valley** are less than 1.5 hours from San Francisco by car, and if the traffic gods smile upon you, you may make it from one end of the valley to the other in about a half hour. Not that you should—there's so much to see and do along the way. The wine country of **Mendocino** and **Lake Counties** lies farther to the north—about a 2.5- to 3-hour drive from San Francisco. While you're visiting wineries in Sonoma and **Mendocino**, plan on taking time to explore the nearby coast, which is rugged, sparsely populated, and extraordinarily beautiful.

You'll need a car to visit the wineries; no bus will take you around, unless you're with an organized tour. Once you're in the wine country, it's easy to get around and almost impossible to get lost, except when searching for small wineries off the beaten track or for those that require an appointment and don't have a sign out front.

When planning a trip, remember that this region, especially Napa Valley, is one of the most popular destinations in California. The best time to visit is off-season (November through May), although it's exciting to see the grape crush (generally in September), when the normally serene landscape is animated with grape pickers moving along the vineyard rows, and the streets are lined with trucks loaded with grapes.

During the peak season and on weekends, most hotels and bed-and-breakfast inns require a minimum two-night stay. Be sure to reserve as early as possible; lodging is limited and can be extremely hard to find on holidays and summer weekends. For help finding vacancies, try calling a referral service (for a list of agencies, see "Accommodations" on page 7).

Much of the pleasure of this type of trip lies in the planning. Start tasting wines at home and read up on those you particularly like. Taste and compare one type of wine from different producers within a region and from different counties—**Napa**, Sonoma, Mendocino, and Lake—to appreciate the differences in style. Don't worry if your wine vocabulary is lacking—people who work with wine every day can be just as perplexed when trying to describe it. After all, it is a purely sensory experience and should be approached with a spirit of curiosity and pleasure.

How To Read This Guide

NORTHERN CALIFORNIA WINE COUNTRY ACCESS® is arranged so you can see at a glance where you are and what is around you. The numbers next to the entries in the following chapters correspond to the numbers on the maps. The text is color-coded according to the kind of place described:

Restaurants/Clubs: Red   **Hotels:** Blue

Shops/ Outdoors: Green   **Sights/Culture:** Black

& **Wheelchair accessible**

Wheelchair Accessibility

Wheelchair accessibility is noted by a & at the end of the entry. An establishment (except a restaurant) is considered wheelchair accessible when a person in a wheelchair can easily enter a building (i.e., no steps, a ramp, a wide-enough door) without assistance. A restaurant is deemed wheelchair accessible *only* if the above applies, *and* if the rest rooms are on the same floor as the dining area and their entrances and stalls are wide enough to accommodate a wheelchair.

Rating the Restaurants and Hotels

The restaurant star ratings take into account the quality, service, atmosphere, and uniqueness of the restaurant. An expensive restaurant doesn't necessarily ensure an enjoyable evening; however, a small, relatively unknown spot could have good food, professional service, and a lovely atmosphere. Therefore, on a purely subjective basis, stars are used to judge the overall dining value (see the star ratings below). Keep in mind that the chefs and owners often change, which sometimes drastically affects the quality of a restaurant. The ratings in this guidebook are based on information available at press time.

The price ratings, as categorized at right, apply to restaurants and hotels. These figures describe general price-range relationships among other restaurants and hotels in this region. The restaurant price ratings are based on the average cost of an entrée for one person, excluding tax and tip. Hotel price ratings reflect the base price of a standard room for two people for one night during the peak season.

Restaurants

★	Good	
★★	Very Good	
★★★	Excellent	
★★★★	An Extraordinary Experience	
$	The Price Is Right	(less than $15)
$$	Reasonable	($15-$20)
$$$	Expensive	($20-$30)
$$$$	Big Bucks	($30 and up)

Hotels

$	The Price Is Right	(less than $100)
$$	Reasonable	($100-$150)
$$$	Expensive	($150-$200)
$$$$	Big Bucks	($200 and up)

Map Key

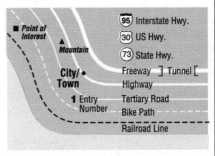

Area code 707 unless otherwise noted.

Getting to the Wine Country

Airports

The closest airports to the wine country with commercial flights are **San Francisco International Airport (SFO), Oakland International Airport (OAK), San Jose International Airport (SJC),** and **Sonoma County Airport** in **Santa Rosa.** No commercial flights are available to Mendocino and Lake Counties; both have airports for small private and charter planes only.

San Francisco International Airport (SFO)

SFO, located south of San Francisco (approximately 1.5 hours from Napa and Sonoma Counties and 2.5 to 3 hours from Mendocino and Lake Counties), is the fifth-busiest airport in the US. The airport can be reached from Highway 101 or Interstate 280 and Highway 380, which connect with Highway 101 and

the airport exits. Long-term airport parking is available off Highway 101 at the San Bruno Avenue East exit. A free shuttle service travels between the parking lots and the airport 24 hours a day. Shuttles on the upper level of the airport provide transportation between terminals every five minutes from 5:30AM to 1AM.

Airport Services

Airport Emergencies	415/876.2424
Business Service Center	415/877.0369
Currency Exchange	415/877.0369
Customs/Immigration	415/876.2816
Ground Transportation Information	415/761.0800
Interpreters	Lower level information booths
Lost and Found	415/876.2261
Parking	415/877.0227
Police	415/876.2424
Traveler's Aid	415/877.0118

Airlines

Air Canada	415/876.7461, 800/776.3000
Alaska	415/875.8600, 800/426.0333
American/American Eagle	415/877.6118, 800/433.7300
America West	415/877.0458, 800/247.5692
Canadian	415/877.5905, 800/426.7000
Continental	415/876.2612, 800/525.0280
Delta	415/877.1017, 800/221.1212
Eva Air	415/876.7422, 800/695.1188
Hawaiian Air	415/877.0134, 800/367.5320
Mark Air	415/876.7449, 800/627.5247
Midwest Express	415/877.0170, 800/452.2022
Northwest	800/225.2525
Southwest	415/877.0112, 800/435.9792
Tower Air	800/221.2500
TWA	415/877.4112, 800/221.2000
United	415/876.3069, 800/241.6522
United Express	415/876.3069, 800/722.5243
USAir/USAir Express	415/877.5543, 800/428.4322
Virgin Atlantic	800/862.8621

Getting to and from San Francisco International Airport

By Bus/Shuttle Bus and shuttle service to and from Napa, Sonoma, and Mendocino Counties is available on the lower level of the airport just outside the baggage claim area. For more information, call the **Ground Transportation Hotline** (800/SFO.2008).

Napa County

Evans Airport Service	255.1559

Sonoma and Mendocino Counties

Sonoma County Airport Express	800/327.2024
Santa Rosa Airporter	545.8015, 800/228.8015
Sonoma Airporter	938.4246

By Car Since you will need a car to visit the wineries, it is best to rent one at the airport and drive to the wine country, rather than take a bus to your destination and rent a car there. The following rental car companies have 24-hour counters in the baggage claim areas. Rental car shuttles pick up and drop off at the center island on the upper level roadway.

Avis	415/877.6780, 800/331.1212
Budget	415/877.4477, 800/527.0700
Dollar	415/692.1200, 800/421.6868
Hertz	415/877.1680, 800/654.3131
National	415/877.4740, 800/227.7368

Oakland International Airport (OAK)

Located five miles south of downtown **Oakland** on Highway 17, off the Hegenburger Drive exit, and an hour from Napa and Sonoma Counties via Highways 80 and 29, **OAK** is smaller and easier to navigate than **SFO.** Less expensive fares are sometimes available as well. Long-term parking is available in the **Economy Lot** on the airport grounds, with free shuttle service to passenger terminals every five minutes, 24 hours a day.

Airport Services

Airport Emergencies	510/569.0740
Business Services	510/577.4000
Currency Exchange	510/635.9164
Customs	415/744.7741
Ground Transportation	510/577.4000
Immigration	415/705.4411
Information	510/577.4000
Interpreters	510/577.4000
Lost and Found	510/577.4095
Parking	510/633.2571
Police	510/569.0740
Traveler's Aid	510/444.6834

Airlines

Alaska	510/577.5812, 800/426.0333
American	800/443.7300
America West	800/235.9292
Delta	510/577.4603, 800/221.1212
Grand Airways	800/634.6616
Martinair Holland	800/627.8462
Southwest	800/435.9792
United	800/241.6522
United Express	800/241.6522

Getting to and from Oakland International Airport

By Bus/Shuttle The **Santa Rosa Airporter** (545.8015, 800/228.8015) provides shuttle service to and from **OAK** and **Santa Rosa**, with transfers to **Healdsburg, Cloverdale, Hopland,** and **Ukiah.** Ground transportation stops are in front of each terminal. **Napa** can be reached by taking **Bay Area Rapid Transit (BART;** 510/465.BART) from the airport to the **El Cerrito Del Norte Station,** catching the *No. 80* **BARTlink** bus to the **Greyhound** station in **Vallejo,** and then taking either **Greyhound** (800/231.2222) or **Napa Transit** (255.7631) to Napa.

By Car Rental car companies have counters in **Terminals 1** and **2.** The following companies have 24-hour counters at the airport:

Alamo	510/639.4730, 800/327.9633
Avis	510/577.6360, 800/331.1212
Budget	510/568.4770, 800/527.0700
Dollar	510/638.2750, 800/421.6868
Hertz	510/639.0200, 800/654.3131
National	510/632.2225, 800/227.7368

San Jose International Airport (SJC)

Though located on Airport Boulevard off Highway 101 in **Santa Clara County,** an hour farther south of the wine country than either **SFO** or **OAK,** SJC's convenience lies in the fact that it offers flights to **Sonoma County Airport** via both **United Express** and **Reno Air Express**. The airport also often has less expensive flights to and from some destinations. Convenient ground transportation options to and from the airport and the wine country are limited to car rentals. Long-term parking is available on the airport grounds. Free shuttle buses take passengers to and from the long-term parking lots and between the terminals every five to 10 minutes from 4AM to midnight.

Airport Services

Airport Emergencies	911
Currency Exchange	408/287.0748
Customs	408/291.7388
Ground Transportation	408/277.4759
Immigration	408/291.7388
Information	408/277.4759
Interpreters	Information booths in terminals
Lost and Found	408/277.5419
Parking	408/291.6788
Police	911

Airlines

Alaska	800/426.0333
American	800/443.7300
America West	800/247.5692
Delta	800/221.1212
Northwest	800/225.2525
Reno Air/Reno Air Express	800/736.6247
Southwest	800/435.9792
TWA	800/221.2000
United	800/241.6522
United Express	800/241.6522
US Air	800/428.4322

Getting to and from San Jose International Airport

By Bus/Shuttle For information on **Greyhound**'s services between the airport and the wine country, call 800/231.2222.

By Car The following rental car companies have 24-hour counters at the airport:

Alamo	408/288.4658, 800/327.9633
Avis	408/993.2360, 800/331.1212
Budget	408/286.7850, 800/527.0700
Dollar	408/280.2201, 800/421.6868
Hertz	408/437.5700, 800/654.3131

Napa County Airport

Only small private and charter planes can use Napa County's airport (2030 Airport Rd, off Hwy 29, Napa, 224.0887, 644.1658).

Sonoma County Airport

United Express and **Reno Air Express** fly to and from Sonoma County's airport (2200 Airport Blvd, off Hwy 101, 524.7240), six miles north of Santa Rosa, via **San Francisco International Airport** and **San Jose International Airport**. **Avis, Hertz,** and **Thrifty** offer car rentals at the airport, but their fleets are small so be sure to make reservations in advance.

Mendocino County Airports

No commercial flights are available to Mendocino County. The following airports are for small private and charter planes only: **Boonville Airport** (Airport Blvd, off Hwy 128, Boonville, 895.9918); **Little River Airport** (43001 Airport Rd, off Hwy 1, Little River, 937.5129); and **Ukiah Municipal Airport** (1411 S State St, at Washington St, Ukiah 463.6293).

Lampson Field Airport, Lake County

Lampson Field Airport (4773 Highland Springs Rd, off Hwy 29, Lakeport, no phone) services small planes.

Bus Stations

For information on **Greyhound** bus service to and from Napa, Sonoma, Mendocino, and Lake Counties, call 800/231.2222. Local bus depots are located at the following addresses:

San Francisco

425 Mission St
(between Fremont and First Sts) ....415/495.1575.

Napa County

While there is no bus station in Napa County, **Greyhound** does make flag stops in Napa, **Yountville,** and **Oakville**. Travelers can also take **Napa Transit** buses from the **Greyhound** station (1500 Lemon St, at the junction of Hwy 780 and the Curtola Pkwy, 643.7661) in Vallejo, 30 minutes south of Napa.

Sonoma County

3854 Santa Rosa Ave (at Todd Rd),
Santa Rosa 586.9512

Mendocino County

99 N Main St (at State St), Willits 459.2210

Lake County

14642 #A Lakeshore Dr
(near Emery St), Clearlake..........................995.0610

Train Station

Northern California's main **Amtrak** station is in Emeryville at 5885 Landregan Street, off I-80 at Powell St (510/450.1080, 800/872.7245).

Getting around the Wine Country

Ballooning See pages 74 and 101 for lists of companies that offer hot-air balloon rides above the wine country.

Bicycles The wine country is crisscrossed with quiet back roads that are ideal for recreational bicycling. Some tour companies not only rent bicycles, helmets, and gloves, but also provide van support along the way for those needing a break from pedaling. In Napa try **Napa Valley Cyclery** (255.3377, 800/707.BIKE); in Sonoma, **Getaway Wine Country Bicycle Tours and Rentals** (942.0332, 800/499.BIKE); and in Mendocino, **Catch a Canoe & Bicycles, Too!** (937.0273).

Boats Napa Riverboat Company Tours (226.2628) makes excursions down the **Napa River** on a 19th-century steamboat (see page 13 for details). Sportfishing and whale-watching expeditions are offered by charter companies along the Mendocino Coast. In **Fort Bragg**, try **Misty II Charters** (996.7161) or **Lady Irma II** (964.3854). In the **Russian River Valley**, kayaks can be rented by the day or weekend at **California Rivers** (838.8919); canoe trips along the **Russian River** can be arranged through **W.C. "Bob" Trowbridge Canoe Trips** (433.7247, 800/640.1386) in Healdsburg. Fishing boats, water skis, and jet skis for exploring **Clear Lake** can be rented at **Lakeport**'s **On the Waterfront** (263.6789).

Buses/Shuttles

Napa County

Bear Flag Express (Yountville)	944.8851
Calistoga Handyvan	963.4229
Napa Valley Transit	800/696.6443
Valley Intracity Neighborhood Express (The VINE)	255.7631, 800/696.6443

Sonoma County

Golden Gate Transit	544.1323
Healdsburg Municipal Transit	431.3309
MTA Coast Bus (Santa Rosa to Point Arena)	884.3723
Santa Rosa CityBus	524.5306
Sonoma County Transit	576.7433, 800/345.7433

Mendocino County

Fort Bragg Dial-a-Ride	964.1800
Mendocino Transit Authority (MTA)/Dial-a-Ride	462.1422
Recording	884.3723
Ukiah Dial-a-Ride	462.3881

Lake County

Clearlake Dial-a-Ride	994.8277
Lakeport Dial-a-Ride	277.9422

Driving Many roads in the regions included in this book are quite narrow, making the mix of tourist vehicles and locals trying to go about their business a frustrating combination. Keep an eye on your rearview mirror, and if you have one or two cars following closely behind, clearly wanting to go faster, pull over to let them pass. This is especially important on roads such as **Highway 128** to the **Anderson Valley** or anywhere along the coast, where many of the roads have only one lane of traffic on either side. Also, the shoulder is not very wide, so watch for bicyclists, particularly when approaching a blind curve.

If you're following a heavy schedule of wine tasting, don't drink too much before getting behind the wheel of a car. Either conscientiously spit the wines out after you taste them as the professionals do (see "Making the Most of Your Winery Visits" on page 106) or appoint a designated driver. Bear in mind that summer heat intensifies the effects of alcohol. Wearing a seat belt is required by law, and children who are under four years old and/or weigh under 40 pounds must ride in a child's car seat.

Parking In general, parking meters allow for either 30-minute, one-hour, or two-hour parking and operate Monday through Saturday from 9AM to 6PM. There are exceptions to this rule, so watch for the occasional meter that is monitored on Sunday. Certain parking zones may not have meters, but are marked as 20-minute, one-hour, or two-hour zones.

Fortunately, there are few places in the wine country where you have to worry about a lack of parking spaces. Most wineries offer ample parking (with designated spaces for people with disabilities) and often have special areas reserved for buses and RVs.

Taxis

Napa County

Valley Cab	257.6444
Yellow Cab	226.3731

Sonoma County

Valley Cab	996.6733
Yellow Cab/George's Taxi	546.3322

Mendocino County

Mendocino Taxi and Delivery	462.8294

Lake County

Clear Lake Cab Company	994.8294

Tours You can't beat the freedom of touring the wine country by car on your own schedule, making brief stops at some wineries, lingering at others, putting together an impromptu picnic with supplies from a country store. But organized tours for individuals or small groups are available, too. Stop by or call any of the visitors' bureaus listed on page 8 for information on tour companies, including **Sonoma Wine Tours** (996.0506), which departs from the plaza in downtown Sonoma, and **Napa Valley Holidays Winery Tours** (255.1050), which offers Bay Area pickup for groups of 10 or more. See "Ballooning,"

"Bicycles," "Boats," and "Trains" in this chapter for more touring options.

Trains The **Napa Valley Wine Train** (253.2111) chugs through the valley on 3.5-hour excursions several times a day. The train departs from Napa, traveling to St. Helena and back along scenic **Highway 29**. See page 18 for more information.

Walking Charming small towns with old-fashioned main streets or squares ideal for exploring on foot can be found throughout the region: Yountville, St. Helena, and **Calistoga** in Napa County; Sonoma and Healdsburg in Sonoma County; Mendocino and Fort Bragg in Mendocino County; and Lakeport and **Kelseyville** in Lake County. Most wineries, however, are located off highways or country roads miles from towns, making wheels the most practical option for visiting.

FYI

Accommodations The following agencies provide free assistance in finding a bed-and-breakfast in the wine country. Bear in mind that some inns have age restrictions; it's best to inquire before you make a reservation.

Accommodation Referral (Napa Valley) 963.VINO, 800/499.8466 (in CA)

Bed-and-Breakfast Inns of Napa Valley 944.4444, 800/793.7959

Bed-and-Breakfast Inns of Sonoma Valley 996.4667, 800/284.6675

Bed-and-Breakfast Style (Napa, Sonoma, and Russian River Valleys) 942.2888, 800/995.8884

Climate Weather varies from region to region in the wine country. A warm summer day in Napa or Sonoma might turn to chilly fog over on the coast, making the "layered look" the most practical option for dressing. The rainy season is generally between December and February. Temperatures range from an average winter low of 61 to a summer high of 92 inland and 40 to 65 in coastal areas.

Drinking The legal age for drinking in California is 21. Liquor is sold in a wide variety of venues, from supermarkets and gourmet food markets to all-night convenience stores and specialized liquor stores and wineshops.

Hours and Admission Charges Opening and closing times for shops, attractions, wineries, coffeehouses, and tearooms, etc. are listed by day(s) only if normal hours apply (from 8 to 11AM and from 4 to 7PM). In all other cases, specific hours will be given (e.g., 6AM-2PM, daily 24 hours, noon-5PM). The majority of wineries do not charge admission; exceptions are noted.

Money The major banks in Napa County include Bank of America, Citibank, Security Pacific, and Wells Fargo; in Sonoma County, look for Bank of America, California First, Security Pacific, and Wells Fargo; and in Mendocino and Lake Counties, Bank of America and Wells Fargo.

Since the wine country is limited when it comes to exchanging money, it is advisable to change it at the point of embarkation—that is, at the airport or in San Francisco. In an emergency, **Thomas Cook Foreign Exchange** has an office in **Corte Madera** (The Village Shopping Center, off Highway 101, 415/924.6009), about a 40-minute drive from the town of Napa; it's open Monday through Saturday. Most banks will exchange traveler's checks written in US dollars; it is much more difficult to exchange traveler's checks written in foreign currency. The San Francisco offices of **American Express** (237 Post St, between Grant Ave and Stockton St, 415/981.5533) and **Thomas Cook Foreign Exchange** (75 Geary St, at Grant Ave, 415/362.3452) are open Monday through Saturday.

Publications For serious coverage of wines and wine regions around the world, consult *The Wine Spectator,* a bimonthly magazine available at newsstands and wineshops. A subscription is $40 per year; call 800/622.2062.

The Wine Advocate, a bimonthly guide to wine, is based on research by one of the most influential wine critics and writers in the business, Robert M. Parker Jr. This publication is only available by subscription and costs $35 per year. Write to *The Wine Advocate,* Box 311, Monkton, MD 21111, or call 410/329.6477.

Other good sources for up-to-date information on wine and wineries are Gerald Asher's well-written column in *Gourmet* magazine and Anthony Dias Blue's lively column in *Bon Appétit* magazine.

Restaurants Fine food and wine go together in the wine country, thanks to an abundance of excellent local produce in the hands of top chefs. "California" or "Wine Country" cuisine typically leans toward Mediterranean in influence, prepared in creative ways with the region's bounty of produce, from Hog Island oysters and Petaluma duck to Sonoma rabbit or lamb and local goat cheese, with lots of fresh vegetables and herbs as sides or in the sauces. Be sure to make reservations in advance where recommended. Most dining spots accept credit cards.

Shopping Don't expect large shopping malls or department stores in the wine country. Instead look for small shops specializing in antiques, hand-crafted items by local artisans, and food-related products, such as locally made olive oils, herb vinegars, mustards, salsas, and more. Some wineries have their own retail shops stocked with wine-related goods, including wine-spiked food products and wine soaps. Shipping is often available, too. Some of the smaller, mom-and-pop establishments do not take credit cards; it's always a good idea to check before making a purchase.

Smoking More and more Californians are becoming nonsmokers, and the sensitivity to smoking is acute. Ask permission before you smoke anywhere indoors. Many restaurants are entirely nonsmoking, as are some inns. When smoking is allowed, it's generally restricted to a special section of the restaurant or to certain rooms of the hotel. If you smoke, be sure to inquire about the establishment's policy when you make your reservation.

Spas The wine country is not only blessed with an ideal grape-growing climate, but also a number of natural hot springs to add to the sybaritic experience. Mud baths, mineral baths, facials, and massages are offered at spas throughout the wine country. Many offer overnight accommodations but allow nonguests to use the spa facilities during specific hours.

Taxes All hotels and overnight lodging (including bed-and-breakfast establishments) are subject to a county- and/or city-imposed tax. The taxes in the wine country range from 6 to 12 percent. Sales tax in California is 7.25 percent.

Telephone Local calls from pay phones are 20 cents, but because the 707 area code encompasses all of Napa, Sonoma, Mendocino, and Lake Counties, many calls within that area code cost more. Find out what is considered a local call before holding any lengthy phone conversations.

Time Zone The wine country is in the pacific time zone, three hours behind New York City.

Tipping In Northern California, it is customary to tip 15 to 20 percent of your restaurant bill including the tax, depending on your satisfaction with the service. Some restaurants automatically tack on a 15 percent gratuity for parties of five or more. A taxi driver is usually tipped about 15 percent, while whoever carries your bags at a hotel might expect $1 to $2 per bag. Whether you tip the housekeeper at your hotel is up to you, but a few dollars per day is typical.

Visitors' Information Centers Wherever you are in wine country, tourist information is always close at hand. In Napa County, visitors' information centers include the **Calistoga Chamber of Commerce** (1458 Lincoln Ave between Washington and Fairway Sts, Calistoga, 942.6333), the **Napa Valley Conference**

& Visitors' Bureau (1310 Napa Town Center Mall off First St, Napa, 226.7459), the **Napa Valley Tourist Bureau** (6488 Washington St between Oak and Mulberry Sts, Yountville, 258.1957, 800/523.4353), the **St. Helena Chamber of Commerce** (1080 Main St at Pope St, St. Helena, 963.4456, 800/767.8528), and the **Yountville Chamber of Commerce & Visitor Information** (6516 Yount St at Washington St, Yountville, 944.0904, 800/959.3604). All are open daily year-round except for the **St. Helena Chamber of Commerce**, which is open Monday through Friday; and the **Yountville Chamber of Commerce & Visitor Information,** which is open Monday through Saturday.

In Sonoma County, tourist information is available at the following centers, all of which are open daily year-round: the **Healdsburg Chamber of Commerce** (217 Healdsburg Ave between Mill and Matheson Sts, Healdsburg, 433.6935), the **Russian River Region Information Center** (14034 Armstrong Woods Rd off Hwy 116, Guerneville, 869.9212, 800/253.8800), and the **Sonoma Valley Visitors' Bureau** (453 First St East between W Napa and W Spain Sts, Sonoma, 996.1090).

Mendocino County visitor centers include the **Fort Bragg/Mendocino Coast Chamber of Commerce** (332 N. Main St between Redwood and Laurel Sts, Fort Bragg, 961.6300, 800/726.2780), which is open Monday through Saturday; and the **Ukiah Chamber of Commerce (Ukiah Valley)** (200 S. School St at Perkins St, Ukiah, 462.4705), which is open Monday through Friday.

In Lake County, visitor information is available at the **Lake County Visitor Information Center** (875 Lakeport Blvd off Hwy 29, Lakeport, 263.9544, 800/LAKESIDE), which is open Monday through Saturday June through September and Tuesday through Friday October through May; and the **Lakeport Chamber of Commerce** (290 S. Main St at Martin St, Lakeport, 263.5092), which is open Monday through Friday.

The Main Event: Wine-Country Festivals

In between winery visits, you may want to take in one of the many fairs, festivals, and other special events that are held each year in wine country. Some are one- or two-day affairs, while others can last as long as a month, but they all offer tourists the opportunity to mix with local residents and get the feel of the area. Here are some of the leading festivities:

May

Spring Fair, Napa

June

Lakeport Revival, Lakeport
Stumptown Days, Guerneville
Russian River Rodeo Days, Guerneville

July

Catalan Festival, Sonoma
Lake County Rodeo, Lakeport
Napa County Fair, Calistoga
Sonoma County Fair, Santa Rosa (July-August)

August

Lake County Fair, Lakeport (August-September)

September

Mendocino County Fair, Boonville

Phone Book

Emergencies

Ambulance/Fire/Police 911

AAA Emergency Road Service 800/222.4357

Dental Referral
All US cities 575.7905

Redwood Empire Dental Society,
Mendocino and Lake Counties 546.7275

Handicapped Crisis Line
(24 hours) 800/426.4263

Highway Patrol
Lake County...279.0103

Mendocino County 937.0808

Napa 253.4906

Santa Rosa 576.2175

Ukiah 463.4717

Hospitals
Community Hospital Emergency
(Santa Rosa) 576.4000

Mendocino Coast District
Hospital Emergency (Fort Bragg) 961.1234

Queen of the Valley Hospital
Emergency (Napa) ....252.4411 ext 2361

St. Helena Hospital
Emergency (St. Helena)..............................963.6425

Sutter Lakeside Hospital (Lakeport) 262.5000

Ukiah Valley Medical Center
Emergency (Ukiah).....................................462.3111

Locksmiths (AAA)...............................800/222.4357

Medical Referral
Physician Referral Service (Redwood Health
Services), Sonoma County 544.2010

Physician Referral Service (The Medical Society),
Mendocino and Lake Counties....................462.1694

Pharmacies (24 hours)
Lucky Sav-On Prescriptions (Napa)............255.7400

Lucky Sav-On Prescriptions (Santa Rosa) ..523.4930

Poison Control Center (24 hours)
Sonoma, Napa, and
Mendocino Counties 800/523.2222

Lake County 800/342.9293

Police (Non-emergency)
Napa County
Calistoga 942.2810

Napa..253.4451

St. Helena...967.2850

Sonoma County
Healdsburg...431.3377

Santa Rosa 543.3600

Sonoma 996.3602

Mendocino County
Fort Bragg 961.2800

Ukiah 463.6242

Lake County
Clearlake 994.8251

Lakeport 263.5491

Visitor Information

American Youth Hostels
Marin County 415/331.2777

San Francisco....................................415/771.7277

Amtrak...800/872.7245

Better Business Bureau
Napa County......................................510/238.1000

Santa Rosa..577.0400

Sonoma, Lake, and
Mendocino Counties 415/243.9999

Greyhound Bus 800/231.2222

Metro Transit ....See "Buses/Shuttles" on page 6.

Road Conditions
Major roads in California 800/427.7623

Northern California Highway Patrol 462.0155

Time ....POP.CORN (or 767 and any four digits)

US Customs (San Francisco)...............415/744.7700

US Passport Office (San Francisco)....415/744.4444

Weather San Francisco Bay Area........415/936.1212;
....415/364.7974

Wine Institute

A very knowledgeable and friendly staff provides
information on the wine industry, including referrals
to classes on related subjects. Free wine-country
booklets and maps are also available. The office (425
Market St, Ste 1000, between Fremont and First Sts,
San Francisco, CA 94105, 415/512.0151) is open
Monday through Friday from 9AM to 5PM.

Napa County

Napa Valley, which was inhabited by six Indian tribes before white settlers arrived in the 1830s, derives its name from an Indian word meaning "plenty." Less than an hour and a half northeast of San Francisco, this world-renowned wine-growing region is bounded by the **Mayacamas Mountains** to the west and the **Vaca** range to the east. It extends some 25 miles from **San Pablo Bay** to the foot of the extinct volcano **Mount St. Helena** to the north. Within these boundaries are world-famous grape-growing districts: **Carneros** (west of the town of **Napa** to the Mayacamas Mountains), **Stags Leap** (east of **Yountville**), and the **Rutherford Bench** (a corridor of vineyards lying west of **Highway 29** between Yountville and **St. Helena**). Other small districts include **Spring Mountain, Diamond Mountain, Howell Mountain,** and **Mount Veeder.** Napa Valley is an agricultural paradise, with a ravishing landscape of gently rolling hills and an assortment of wineries that consistently surpass their European counterparts in international competitions. Add to that a wealth of fine restaurants, intriguing shops, sites of literary and historic interest, and recreational opportunities galore—and you've got "plenty" indeed.

The tradition of wine making in Napa Valley goes back more than a century and a half—early in American history, but a mere blink of the eye by European standards. In 1838 the trapper, explorer, and Napa Valley pioneer George C. Yount planted vines obtained from General Mariano Vallejo's estate in Sonoma on part of the huge land grant he had received from the Mexican government. Yount produced his first wine in 1841; the grape was not the Chardonnay or the Cabernet Sauvignon the valley is known for today, but the Mission grape brought to Northern California by Franciscan fathers in 1823 and used primarily for sacramental wines.

By 1880 the wine business was booming. Napa Valley wines were served in the best restaurants in San Francisco and New York. More than 10,000 acres were planted with vines, and the number of wineries had quickly grown to an astonishing 175—together they produced the equivalent of one million cases of wine a year. The valley's pioneering wine makers, from France, Italy, and Germany, had laid the foundations for today's thriving wine industry, using grape varieties and skills borrowed from their homelands.

Today Napa's wines, particularly Chardonnay and Cabernet Sauvignon, are known and respected all over the world. The vineyards cover 32,000 acres and the valley boasts more than 250 wineries, ranging from tiny mom-and-pop establishments where the cellar is practically part of the house to immense operations owned by corporations and holding companies. In recent years the international presence in Napa Valley has increased. Some wineries are owned outright by European families or companies, while others are joint ventures with European wineries.

As celebrated as it is, Napa Valley accounts for only five percent of the wine grapes harvested in California. The valley's wineries, for the most part, have made every effort to concentrate on quality over quantity. As a new generation of wine makers takes the helm, many of them trained at the **School of Enology** at the prestigious **University of California at Davis,** they continue to learn from each other, making improvements in both wine production techniques and viticulture.

Since the 1950s Napa County has grown from a sleepy country outpost, a paradise enjoyed by the privileged few residents of the valley, to a prime vacation destination that attracts more than four million visitors each year. Driving along either of the county's two main arteries, Highway 29 or the **Silverado Trail** (one of California's most beautiful drives), you will pass tractors chugging along at their own pace and trucks stacked with oak barrels from the forests of Burgundy or with premium wines on their way to fine shops and restaurants. Sleek sports cars race past pickups, while bicyclists cling to the edge of the road.

Wineries vie with each other to attract visitors by creating lavishly appointed tasting rooms, award-winning architecture, informative tours, special tastings, displays on Napa Valley history, and world-class art collections. There is just as much friendly competition among the restaurants. Chefs here have developed a distinctive wine-country fare based on premium local ingredients and dishes carefully designed to showcase the wines. Elegant establishments such as **Domaine Chandon Restaurant**, **Auberge du Soleil Restaurant**, and **The Restaurant at Meadowood** rub shoulders with sassy bistros such as **Mustards Grill**, **Tra Vigne**, and **Brava Terrace**. And you can still find intimate restaurants where hand-crafted personal cuisine is the rule, such as **The French Laundry** in Yountville or **Trilogy** in St. Helena, along with down-home spots like **The Diner** in Yountville.

One Napa Valley experience not to be missed is a wine-country picnic. You can collect the makings at a number of spots, including **Cantinetta Tra Vigne** or the granddaddy of the Bay Area gourmet shops, **Oakville Grocery Co.** Many wineries provide picnic areas for their visitors; one of

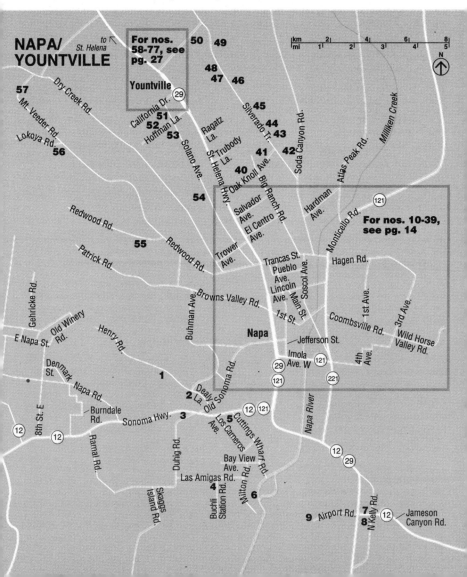

the best, **Château Montelena**'s Chinese pagodas located on tiny islands in the middle of a small lake, requires reservations. But spots along the Silverado Trail and parks in Yountville, St. Helena, and **Calistoga**, along with **Bothe–Napa Valley State Park** and the rugged **Robert Louis Stevenson State Park**, offer more secluded sites.

It's no secret that on many weekends, especially in the summer, Highway 29 is one big traffic jam. But most people visit only a few dozen of the prominent wineries along this road; some never manage to get off the main drag, and most never make it to what the locals call the "up-valley" (the section of the valley located north of St. Helena). To avoid the crowds, a good strategy is to head north first and work your way south, cutting over to the parallel (and much more scenic) Silverado Trail whenever possible. If you want to visit the most popular wineries such as **Robert Mondavi** and **Beringer,** plan your trip early in the day.

Many visitors try a different method of exploration and map out an itinerary by bicycle. It takes longer to cover the territory this way, of course, but you'll experience the tranquil landscape up close, stopping along the way for winery visits and tastings. And then there is the controversial **Napa Valley Wine Train** (when it was proposed, residents feared increased traffic, the circuslike atmosphere it would bring, and the added strain on an already stressed environment), which carries passengers in luxurious Pullman lounge cars; during the three-hour tour, riders sip Napa Valley wines, enjoy an elegantly presented meal, and view the region from the windows of the train.

A Napa County ordinance designed to control development and tourism in the valley limits drop-in public tours and tastings primarily to those wineries that were already doing so before 1991. All other wineries may allow tours and tastings *by appointment only.* But don't let this requirement dissuade you from visiting. "By appointment" simply means calling ahead. More than a hundred small wineries offer tours and tastings that are intimate and unrushed. Your tour guide may well be the winery owner or wine maker, and often the tour may be custom-tailored to your interests, perhaps including a vineyard walk or a barrel tasting of the latest vintage.

1 Codorníu Napa Napa Valley's newest premium sparkling winery fits snugly into its site at the foot of Miliken Peak. The dramatic, $22-million winery and its product were named in honor of the Spanish owner, the House of Codorníu, which has been making wines in the Catalán region of Spain for more than 400 years. The ultramodern building was designed by Barcelona architect **Domingo Triay,** who also designed Codorníu's Raimat estate in Spain. From a distance, it's hard to make out the modernistic structure, for the architect built the ecologically sound winery right into the hillside and covered the top with an earthen berm planted with drought-resistant California grasses to create the cool, stable conditions ideal for producing and storing high-quality sparkling wine. A series of terraces leads into the winery past columns and reflecting pools; and the view from inside is a stunning panorama of the Carneros district. The wine maker is a young San Franciscan, Janet Pagano, who honed her skills at several other California wineries, including **Domaine Mumm.** Tours of the winery, which are designed to give an overview of *méthode champenoise* wine making, are followed by a tasting of its first premium sparkling cuvée. ♦ Fee. Tasting and tours daily. 1345 Henry Rd (west of Dealy La), Napa. 224.2668 &

2 Carneros Creek Winery A barnlike building just off Old Sonoma Road marks this small Carneros-district producer. The emphasis here is on Chardonnay and Pinot Noir, though the winery also makes Cabernet Sauvignon and Merlot. A tasting room was added in 1994. A few picnic tables are in a lovely setting under a pergola (overhead trellis) twined with trumpet vines. ♦ Fee. Tasting and sales daily. 1285 Dealy La (between Old Sonoma and Henry Rds), Napa. 253.9463 &

3 Domaine Carneros Founded in 1987 by the French Champagne house Taittinger, this winery (pictured above) is devoted to making sparkling wines by the traditional *méthode champenoise*. Managing director and wine maker Eileen Crane has extensive experience making sparkling wine in California. Designed by **Thomas Faherty & Associates** of St. Helena, the massive winery was inspired by the Château de la Marquetterie, a historic 18th-century residence owned by the Taittinger family in Champagne. A grand cement staircase leads from the parking lot to the elegant reception and tasting room where visitors can relax with a glass of Domaine Carneros Brut at tables decorated with vases of flowers. Downstairs is a gallery with views of the bottling line and fermentation stages, along with historical photos of the harvest in Champagne. ♦ Fee. Tasting, sales, and tours daily. 1240 Duhig Rd (just south of Hwy 12), Napa. 257.0101; fax 257.2030 &

4 Bouchaine Vineyards Perched on a hillside overlooking San Pablo Bay, Gerret Copeland's small, modernized winery tucked into an existing older building specializes in Carneros-grown Pinot Noir and Chardonnay made by traditional Burgundian methods. It also has started to produce a small amount of Alsatian-style Gewürztraminer. The original wine estate at this site dates from 1899. ♦ Tasting and tours by appointment only. 1075 Buchli Station Rd (at Las Amigas Rd), Napa. 252.9065; fax 252.0401 &

GARNET
1989
Carneros Pinot Noir

AINTSBURY

PRODUCED AND BOTTLED BY SAINTSBURY
NAPA, CALIFORNIA, USA   ALCOHOL 12.9% BY VOLUME

5 Saintsbury Named in honor of the 19th-century wine connoisseur and writer George Saintsbury, best known as the author of *Notes on a Cellar Book*, this Carneros-district winery is housed in a weathered redwood building. Partners Richard Ward and David Graves are dedicated to making Burgundian-style Pinot Noir and Chardonnay. The Chardonnay is fermented and aged in barrels coopered in France. The partners make two styles of Pinot Noir: the fresh and lively Garnet and the more classic Carneros Pinot Noir. All their wines are first rate and are sold at excellent prices. ♦ Limited tours M-F by appointment only. 1500 Los Carneros Ave (off Hwy 12), Napa. 252.0592; fax 252.0595 &

6 Napa Riverboat Company Tours Hop on board for a two-and-a-half-hour excursion down the Napa River to the Third Street Bridge and back on an original 19th-century steamboat. A Saturday night four-course dinner cruise features Dixieland and jazz bands; Sunday brunch cruises are offered, too. ♦ Call for information on prices, departure times, and special charter programs. 1200 Milton Rd (off Cuttings Wharf Rd), Napa Valley Marina. 226.2628

7 Hakusan Sake Gardens It's ironic that the first tasting room you'll come to along Highway 29 doesn't serve wine made from grapes. Rather, it serves sake, Japan's traditional wine, which is made from rice. At this 20-acre, $21-million facility, a short video explains how the winery produces sake from the inner kernel of short-grained rice grown in the Sacramento Valley. It is followed by a tasting of warm and cold sake. Spend a quiet moment in the beautiful raked-sand Japanese gardens before heading up the valley. ♦ Tours (available in Japanese and English), tasting, and sales daily by appointment only. Hwys 29 and 12 (entrance at N Kelly Rd), Napa. 258.6160; fax 258.6163 &

8 Chardonnay Club This championship 18-hole golf course (5,300-7,150 yards, par 72, rated 73.5) regularly appears on *California Golf* magazine's list of the 25 best courses in the state. Golf shops, a clubhouse with a grill and restaurant, a snack bar, and a practice range are available. ♦ Daily. Reservations must be made at least two weeks in advance. 2555 Jameson Canyon Rd (off Hwy 29), Napa. 257.8950; fax 257.0613

9 Bridgeford Flying Service Fly over the wine country in a five-passenger Cessna Skyhawk, Centurion, or Skylane for bird's-eye views of vineyards and historic wineries. The Napa tour heads north along one side of the valley as far as Calistoga, returning down the other side. An alternate coastal tour flies over the Golden Gate Bridge, along the coast to Point Reyes, Bodega Bay, and Jenner, returning via the Russian River wine district and Napa Valley. Charter flights, lessons, and rentals are available, too. ♦ Reservations required. Napa County Airport, 2030 Airport Rd (off Hwy 29), Napa. 224.0887, 644.1658; fax 257.7770 &

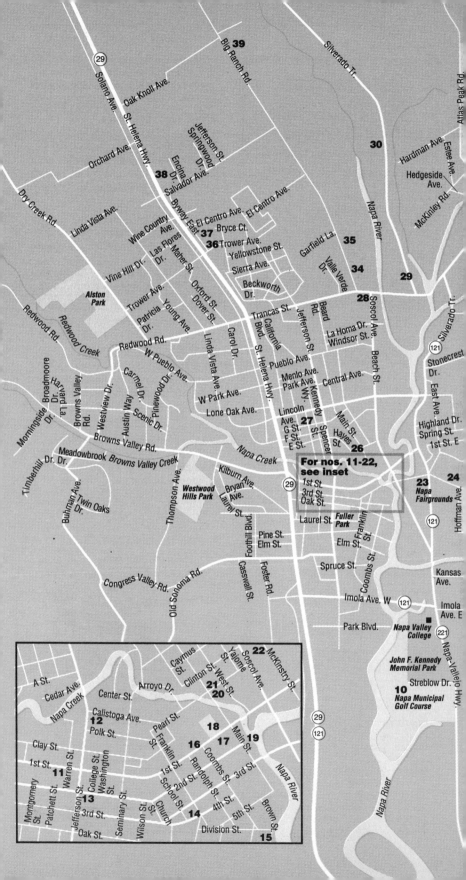

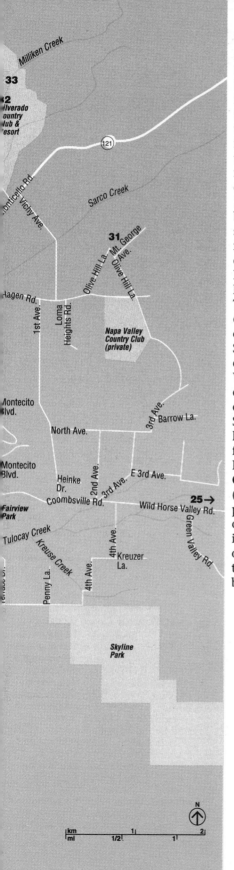

Milliken Creek

33

32
Silverado
Country
Club &
Resort

121

Monticello Rd.

Sarco Creek

Vichy Ave.

31

Mt. George Ave.

Olive Hill La.

Olive Hill La.

Hagen Rd.

1st Ave.

Loma Heights Rd.

Napa Valley
Country Club
(private)

Montecito
Blvd.

North Ave.

3rd Ave.

Barrow La.

Montecito
Blvd.

Heinke
Dr.

2nd Ave.

3rd Ave.

E 3rd Ave.

Coombsville Rd.

Wild Horse Valley Rd.

25 →

Fairview
Park

Tulocay Creek

Kreuse Creek

Penny La.

4th Ave.

4th Ave.

4th Ave.

Kreuzer
La.

Green Valley Rd.

Skyline
Park

N

km
mi

1/2

1

1

2

Napa

The city of Napa was founded by Nathan Coombs, a member of the infamous Bear Flag Party that declared the Republic of California independent from Mexico in 1846. Two years later Coombs surveyed Napa's original town site. The first building went up in 1848, but its owner rushed off to the gold fields to seek his fortune, returning disillusioned a year later to open the **Empire Saloon.** By the mid-19th century, the valley's wine business was flourishing and a steamship line carried its products from Napa to San Francisco. Because of its location at the head of the **Napa River**, the city of Napa controlled the local wine trade for almost a century. Today it is a riverfront city of about 64,000 people, with a rich heritage of Victorian domestic architecture. Stroll through the restored downtown district and you'll pass Victorian mansions, a Gothic-style church, historic bridges, and 19th-century commercial buildings. Self-guided walking tours of Napa's historic structures are available for a nominal fee at **Napa County Landmarks** and **Napa Valley Conference & Visitors' Bureau** (see page 17 for both). Future plans for Napa include development of the Napa River, with public docks, inlets, walking paths, and restaurants overlooking the river-banks.

10 Napa Municipal Golf Course A public 18-hole championship golf course (6,571 yards, par 72, rated 71.5), driving range, pro shop, and rental clubs and carts are available here, as well as a coffee shop and snack bar. Reservations may be made a week in advance or on the morning of the day of play (you also can come without a reservation, but you may have to wait for an open spot). No spectators are permitted. ♦ Daily. 2295 Streblow Dr (next to Napa Valley College and JFK Memorial Park). 255.4333

11 Beazley House $$ In the heart of a fine old neighborhood of dignified houses and tree-lined streets, this Colonial Revival building (see drawing above) has had few owners since it was built in 1902, which has helped it to retain its original character. On a half acre of land, the inn boasts 10 large guest rooms with high ceilings, comfortable period furnishings, handmade quilts, and private baths. Five of the rooms are in the main house and the rest are in the newer carriage house at the rear. The master bedroom in the main house and several rooms in the carriage house feature fireplaces and Jacuzzis, and the **West Loft,** a favorite with many guests, features a 15-foot cathedral ceiling and a stained-glass window over the king-size bed. Innkeepers Jim and Carol Beazley will sit down with guests to map out an itinerary of the best Napa Valley has to offer. Breakfast here includes fresh fruits, homemade muffins, and a special **Beazley House** coffee blend sold at the **Napa Valley Coffee Roasting Company** (see page 17). Smoking is not allowed. ♦ 1910 First St (at Warren St). 257.1649, 800/559.1649; fax 257.1518 ♿

12 Old World Inn $$ This exquisitely preserved 1906 Napa residence has been transformed into an eight-room bed-and-breakfast inn by proprietor Diane Dumaine. The building's exterior reflects a mixture of architectural styles, from its Colonial Revival porch columns to the two-story Queen Anne corner tower. Inside, the inn is lavishly adorned with pastel colors, draped fabrics, and the kind of stuff Grandma would never let you touch. Each individually decorated room features a private bath (most with a claw-foot tub and shower), and some have either full- or quarter-canopied queen-size beds. One room even has its own Jacuzzi, and there's also a large Jacuzzi outside for all guests to soak in after a long day of wine tasting. A full breakfast is served, as well as wine and cheese in the afternoon, a late-afternoon tea, and a popular self-serve late-night dessert buffet. No smoking is allowed. ♦ 1301 Jefferson St (at Calistoga Ave). 257.0112

13 La Boucane ★★$$$ In a fine, 19th-century house with burgundy awnings, Jacques Mokrani offers classic French dinners. Specialties range from prawns Provençal (sautéed with Cognac, tomatoes, lemon, and garlic) and salmon poached in Champagne and cream to sweetbreads in a Port sauce and duck *à l'orange.* For dessert, try the strawberries in red wine or the soufflé glacé praline. With its flowered wallpaper, beautifully set tables, and dark bistro-style chairs, the place feels like a French provincial restaurant that has been transplanted to California wine country. ♦ French ♦ M-Sa dinner; closed in January. 1778 Second St (at Jefferson St). 253.1177

14 ABC/Alexis Baking Company and Cafe ★$ The friendly staff at this casual cafe offers a limited menu of pizzas, hamburgers, roast chicken, salads, soups, and good homemade breads and desserts, along with a short wine list. Counter service is available, too. Don't miss the bathrooms, which have been painted by local artists with whimsical designs of flying pizzas, angels, and hamburgers. No smoking is allowed. ♦ Eclectic ♦ Daily breakfast, lunch, and takeout. 1517 Third St (between Franklin and School Sts). 258.1827; fax 258.1916 ♿

15 Churchill Manor $$ Built in 1889 for Napa banker Edward S. Churchill, this spectacular Colonial Revival mansion (see drawing above) with stately columns and a spacious veranda is listed on the National Register of Historic Places. Now an elegant bed-and-breakfast inn run by Joanna Guidotti—who has planted daffodils, roses, freesias, and an herb garden on the beautifully manicured grounds—the three-story house boasts 10 guest rooms, all with private baths. The largest is the original master bedroom, with a carved French armoire and king-size bed, plus a fireplace framed with gold-laced tiles. Full breakfast (fruit tray, fresh-squeezed orange juice, homemade blueberry muffins or croissants, and a quiche or egg dish, plus herb teas and coffees) and afternoon tastings of Napa Valley wines are offered in the solarium. Bicycles, including two tandems, and croquet equipment are available for guests. ◆ 485 Brown St (between Oak and Division Sts). 253.7733; fax 253.8836 &

16 Napa County Historical Society Conceived on a pioneer picnic at the **Old Bale Mill** in 1948, the historical society has a library of books on Napa Valley history, manuscripts, and hundreds of old photographs of pioneer settlers and historic sites, plus an archive of historical newspaper clippings. Housed in the **Goodman Library Building** (see drawing above), designed by local architect **Luther M. Turton** at the turn of the century, it also includes a small museum of Napa Valley artifacts. Pick up the inexpensive short guide *California Historic Landmarks of Napa County*, along with notecards and posters of noteworthy sites. ◆ Tu, Th noon-4PM. 1219 First St (between Coombs and Randolph Sts). 224.1739

17 Napa County Landmarks The city of Napa has a rich heritage of carefully restored historic buildings. Self-guided Landmark Walks explore **City Hall**, the **Old Courthouse,** and well-preserved Victorian neighborhoods. Maps for these self-guided tours in Napa, as well as walks in Yountville, St. Helena, and Calistoga are available here and at the **Napa Valley Conference & Visitors' Bureau** (see below) for a nominal fee. The organization offers guided walks through Napa neighborhoods for a small charge on Saturday from 10-11:30AM, May through September; refreshments are served afterward. ◆ M-F. 1026 First St (between Main and Coombs Sts), or write to Box 702, Napa, CA 94559. 255.1836 &

18 Napa Valley Conference & Visitors' Bureau Information on restaurants, wineries, lodging, attractions, and activities, plus hints about transportation and travel in Napa Valley, is provided at this office. You may also pick up free information on a self-guided walking tour of Napa's historic buildings here. ◆ Daily. 1310 Napa Town Center Mall (off First St), Napa, CA 94559. 226.7459 (no calls taken on weekends; only walk-in visitors); fax 255.2066 &

19 Downtown Joe's ★$$ After a day of wine tasting, a cool glass of Tail Waggin' Ale or Ace High Cream Ale at this riverfront pub is a refreshing change, particularly at an outdoor table overlooking the Napa River. The ginger ale and root beer served here are brewed on the premises. The menu features salads, homemade ale bread, burgers, porterhouse steak, fresh pasta, and seafood. ◆ American ◆ Daily breakfast, lunch, and dinner. 902 Main St (at Second St). 258.2337; fax 258.8740 &

19 Napa Valley Coffee Roasting Company $ This coffee emporium, owned by partners Denise Fox and Leon Sange, is housed in a beautifully restored brick building in downtown Napa. The cozy space is decorated with marble bistro tables, old-fashioned coffee tins, signs, and other memorabilia. Faithful patrons drop in to enjoy an espresso or a cappuccino made from green coffee beans that have been imported from plantations all over the world and roasted right in the store. In addition to espresso drinks and the house coffee, which changes several times throughout the day so you may sample different types, you'll find a stash of freshly baked goodies from local bakeries: blueberry muffins, dynamite chocolate-coconut macaroons, lemon poppy-seed cake, and, sometimes, crunchy biscotti to dip into your coffee Italian-style. ◆ Cafe ◆ Daily 7AM-6PM. 948 Main St (at First St). 224.2233; fax 224.9276 &

19 Veterans Memorial Park This grassy slope overlooking the Napa River at the Third Street Bridge makes a good impromptu city picnic spot. ◆ Main St (between Third and Second Sts)

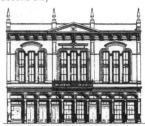

20 Napa Valley Opera House This Italianate late-19th-century opera house (pictured above), designed by architects **Joseph** and **Samuel Newson** and **Ira Gilchrist,** is one of the last second-story theaters left in California. A City of Napa Landmark, it is listed on the National Register of Historic Places. Built in

1879, it opened in 1880 with a performance of *HMS Pinafore,* but because "opera house" at that time was synonymous with vaudeville hall, there were many minstrel shows, political rallies, and dog-and-pony shows held here, too. The opera house is undergoing extensive renovation, with plans for a 500-seat performing arts center and commercial space downstairs. The completion date has yet to be determined. ◆ 1018 Main St (at Pearl St). 226.7372; fax 252.2813

21 Napa Valley Traditions Here's another place to get your caffeine fix. The coffee beans come from the top-quality San Francisco roaster Mountanos Bros., and you'll also find espresso and tea at this shop. The demonstration kitchen provides lessons in making wine jellies and other treats. Gift baskets can be assembled here, too. A wine tasting shop under the same ownership is around the corner at 908 Pearl St (255.8544). ◆ Daily. 1202 Main St (at Pearl St). 226.2044; fax 226.2069 ♿

22 Napa Valley Wine Train

Napa Valley's answer to the Orient Express barely made it out of the station, as it was fought by locals who feared the traffic jams and carnival-like atmosphere it might engender. But the train finally got on track, and though it still has its detractors, it has proved less disruptive than many thought it would be. During the three-hour, 36-mile ride, passengers relax in luxurious Pullman lounge cars and dining cars replete with etched glass, fine fabrics, shiny brass, and mahogany. You can board for a Champagne brunch, lunch, or dinner run, with both fixed-price menus and à la carte items. A good selection of Napa Valley wines is available during the trip. Call for timetables, rates, and reservations. No smoking on board. Back at the station, a shop stocks more than 200 Napa Valley wines, which the operators will gladly ship anywhere in the US. ◆ Daily excursions. Reservations and deposit required. 1275 McKinstry St (off First St). 253.2111, 800/427.4124; fax 253.9264 ♿

23 Napa Fairgrounds The two-day Spring Fair in May features a fiddling contest, 4-H animal husbandry exhibitions, Highland dancers, a high-school rodeo, a horse show, Renaissance games for children, a demolition derby, and a children's circus. The Napa Town & Country Fair, held here for five days every August, ranks among the best in the country, with a demolition derby, a rodeo, live entertainment, and plenty of country-style exhibits, including displays of flowers, crafts, baked goods, homemade jams, and livestock and animals. The highlight of the fair is the wine tasting, where you may sample the wares of almost every Napa Valley producer. Numerous other activities and events are held here year-round. ◆ Call for the current schedule. 575 Third St (off the Silverado Tr). 253.4900 ♿

24 Tulocay Winery Chardonnay, Pinot Noir, Zinfandel, and a rich, intense Cabernet Sauvignon are produced here. The winery, adjacent to the family home, is so small that the telephone number is the same for both. ◆ Tasting, sales, and tours by appointment only. 1426 Coombsville Rd (off the Silverado Tr). 255.4064 ♿

25 Wild Horse Valley Ranch Pack up your picnic lunch and go horseback riding. This well-equipped riding facility not only boasts more than 50 miles of trails, it also has a racetrack, a polo field, and a cross-country jumping course. Classes for riders of all levels are available. Two-hour trail rides are offered three times daily (except on Tuesday). ◆ Daily. Reservations required. Wild Horse Valley Rd (at the end of Coombsville Rd, 20 miles east of town on Hwy 121). 224.0727; fax 224.8689

26 Hennessey House Bed & Breakfast $$ Formerly the residence of a local physician, this Eastlake Queen Anne Victorian is on the National Register of Historic Places. Today, it is a gracious bed-and-breakfast inn run by Laurianne Delay and Andrea LaMar, who used to work in the financial industry in New York. The inn has 10 guest rooms, all with private baths, queen-size featherbeds with old-fashioned quilts, period antiques, and many other elegant Victorian details. The four large rooms in the carriage house also feature whirlpool tubs, and a few have fireplaces or private patios. A hearty country breakfast (homemade granola and yogurt, fruit, and a hot entrée such as pancakes, baked eggs, or French toast) is served in the dining room, with its rare, hand-painted, stamped-tin ceiling. **Napa Valley Wine Train** and golfing packages are available. No smoking is allowed. ◆ 1727 Main St (between Yount and Jackson Sts). 226.3774; fax 226.2975

27 Arbor Guest House $$ This white-frame structure built in 1906 makes a charming bed-and-breakfast, with three guest rooms in the main house and two in the restored carriage house out back. All have private baths and graceful period furnishings, including queen-size beds with handmade quilts; three rooms also have fireplaces. In the main house, **Winter Haven** features a two-person spa in the corner, velvet Victorian chairs next to a cozy fire-place, and an Amish quilt on the bed. In the carriage house, **Rose's Bower** boasts a carved mahogany bed, ribboned wallpaper, cut-glass lamps, and rose-patterned French fireside chairs by the hearth. Enjoy breakfast (homemade scones or coffee cake, a baked egg dish, and fruit) in the garden, where a walkway edged with lavender trumpet vines leads from the main house to the carriage house. No smoking is allowed. ♦ 1436 G St (between Spencer and Georgia Sts). 252.8144 ♿

28 Von Uhlit Ranch Harvest your own apples, pears, prunes, pumpkins, almonds, and walnuts in season. Grapevine wreaths and fresh and dried flowers are also sold here. ♦ Daily noon-4PM. 3011 Soscol Ave (off Trancas St). 226.2844 ♿

29 Hoffman Farm Pick your own organically grown pears, prunes, plums, and walnuts in season. ♦ Daily July-Nov. 2125 Silverado Tr (off Trancas St). 226.8938 ♿

30 Silverado Hill Cellars Wine maker John Nemeth indulges his love of the Chardonnay grape at this small winery set behind a wrought-iron gate along the Silverado Trail. Three vintages of Chardonnay are usually available for tasting. Nemeth's Winemaker's Special vintages are only available here. ♦ Tasting and sales daily; tours by appointment only. 3105 Silverado Tr (north of Trancas St). 253.9306 ♿

31 John's Rose Garden Allow at least an hour to visit John Dallas's garden and nursery with more than 500 kinds of roses, many of them old varieties. The best time to visit is in May and June, when most roses are in full bloom. ♦ Daily by appointment only. 1020 Mount George Ave (off Olive Hill La). 224.8002 ♿

32 Silverado Country Club & Resort $$$$ An extensive luxury resort complex and country club occupies the 1,200-acre estate purchased in 1869 by Civil War general and US senator John Miller. His imposing mansion (built around an adobe house) has become the resort's clubhouse, with views of huge oak trees, palms, and the surrounding hills and mountains from the back terrace.

Clusters of junior suites and one-, two-, and three-bedroom condominium suites (280 total) designed with privacy in mind are grouped around eight swimming pools and garden areas. The most popular units are on the clubhouse side and are an easy walk to the tennis courts, clubhouse, and golf courses, while **Oak Creek East**, one of the newer areas, is the most secluded. The presidential suite (with four bedrooms) is a good choice for those who want accommodations as large as a house. The rental units are individually owned by members but furnished according to club guidelines, with contemporary furniture, private baths, deck furniture, and full kitchens. The exteriors won't knock you off your feet (they're more reminiscent of a middle-class suburban neighborhood than of a posh resort), but they're quite comfortable and feel just like home—if home is a cushy condo with room service, that is.

The club is a paradise for golf and tennis buffs—that's the real reason people come here. Its two challenging 18-hole championship golf courses, designed by Robert Trent Jones Jr., are among the best in the country, and the 20 plexipaved tennis courts—more than anywhere else in Northern California—make it one of the nation's top 10 tennis facilities. An added bonus: Head concierge Laurie Gordon is a native and knows the area as only an insider can. ♦ 1600 Atlas Peak Rd (off Monticello Rd). 257.0200, 800/532.0500 (reservations only); fax 257.5400 ♿

Within the Silverado Country Club:

Vintners Court ★★$$$$ This formal restaurant has an elegant dining room featuring an oversized chandelier, potted palms, and a dramatic white grand piano. The walls are lined with wine lockers where prominent Napa Valley vintners stash their private reserves. Start with one of the simple appetizers, such as grilled marinated vegetables with buffalo-milk mozzarella or cold poached asparagus and Belgian endive. Then move on to an entrée, which might include grilled ahi tuna with a macadamia nut–cilantro pesto, and chicken breast stuffed with goat cheese, chorizo sausage, and Anaheim chilies, or pork tenderloin topped with a raspberry-peppercorn sauce. If you're splurging on a bottle of top California red, play it safe and order the herb-encrusted rack of lamb or the mixed grill. On Friday night, a popular, elaborate seafood buffet is served, and the Sunday brunch features more than 40 items, including an omelette bar and made-to-order waffles. ♦ California ♦ W-Sa dinner; Su brunch and dinner. Reservations recommended. 257.5428 ♿

Royal Oak Restaurant ★$$$ Cooks prepare prawns, swordfish, salmon, mesquite-grilled steaks, and triple-cut lamb chops in the open kitchen of this restaurant. The steaks and seafood are fine, but the desserts seem designed for kids with a sweet tooth rather than for adults. ♦ American ♦ Daily dinner. Reservations recommended. 257.5427 ಕ

SILVERADO BAR & GRILL

Silverado Bar & Grill ★$ The best bet at the **Silverado Country Club** is this casual restaurant, which serves breakfast all day long. The menu also offers burgers and salads. If you want the classic version of a club sandwich, you'll find it here. ♦ American ♦ Daily breakfast and lunch. 257.0200, ext. 5380 ಕ

33 William Hill Winery Founded in 1974, this Napa winery makes consistently well crafted wines, and produces both regular and reserve bottlings of Chardonnay and Cabernet Sauvignon. With the 1989 vintage, the winery also began producing Pinot Noir and Chardonnay from grapes grown in Oregon. Food and wine pairings are sometimes offered here on weekends. ♦ Tasting and sales daily; tours by appointment only. 1761 Atlas Peak Rd (off Monticello Rd about a half mile north of the Silverado Country Club & Resort). 224.4477; fax 224.4484 ಕ

34 Bucher Ranch Cut your own Christmas trees at this ranch—you can choose from Douglas fir and Scotch pine. ♦ Daily from the day after Thanksgiving to 24 Dec. 2106 Big Ranch Rd (off Trancas St). 224.5354

35 Napa Valley Christmas Tree Farm Here are more Christmas trees to cut yourself: Douglas fir, Scotch pine, Monterey pine, precut Noble fir, Silver Tip fir, and White fir. ♦ Daily from the day after Thanksgiving to 24 Dec; tours by appointment only. 2134 Big Ranch Rd (off Trancas St). 252.1000

36 John Muir Inn $$ Located at a busy crossroads on Highway 29 at the south end of Napa Valley, this contemporary inn has 59 guest rooms with modern decor, cable TV, and private baths (some with whirlpool spas). Relax in the swimming pool and hot tub after the day's excursion. A continental breakfast is served. ♦ 1998 Trower Ave (at Hwy 29). 257.7220, 800/522.8999; fax 258.0943 ಕ

37 Napa Valley Cyclery Rent your wheels here: 15-speed mountain-style ATBs (all-terrain bikes) and 21-speed touring bikes and tandems, plus burly trailers that will carry two children and gear. Delivery and one-way rentals are available, too. The shop also offers treks with **Napa Valley Bike Tours** that cater to beginner and recreational riders, as well as experienced cyclists. Tours include rental of a mountain-style bicycle and helmet, a catered picnic overlooking the valley, and a support van to carry wine purchases or too-pooped-to-pedal riders. Led by tour director Lori Townsend, the 9AM-4PM excursion covers nearly 25 miles of the Silverado Trail, stopping off at four wineries for tours and tasting. ♦ Daily. Reservations recommended. 4080 Byway East (off Hwy 29 at Trower Ave). 255.3377, 800/707.BIKE; fax 255.3380 ಕ

What is Wine?

The grape's contribution:

Skin = 8 percent

Adds color, flavor (bitterness and astringency), and aroma. Much of the tannins in red wine and all of the color comes from the skins

Seed = 4.5 percent

Crushing these adds tannins and oils

Pulp = 80 percent juice and 4.5 percent suspended solids

Stems and Stalk = 3 percent of cluster

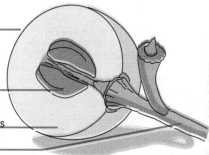

COURTESY OF THE SONOMA COUNTY WINERIES ASSOCIATION

38 La Residence Country Inn $$$ This country inn features 20 guest rooms on a two-acre estate just off Highway 29. The 1870 Gothic Revival mansion (illustrated below) has nine rooms, seven with private baths. All are furnished with period American antiques, patterned wallpaper, sweeping drapes, and queen-size beds; some rooms, such as No. 6, have fireplaces and entrances onto the second-floor veranda. The remainder of the rooms are in **Cabernet Hall,** a newer building styled after a French barn. These airy, spacious rooms with private baths are comfortably furnished with French and English pine antiques and queen-size beds and designer prints, such as Laura Ashley and Pierre Deux. The large swimming pool between the two buildings is flanked by an arbor and a gazebo twined with wisteria. Guests sit down to breakfast (orange juice, a fresh fruit course, and an entrée such as French toast with berries and jam or scrambled eggs served with caramel nut rolls) in the inn's French country–style dining room. ♦ 4066 St. Helena Hwy (just north of Salvador Ave). 253.0337; fax 253.0382 &

38 Bistro Don Giovanni ★★★$$ Owner/executive chef Donna Scala and her husband and co-owner, Giovanni Scala, were previously partners in the very popular **Piatti** restaurant up the road in Yountville before opening up this bistro. The menu features such tasty appetizers as tuna tartare with croutons and leeks vinaigrette with tomatoes. Main courses may include penne pasta with yellowfin potatoes, sun-dried tomatoes, and fresh pesto, as well as pan-seared scallops and grilled shrimp, braised lamb shanks, and filet mignon. The large bar, although sometimes noisy, is a great hangout for sipping wines and unwinding from a day of sightseeing. ♦ Italian ♦ Daily lunch and dinner. Reservations recommended. 4110 St. Helena Hwy (just north of Salvador Ave). 224.3300; fax 224.3395 &

39 Monticello Cellars Virginian Jay Corley pays tribute to Thomas Jefferson, a great wine connoisseur, at this brick replica of his famous estate. Jefferson certainly would have appreciated the wines, especially the two distinguished Cabernet Sauvignons— Jefferson Ranch and Corley Reserve. An excellent Chardonnay is also made here. The tasting room sells books about Jefferson, Monticello, and the former president's travels through the French wine country. Visitors may picnic at several tables set out on a lawn beside the **Jefferson House.** ♦ Fee. Tasting, sales, and tours daily. 4242 Big Ranch Rd (off Oak Knoll Ave). 253.2802; fax 253.1019 &

Trefethen

40 Trefethen Vineyards Built in 1886, the tall, rust-colored winery building, shaded by centuries-old oak trees, is the last example of a three-level gravity-flow winery in California built entirely of wood. The Trefethen family, who restored the vineyards and winery in the early 1970s, have set up an outdoor exhibition of antique farm equipment near the building. All the wines, including a fine oaky Chardonnay and well-made Cabernet, Pinot Noir, and Riesling, are produced from grapes grown exclusively on this 600-acre estate at the cool southern end of Napa Valley. Special Library Selections of older vintages are sometimes available. For everyday drinking, the Eschol Red and Eschol White are always good values. ♦ Tasting daily; tours by appointment only. 1160 Oak Knoll Ave (off St. Helena Hwy). 255.7700; fax 255.0793 &

41 Oak Knoll Inn $$$ This luxurious, well-run bed-and-breakfast is set amidst 600 acres of Chardonnay vines. Built of field stones collected from nearby vineyards, the impressive French country–style inn has four spacious guest rooms. Each has high wooden ceilings, lush carpeting, a king-size bed, a full fireplace with a comfortable sofa set in front, and a private bath tiled in granite. Tall French doors open onto a broad wooden veranda with a view of the vineyards and the mountainous

La Residence Country Inn

Stags Leap district beyond. To make this wine-country retreat even more appealing, there is a large outdoor pool, an outdoor Jacuzzi, and a gazebo for poolside picnics. Another nice touch is the croquet setup on the front lawn. Innkeeper Barbara Passino will serve her full breakfast either in the dining room in front of the fireplace, on the veranda, or in your room. ♦ 2200 Oak Knoll Ave (between the Silverado Tr and Big Ranch Rd). 255.2200

42 Altamura Vineyards and Winery This tiny winery has concentrated on hand-crafted Chardonnay since its founding in 1985, although now it also produces a Cabernet Sauvignon. Vintner Frank Altamura, a Napa Valley native, picked up his wine-making skills at **Caymus Vineyards** in Rutherford. ♦ Tasting and tours daily by appointment only. 4240 Silverado Tr (at Oak Knoll Ave). 253.2000 ♿

43 Signorello Vineyards Owned by San Francisco native Raymond E. Signorello, this small winery in the Stags Leap district (east of Yountville) produces Chardonnay, Sauvignon Blanc, and Zinfandel, along with limited quantities of Cabernet, Pinot Noir, Merlot, Sémillon, and the white Rhône variety Viognier. ♦ Tasting and tours by appointment only. 4500 Silverado Tr (north of Oak Knoll Ave). 255.5990

44 Chimney Rock Golf Course This privately owned nine-hole golf course (par 36) is surrounded by vineyards; it can also be played as an 18-hole course. ♦ Daily. Open to the public. 5320 Silverado Tr (north of Oak Knoll Ave). Reservations recommended. 255.3363; fax 257.2036

45 Chimney Rock Winery
After decades in the international soft drink and hotel business, in 1980 Hack and Stella Wilson decided to  become vintners. They planted grapevines on nine of the 18 holes of their **Chimney Rock Golf Course,** which just happened to be on prime vineyard land. Nestled in a grove of poplar trees, the distinctive Cape Dutch architecture of the hospitality center and winery (illustrated below) features steep roofs and gables with gracefully curving arches. Adorning the cellars is a frieze of Ganymede, cupbearer to Zeus; sculpted by Michael Casey, the resident artist for the California State Capitol restoration in Sacramento, it is a copy of a work by 18th-century German sculptor Antón Anreith. The winery produces a supple Bordeaux-style Cabernet and a barrel-fermented Chardonnay, as well as a Fumé Blanc. ♦ Fee. Tasting and sales daily; tours by appointment only. 5350 Silverado Tr (north of Oak Knoll Ave). 257.2641; fax 257.2036 ♿

45 Clos du Val Winery Known for its Cabernet Sauvignon (especially the reserve), velvety Merlot, and graceful Zinfandel, this winery has had a French wine maker, Bernard Portet, at the helm since its founding in 1972. Portet grew up at Château Lafite-Rothschild in Bordeaux, where his father was cellar master, and successfully combines Bordeaux tradition with California technological innovation. The tasting-room staff is friendly and personable. An added attraction is the series of witty wine-related postcards and posters on wine themes by artist Ronald Searle. Relax at the picnic tables under old oak trees. ♦ Tasting and sales daily; tours by appointment only. 5330 Silverado Tr (north of Oak Knoll Ave). 252.6711; fax 252.6125 ♿

Chimney Rock Winery

Wine Making: From the Grape to the Bottle

There are almost as many methods for making wine as there are wine makers. And different procedures can produce totally different wines—even when they're made from the same grapes. This basic chart outlines the major stages for making white and red wine.

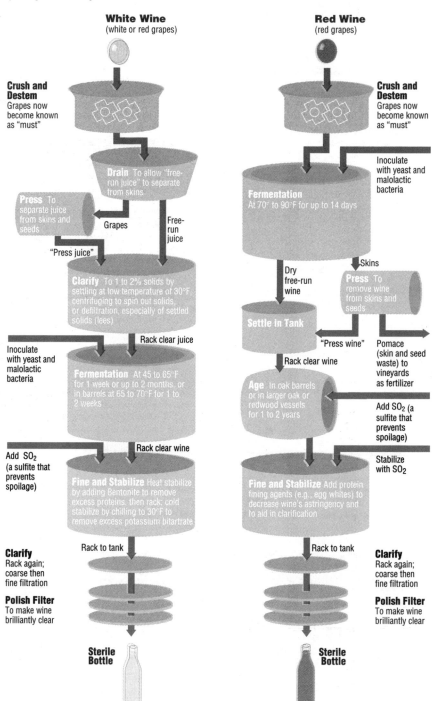

COURTESY OF THE SONOMA COUNTY WINERIES ASSOCIATION

46 Stag's Leap Wine Cellars In the now-famous Paris tasting of 1976, California wines competed with top French vintages in a blind taste test. Much to the chagrin of French producers and tasters alike, the best Cabernet Sauvignon was not a pedigreed Bordeaux but a California wine—the 1973 Cabernet Sauvignon from this winery, which had been founded only the year before. Vintners Warren and Barbara Winiarski have continued to produce consistently world-class Cabernets; their Cask 23 is among the most coveted and expensive California wines. They also make Chardonnay, Johannisberg Riesling, Sauvignon Blanc, Petite Sirah, and Merlot. The tasting room often has some older vintages for sale. The lovely winery is set in a terraced hillside sheltered by trees. ♦ Fee. Tasting and sales daily; tours by appointment only. 5766 Silverado Tr (between Oak Knoll Ave and Yountville Cross Rd). 944.2020; fax 255.7501 &

47 Pine Ridge Winery Sample Cabernet Sauvignon, Merlot, Chardonnay, and a crisp Chenin Blanc in the small, rustic tasting room on the western edge of the Stags Leap area. If you have time, tour the aging cellars dug into the terraced hillside. There also is a shady picnic area and swings for the kids. A trail leads up to the ridge that gives the winery its name. ♦ Fee. Tasting and sales daily; tours 10:15AM, 1PM, and 3PM by appointment only. 5901 Silverado Tr (between Oak Knoll Ave and Yountville Cross Rd). 252.9777; fax 253.1493 &

In the late 19th century, peregrine falcons nested on Mount St. Helena. But by the 1950s the bird of prey's numbers had been reduced to just 10 breeding pairs in all of California, primarily due, it is believed, to the widespread use of the insecticide DDT. In 1977 a pair settled on Mount St. Helena, and peregrine falcons have been doing well on the mountain ever since. Watch them dive over the skies above the extinct volcano; they can reach speeds of 180 to 217 miles per hour and are considered the fastest animals in the world.

Restaurants/Clubs: Red   Hotels: Blue
Shops/ ♦ Outdoors: Green   Wineries/Sights: Black

48 Silverado Vineyards Set high on a knoll west of the Silverado Trail, this Spanish-style fieldstone winery with a tiled fountain and an entrancing view of the valley is known for its Cabernet and Chardonnay, notably the special reserves produced only in outstanding vintages. The winery also makes Sauvignon Blanc and Merlot. The regular Cabernet is a great value. The winery is owned by the Walt Disney family, who sold grapes from their vineyards before constructing the current building in 1981. ♦ Tasting and sales daily. 6121 Silverado Tr (between Oak Knoll Ave and Yountville Cross Rd). 257.1770 &

49 Shafer Vineyards Grape growers–turned-vintners John and Elizabeth Shafer produce excellent Cabernet, Merlot, and Chardonnay from hillside vineyards in both the Stags Leap and Carneros districts. Their top wine is the Hillside Select Cabernet Sauvignon. ♦ Tours M-F by appointment only. 6154 Silverado Tr (between Oak Knoll Ave and Yountville Cross Rd). 944.2877 &

49 Robert Sinskey Vineyards One of the original partners in the now-defunct **Acacia Winery,** Robert Sinskey founded his own Stags Leap district winery in 1986 and has been garnering a fine reputation for his well-crafted Pinot Noir, Merlot, and Chardonnay. The modern stone-and-redwood winery with a 35-foot-high cathedral ceiling and columns twined with wisteria was designed by **Oscar Leidenfrost.** It's nice to stop and sit on the edge of the koi pond or walk around the small rose garden before heading inside for some serious tasting. A deck to one side offers picnic tables and a view of the valley. ♦ Fee. Tasting and sales daily; tours by appointment only. 6320 Silverado Tr (between Oak Knoll Ave and Yountville Cross Rd). 944.9090; fax 944.9092 &

50 S. Anderson Vineyards Founded in 1971, this small, family-owned winery reminiscent of a one-room schoolhouse specializes in Chardonnay and sparkling wines made by the traditional *méthode champenoise.* A spectacular 7,000-square-foot aging cave has been tunneled out of a volcanic-rock hillside overlooking the estate's vineyards. ♦ Fee. Tasting and sales daily; tours daily 10:30AM and 2:30PM. 1473 Yountville Cross Rd (between the Silverado Tr and Hwy 29). 944.8642 &

51 Château Chèvre Winery The name means "goat castle," after the herds that once roamed the property. The concrete winery building used to be the barn, and the bottling line has taken over the milk room. Best known for its Cabernet Franc and Merlot, it also produces Sauvignon Blanc, the classic accompaniment to goat cheese. ♦ Tasting and sales by appointment only. 2030 Hoffman La (off Solano Ave). 944.2184

52 Bernard Pradel Cellars Owner/wine maker Bernard Pradel hails from Burgundy, where Pinot Noir is king. But here he eschews that noble red grape for another: Cabernet Sauvignon, the favored grape of Bordeaux. He also makes Chardonnay and an unusual late-harvest Sauvignon Blanc. ♦ Sales daily by appointment only. 2100 Hoffman La (off Solano Ave). 944.8720; fax 944.0354 &

53 Lakespring Winery Impressive Merlot and pleasant Cabernet Sauvignon, Sauvignon Blanc, and Chardonnay are produced by this small winery owned by San Francisco's Battat brothers. ♦ Sales daily; tours by appointment only. 2055 Hoffman La (off Solano Ave). 944.2475 &

54 Newlan Vineyards Award-winning reds keep on coming from this small winery founded by the Newlan family in 1980. Owners Bruce and Jonette Newlan and wine maker Glen Newlan produce Cabernet Sauvignon, Pinot Noir, and Zinfandel, along with two whites: Chardonnay and a Late Harvest Johannisberg Riesling. The beautiful carved door that leads to the tasting rooms once graced the entrance of an old church. ♦ Tasting and sales daily; tours by appointment only. 5225 Solano Ave (south of Hoffman La). 257.2399 &

55 Hess Collection Winery This restored, historic stone winery is not to be missed, despite the 15-minute drive from the main road. In 1978 Swiss mineral-water magnate Donald Hess took a long lease on the old **Christian Brothers Mont LaSalle Cellars** on Mount Veeder and produced a spectacular 1983 Reserve Cabernet Sauvignon. His elegant estate-bottled Chardonnay is just as impressive. A passionate art collector, Hess stored much of his extensive collection of contemporary European and American art at his headquarters in Bern, Switzerland, until he decided to showcase his wines and art under one roof. The old stone building has been completely renovated to house both the winery and a private museum of contemporary art. The 130-piece collection is devoted to the work of 29 artists, including Francis Bacon, Robert Motherwell, Frank Stella, Theodoros Stamos, and Magdalena Akabanowitz. A well-designed,

self-guided tour takes you through the museum and includes glimpses of the cellars where Hess's Chardonnays and Cabernets ferment and age, ending in the handsome tasting room, where wines and mineral water are served. Highly recommended. ♦ Fee. Tasting, sales, and tours daily. 4411 Redwood Rd (off Hwy 29). 255.1144 &

56 Mayacamas Vineyards A formidable road takes you to this historic property with terraced vineyards high on the slopes of the extinct volcano Mount Veeder. The three-story stone building, set in the volcano's crater, was built in 1889 for John Henry Fisher, a native of Stuttgart, Germany. The winery was re-established in 1941 when the British chemist Jack Taylor restored it and replanted the vineyards. It has been owned by banker-turned-vintner Bob Travers and his wife, Nonie, since 1968. The winery is known for its rugged, intense Cabernet and rich, oaky Chardonnay, both of which age remarkably well. It also makes Pinot Noir and Sauvignon Blanc. ♦ Tasting and tours M-F by appointment only. 1155 Lokoya Rd (off Mount Veeder Rd). 224.4030; fax 224.3979 &

57 Château Potelle This winery located on scenic Mount Veeder produces Chardonnay, Sauvignon Blanc, Cabernet, and Zinfandel from grapes grown on its mountain vineyards. French proprietors Jean-Noël and Marketta Fourmeaux du Sartel named the winery after the family's 11th-century castle in France. Reservations are required for the winery's picnic area, which has a panoramic view of mountains and vineyards. Call for directions; it's much faster via the Oakville Grade. ♦ Tasting and sales M, Th-Su; tours by appointment only. 3875 Mount Veeder Rd (near Dry Creek Rd). 255.9440; fax 255.9444 &

Bests

André Tchelistcheff
Enologist

A Sunday brunch or lunch on the **Napa Valley Wine Train** in the spring.

Also in spring, a leisurely drive from **Napa** to **Calistoga** on the **Silverado Trail.**

A tour of **Domaine Chandon** and lunch or dinner at the **Domaine Chandon Restaurant.**

A visit to **The Hess Collection** art gallery and winery.

The excitement, hopes, and anxieties of harvest season—mid-September through October—in **Napa Valley,** and the fall colors in the vineyards after harvest.

Yountville/Oakville/ Rutherford

Just after the outskirts of **Napa** give way to vineyards, Yountville appears east of **Highway 29**. Founded by George Calvert Yount, a pioneer and adventurer who traveled to California from North Carolina, it is now a town of 3,500 people. Yount, after visiting Mexican general Mariano Vallejo at his Sonoma ranch, became the first American to settle in **Napa Valley** and the first to receive a land grant from the Mexican government—12,000 acres in the heart of the valley called **Rancho Caymus.** With the help of local Indians, he also planted the first grapevines in Napa Valley with cuttings he obtained from General Vallejo. By 1855, a town had grown up on the southern borders of Rancho Caymus, which Yount dubbed **Sebastopol** (not to be confused with the Sebastopol in Sonoma County). In 1867, two years after Yount's death at age 71, the town's name was changed to Yountville in his honor.

A short jaunt from Yountville up Highway 29 are the twin towns of Oakville and Rutherford, where some of the world's best Cabernet Sauvignon vines thrive in a microclimate similar to France's Bordeaux region. Don't hurry through this area on your way to **St. Helena** or you'll miss such great wineries as **Robert Mondavi** and **Beaulieu.** And if their beautiful buildings and highly touted wines aren't enough to entice you, a stay or a meal at **Auberge du Soleil,** one of the valley's best inns/restaurants, surely will. Summer and harvesttime (August through October) are the busiest times to visit.

58 Domaine Chandon The French Champagne house Moët et Chandon, with more than two centuries of experience, has been making sparkling wine in Napa Valley since 1977. Here in California, this winery has pioneered the use both of exclusively classic varietals in its sparkling wines and of certain production techniques. More than six million bottles of sparkling wine are produced here annually.

The top of the line is the toasty reserve; the best value is the Blanc de Noirs. Wine maker Dawnine Dyer also produces very limited quantities of Chandon Club Cuvée, aged a minimum of six years on the lees, or yeast, a process that gives it a more complex flavor. Tours explain how sparkling wine is made by the traditional *méthode champenoise* and include a visit to a museum devoted to the history of Champagne. Come just to stroll around the extensive, beautifully landscaped gardens or enjoy the winery's informal bar, **Le Salon,** where Domaine Chandon sparkling wine is sold by the glass and by the bottle, along with sparkling-wine cocktails, mineral water, and juice. ♦ Fee. Tasting, sales, and tours daily May-Oct; W-Su Nov-Apr. One California Dr (off Hwy 29), Yountville. 944.2280 &

YOUNTVILLE

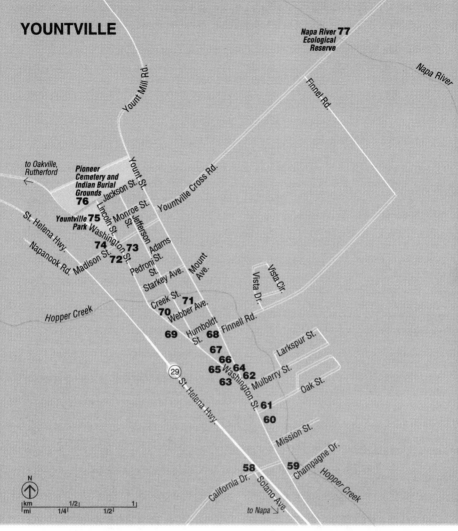

Within Domaine Chandon:

Domaine Chandon Restaurant ★★★
$$$ Chef Philippe Jeanty, a native of Champagne, has headed the kitchen staff here since the restaurant opened in 1977. With its candlelit tables and sweeping views of the vineyards, the restaurant remains one of the most romantic settings in Napa Valley. In warm weather you may also dine outdoors. Jeanty favors a light, flavorful style of cooking using prime local ingredients, and is committed to the simple idea that food should go with wine. With a glass of Brut, try his alder-and-hickory-smoked Norwegian salmon with caramelized onion brioche or the house-smoked red trout fillet drizzled with olive oil and served with warm potato slices. For red wines, he offers a dry-aged sirloin of beef, charred rare, or Sonoma farm-raised lamb served with a roasted shallot-and-garlic tart. The venison tournedos wrapped in pancetta are perfect with a robust red wine. Another thoughtful touch is a cheese course, the ideal way to finish off that fine bottle of Cabernet. The desserts can be disappointing and too sweet, but the crème brûlée scented with lavender is fine. The fare is more casual at lunch: several soups, inventive salads, even a pizza on occasion, and such entrées as grilled Sonoma rabbit and chicken potpie. The service is attentive without being pretentious, and the extensive wine list offers a number of Napa Valley's best wines at good prices. ♦ California ♦ M-Tu lunch and dinner; W-Su dinner Feb-Dec. Reservations recommended; jacket required at dinner. 944.2892 &

59 The Massage Place Therapeutic massages using a combination of Swedish/Esalen techniques are offered here. ♦ M-F by appointment only. 6428 Washington St (between Champagne Dr and Mission St), Yountville. 944.1387

Restaurants/Clubs: Red   **Hotels:** Blue
Shops/ ⵍ Outdoors: Green   **Wineries/Sights:** Black

THE DINER

60 The Diner ★★$ There's plenty to like about this down-home restaurant, with its colorful collection of vintage Fiestaware pitchers, roomy booths, and a long counter where you may settle in with the morning paper and a plate of great cornmeal pancakes and smoky links. Breakfast (served all day), which includes a particularly fine rendition of *huevos rancheros,* is enough to put this unpretentious place on the map. Lunch brings on an array of hearty sandwiches and oversized enchiladas, burritos, and tostadas, while dinner focuses on fresh fish and south-of-the-border–inspired dishes. The superlative buttermilk shake, which tastes just like cheesecake, is quite a treat. The power behind this appealing diner is Cassandra Mitchell, a fourth-generation San Franciscan. ♦ Eclectic ♦ Tu-Su breakfast, lunch, and dinner. 6476 Washington St (between Mission and Oak Sts), Yountville. 944.2626 ♿

60 Piatti ★★★$$$ One of the most popular restaurants in the valley, this place (which has expanded to seven other locations, including in Sonoma and Montecito) serves soul-warming Italian fare in a casual setting. With lavish garlic braids and garlands of hot red peppers, witty trompe l'oeil paintings of food on the walls, and a wood-burning pizza oven, it feels like an idealized trattoria. But what impresses most is the menu, filled with gutsy regional dishes that are hard to find even in Italy these days: real Roman bruschetta (grilled country bread topped with garlic, olive oil, basil, and tomato), black risotto cooked with cuttlefish ink, and *pappardelle* (wide ribbon noodles) sauced with braised rabbit, chard, and wild mushrooms. The menu changes seasonally, but a good bet is the grilled chicken breast *al mattone* (literally, "under a brick") served with roasted-garlic mashed potatoes and thyme gravy. Great appetizers, grilled fish, and pizzas from the wood-burning oven are also available—and save room for dessert, particularly the heavenly tiramisù. The well-chosen wine list includes the best of California and Italy. ♦ Italian ♦ Daily lunch and dinner. Reservations recommended. 6480 Washington St (between Mission and Oak Sts), Yountville. 944.2070 ♿. Also at: the Salvador Vallejo Adobe, First St W (at W Spain St), Sonoma. 996.2351; fax 996.3148 ♿

61 Napa Valley Tourist Bureau Stop here for free information on reservations for lodging, balloon flights, mud baths, and other diversions in Napa Valley. The staff has up-to-date information on which wineries have tasting fees or require appointments for tours and can help you decide which ones might interest you most. Maps, books, and guides are also available. ♦ Daily. 6488 Washington St (between Oak and Mulberry Sts), Yountville. 258.1957, 800/523.4353; fax 944.8710

62 Yountville Chamber of Commerce & Visitor Information You'll find free maps of Yountville here, as well as brochures on wineries and activities in the area. Information on wedding packages is also available. ♦ M-Sa. 6516 Yount St (at Washington St), Yountville. 944.0904, 800/959.3604 (recording); fax 944.4465 ♿

63 Whistle Stop Center The old **Southern Pacific** train station, built in 1889, has been restored as a shopping center that houses several stores. ♦ 6505 Washington St (at Yount St), Yountville. 944.9624 ♿

Within the Whistle Stop Center:

Overland Sheepskin Company This shop sells superb sheepskin rugs, coats, hats, mittens, and slippers, all made in Taos, New Mexico. Coats are made from *entre fino*—the finest European sheepskin—in a variety of styles, but come in only one price range: high. The prices of the shearling gloves and the beautifully crafted shearling-lined booties are more down-to-earth. You'll find men's and women's styles, plus authentic Panama hats (which aficionados know actually come from Ecuador), oilskin raincoats from Australia, and handsome leather luggage for world-class adventurers. And don't miss the unusual all-leather animals (including hippos, tigers, and horses), made in India. ♦ Daily. 944.0778; fax 944.9644 ♿

64 Anestis' ★$$$ This large restaurant with a modern decor concentrates on food with a Mediterranean touch, including pasta, fish with fresh salsa, and poultry and meats roasted on an imported French rotisserie. At lunch, stop in for a quick mesquite-grilled burger or pita-bread sandwich. There's a large selection of such spit-roasted items as duckling, leg of lamb, and prime rib for dinner. The wine list is perfunctory. ♦ Mediterranean ♦ Daily lunch and dinner. 6518 Washington St (at Yount St), Yountville. 944.1500; fax 944.8613 ♿

Vintage 1870

65 Vintage 1870 When Gottlieb Groezinger's Yountville winery was built in 1870, it was hailed as the largest and best equipped in the valley. Today, the brick winery and the old train station next to it are a handsome shopping complex, with more than 45 specialty stores, gift shops, and boutiques (which seem to change every few months). Muzak is piped inside and outside the building, and many shops concentrate on silly souvenirs, so it takes determination to find the few interesting places inside. And the overpowering scent of popcorn and cheap snacks doesn't add to the complex's appeal. ♦ Daily. 6525 Washington St (between Mulberry and Humboldt Sts), Yountville. 944.2451; fax 944.2453 &

Within Vintage 1870:

Adventures Aloft This company offers balloon flights above Napa Valley with a catered light brunch and Champagne. ♦ Reservations required (preferably two weeks in advance). 255.8688; fax 944.0540

A Little Romance Victoriana lovers will swoon over the Battenberg-lace duvet covers, flowered chintz coverlets, antique quilts, old-fashioned hatboxes, profusion of pillows, reproductions of Victorian tea sets, and books on country houses and related subjects found in this boutique. ♦ Daily. 944.1350 &

Blue Heron Gallery Located in the complex's courtyard, this shop features a mélange of art, including pottery, sculpture, oil and watercolor paintings (many of Napa Valley scenes), prints, and even handmade clocks. ♦ M, W-Su. 944.2044 &

Red Rock Grill ★$ Burgers, salads, and sandwiches are served in a restored railroad depot with a pleasant outdoor wooden deck that's laced with wisteria. The concept here is American-style pub grub. At breakfast, the kitchen turns out classic egg dishes and omelettes. Lunch brings on fish and chips, fried calamari, and more. And at dinner you may choose from all of the above plus barbecued ribs and steaks. There's also a good selection of domestic beers and ales, including San Francisco's Anchor Steam and Chico's Sierra Nevada Pale Ale. ♦ American ♦ Daily breakfast, lunch, and dinner. 944.2614; fax 252.9278 &

66 Groezinger Wine Company A good selection of current Napa Valley releases, along with selected older wines, are offered in this shop. The tasting bar is at its busiest in the summer and may serve up to a hundred wines by the glass. The staff is helpful and knowledgeable. They'll ship wines almost anywhere in the US, too. ♦ Daily. 6528 Washington St (between Mulberry and Humboldt Sts), Yountville. 944.2331; fax 944.1111 &

67 Beard Plaza Art galleries, gift shops, and a hair salon are featured in this small shopping complex. ♦ Daily. 6540 Washington St (between Mulberry and Humboldt Sts), Yountville &

68 Maison Fleurie $$$ The balcony of this cozy brick building, which has been operating as a hotel since 1873, once graced the old French Hospital in San Francisco. Now a French country inn owned by Four Sisters Inns, the property boasts 13 rooms in the main building and two newer annexes, all with private baths and furnished with antiques. There is also a large swimming pool and a Jacuzzi for hotel guests. Innkeeper Roger Asbill serves a full breakfast in the dining room. No smoking is permitted. ♦ 6529 Yount St (between Finnel Rd and Humboldt St), Yountville. 944.2056

69 Vintage Inn $$$ This inn on a 23-acre estate was once part of the Spanish land grant that pioneer George C. Yount received from General Vallejo. Designed by **Kipp Stewart**, who also created the sybaritic Ventana Inn in Big Sur, the inn boasts 76 guest rooms and four villas. Fireplaces, pine armoires, private baths with Jacuzzis, ceiling fans, refrigerators, and private patios or verandas in every room make this a comfortable base for exploring the wine country. Other amenities include a 60-foot lap pool and spa heated year-round, two tennis courts, and bikes for rent. The concierge will arrange for private tours of wineries, mud baths, and hot-air balloon rides. A Champagne continental breakfast is served. ♦ 6541 Washington St (between Humboldt St and Webber Ave), Yountville. 944.1112, 800/351.1133 in CA, 800/982.5539; fax 944.1617 &

70 Bordeaux House $$ Designed in the 1970s by architect **Robert Keenan**, this unusual red-brick inn sits on a quiet residential street. The seven guest rooms feature queen-size beds, fireplaces, and private baths; the best is the **Chablis Room** upstairs, which has its own balcony. Innkeeper Jean Lunney serves a continental breakfast (muffins or other pastries, granola, yogurt, juice, and coffee) each morning in the common room. ♦ 6600 Washington St (between Webber Ave and Creek St), Yountville. 944.2855 &

70 The French Laundry ★★★$$$$ Situated in a historic stone building that was once a laundry, this intimate but unfussy restaurant has long been a favorite among the valley's food connoisseurs. Thomas Keller, former chef/owner of the popular Rakel restaurant in New York City, prepares superb French haute cuisine. A meal here is a leisurely affair; the table is yours for the evening. The prix-fixe menu, which changes daily, is generally four or five courses. Appetizers, such as carpaccio of Atlantic salmon or sautéed rabbit livers, are almost always intriguing. The main course may be slow-cooked veal breast with roasted root vegetables or pan-roasted California sturgeon with a cassoulet of white beans and glazed pearl onions. Desserts might include bitter chocolate marquise cannolis and ginger sabayon, crème brûlée with candied bartlett pears, and home-style cinnamon-sugared doughnuts. ◆ French ◆ Tu-Su dinner. Reservations required. 6640 Washington St (at Creek St), Yountville. 944.2380 &

71 Webber Place $$ Built in 1850 at the edge of old Yountville, this red farmhouse (illus- trated below) enclosed by a white picket fence has been turned into a homey and unpre- tentious bed-and-breakfast inn by its owner, artist Diane Bartholomew. In the morning, her comfortable kitchen smells of good coffee, biscuits, and bacon, and on sunny afternoons she serves tea and homemade cookies on the front porch. The four lovely guest rooms have ornate brass beds covered with antique quilts. Two of the rooms share a deep, old-fashioned tub; the other two have similar tubs tucked in alcoves. The upstairs rooms have views of treetops and the sky; the large **Veranda Suite** downstairs boasts a queen-size featherbed and down comforter, its own entrance, and a shady private veranda. At press time, plans were in the works to add five new cottages with queen-size beds and fireplaces, as well as a swimming pool and spa. ◆ 6610 Webber Ave (between Jefferson and Yount Sts), Yountville. 944.8384, 800/647.7177

72 Washington Square A dozen shops and a few restaurants fill this small shopping center. ◆ Daily. 6795 Washington St (at Madison St), Yountville. 944.0637; fax 944.0941 &

Within Washington Square:

NAPA VALLEY GRILLE

Napa Valley Grille ★$$ Chef Bob Hurley is at the helm of this pleasant restaurant offering a lunch and dinner menu that changes daily but always includes good salad and pasta dishes. At lunch, you may choose from a wide variety of sandwiches, such as grilled chicken and roasted chilies on rosemary focaccia, hamburgers topped with Sonoma jack cheese, and grilled eggplant layered with provolone and pesto. The main courses at dinner may include pepper-crusted rack of pork, grilled certified Angus top sirloin with Cognac sauce, and grilled salmon served with snap-pea coulis. Equally engaging is the Sunday brunch menu, which features many tempting choices, including Dungeness crab cakes with poached eggs, *huevos rancheros,* and fresh berry blintzes topped with crème fraîche. The outdoor patio is a popular seating area in good weather. ◆ California ◆ M-Sa lunch and dinner; Su brunch and dinner. 944.2330 &

Massage Werkes Here you can indulge in an hour-long body massage given either in a combination Swedish/Esalen technique or in Chuaka, a rubdown that you can feel right down to your bones. Herbal facials are available as well. ◆ Daily by appointment only. 944.1906

Webber Place

73 Katz & Company Gorgeous food-related items are the specialty of this shop owned by Albert and Kim Katz. All of the products are made either by the Katzes in the shop's open kitchen or by local chefs. The shelves are lined with beautifully bottled Napa Valley olive oil, herb and wine vinegar, fruit preserves, chutneys, beeswax candles, ceramic pears, and other artistic creations, all of which can be packed in the store's handmade birch baskets for the perfect wine country gift. Order an espresso or fresh pastry at the counter and relax a bit at the large farm table in the back of the shop. Mail order is available, too. ♦ Tu-Su. 6770 Washington St (between Pedroni and Madison Sts), Yountville. 944.1393, 800/455.2305; fax 944.1263 &

74 Napa Valley Lodge $$$ Tucked into the quiet north end of Yountville, this pleasant, well-run 55-room inn was built in Spanish-hacienda style, with wooden balconies, private baths, and a terra-cotta roof. Special touches include honor bars and VCRs in each room, small two-room suites for families, and a helpful staff that will arrange bicycle rentals and other wine-country activities. Many rooms have vineyard views. Health activities include a large pool, sauna, and small fitness room. ♦ 2230 Madison St (at Washington St), Yountville. 944.2468; fax 944.9362 &

In 1861 the governor of California commissioned Agoston Haraszthy to travel to Europe and bring back vines suitable for planting in California vineyards. Six months later he was back, awaiting shipment of 100,000 vines from more than 300 varieties he had collected in France, Switzerland, Italy, and Germany.

75 Yountville Park This small park has shaded picnic tables, barbecue grills, and a children's playground. ♦ Washington St (between Madison and Jackson Sts), Yountville. 944.8851

76 Pioneer Cemetery and Indian Burial Grounds The early history of the valley can be traced in the tombstones here, which include a monument to town founder George C. Yount. Part of this 1848 cemetery serves as the burial grounds for the local Wappo Indian tribe. ♦ Off Jackson St (between Washington and Yount Sts), Yountville

77 Napa River Ecological Reserve Shady picnic spots under a grove of oak and sycamore trees beside the Napa River can be found here. ♦ Off Yountville Cross Rd (at the bridge)

Goosecross Cellars

78 Goosecross Cellars Napa Valley Chardonnay is the specialty of this small winery overlooking 20 acres of grapes and a rose garden. Guests are welcome to stroll through the vineyards after visiting the cellar. ♦ Tasting and sales daily; tours by appointment only. 1119 State La (off Yountville Cross Rd), Yountville. 944.1986; fax 944.9551 &

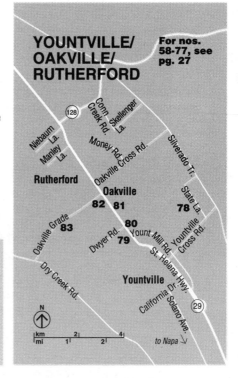

YOUNTVILLE/ OAKVILLE/ RUTHERFORD

For nos. 58-77, see pg. 27

79 Mustards Grill ★★★$$ The quintessential wine-country restaurant, it's been a smash hit since the team of Cindy Pawlcyn (who devises all the menus), Bill Upson, and Bill Higgins opened it in 1983. (Other popular dining spots these three have created include **Tra Vigne** in St. Helena and Fog City Diner in San Francisco.) Its major assets are a carefully chosen, well-priced wine list and a menu that always induces you to order far more than you had intended. The grill is open all day for late lunches and California-style grazing. And like most restaurants that have been extremely popular for several years, there are days when the fare isn't up to snuff and the service isn't as attentive as it should be. But fortunately this is the exception rather than the rule, and this place has maintained its spot on the roster of the best wine-country restaurants.

The menu changes frequently, but you can count on a superlative burger and ethereal onion rings (order them with homemade ketchup). Consider rabbit and pistachio sausages with pear chutney and a potato-shallot pancake or grilled stuffed pasilla peppers with tomatillo salsa to start. Move on to calf's liver with caramelized onions and bacon (a great dish to enjoy with a robust Napa Valley red); braised oxtail with sun-dried tomatoes and caper sauce; or grilled Sonoma rabbit with red peppers, fennel, and saffron. The side dishes—don't overlook the mashed potatoes or roasted garlic—are all terrific. And if you have room, go for the desserts, which may include a fresh blueberry crisp with lemon ice cream or strawberry, banana, and chocolate sorbets with a cookie. In the late afternoon this is a good spot to sit at the bar and eat while watching a ball game on TV. ♦ California ♦ Daily lunch and dinner. Reser-vations recommended. 7399 St. Helena Hwy (at Yount Mill Rd), Yountville. 944.2424 占

79 Oleander House $$ The four rooms at this bed-and-breakfast in a contemporary French country–style home just off Highway 29 are furnished with Laura Ashley fabrics and antiques. Each has a queen-size bed, private bath, fireplace, and balcony. A bonus: It's virtually next door to **Mustards Grill**, so you can stroll home to bed after a filling dinner. Innkeepers Louise and John Packard prepare a full breakfast of fresh orange juice, fruit, homemade pastries, and an entrée such as an herb omelette or French toast with raspberries. Smoking is not allowed. ♦ 7433 St. Helena Hwy (at Yount Mill Rd), Yountville. 944.8315; fax 944.2279

80 McAllister Water Gardens Re-create scenes from Monet's paintings in your own backyard with the help of this nursery, which specializes in water lilies and pond plants. ♦ F-Su Mar-Sept. 7420 St. Helena Hwy (north of Yountville Cross Rd), Yountville. 944.0921

81 Robert Pepi Winery In this contemporary winery, Robert Pepi and family produce a range of good wines, including Sangiovese (an Italian varietal), Sauvignon Blanc, and a Cabernet from Vine Hill ranch. ♦ Tasting and sales daily. 7585 St. Helena Hwy (between Yountville and Oakville Cross Rds), Oakville. 944.2807; fax 944.5628 占

82 Pometta's Deli Bicyclists make pit stops at this unassuming roadside Italian deli for barbecued-chicken sandwiches, whole-roasted chicken with barbecue spices, and

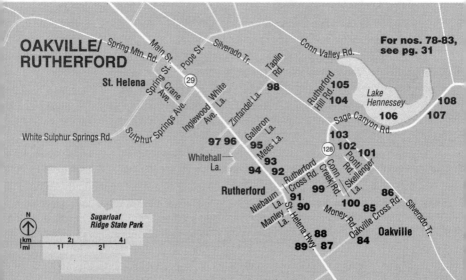

For nos. 78-83, see pg. 31

OAKVILLE/
RUTHERFORD

Spring Mtn. Rd.
Main St.
Pope St.
Silverado Tr.
Taplin Rd.
Conn Valley Rd.
St. Helena
Spring St.
Crane Ave.
Inglewood Ave.
White La.
Zinfandel La.
29
98
Rutherford Hill Rd.
105
104
Lake Hennessey
108
Sage Canyon Rd.
106
107
White Sulphur Springs Rd.
Sulphur Springs Ave.
Galleron La.
Mees La.
103
102
128
101
97 96
95
93
94 92
Whitehall La.
91
Rutherford Cross Rd.
99
Conn Creek Rd.
Ponti Rd.
Skellenger La.
100 85
86
Rutherford
Niebaum La.
90
St. Helena Hwy
Manley La.
Money Rd.
84
Oakville Cross Rd.
Silverado Tr.
Oakville
N
Sugarloaf Ridge State Park
88
89 87
km 2 4
mi 1 2

Pometta's Napa Valley Muffuletta sandwiches (ham, salami, two cheeses, and a special olive spread), along with an array of Italian deli salads. You can get your food to go or eat on the outdoor patio. ♦ Daily. 7787 St. Helena Hwy (at Oakville Grade), Oakville. 944.2365; fax 944.1513 &

83 Vichon Winery This Spanish Colonial–style winery, owned by the Robert Mondavi family, is tucked away high on a hill with a stunning view of the vineyards. It produces Chardonnay, Cabernet Sauvignon, Merlot, and Chevrignon. There are several tables in a small, but pretty, shady picnic grove and a boccie court for visitors. ♦ Fee for tasting older vintages. Tasting and sales daily; tours by appointment only. 1595 Oakville Grade (off Hwy 29), Oakville. 944.2811; fax 944.9224 &

84 Silver Oak Wine Cellars This small winery specializes in the production of only one varietal—a rich, powerful Cabernet Sauvignon made in three sites: Napa Valley, Alexander Valley, and the small Bonny's Vineyard. The result: three knockout Cabernets, aged three years in oak and two years in the bottle before they're released. It's worth a special trip to taste these beauties. ♦ Fee. Tasting and sales M-Sa; tours M-F 1:30PM by appointment only. 915 Oakville Cross Rd (at Money Rd), Oakville. 944.8808

85 Groth Vineyards and Winery The top-ranking Cabernet Sauvignon made here is produced by Atari computer maven Dennis Groth, his wife, Judith, and wine maker Michael Weiss. Their Cabernets are among the most sought after in California; Sauvignon Blanc and Chardonnay are also produced here. ♦ Tasting and tours Tu-Sa by appointment only. 750 Oakville Cross Rd (between Money Rd and the Silverado Tr), Oakville. 944.0290; fax 944.8932 &

86 Girard Winery One of California's best wineries, this family-owned property has supplied grapes to a number of top Napa Valley vintners and now produces its own rich, barrel-fermented Chardonnay. It also makes an impressive Cabernet Sauvignon, including a notable reserve, a small amount of Sémillon, and a Pinot Noir made from Oregon grapes, available only at the winery. ♦ Tasting and sales daily; tours M-F by appointment only. 7717 Silverado Tr (north of Oakville Cross Rd), Oakville. 944.8577 &

87 Stars Oakville Cafe ★★★$$; Ever-popular chef/restaurateur Jeremiah Tower has brought fame and fine food to the tiny town of Oakville. He also has brought his all-star team of executive chef Marc Franz and executive pastry chef Emily Luchetti from his award-winning Stars restaurant in San Francisco. Since this cafe opened a few years ago, Franz and Luchetti have been doing double duty, working at both restaurants. There are no pretenses of big-city life at this earth-colored cafe; it focuses on being simple and rustic, a befitting approach given its small-town setting.

The lunch and dinner menus (which change daily) are influenced by the produce and herbs available from surrounding farms and the restaurant's own vegetable gardens. Several dishes come from the kitchen's wood-burning ovens and may include such entrées as whole roast squab or a roasted shellfish platter, and many are reminiscent of the California cuisine served at Stars. And, of course, there is a top-notch selection of California and imported wines to choose from. An expansive patio provides alfresco dining, and guests are welcome to stroll through the artfully landscaped gardens filled with olive trees, lemon trees, lavender, flowers—and even an aviary. ♦ California ♦ Daily lunch and dinner. Reservations recommended. 7848 St. Helena Hwy (at Oakville Cross Rd), Oakville. 944.8905 &

87 Oakville Grocery Co. This is the place to shop for a sumptuous picnic. It's stocked with a vast array of gourmet goodies (with gourmet-level prices): wonderful pâtés, cold cuts, caviar, crusty country breads, crackers, and carefully tended cheeses, including local jack and goat. You may also opt for the prepared sandwiches, such as turkey and pesto or roast beef with blue cheese on Italian flat bread (they usually sell out by about 1PM). A tiny produce section stocks tender leaf lettuces, fresh herbs, and ripe summer fruit. Also note the top-quality olive oils and vinegars, and don't miss the desserts (truffles, tarts, cookies), which come from local bakeries. With two days' notice, the staff will put together any kind of picnic fantasy: everything from bicycle box lunches to lavish honeymoon picnics. The latest addition to the store is a small espresso bar tucked in the corner. This top-notch grocery store is the granddaddy of gourmet shops in the Bay Area. ♦ Daily. 7856 St. Helena Hwy (at Oakville Cross Rd), Oakville. 944.8802, 800/736.6602 fax 944.1844 ♿

88 Turnbull Wine Cellars This small winery is housed in an award-winning, barnlike structure designed by San Francisco architect **William Turnbull,** who used to be a partner in the winery with San Francisco attorney Reverdy Johnson. Their first vintage was in 1979. Patrick O'Dell is now the owner, and Kristin Belair is the wine maker. The winery produces a Cabernet Sauvignon with a pronounced minty, eucalyptus character. Vineyard Selection 67 comes from the last block of old vines on the property. ♦ Sales daily; tasting and tours by appointment only. 8210 St. Helena Hwy (north of Oakville Cross Rd), Oakville. 963.5839; fax 963.4407 ♿

88 Evensen Vineyards & Winery A half-timbered, Alsatian-style building houses the cellar where Richard Evensen and family produce a Gewürztraminer wine that nicely complements the setting. ♦ Tasting and sales by appointment only. 8254 St. Helena Hwy (north of Oakville Cross Rd), Oakville. 944.2396

89 Robert Mondavi Winery If there's one person who has put California on the international wine map, it is the ebullient Robert Mondavi—he seems to have spread the gospel of Napa Valley wine to every country in the world. Even in the early years he believed that California was capable of making world-class wines, and his vision and tireless promotional efforts have cultivated much of the success of Napa Valley's image both in this country and abroad. In his own winery, Mondavi has been an innovator in technology, viticulture, and marketing. His greatest coup may have been the joint venture he formed with Baron Philippe de Rothschild of Mouton-Rothschild in Bordeaux to produce Opus One, a Bordeaux-style Cabernet blend with cachet to burn. (Across the street is Mondavi's **Opus One** winery; tours of this fascinating structure are available Monday through Saturday by appointment only; call 944.9442.)The mission-style winery building (see drawing below), designed by **Cliff May** in 1966, graces the ubiquitous Mondavi label, and the firm turns out a vast array of benchmark Napa Valley wines, from straightforward varietals to exquisite reserves. This is the first stop on everyone's wine route—the tasting room and tours are packed with visitors year-round, but a reservation system for tours helps manage the crowds. In addition to the usual one-hour tour given by well-prepared guides, there's a three- to four-hour, in-depth tour and tasting several times a week (less often in winter). ♦ Tasting, sales, and tours daily. Reservations recommended for tours. 7801 St. Helena Hwy (north of Oakville Cross Rd), Oakville. 259.WINE ♿

Within Robert Mondavi Winery:

The Great Chefs at Robert Mondavi Winery This first-class cooking school invites the top chefs from France and the US to teach master-level classes ranging from two or three days to one week in a posh wine-country setting. The school originated in 1976 as the "Great Chefs of France." In 1983 a "Great Chefs of America" series was added, and in 1986 the two were merged under the present name.

Robert Mondavi Winery

Most of France's three-Michelin-star chefs have taught at the school at one time or another, as have such homegrown stars as Alice Waters of Chez Panisse in Berkeley, Wolfgang Puck of Spago's in Los Angeles, Jeremiah Tower of Stars in San Francisco, and Mark Miller of Coyote Cafe in Santa Fe. Each year, three to five "Great Chefs" programs of varying length are scheduled. Classes are deliberately kept small and students are a mix of cooks, chefs, and die-hard food fans from around the world. After each class, participants sit down to a meal based on the cooking demonstrations. Fine china and linen and Christofle silverware are the order of every day, and the decor of the **Vineyard Room** is transformed to match the theme of each meal, often with live music. Needless to say, the wine flows freely—and Robert Mondavi and his wife, Margrit Biever, are generous with the good stuff. For most classes, accommodations and local transportation are provided. ♦ For further information, contact Axel Fabre, Director, "The Great Chefs at Robert Mondavi Winery," Box 106, Oakville, CA 94562 (944.2866) ♿

Cakebread Cellars

90 Cakebread Cellars This small, family-owned winery housed in a simple redwood barn was designed and built in 1986 by San Francisco architect **William Turnbull.** Jack and Dolores Cakebread, with sons Bruce as wine maker and Dennis as business manager, specialize in regular and reserve Cabernet Sauvignon, Chardonnay, and Sauvignon Blanc. ♦ Tasting, sales, and tours daily by appointment only. 8300 St. Helena Hwy (between Oakville Cross and Rutherford Cross Rds), Rutherford. 963.5221 ♿

90 Sequoia Grove Vineyards The James Allen family owns this small winery housed in a 19th-century barn shaded by sequoia trees that are over a hundred years old. Three generations of the family work the vineyards and the winery, producing Chardonnay, Cabernet Sauvignon, and Gewürztraminer. Old Chardonnay vines by the river provide grapes for the winery's estate bottlings. ♦ Tasting, sales, and self-guided tours daily. 8338 St. Helena Hwy (between Oakville Cross and Rutherford Cross Rds), Rutherford. 944.2945; fax 963.9411 ♿

90 St. Supéry Vineyards and Winery Budding enologists will enjoy the walk-through display vineyard, where they can see different grape varieties and various examples of pruning and

trellising. Inside the functional modern winery building, an informal exhibition is devoted to promoting the arts in Napa Valley. Shows change every month and range from exhibits by individual local artists to group shows with participating Napa Valley galleries; occasionally artisans may demonstrate fabric painting or a variety of other textile crafts. The Queen Anne Victorian farmhouse on the property has been restored in period furnishings as a living museum of 1880s' viticultural life in Napa Valley. The self-guided tour includes exhibits on soil types, growing conditions, and climate, plus a lesson in wine jargon. Wines include Chardonnay, Sauvignon Blanc, and Cabernet Sauvignon. ♦ Tasting, sales, and tours daily. Reservations recommended for tours. 8440 St. Helena Hwy (between Oakville Cross and Rutherford Cross Rds), Rutherford. 963.4507; fax 965.2147 ♿

Harvesttime in Napa

Although lush vineyards appear to blanket the entire **Napa Valley,** grapes are not the only crop harvested here. Small plots are still devoted to fruit orchards, vegetable gardens, and berry patches. And from May through November, you can visit the Napa Valley farmers' markets on Tuesday and Friday mornings from 7:30AM to noon to sample and purchase the fruits of these farmers' labors. During the summer months there are also a few produce stands set up along the **Silverado Trail.** For a free map and list of farms that sell their produce directly to visitors, send a self-addressed, stamped envelope to **Napa County Farming Trails,** 4075 Solano Avenue, Napa, CA 94558, or call 224.5403.

What's in Season When

	Jun	July	Aug	Sep	Oct	Nov	Dec
Apples		✓	✓	✓	✓	✓	✓
Basil		✓	✓	✓	✓		
Berries	✓	✓					
Figs			✓	✓	✓		
Grapes				✓	✓		
Kiwi						✓	✓
Melons	✓	✓	✓	✓	✓		
Nectarines	✓	✓	✓	✓			
Peaches		✓	✓				
Pears					✓	✓	
Persimmons						✓	
Plums		✓	✓				
Pumpkins					✓	✓	
Tomatoes			✓	✓	✓		
Vegetables	✓	✓	✓	✓	✓	✓	
Walnuts					✓	✓	✓
Xmas Trees						✓	✓

90 Peju Province Winery Founded in 1983, this family-owned winery produces Cabernet Sauvignon, French Colombard, Chardonnay, and Sauvignon Blanc. ◆ Tasting, sales, and self-guided tours daily. 8466 St. Helena Hwy (between Oakville Cross and Rutherford Cross Rds), Rutherford. 963.3600; fax 963.8680 ⏱

91 Rutherford Square Now the site of a post office, this small piece of land was once part of Rancho Caymus, the original land grant given to pioneer George Yount by General Vallejo more than a hundred years ago, and was developed by local sculptor Mary Tilden Morton. ◆ St. Helena Hwy and Rutherford Cross Rd, Rutherford

91 Rancho Caymus Inn $$ Sculptor Mary Tilden Morton (whose family founded the Morton Salt Company) built this rustic 26-unit Spanish Colonial–style hotel (pictured above), where **Flora Springs** winery proprietor John Komes is the owner/innkeeper. The two-story building is constructed around a central courtyard with a fountain and wisteria-covered balconies. Morton planned each room as a separate work of art, hiring local carpenters and craftspeople skilled at creating stained glass, wrought iron, and ceramics. She designed and built the adobe fireplaces and collected crafts from Ecuador, Peru, and Mexico to decorate the rooms and suites (all with private baths). The four master suites, each named for a local historical figure, feature Jacuzzis, full kitchens, and large balconies, and are ideal for long stays. ◆ 1140 Rutherford Cross Rd (off St. Helena Hwy), Rutherford. 963.1777, 800/845.1777; fax 963.5387 ⏱

RUTHERFORD GRILL

91 Rutherford Grill ★★$$; Right next door to the **Beaulieu** tasting room (see below), this large, casual restaurant with a handsome bar, burgundy leather booths, and a sleek open kitchen serves wood-fired, spit-roasted chicken, fresh fish, steak, and a good seared tuna salad. Don't miss the blue-cheese potato chips. Wines from the lengthy list can be ordered by the glass or bottle. The whole roast chicken can be ordered to go—perfect for picnicking. ◆ American ◆ Daily lunch and dinner. 1180 Rutherford Cross Rd (off St. Helena Hwy), Rutherford. 963.1793 ⏱

Restaurants/Clubs: Red   Hotels: Blue
Shops/ 🍷 Outdoors: Green   Wineries/Sights: Black

92 Beaulieu Vineyard Don't miss this historic Rutherford estate prominently located on St. Helena Highway. Founded in 1900 by the French émigré Georges de Latour, who gave it a French name (meaning "beautiful place"), the winery is now known for its Chardonnay, Sauvignon Blanc, and especially its Cabernet Sauvignon. The Rutherford and Georges de Latour Private Reserve are the benchmark California Cabernets, which have a long track record for their aging potential. In addition, Gamay Beaujolais, Merlot, Pinot Noir, and a sweet Muscat de Frontignan are made here. There's also a small tasting room next door that showcases the reserve wines, namely older and current vintages of the Georges de Latour Private Reserve and Carneros Reserve Chardonnay and Pinot Noir. Wines from **Quail Ridge** winery in Rutherford can also be tasted here. ◆ Wine tasting in the main room is free, but there is a small charge for the reserve wines. Tasting, sales, and tours daily. 1960 St. Helena Hwy (north of Rutherford Cross Rd), Rutherford. 963.2411; fax 963.5920 ⏱

93 Napa Valley Grapevine Wreath Company This is a great spot to find wreaths made from twined grapevine cuttings in many shapes (hearts, or, at Christmastime, trees and reindeer) and sizes (up to 36 inches across or even larger by special order). There is also an assortment of baskets available, and fresh produce is sold here May through October. ◆ Daily. 1796 St. Helena Hwy (north of Rutherford Cross Rd), Rutherford. 963.0399

94 Grgich Hills Cellar A dapper émigré vintner from Yugoslavia, Miljenko (Mike) Grgich is among the pioneers who established the reputation of Napa Valley wines in the early 1970s. He began his career at **Château Montelena** (he made the 1973 Chardonnay that won the famous Paris tasting of 1976) and then opened his own winery with partner Austin Hills (of the Hills Bros. Coffee family) in 1977 in a functional Spanish Colonial building along Highway 29. Grgich is an undisputed master of Chardonnay and has priced his wines accordingly. He also makes a distinguished Fumé Blanc, a full-bodied Cabernet, and a Zinfandel from old vines. On weekends you may taste older library wines, and selected older vintages are for sale. This should be a mandatory stop on your wine itinerary. ◆ Fee for tasting older wines. Tasting

GRGICH HILLS

and sales daily; tours by appointment only. 1829 St. Helena Hwy (north of Rutherford Cross Rd), Rutherford. 963.2784 ♿

95 Franciscan Vineyards This state-of-the-art building is the headquarters of four California properties where you can stop and taste wines from **Franciscan Vineyards, Estancia, Pinnacles,** and **Mount Veeder** wineries. **Franciscan's** flagship wine is the Franciscan Oakville Estate Meritage, a blend of red Bordeaux varietals, and Cuvée Sauvage, a Chardonnay fermented in French oak barrels by the naturally occurring wild yeast present in the vineyard. The winery is owned by the Eckes family, which has been involved in wine making and brandy distilling in Germany for five generations, and by Agustin Huneeus, president of **Franciscan.** ♦ Fee. Tasting and sales daily. 1178 Galleron La (at St. Helena Hwy), Rutherford. 963.7111; fax 963.7867 ♿

96 Whitehall Lane Winery Wine maker Arthur Finkelstein founded this small winery on the northern edge of the Rutherford Bench district in 1979. The Leonardini family now owns the place; Gary Galleron is the wine maker. The winery produces a good Cabernet and Merlot, as well as Chardonnay and special bottlings of Pinot Noir and Cabernet Franc. ♦ Tasting and sales daily; tours daily 1PM and 4PM. 1563 St. Helena Hwy (at Whitehall La), St. Helena. 963.9454; fax 963.7035 ♿

96 Ink House $$$ Wealthy local landowner Theron H. Ink built this Italianate Victorian bed-and-breakfast (pictured above) in 1884. Now owned by Ernie Veniegas, a former director of the **Honolulu Symphony** and the **Hawaii Opera Theater,** the inn boasts understated period decor and antique furnishings. The four guest rooms of varying sizes have private baths and antique brass-and-iron beds. The breezy observatory on the third floor is a perfect spot from which to watch hot-air balloons floating over the valley. The continental breakfast includes fresh-baked bread and herb teas. ♦ 1575 St. Helena Hwy (at Whitehall La), St. Helena. 963.3890

VINTAGE 1989

FloraSprings

Napa Valley
CHARDONNAY

ESTATE GROWN, PRODUCED AND BOTTLED BY FLORA SPRINGS WINE CO ST. HELENA, CA   ALCOHOL 13.4% BY VOLUME

97 Flora Springs Wine Company Founded in the 1880s by the Rennie brothers of Scotland, the old stone winery now houses a state-of-the-art cellar. The present winery, owned and run by three generations of the Komes and Garvey families, produces top-rated Chardonnays in a French Burgundy style and an exceptional Sauvignon Blanc. Wine maker Ken Deis's blend of Cabernet Sauvignon, Merlot, and Cabernet Franc is called Trilogy. Depending on visitors' interests, tours may include both the vineyards and the cellar. There's a picnic area here, too. ♦ Tasting and tours by appointment only. 1978 W Zinfandel La (at St. Helena Hwy), St. Helena. 963.5711; fax 963.7578 ♿

Best Cellars

Some of the choicest wine tastings take place not at the wineries, but in the wine-country restaurants. Listed below are the restaurants with the best rosters of wines. This is where to look for those hard-to-find bottles, wines from vintners with a very limited production, and selected older vintages.

All Seasons Cafe, Calistoga	942.9111
Auberge du Soleil Restaurant, Rutherford	963.1211
Domaine Chandon Restaurant, Yountville	944.2892
John Ash & Co., Santa Rosa	527.7687
Mixx, Santa Rosa	573.1344
Napa Valley Grille, Yountville	944.2330
The Restaurant at Meadowood, St. Helena	963.3646
Silverado Tavern, Calistoga	942.6725
Terra, St. Helena	963.8931
Trilogy, St. Helena	963.5507

The exact origin of Zinfandel, which has become one of the most beloved grapes in California, is unknown. Scholars are certain it's a *Vitis vinifera* (nonnative) variety that somehow got to California in one of the shipments of vine cuttings that pioneer Sonoma vintner Agoston Haraszthy sent back from Europe. In shape and foliage, Zinfandel closely resembles Primitivo, a grape variety from the northern Italian region of Piedmont, but the wine flavors it produces are very different—and therein lies the mystery.

98 Mario Perelli-Minetti Winery This tiny family-owned winery produces only Cabernet Sauvignon and Chardonnay. Owner Mario Perelli-Minetti comes from one of California's oldest wine families. He was actually born in the Sonoma County winery built by his father, Antonio, who graduated from the Royal Academy of Viticulture and Enology at Conegliano, Italy. From 1902 until his death in 1976, Antonio was active in viticulture and wine making in California and Mexico. ♦ Tasting and sales F-Su. 1443 Silverado Tr (at Zinfandel La), St. Helena. 963.8762 ♿

99 Caymus Vineyards

Charlie Wagner and his son Chuck, second- and third-generation wine makers, run a no-nonsense operation that just happens to turn out some of California's best Cabernets. Drive past the ranch-style house to the small tasting room. This was one of the first vintners to produce a Pinot Noir Blanc, called *oeil de perdrix* ("eye of the partridge"), and is best known for its outstanding Cabernet Sauvignon (the Special Selection is always one of California's greatest). It also makes a good Sauvignon Blanc and Zinfandel. ♦ Fee. Tasting and sales daily. 8700 Conn Creek Rd (off Rutherford Cross Rd), Rutherford. 963.4204 ♿

FROG'S LEAP

100 Frog's Leap Founded in 1981 on the site of an old frog-raising farm (hence the name) along Mill Creek Road in St. Helena, this winery moved south to new quarters in 1994. Owners John and Julie Williams have restored the historic red barn to its original condition and continue to use the organic farming methods for which they are well known. Their best wines are the Cabernet Sauvignon and Sauvignon Blanc, but the Chardonnay is not far behind. They also make a spicy Zinfandel and Merlot.

When the Williamses started their winery, they didn't have much money, so they looked for an unknown artist to design their wine labels in exchange for a small fee and a few cases of wine. Charles House accepted their offer—and it was a decision he will never forget (or regret). His labels have won national graphic-design awards and are now part of the Smithsonian Institution's permanent collection, bringing fame to both House and the wines. The winery provides a great tour. ♦ Sales and tours M-F by appointment only.

8815 Conn Creek Rd (off Rutherford Cross Rd), Rutherford. 963.4704 ♿

101 ZD Wines

Former aerospace engineers Gino Zepponi and Norman de Leuze took the first letters of their last names to form their logo when they started making wine in Sonoma in 1969. They moved their operation to the Silverado Trail in 1979. Now run by de Leuze and his wife Rosa Lee, the winery's star continues to be an opulent barrel-fermented Chardonnay. Also look for its Pinot Noir and powerful Estate Cabernet Sauvignon. ♦ Fee. Tasting and sales daily; tours by appointment only. 8383 Silverado Tr (between Oakville Cross and Rutherford Cross Rds), Napa. 963.5188; fax 963.2640 ♿

102 Mumm Napa Valley This joint venture between the French Champagne producer G.H. Mumm and the Seagram wine company Domaine Mumm, directed by French wine maker Guy Devaux and his American counterpart Greg Fowler, produces several pleasant sparkling wines made by the traditional *méthode champenoise*. The winery building, with its steep-pitched roof and redwood siding, is reminiscent of the traditional Napa Valley barn. You may taste either the Brut Prestige or the Blanc de Noirs in the salon overlooking the vineyard, where Champagne flutes and crystal wine buckets are also available. There is a large porch open to the vineyards with views of the Mayacamas Mountains, and, in warm weather, a patio area is set with shaded tables. The winery produces a Prestige Cuvée called Mumm Grand Cordon, and, in certain years, a vintage-dated reserve—a blend of Chardonnay and Pinot Noir—that's aged two years on the yeast. ♦ Fee. Tasting, sales, and tours daily; private tours and tastings are available by appointment only. 8445 Silverado Tr (between Oakville Cross and Rutherford Cross Rds), Rutherford. 942.3400; fax 942.3469 ♿

103 Villa Mount Eden Winery Managed by Château Ste. Michelle in Washington, this winery concentrates on limited-production wines: Chardonnay, Chenin Blanc, and a usually excellent Cabernet Sauvignon, under the direction of talented wine maker Mike McGrath. At press time, the winery was sharing facilities with **Conn Creek Winery** (see page 39), but it's looking for a new larger location. ♦ Tasting and sales daily; tours by appointment only. 8711 Silverado Tr (between Oakville Cross and Rutherford Cross Rds), Rutherford. 944.2414; fax 963.7840 ♿

103 Conn Creek Winery Well-crafted reds are the specialty of this small winery along the Silverado Trail. Look for wine maker Robert Pepi's Cabernet Sauvigon and Zinfandel. Chardonnay, Sauvignon Blanc, and Merlot are also produced. ♦ Tasting and sales daily; tours by appointment only. 8711 Silverado Tr (between Oakville Cross and Rutherford Cross Rds), Rutherford. 963.9100 &

104 Auberge du Soleil $$$$ Without question this French country–style inn is the wine country's best resort—and certainly one of its most expensive as well. Despite the high price tag and magnificent appointments, however, the atmosphere is engagingly casual. And because of the privacy it affords, **Auberge** has become a honeymoon haven.

The breathtaking setting for this wine-country retreat is a 33-acre hillside olive grove overlooking Napa Valley. Architect **Sandy Walker** and the late designer Michael Taylor built 11 spacious villas (housing 50 one- and two-room accommodations), each named after a region of France; indeed, once inside one of these very private and romantic *maisons,* you'll feel as if you've been transported to a hill town in southern France. Every suite or room has its own entrance, fireplace, and French doors that open onto a completely private veranda overlooking the wine country. Windows are set deep into earth-toned stucco walls, much like a Provençal farmhouse. Hand-glazed terra-cotta tiles cover the floors, frame the fireplaces and bathtubs, and even top the bureaus and counters, and couches with soft, large cushions and pigskin chairs fill the high-ceilinged rooms. The beds are covered with thick cotton chenille in sizzling peaches, pinks, and yellows, and the enormous bathrooms have oversized tubs. The deluxe rooms are a third larger than the standard rooms and feature whirlpool baths, but otherwise there's not much difference between the two. The suites are the most romantic rooms, although they don't include whirlpool tubs.

The extensive grounds are planted with a profusion of flowers as well as a vegetable garden used by the restaurant's chef. A half-mile sculpture trail winds around the western end of the resort and features a variety of works by Northern California artists. The swimming pool has a heart-stopping, panoramic view, and there's a tiny exercise room with an equally stunning view, a basic spa with two steam rooms, showers, lockers, and a massage room (massages may be given in your room, too), and a full-service beauty salon. The property also features picnic tables and three tennis courts. Don't miss sitting outside on the bar's terrace when the weather is mild—it's the best place in the valley to linger over a glass of wine at sunset. This "Inn of the Sun" is a member of the prestigious international Relais & Châteaux hotel association. Concierge and 24-hour room service are available. ♦ 180 Rutherford Hill Rd (off the Silverado Tr), Rutherford. 963.1211, 800/348.5406; fax 963.8764 &

Within Auberge du Soleil:

Auberge du Soleil Restaurant ★★★ $$$$ When this restaurant first opened in 1981 with the late Japanese chef Masa Kobayashi at the helm, it became an instant hit with both restaurant critics and romantics. After Kobayashi left to open his own restaurant, this dining spot had its ups and downs for awhile, but executive chef David Hale, who worked alongside popular Swiss-trained Udo Nechutnys here for a year, has now won wide acclaim. Hale's menu changes with the seasons and incorporates vegetables and herbs from his garden at the inn. Dinner might begin with calamari ceviche with orange crème fraîche and *habañero* chili–avocado sauce, a warm goat-cheese tart, or pan-seared duck liver with lemon-thyme brioche and huckle-berries, followed by such main courses as Champagne-poached golden trout with shrimp-chive stuffing and zante grape-chanterelle sauce, or pan-roasted lamb loin served with crisp mint pasta and portobello mushroom ragout. Lunch often includes a pizza and pasta of the day and such inventive sandwiches as the corn-fried soft-shell crab sandwich served with poppy-seed melon slaw. The dining room, with its sculptural bouquets of seasonal flowers, comfortable banquettes, and seemingly endless views of the valley, has always been one of the most romantic in the area, particularly when you're seated at a table on the terrace. ♦ California ♦ Daily breakfast, lunch, and dinner. Reservations recommended; no shorts after 6PM &

> "Not only does one drink wine, but one inhales it, one looks at it, one swallows it. . . and one talks about it."
>
> King Edward VII

RUTHERFORD HILL

1978
Napa Valley
CABERNET SAUVIGNON

PRODUCED AND BOTTLED BY RUTHERFORD HILL WINERY
RUTHERFORD, CALIF. USA • ALCOHOL 12.7% BY VOLUME

105 Rutherford Hill Winery Take an informative tour through this contemporary wood winery, including a walk through the extensive aging caves carved a half mile into the cliffs behind the winery. Tunnel specialist Alf Burtleson spent 13 months on the job, using an English drilling machine to burrow into the hard-packed earth and rock. Wine makers Kevin Robinson and Kent Barthman focus on Merlot, Chardonnay, Cabernet Sauvignon, and a Zinfandel Port. The picnic grounds, under the oaks and in an olive grove, share the same panoramic view as **Auberge du Soleil.** ♦ Tasting and sales daily; tours M-F 11:30AM, 1:30PM, and 3:30PM; Sa-Su 11:30AM, 12:30PM, 2:30PM, and 3:30PM. 200 Rutherford Hill Rd (off the Silverado Tr), Rutherford. 963.7194; fax 963.4231 ♿

106 Lake Hennessey Picnic Grounds If the lake has been stocked with trout, as it generally is each spring, you could catch a fish and fry it up right here in the barbecue pits in the picnic area. This is a reservoir for local drinking water, so no swimming is allowed; however, you can take a dip in the creek that runs alongside the picnic grounds. ♦ Sa, Su, and holidays Memorial Day through Labor Day weekend. Off Hwy 128, 3 miles east of Rutherford. 257.9529

107 Long Vineyards This tiny family winery on Pritchard Hill east of the Silverado Trail was founded in 1978 by Zelma Long, one of California's most prominent wine makers and president of **Simi Winery** in Sonoma County, and her former husband, Bob Long. Zelma is now a consultant at the winery, and Bob and wine maker Sandi S. Belcher continue to produce first-class Chardonnay, Riesling, Cabernet Sauvignon, Sauvignon Blanc, and Pinot Grigio, all of which are hard to find because quantities are so limited and sought after by connoisseurs. Another bottle to covet is the opulent late-harvest Johannisberg Riesling, produced only in years when conditions are right. ♦ Tours by appointment only. 1535 Sage Canyon Rd (off the Silverado Tr), St. Helena. 963.2496; fax 963.2907 ♿

108 Chapellet Vineyard Donn and Molly Chapellet's pyramid-shaped winery, founded in 1967 and located on a spectacular site on Pritchard Hill, is devoted to four wines: a crisp Chenin Blanc, Chardonnay, Merlot, and a very good Cabernet. ♦ Tours by appointment only. 1581 Sage Canyon Rd (off the Silverado Tr), St. Helena. 963.7136; fax 963.7445 ♿

Sandi S. Belcher
Wine Maker/Grapegrower, Long Vineyards, St. Helena

Breakfast at **The Diner** or onion rings at **Mustards Grill** in **Yountville.**

Watching the cormorants nesting in a lone Digger pine tree on the south shore of **Rutherford**'s **Lake Hennessey** each night at dusk.

Breakfast at **The Diner** in Yountville.

A glass of wine on the deck of **Auberge du Soleil** in Rutherford during frost season.

Lunch, dinner, drinks at **Tra Vigne** in **St. Helena.**

Hiking to the top of **Bothe–Napa Valley State Park** on **Highway 29** north of St. Helena (with a camera) for a view up and down the valley.

Rafting the **Russian River** to **Healdsburg Memorial Beach.**

Sauntering through the caves of **Beringer Vineyards** in St. Helena for the wonderful smells. And visiting their **Rhine House** for a look at the stained-glass windows and the sensual wooden staircase—a nicely preserved touch of history.

Taking a peek at the fountain at **Franciscan Vineyards** in Rutherford.

A springtime stroll through the **St. Helena Cemetery** to look at the flowering bulbs and trees and the good view of the east side of the valley.

A visit to the **Napa Valley Wine Library** in St. Helena.

R. Curtis Ellison, M.D.
Professor of Medicine & Public Health, Boston University School of Medicine

Sitting before a roaring fire in your cottage at **Meadowood Resort** on a cool October night. . . after an exhausting afternoon on the croquet court. ("All white apparel, sir, if you please!") And sipping a glass of beautifully made Cabernet Sauvignon from **Merryvale Vineyards.** (St. Helena)

After the excellent tour at the **Robert Mondavi Winery,** calling back the wine server in the tasting room: "Are you sure this is the '89 Pinot Noir? It seems more like the '90 to me." And being right! (Oakville)

Munching on the great bread served at **Piatti** after dipping it into the green, extra-virgin olive oil. . . and hoping the entrée doesn't come too soon. (Yountville)

Finding out when you arrive at **Tra Vigne:** "As a matter of fact we *do* have fresh mozzarella tonight." (St. Helena)

Reveling in the brilliantly colored mustard growing between the rows of vines in the organically farmed vineyards of **Fetzer**. . . and then walking through their gardens of fantastic vegetables. (Redwood Valley)

Happening upon the tiny wineries, such as **Villa Helena,** where the owner/wine maker/tour guide (all the same person) lets you barrel taste the Chardonnay, and describes what he or she is striving for. (St. Helena)

Learning to appreciate the aroma and bouquet of wine at the wonderful **"Smellavision"** units at **St. Supéry.** (Rutherford)

Dan Berger
Wine Columnist, *Los Angeles Times*

Sipping a bottle of chilled Navarro Gewürztraminer before a crackling fire in a cabin at **Bear Wallow,** hidden in the hills between **Philo** and the coast of **Mendocino.** Bear Wallow is a nearly unknown respite from the world: no phones, no TVs, no radio. But it has a one-match fireplace, windows to the trees, fresh air, and a bottle of sherry on the kitchen table of every cabin.

Four miles east is **Boonville,** a lost-in-time town of ultimate charm that has one of the best restaurants in Northern California (the **Boonville Hotel Restaurant & Bar**), as well as some of the best locally grown apples (at **Gowan's Oak Tree**), and real people at the **Horn of Zeese Coffee Shop.** The wines of this region are among the best in the US.

The massive Spanish omelette (with sourdough toast) on a Saturday morning in September at **The Diner** in **Yountville.** The breakfast at this cafe is the best in Northern California, making the hard bench seats only a minor inconvenience. Don't get there too late or you'll have to wait (and don't miss the fried potatoes or the pancakes).

A walk through **Armstrong Redwoods State Reserve** near **Guerneville** on a spring morning with espresso in a Thermos and a sticky bun from the **Downtown Bakery & Creamery** in Healdsburg. (**Armstrong Woods,** a gem in western **Sonoma County,** is so little known that even some locals are unaware of it.)

An early-morning drive from **Santa Rosa** west over Coleman Mountain Road in January, with the wind raking the leaves and newborn lambs frolicking on unsure legs. On the way home, make sure you stop at **Kozlowski Farms** near **Forestville** to buy a basket of fresh blueberries—which will never make it back to town alive.

Dinner at **Tra Vigne** in **St. Helena** preceded by their homemade sardines, house-cured olives, fresh-baked olive bread dipped in olive oil, and sips of Spottswoode Sauvignon Blanc. Its sister restaurant, **Mustards Grill,** located down the road, may be the best example of California cuisine in the state, but for intensity of flavor Tuscan-style, **Tra Vigne** has it, with an amazing array of pastas, plus chicken, seafood, and a wait staff both efficient and full of fun. I could eat here three times a week and never get bored.

A night at the modern-eclectic **Stevenswood Lodge** on the **Mendocino Coast,** followed the next morning by breakfast at **Cafe Beaujolais** (reservations recommended). Margaret Fox's amazing morning-food preparations are legendary, so even midweek it's not easy to get a seat here. But the baked goods, scrapple, and even the mundane things are cooked to perfection, with freshly ground coffee you can smell up the street.

An impromptu picnic lunch on the lawn in the **Sonoma** town square with all the accoutrements: a bottle of wine from a local winery, a loaf of sourdough bread still warm from the oven from the **Sonoma French Bakery** across the square, and a block of Ig Vella's hard dry Sonoma Jack cheese from the cheese shop around the corner. Try the hearty Haywood Zinfandel or one from **Gundlach-Bundschu** for a treat with the cheese.

The perfection of Diane Pariseau's cooking at calm, quiet **Trilogy** in St. Helena, paired with a bottle of wine (from an intriguing wine list) that's served in splendid tall wine goblets with ultrathin rims and stems. The word sublime comes to mind. . .

A Saturday art tour of **Napa Valley,** starting with the amazingly diverse **Hess Collection** at the southern end of the valley, followed by an afternoon seminar in the caves at **Clos Pegase,** listening to the enthusiastic Jan Shrem give his slide presentation on wine as an art form and art in the world of wine.

Taking a loaf of bread, a hunk of cheese, and a glass of a local red to **Jack London State Historic Park** in Sonoma County's **Valley of the Moon** in September. Follow that with a blackberry-picking walk along the side roads.

James Conaway
Author, *Napa: The Story of an American Eden*

Breakfast at **The Diner** in **Yountville** (*caffè latte* and corn cakes).

Lunch at **Piatti** in Yountville (a glass of Chardonnay and capellini with fresh tomatoes, garlic, and basil).

A dip in any of the hot springs in **Calistoga,** without the mud bath (herbal wrap optional).

A glass of Domaine Mumm on the deck of **Auberge du Soleil** in **Rutherford.**

Dinner at **Mustards Grill** in Yountville (grilled asparagus and Sonoma rabbit, accompanied by an honest Napa red).

St. Helena

This small town in the heart of **Napa Valley** got its start around 1846, when Edward Bale built a flour mill beside a creek three miles north of the present town. Bale was an impoverished British surgeon who sailed to California aboard a whaling vessel and later married into General Mariano Guadelupe Vallejo's family. The land was part of **Rancho Carne Humana**, an immense Spanish land grant covering around 20,000 prime acres—virtually all of northern Napa Valley—which Bale received in 1839. He later sold a hundred acres to a fellow Englishman, J.H. Still, who promptly opened a general store. That became the nucleus of the town, which took its name from **Mount St. Helena.** Here you will find several of the best restaurants in the wine country, a number of historic wineries, and the **Napa Valley Wine Library**, which preserves the history of the area in its books, papers, and oral histories.

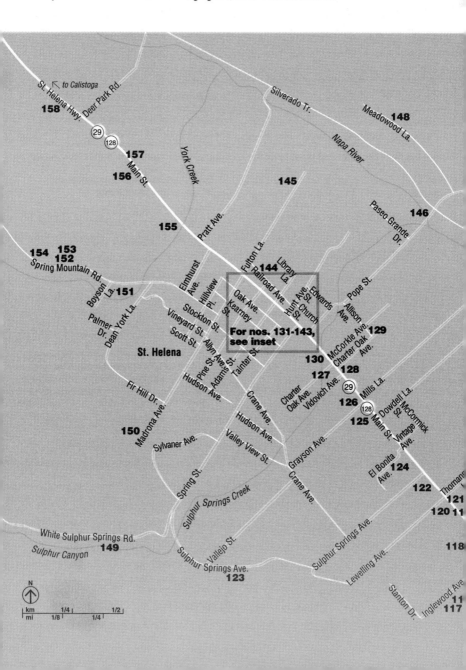

Main Street, with its stately, 19th-century stone buildings, is a portion of the valley's main highway, and has been a significant thoroughfare since the days of the horse and buggy. The infamous Black Bart, who taught school and wrote poetry when he wasn't busy robbing stagecoaches (he thoughtfully left bits of verse at the scenes of his crimes), passed through here before his capture in 1883. On a more romantic note, author Robert Louis Stevenson and his new bride, Fanny, also made their way through the town en route to nearby Calistoga, where they spent their honeymoon in the summer of 1880.

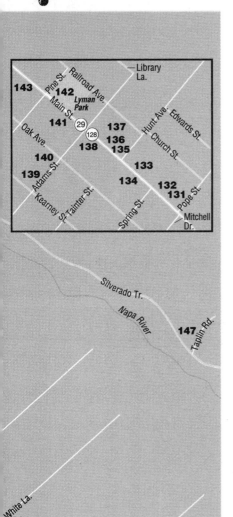

109 Raymond Vineyard and Cellar Full-bodied Chardonnay and Cabernet, plus Sauvignon Blanc, are made here by one of the oldest wine-making families in the valley. Fourth-generation vintners Roy Raymond Jr. and Walter Raymond, along with Kenn Vigoda, oversee all aspects of the vineyard and winery operation. Their top wines are the private reserves; older vintages of their notable Cabernet Sauvignon Private Reserve are sometimes available at the winery. ♦ Tasting and sales daily; tours by appointment only. 849 Zinfandel La (off St. Helena Hwy). 963.3141; fax 963.8498 &

110 Shady Oaks Country Inn $$ This inn features two guest rooms in a 1920s house and two more in an 1800s stone winery building, all with private baths and furnished with country-style antiques. A Champagne breakfast, including eggs Benedict and Belgian waffles, is served in the parlor or on the patio overlooking the garden and vineyards, which is shaded with a century-old wisteria. ♦ 399 Zinfandel La (off St. Helena Hwy). 963.1190 &

111 Shadow Brook Winery Housed in a rustic barn, this tiny winery is best known for its Chardonnay, but it also produces Pinot Noir and a small amount of Merlot. A picnic area is available for visitors. ♦ Tasting and sales by appointment only. 360 Zinfandel La (off St. Helena Hwy). 963.2000

112 Zinfandel Inn $$$ Don't let the fancy stonework and formal entrance fool you: Inside you won't find a stuffy castlelike interior, but a quaint, quiet, three-room bed-and-breakfast inn that has all the comforts of home. The property is well tended by proprietors Jerry and Diane Payton. Two of the rooms feature fireplaces, and the **Zinfandel Suite** also has a large indoor whirlpool tub and a private balcony overlooking the garden; all have private baths. A swimming pool provides welcome relief on hot summer days, and there's an outdoor Jacuzzi. A full breakfast is served in the formal dining room. ♦ 800 Zinfandel La (at Victoria La). 963.3512; fax 963.5310

Restaurants/Clubs: Red   Hotels: Blue
Shops/ 🍴 Outdoors: Green   Wineries/Sights: Black

43

113 Milat Vineyards Chardonnay, Chenin Blanc, Zinfandel, Zivio (a blush Zinfandel), and Cabernet are produced by this small winery. ♦ Fee. Tasting and sales daily. 1091 St. Helena Hwy (at Stice La). 963.0758, 800/54.MILAT; fax 963.0168 &

114 V. Sattui Winery The fourth generation of the Sattui family offers 10 of their wines to taste at this 1885 winery with yard-thick stone walls, hand-hewn timbers, and four underground cellars. It's also a popular stop for people who want great picnic fare: The large, well-organized cheese shop and deli offers more than 200 imported and domestic cheeses, a variety of cold cuts, straightforward salads, and desserts such as truffles and oversized cookies. Enjoy your booty at the winery's shady picnic area alongside the highway. Wine- and cheese-related gifts are available, too. ♦ Tasting daily. 1111 White La (at St. Helena Hwy). 963.7774; fax 963.4324 &

115 St. Helena Wine Merchant A wide range of California and imported wines are sold at good prices in this large shop that specializes in vintages from small-production wineries that can be hard to find outside of California. At any given time, you can choose from 400 to 500 estates (more than 300 Cabernets alone). You'll also find the latest releases from up-and-coming wineries. The knowledgeable staff is ready to advise, and they'll ship your purchases home, too. ♦ Daily. 699 St. Helena Hwy (at Inglewood Ave). 963.7888; fax 963.7839 &

116 Villa Helena Winery Viognier (a white Rhône Valley varietal), Charbono (a red table wine), and Dulcinea (a late-harvest dessert wine with a blend of Sémillon and Sauvignon Blanc) are the specialties of this small producer. They also make Chardonnay and Cabernet Sauvignon. ♦ Tasting and sales daily by appointment only. 1455 Inglewood Ave (off St. Helena Hwy). 963.4334; fax 963.4748

117 La Fleur Bed and Breakfast $$ Designer prints decorate the seven guest rooms in this 1882 powder-blue Queen Anne Victorian surrounded by vineyards. Each room has a queen-size bed, private bath, and view of the vineyards or rose garden; four have fireplaces. A full breakfast is served in the sunny solarium, where most days you can see hot-air balloons drifting through the sky in the distance. ♦ 1475 Inglewood Ave (off St. Helena Hwy). 963.0233

The Benedictine monk Dom Pérignon is credited with perfecting the secondary fermentation stage of Champagne making, which took place at the abbey of Hautvillers near Epernay in the Champagne region of France in the late 17th century.

118 Sugarhouse Bakery Rudy and Therese Frey have been turning out delicious cross-hatched loaves of Swiss farmhouse bread, coarse rye, and potato bread since 1970. They also make sweet cinnamon rings, strudels, and stollens, plus brownies and Swiss *leckerli* (gingerbread) cookies. For picnics, order sandwiches on the fresh house-baked rolls. Special breads and sweets are available at Christmas and Easter. ♦ W-Su. 587 St. Helena Hwy (north of Inglewood Ave). 963.3424 &

119 Heitz Wine Cellars

Established in 1961 by Joe and Alice Heitz, this winery is known for its big, full-bodied Cabernets, especially those made from two specially selected Cabernet Sauvignon vineyards—**Bella Oaks** and **Martha's Vineyard.** The latter is noted for its unique bouquet of eucalyptus and mint. ♦ Tasting and sales daily; tours M-F 2PM by appointment only. 436 St. Helena Hwy (between White and Thomann Las). 963.3542 &

SUTTER HOME

1988 CALIFORNIA
WHITE ZINFANDEL

VINTED AND BOTTLED BY SUTTER HOME WINERY
ST. HELENA, NAPA VALLEY, CALIFORNIA BW 1007
ALCOHOL 9% BY VOLUME. CONTAINS SULFITES

120 Sutter Home Winery Established in 1874 by Swiss-German immigrant John Thomann and purchased by the Sutter family in 1906, this winery, housed in a complex of gussied-up Victorian buildings, has been under the sole ownership of the Trinchero family since 1947. It is best known for Zinfandels, with its Amador County Zinfandel and White Zinfandel, a wine tailor-made for a mass audience, being the most popular. Chardonnay, Cabernet, and a slew of other wines are also produced here. Visitors are welcome to take a self-guided tour of the **White Zinfandel Garden,** with more than 800 varieties of flora, including a hundred varieties of roses, daylilies, azaleas, columbines, and an extensive herb garden. The visitors' center is a big operation: T-shirts, baseball jackets, Victorian gift tins of wines, specialty foods, umbrellas—they've got it all. ♦ Tasting and sales daily. 277 St. Helena Hwy (at Lewelling Ave). 963.3104 ♿

121 Louis M. Martini Winery This is one of the oldest wineries in Napa Valley. It was founded in 1922 by Louis M. Martini and is still run by the Martini family. The founder's grand-daughter, Carolyn, is now president; his grandson, Michael, is the wine maker. After a period of decline, the winery is making a strong comeback. Its Los Niños, a Cabernet Sauvignon made from the oldest vines on **Monte Rosso** vineyard high in the Mayacamas Mountains, is meant to age until *los niños*—children born the year of the vintage—are at least 21 years old. It is **Martini**'s benchmark wine; the regular bottling is called North Coast Cabernet. ♦ Tasting, sales, and tours daily. 254 St. Helena Hwy (at Thomann La). 963.2736; fax 963.8705 ♿

122 Harvest Inn $$$ If the Catalán modernist architect **Antoni Gaudí** worked in brick, he might create something like this fantasy hotel just off Highway 29. The bricks came from turn-of-the-century San Francisco houses, old cobblestones were used to build the myriad fireplaces, and more than $1 million was spent on antiques (mostly oak refinished to look brand new). Alas, the effect is just a bit ho-hum. Rooms with names such as **Romeo and Juliet,** the **King of Hearts,** the **Earl of Ecstasy,** and the **Count of Fantasy** are scattered over several buildings on the spacious grounds, and feature private baths, ornate fireplaces, hardwood floors, and decks or patios. West-facing rooms have hillside views. Overstuffed leather sofas are pulled up around a baronial fireplace in the main hall, which sports a wine bar with a dozen wines by the glass. The inn has two swimming pools with Jacuzzis, plus private Jacuzzis in some of the deluxe rooms. ♦ One Main St (at Sulphur Springs Ave). 963.9463, 800/950.8466; fax 963.4402 ♿

Villa St. Helena

123 Villa St. Helena $$$ You might feel like Jane Eyre approaching Gateshead mansion as you enter this expansive Mediterranean-style villa tucked away high in the hills of the Mayacamas Mountains above St. Helena. International architect **Robert M. Carrere** was commissioned in 1941 to create this fantastic villa—his last major work—on a 20-acre site. In the 1940s

and 1950s, Hollywood celebrities and the political elite favored it as their country hideaway. Now three of the rooms comprise a bed-and-breakfast inn for those who want to escape civilization and experience true peace and solitude while enjoying panoramic views of Napa Valley. The unusual but beautiful architecture of this grand house is its strong point; the ambience, however, is rather cold and eerie. As you stroll through the wide hallways and peer into the numerous rooms you can't help but imagine what the likes of Gloria Swanson or Rita Hayworth and their entourages would have brought to this great villa. It's an intriguing place, but definitely not for everyone; you may want to inquire about a quick tour before planning a long retreat here. A continental breakfast is served, and hiking trails and tennis courts are nearby. ♦ 2727 Sulphur Springs Ave (2 miles west of St. Helena Hwy). 963.2514 ♿

124 El Bonita Motel $ Built in the 1930s and extensively remodeled in 1994, this 20-unit motel retains its original Art Deco feel on the outside, while inside the rooms are decorated in pastels, with such modern conveniences as private baths, cable TV, microwaves, and refrigerators, plus whirlpool tubs in some rooms. The units with kitchens are the best deal in the valley for families. The gardens surrounding the motel are always in bloom; there's also a kidney-shaped pool. ♦ 195 Main St (at El Bonita Ave). 963.3216, 800/541.3284 ♿

125 Vintage Hall/Napa Valley Museum Located in the old **St. Helena High School Building** for the time being, this museum presents a permanent exhibit on Napa Valley's land, people, and industry, as well as changing displays on the area's culture and history. Previous exhibits have included prints of California native plants by artist Henry Evans, a photography exhibit of rare Napa Valley plants from **The Native Plant Society Collection,** and an exhibit devoted to the Wappo Indian tribe. One of the museum's most important services is the **Trunk Program,** where docents travel to schools to present programs about the cultural and agricultural heritage of Napa Valley. The museum has acquired a four-acre site adjacent to **Domaine Chandon** in Yountville as its future home, and the board of directors is devoting much of its time and effort to raising funds for the proposed building (slated to open at press time). ♦ Free. Daily. 473 Main St (at Grayson Ave). 963.7411

126 A&W Restaurant & Ice Cream Parlor $ Burgers, hot dogs, chili dogs, sandwiches, onion rings, french fries, and old-fashioned root beer floats in frosted mugs: This, in short, is the high-school hangout. ♦ Fast food ♦ Daily breakfast, lunch, and dinner. 501 Main St (at Grayson Ave). 963.4333 ♿

127 Dansk Factory Outlet Save up to 60 percent on seconds, discontinued patterns, overstocks, and limited editions of Dansk dinnerware, flatware, crystal wineglasses, wooden salad bowls and carving boards, cookware, and gifts. They'll ship your purchase anywhere in the US. ♦ Daily. 801 Main St (at Charter Oak Ave). 963.4273 &

128 Ristorante Tra Vigne ★★★★$$
This place, whose name means "among the vines" in Italian, has been one of the hottest dining spots in the wine country since the day it opened. The beautiful brick building is actually situated among some grapevines (which often conceal the restaurant's sign), and the restaurant is spacious and lively with a stylish ambience, popular with visitors and residents alike. Garlands of pepper and garlic, hanging sausages and hams, and a broad terrace shaded with a black-and-white awning give it the look of a post-modern Italian movie set. The large menu is constantly changing, but there is always a long list of antipasti, salads, pasta, and pizzas (the cooking is sometimes uneven, but when this place is on, it is a memorable wine-country experience).

While you can have just a dish or two at the bar or regroup over a glass of wine on the terrace, it's more fun to gather with friends and sample everything on the menu: warm spinach-and-escarole salad with goat cheese, oven-dried figs, and pancetta dressing; polenta with wild mushrooms in aceto-balsamic vinegar sauce; grilled rabbit with mustard, sage, and grappa-soaked cherries; rustic pizza from the wood-burning oven with caramelized onions, thyme, and gorgonzola; or chef Michael Chiarello's house-cured sausage served with fresh mozzarella and a tomato-onion-herb sauce. *Dolci* (sweets) include anise-almond biscotti to dip in a Tuscan dessert wine, freshly made Italian-style ice creams and sherbets, and a winning *semifreddo* (hazelnut and vanilla ice cream doused with espresso). The wine list features an all-star selection of Italian and California wines plus great grappas. The pizzas and selected other dishes are also available to go. No smoking is allowed. ♦ Italian ♦ Daily lunch and dinner. Reservations recommended. 1050 Charter Oak Ave (at Main St). 963.4444; fax 963.1233 &

Within Ristorante Tra Vigne's courtyard:

Cantinetta Tra Vigne ★★★$ Have a light bite and a glass of wine or an ice-cold draft beer and shop for hard-to-find Italian groceries at this upscale deli and wineshop. The wood-paneled bar on one side serves aperitifs, strong espresso drinks, and the special house campari. There is also a wonderful selection of wines by the glass. Step up to the counter to order *panini* (Italian sandwiches), focaccia (pizza bread), savory pies, whole-roasted garlic heads to spread on bread Italian-style, and other items to go. Every night there's a different take-out entrée. And at the deli counter look for goat cheese from **Laura Chenel's Chèvre** in Sonoma, handmade Calabrese-style salami, fresh wild mushrooms, dried porcini mushrooms, and special dried beans for *pasta e fagioli* (pasta and beans). The perfect wine-country gift? **Tra Vigne**'s own dried tomato conserves, virgin olive oil, and flavored wine vinegars. There is also a good selection of top California, Oregon, and Italian wines, plus books on Italian wines and cooking. ♦ Italian ♦ Daily lunch and dinner. 963.8888 &

128 Merryvale Vineyards Visit this winery in its historic stone building and try the award-winning, barrel-fermented Chardonnay. Profile is a blend of the Bordeaux varietals Cabernet Sauvignon, Cabernet Franc, and Merlot from vineyards in and around the Rutherford Bench area. Under wine maker Bob Levy, a special label has been established to designate premium varietal wines. The tasting room also sells a Zinfandel-spiked pasta sauce and ketchup, a Dijon Chardonnay mayonnaise, and other goodies under the winery label. Olive oil from the **Tra Vigne** restaurant next door is also on sale here. On Saturday morning the winery offers a component-tasting class in which participants learn how to taste tannin, sugar, and tartaric acid in wines. ♦ Fee. Tasting and sales daily; tours and Saturday component-tasting class by appointment only. 1000 Main St (at Charter Oak Ave). 963.7777; fax 963.1949 &

129 Napa Valley Olive Oil Mfg. This hole-in-the-wall shop is one of those off-the-beaten-path wine-country treasures. Osvaldo, Ray, and Leonora Particelli and Policarpo Lucchesi have been selling their dark golden-green California olive oil (regular and extra-virgin) at a very modest price since the 1930s. They also sell a variety of nuts, dried fruit (even dried strawberries and cherries), homemade antipasto, freshly grated imported parmesan, the sharper pecorino romano, imported De Cecco pasta, and dried porcini mushrooms. For picnics they have Sciambra bread from Napa, cheese at good prices, and plenty of whole salami, prosciutto, and mortadella. The hand-rolled grissini (bread sticks) and focaccia (pizza bread) come from Cuneo

Bakery in San Francisco's North Beach. Fresh mozzarella drizzled with their extra-virgin olive oil makes a terrific first course. For dessert try the *torrone* (nougat), biscotti, amaretti cookies, or the famous chocolate *baci* (kisses) from the Italian chocolate firm Perugina. To find this hidden shop, look for the picnic tables with umbrellas next to the parking lot. ♦ Daily. 835 Charter Oak Ave (at Allison Ave). 963.4173

130 Taylor's Refresher $ Since 1949 this roadside stand with a picnic area has been dishing out hamburgers (and now veggie burgers), hot dogs, corn dogs, french fries, and homemade burritos and tacos. You can get shakes, malts, and floats here, too. ♦ Fast food ♦ Daily breakfast, lunch, and dinner. 933 Main St (near McCorkle Ave). 963.3486 ♦

131 St. Helena Chamber of Commerce Information on St. Helena and Napa Valley, including lodging, restaurants, wineries, and bike routes, is available here. ♦ M-F. 1080 Main St (at Pope St). 963.4456, 800/767.8528 (recording); fax 963.5396 ♦

132 St. Helena Cyclery Rent hybrid bikes (a mountain/touring cross) complete with helmets, side bags, and locks. The store doesn't take reservations, so arrive early, especially on weekends. Colorful biking togs, accessories, and books on biking in the wine country are for sale, too. ♦ Daily. 1156 Main St (at Spring St). 963.7736; fax 963.5099 ♦

132 Noble Building The hipped roof and double dormers mark this 1903 landmark as an example of Dutch Colonial architecture. Designed by **Luther Mark Turton,** who created more than 50 homes and buildings in the valley, it has housed a furniture store, an undertaking establishment, and a chicken hatchery at various times in its history. Now it's home to several small businesses. ♦ 1200-1204 Main St (at Spring St)

133 Calla Lily Debra Caselli has special sources in Europe for her luxury table and bed linens. Among the treasures here are exquisite Italian linen tablecloths with matching napkins handwoven in Renaissance patterns; silky Belgian cotton percale sheets (300-thread count), which can be monogrammed in more than 200 thread colors; Egyptian-cotton towels; wool-filled bed pads; and bedcoverings and pillow shams in jacquard cotton or subtle Marseilles piqué. Caselli will make custom sheets and bedcoverings in her high-quality fabrics, too. ♦ Daily. 1222 Main St (between Pope St and Hunt Ave). 963.8188 ♦

Louis Pasteur's discovery of yeast as the source of fermentation provided the key to consistency in wine making.

STILLWATERS

133 Stillwaters Owner Ron Sculatti stocks his shop with a unique mix of outdoor clothing and adventurous toys for those on the sporting edge, particularly items with a fly-fishing theme: state-of-the-art graphite poles that telescope down to 26 inches, elegant bamboo rods that come apart in two sections, hand-crafted decoys, binoculars, and exotic handmade Tiffany-style lamps shaped like swans and pheasants. Columbia Crest outerwear, Teva and Birkenstock shoes, hats, vests, boxers, and leather goods are also sold. The pocket fish knife is a handy item. ♦ Daily. 1228 Main St (between Pope St and Hunt Ave). 963.1782; fax 963.2567 ♦

133 Trilogy ★★★★$$ Chef/owner Diane Pariseau keeps her restaurant small so she and fellow chef Larry Quirit can personally cook almost every dish. The graceful, spare dining room with less than a dozen tables is especially lovely at lunch, and a good deal of wine-country business is conducted at this unpretentious spot. The extensive, reasonably priced list of California wines is just as big a draw as the light and flavorful dishes, which are always beautifully presented. The appetizers are intriguing, especially Pariseau's signature wild-mushroom ragout served with fresh corn crepes, and the grilled fennel, eggplant, and red bell peppers. The soups are always wonderful, as are the fish dishes, such as steamed salmon with lemongrass, ginger, garlic, and sesame oil or chilled rock shrimp with couscous and red bell-pepper puree. Red-wine lovers will find dishes such as pheasant with chanterelle mushrooms, roast rack of lamb with whole-grain mustard and rosemary, and sautéed medaillons of veal with shiitake mushrooms and sage. A four-course prix-fixe menu served with or without wine at each course is also offered. The restaurant has a small patio area where you can stop for a glass of wine and a few appetizers. ♦ California ♦ Tu-F lunch and dinner; Sa-Su dinner. Reservations recommended. 1234 Main St (at Hunt Ave). 963.5507 ♦

134 Valley Exchange Head toward the back of this store—past the bird feeders, terra-cotta pots, baskets, and more—for almond-studded biscotti from San Francisco's La Tempesta bakery. ♦ Daily. 1201 Main St (between Spring St and Hunt Ave). 963.7423 ♦

134 St. Helena Antiques Among the finds here are antique corkscrews, 19th-century French bottle-drying racks and wine carriers, crystal decanters, old ice cream and butter molds in the shape of a cluster of grapes, handmade English basketry wine carriers for four or six bottles, and garden furniture. ♦ Daily. 1231

Main St (between Spring St and Hunt Ave). 963.5878

134 Mosswood Top-of-the-line garden tools, most imported from England, plus French galvanized watering cans, garden gloves, and other essentials for the upscale gardener are sold in this shop. There's also a large selection of birdbaths, fountains, and statues in various materials, plus hand-crafted accents for the home and garden. In the solarium out back, you can find exotic orchids, ivy and myrtle topiaries, and other ornamental plants. The children's section, which is devoted to toys and educational games with a nature focus, is quite good. ♦ Daily. 1239 Main St (between Spring St and Hunt Ave). 963.5883; fax 963.5883 &

134 My Favorite Things Handwoven throws, wooden arks, hand-painted pottery and glass jars, and children's carved wooden trains, plus nostalgic picture frames and needlepoint pillows, are some of the treasures you'll discover at this boutique. ♦ Daily. 1289 Main St (between Spring St and Hunt Ave). 963.0848 &

135 Magnolia Cafe ★★$ Large French doors open into Betty Scott's sunny cafe; decorated with terra-cotta floors, green wooden chairs, and magnolias, it also boasts a faux-stone fresco painted on the walls by Scott's husband Michael, an artist who owns **Armadillo's** (see below) around the corner. Daily specials are posted on a chalkboard at the counter; you can choose from a changing selection of gourmet sandwiches, salads, homemade soups, espressos, and even peanut butter and jelly for the kids. Call ahead for boxed lunches to go. ♦ Eclectic ♦ Daily breakfast, lunch, and dinner. 1118 Hunt Ave (off Main St). 963.0748 &

136 Armadillo's ★★$ Great California-Mexican cuisine is served in this popular restaurant owned by Michael Scott and Tony Velazquez. Scott is the talent behind the whimsical decor, from the colorful frescoes on the walls and the

brightly painted tables and chairs to the kinetic *rufugio* broom sculptures and booths covered with traditional Mexican blankets. Velazquez, originally from Jalisco, Mexico, takes over in the kitchen, using only fresh local ingredients to create his homemade sauces, tortilla chips, and refried beans. ♦ Mexican ♦ M-F lunch and dinner; Sa-Su breakfast, lunch, and dinner. 1304 Main St (between Hunt Ave and Adams St). 963.8082 &

136 Green Valley Cafe & Trattoria ★$$ With its long green bar and vintage opera posters, this cafe feels like a trattoria somewhere in the Italian countryside. The day's specials are chalked on a blackboard and might include fried calamari, gnocchi in Gorgonzola sauce, or ravioli with meat and porcini-mushroom sauce. Generous portions are the rule. Skip the cappuccino, though—it's too weak and foamy. ♦ Italian ♦ Tu-Sa lunch and dinner. 1310 Main St (between Hunt Ave and Adams St). 963.7088 &

136 St. Helena Star Building St. Helena's only local newspaper has called this historic Old West–style building home since 1900. ♦ 1328 Main St (between Hunt Ave and Adams St). 963.2731

136 Liberty Theatre Though this cozy small-town theater dates from 1918, the original facade and interior were remodeled in the 1950s. Today the theater, which seats 172, shows current releases and classic films in runs of from two days to one or two weeks. It also features comfortable rocking lounge chairs, Dolby stereo sound, and fresh popcorn with real butter. ♦ 1340 Main St (between Hunt Ave and Adams St). 963.3946

136 I.O.O.F. Building Built in 1885, this remains one of the largest stone buildings in town. The brick facade boasts details such as lions' heads, brackets, and rosettes. Part of the base is painted cast iron. The upstairs area still houses the **Odd Fellows** meeting hall. ♦ 1350 Main St (between Hunt Ave and Adams St)

136 Steve's Hardware & Housewares Since 1878 this old-fashioned hardware store has been a fixture in St. Helena, offering picnic supplies and inexpensive cooking equipment such as knives, Styrofoam coolers, enamel coffeepots for the campfire, wineglasses (in plastic versions, too), pocket corkscrews, and other handy necessities. ♦ Daily. 1370 Main St (between Hunt Ave and Adams St). 963.3423; fax 963.2258 &

137 Showley's ★★★$$$; Owners Grant and Sharon Showley had a hard act to follow when they bought **Miramonte** from the talented, Swiss-born chef, Udo Nechutnys, and changed the name to **Showley's at Miramonte.** Now simply called **Showley's**—a tribute to how well the restaurateurs' efforts have been received— the successful eatery offers an inventive menu that focuses on local ingredients and clean, uncomplicated flavors. Entrées may include risotto of duck, parmesan cheese, and pine nuts; grilled pizza topped with figs and cambazola blue cheese; fresh fettuccine with quail; and veal sweetbreads in Madeira and whole-grain mustard sauce. The homemade desserts range from berry cobbler to caramel pecan passion ice cream topped with meringue and chocolate sauce. A big attraction here is the brick patio shaded by a century-old fig tree. ♦ California ♦ Tu-Su lunch and dinner. Reservations recommended. 1327 Railroad Ave (between Hunt Ave and Adams St). 963.1200; fax 963.8864 &

137 Terra ★★★★$$$ Lissa Doumani and her husband, Hiro Sone, a Japanese chef who worked with Wolfgang Puck at Spago in Los Angeles, have created one of the best restaurants in Napa Valley, long a favorite among locals. If you enjoy truly fine food and wine, this place is a *must* on your wine-country itinerary. Sone's cooking is subtle and marvelously flavorful, featuring well-crafted, intelligently conceived dishes such as Nantucket bay scallop tartare with caviar, wonton of duck liver with wild-mushroom sauce, grilled medaillon of lamb with anchovy-and-black-olive sauce, and roasted sea bass with shallot-butter sauce and chanterelle mushrooms. The two dining rooms, set in a historic stone building, have an elegant, understated ambience. Doumani is warm and welcoming; the service,

professional and unobtrusive. The extensive California wine list features many hard-to-find selections from small estates. ♦ California ♦ M, W-Su dinner. Reservations recommended. 1345 Railroad Ave (between Hunt Ave and Adams St). 963.8931 &

138 Hotel St. Helena $$ Built in 1881, this inn boasts 18 comfortable, old-fashioned guest rooms decorated with period wallpapers, fabrics, and accessories. Every effort is made to make guests feel at home. Some rooms share large bathrooms; others have private baths. A continental breakfast is included. ♦ 1309 Main St (between Hunt Ave and Adams St). 963.4388; fax 963.5402

138 St. Helena Masonic Lodge The most elaborate building on Main Street, this fancy Victorian structure was erected in 1892 by **M.G. Ritchie** and bought by the Masons in 1972. The influence of British architect **Charles Eastlake** is obvious in such repetitive motifs as turned spindles and concentric circles. The facade is brick over structural stone, the bays are wood, and the sides show the use of stone repeating some of the wood designs. ♦ 1327-1337 Main St (between Hunt Ave and Adams St)

138 Model Bakery The best bread in the valley comes from this bakery's old-fashioned brick oven. Look for *pain de campagne* (half-wheat, half-white sourdough), sour rye, crusty sweet or sourdough baguettes, plus terrific poppy- or sesame-seed sandwich rolls. If you're thinking of a picnic, owner Karen Mitchell offers croissants stuffed with either ham and cheese or spinach and feta, brie sold by the slice, a changing selection of sandwiches, and several types of pizza—call to reserve a small individual pizza to go. For dessert, she has chocolate chocolate-chip cookies, oatmeal-raisin cookies, almond-studded biscotti, and, in the summer, lovely fruit tarts. Bring in your Thermos and she'll fill it with coffee or espresso brewed from freshly roasted beans. Seating is also available in the bakery. ♦ Tu-Su. 1357 Main St (between Hunt Ave and Adams St). 963.8192 &

Restaurants/Clubs: Red   **Hotels:** Blue
Shops/ ♥ Outdoors: Green   **Wineries/Sights:** Black

138 **Gallery on Main Street** Barbara Ryan concentrates on the works of local artists, especially wine-related art, in this Napa Valley gallery. ♦ M-Sa. 1359 Main St (between Hunt Ave and Adams St). 963.3350 &

138 **Main Street Books** This shop features a small, well-edited selection of wine books, including *Norman's Napa Valley Adventures,* a coloring-and-activity book for children. There is a good California travel section, too. ♦ M-Sa. 1371 Main St (between Hunt Ave and Adams St). 963.1338 &

139 **The Cinnamon Bear** $$ The teddy bear—the best plaything ever invented, according to some—is the motif at this bed-and-breakfast, with teddies of every size and description scattered throughout the 1904 bungalow where St. Helena's longtime mayor Walter Mezner lived for many years. Willow furniture graces the broad veranda, and the four guest rooms (three upstairs and one down) have 1920s antiques, queen-size beds, and private baths. A full breakfast is served. ♦ 1407 Kearney St (at Adams St). 963.4653

139 **Chestelson House** $$ Just off Main Street, this small 1904 Victorian (pictured above) offers the welcoming ambience of a family home. Owner Jackie Sweet draws on her previous experience as a successful caterer and cooking instructor to plan creative, mouth-watering meals, which might include bran muffins with praline butter, peach shortcake, her signature baked stuffed eggs, French toast filled with ricotta, and fruit, juice, and coffee. The three light, spacious bedrooms are elegant and unfussy, with queen-size beds, Roman blinds or French shutters, and private baths. Each room is named for a different verse in Robert Louis Stevenson's *A Child's Garden of Verses.* Sweet also keeps picnic baskets for guests to use. ♦ 1417 Kearney St (at Adams St). 963.2238, 800/959.4505

140 **Napa Valley Coffee Roasting Company** $ Light floods through the French windows at this attractive corner cafe, making it a great spot for breakfast or whiling away the afternoon. Settle in at one of the marble bistro tables for some of the best espresso drinks in the valley. Partners Denise Fox and Leon Sange roast the more than 20 varieties of coffee beans at their downtown Napa location. (Forget the Napa Valley T-shirts and take home a pound or two of great coffee for a different kind of wine-country souvenir.) They offer freshly squeezed orange juice, the cappuccino of your dreams, bagels with cream cheese and chutney, crumbly scones, flaky Danishes, and toasted bread from the popular Berkeley bakery Acme Baking Company. And if that isn't enough, they have outdoor seating on the porch, and a shelf of good reads provided by **Main Street Books** (see above). If the weather's hot, stop in for the refreshing double espresso granita, a rough slush of frozen coffee crystals topped with *panna* (whipped cream)—now that's truly *la dolce vita.* ♦ Cafe ♦ Daily breakfast and snacks. 1400 Oak Ave (at Adams St). 963.4491; fax 963.1183 &

141 **Vanderbilt and Company** For the stylish picnic, this housewares-and-garden shop has a great collection of paper plates and matching napkins in grape, flower, or lettuce patterns; nifty Italian plastic plates that mimic old majolica pottery (cracks and all); plastic Champagne flutes and wineglasses (a necessity around pool areas); and handsome wicker picnic baskets. If you really want to go whole hog, they have lovely jacquard linens from **Le Jacquard Français,** hand-painted tablecloths, rustic terra-cotta, Italian hand-blown wineglasses, and white-on-white grape-leaf majolica from Deruta, a town in Umbria, Italy, which has specialized in this type of pottery since the Middle Ages. ♦ Daily. 1429 Main St (between Adams and Pine Sts). 963.1010 &

142 **Pairs Parkside Cafe** ★★★$$ Many a gastronome has been dazzled by this small, cheery, sizzling-yellow cafe/caterer since it opened its doors a few years ago—no small feat given the culinary competition in the wine country. Co-owner/chef Craig Schauffel, who graduated with honors from The Culinary Institute of America in Hyde Park, New York, runs the place with his brother Keith.

Entrées on the ever-changing menu may include garlic-roasted mussels and sweet corn broth with roasted red pepper aioli, rosemary-roasted chicken breast with mashed potatoes and a sweet corn and carrot ragout, and a grilled basil burger served with smoked-tomato ketchup and shoestring potatoes. The Schauffel brothers are as serious about their wine as they are about their food, and they offer a very good list, including 20 wines by the glass—all of which are poured into fine Riedel glassware. There is a small wine bar. Take-out and catering service is available, too. ♦ California ♦ Daily lunch and dinner. 1420 Main St (between Adams and Pine Sts). 963.7566; fax 963.7567 &

142 Lyman Park You'll find picnic tables, barbecue pits, and a playground for kids here, as well as a gazebo where live concerts are sometimes held in the summer. ♦ Main St (between Adams and Pine Sts)

143 Ambrose Bierce House $$ The modest exterior of this 1872 Victorian home hides a hospitable, superbly restored guesthouse/mini-museum crammed with memorabilia of 19th-century writer Ambrose Bierce and friends (including Lillie Langtry, Eadweard Muybridge, and Lillie Coit). Bierce lived here for 13 years, plotting ghost stories before his mysterious disappearance in Mexico in 1913. The inn has two suites upstairs, each with a queen-size bed and private bath. The largest and most comfortable is, of course, named for Bierce. Innkeeper Jane Gibson offers concierge services and serves a sumptuous continental breakfast featuring freshly squeezed juice, fruit, homemade scones or croissants, and a special blend of coffee. ♦ 1515 Main St (between Pine St and Fulton La). 963.3003

144 Silverado Museum This museum is devoted to the beloved Robert Louis Stevenson, author of *A Child's Garden of Verses* and *Treasure Island* (among other works), who spent his honeymoon in an abandoned bunkhouse at the old **Silverado Mine** on Mount St. Helena in 1880. Founded by bibliophile Norman Strouse, it has a touching and quirky collection of more than 8,000 items acquired from heirs and friends of Stevenson: original letters, manuscripts, first editions, paintings, sculpture, photographs, and memorabilia. You'll see the copy of *A Child's Garden of Verses* that he presented to his wife, Fanny; the parmesan-cheese case his father used (which he later mentioned in *Treasure Island*); a lead toy soldier and a miniature tea set he played with more than a century ago; and the name board from the ship *Equator*, which carried the Stevenson family from Hawaii to Samoa in

1889. Also on view are the gloves that fellow author Henry James left behind during a visit, which Fanny gleefully appropriated and put in an envelope with the note: "Henry James' gloves left in my house and dishonestly confiscated by me. FS." ♦ Fee. Tu-Su. 1490 Library La (off Adams St). 963.3757; fax 963.0917 &

144 Napa Valley Wine Library

For anyone interested in wine lore, this 6,000-volume collection of books, tapes, and reference materials on wine and viticulture is definitely worth a visit. Browsers and borrowers alike are welcome. ♦ M-Sa. 1492 Library La (off Adams St). 963.5244; fax 963.5264 &

Associated with the Napa Valley Wine Library:

Napa Valley Wine Library Association
The $20 annual membership fee gives you access to the specialized wine library, a subscription to a newsletter listing new wine books in the collection, and an invitation to the gala tasting in August—in itself well worth the price of membership. ♦ Box 328, St. Helena, CA 94574. 963.5145

Napa Valley Wine Library Association Courses Weekend courses are offered in May and June, including an informal introduction to wine appreciation presented by wine professionals from Napa Valley wineries. Lectures, field trips, and tastings cover sensory evaluations of wines, grape varieties, and production. The fee includes a year's membership in the association. ♦ Box 207, St. Helena, CA 94574

144 Napa Valley Farmers' Market Shop for exotic leaf lettuce, vine-ripened tomatoes, and handmade cheeses and breads at this Friday morning farmers' market in the parking lot of the **Old Railroad Depot** behind Dansk Square. It's a certified farmers' market, which means that all goods must be grown or made by the farmer selling them. This is a great chance to see firsthand some of the top-notch ingredients that go into wine-country cooking. It's also fun to rub elbows with innkeepers, chefs, vintners, and other local folk who make a point of shopping here. ♦ F 7:30AM-11:30AM May-Nov. Railroad Ave (off Pine St). 963.7343

145 Calafia Cellars Named for an Amazonian queen, this winery produces small quantities of Cabernet and Merlot. ♦ Sales and tastings by appointment only. 629 Fulton La (off Main St). 963.0114

146 Stonesbridge Park This small park on the banks of the Napa River is a good place to sit and enjoy a picnic lunch. ♦ Pope St (near the Silverado Tr)

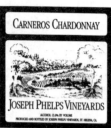

CARNEROS CHARDONNAY

JOSEPH PHELPS VINEYARDS

ALCOHOL 13.0% BY VOLUME
PRODUCED AND BOTTLED BY JOSEPH PHELPS VINEYARDS, ST. HELENA, CA

147 Joseph Phelps Vineyards Construction magnate Joseph Phelps built a few wineries for other people before he decided to construct his own in 1974 on the former **Connolly Hereford Ranch** in Spring Valley. The redwood winery is so cleverly designed that it almost disappears into the hillside to the east of the Silverado Trail. Wine maker Craig Williams produces excellent vintages, including an outstanding late-harvest Riesling, a Bordeaux-style blend called Insignia, and several vineyard-designated Cabernet Sauvignons. There's also a Vin du Mistral label for Rhône-style wines, including a Syrah, a violet-scented Viognier (white), a Grenache, and a blend of Mourvèdre, Grenache, and Syrah that's dubbed Rouge— for red. ♦ Tasting and tours M-F by appointment only. 200 Taplin Rd (off the Silverado Tr). 963.2745; fax 963.4831 ♿

147 The Farmhouse $$ In the midst of **Joseph Phelps Vineyards** sits this graceful bed-and-breakfast, built around an inner courtyard draped with wisteria. Decorated in an understated country style, the three guest rooms, all with private entrances and baths, have queen-size beds with cheerful duvets and plump pillows. The **Blue Room** is the largest, and has windows across two sides and a view of vines with wildflowers growing on them. The spring-fed swimming pool is in a spectacular setting framed by fruit trees and a gnarled olive tree. Breakfast, prepared by innkeeper Hannah Nunn, might feature homemade pear or fig jam from the farm's own trees. In the evenings, she and her husband, Ron, may serve **Phelps** wines with cheese in front of the fire. There are several nice walks through Spring Valley; as a guest you may hike through acres of **Joseph Phelps Vineyards**. ♦ Friday and Saturday nights only; closed November through May. 300 Taplin Rd (off the Silverado Tr). 963.3431

148 Meadowood Resort $$$$ Originally a private country club for well-to-do Napa Valley families, this luxurious retreat has great charm and style. After a fire destroyed the old clubhouse, Sausalito architect **Kirk Hillman** rebuilt it, using elements of New England's grand turn-of-the-century cottages. Trimmed in white, with tiers of gabled windows and wraparound porches, the two main lodges and the 18 smaller lodges scattered over the 256-acre, heavily wooded property evoke a feeling of old money and tradition and attract the likes of Danielle Steel and the Mondavi family. General Manager Jorg Lippuner's professionalism is evident in the staff's attention to detail and the Old-World sense of service. The 99 rooms range from one-room studios to large four-bedroom suites (most with stone fireplaces); all have private baths, porches, beds covered in chintz with matching pillows and plump down comforters, thick terry robes, wet bars, coffeemakers, and toasters. The grounds include a perfectly maintained and challenging nine-hole golf course and two international-regulation croquet lawns, as well as seven championship tennis courts strung along the foot of the lush hillside. There are also two heated pools, including a 25-yard lap pool, and a 102-degree whirlpool. Another attractive amenity is the health spa, which features a well-stocked weight room, aerobics classes, steam rooms, saunas, and a spa boutique.

The **Croquet Classic at Meadowood** is held here every July, and the resort is also the site of the elegant annual Napa Valley Wine Auction in June. In addition to golf, tennis, and croquet pros, the resort has John Thoreen, an unpretentious and down-to-earth wine expert, to advise guests on winery itineraries or to conduct tastings for groups. Book well ahead for summer stays and weekend getaways. The property is a member of the prestigious international Relais & Châteaux hotel association, as well as the Small Luxury Hotels of the World and the Preferred Hotels & Resorts Worldwide organizations. ♦ 900 Meadowood La (off Pope St). 963.3646, 800/458.8080; fax 963.3532 ♿

Within the Meadowood Resort:

The Restaurant at Meadowood ★★ $$$$ This grand, conservatively elegant dining room accented with shades of pink and burgundy overlooks **Meadowood**'s tree-lined property and pristine golf course. The chef is native Californian Roy Breiman, who has a passion for Provençal cuisine and worked as a chef in the south of France before coming here. Breiman's menu changes daily, and he keeps it fairly small to ensure the quality of each dish. His lunch menu, which usually provides diners with three choices of appetizers, main courses, and desserts, might include a starter of chilled tomato soup with seared ahi tuna, anchovy, and basil, followed by roasted sea bass with bay leaves, baby fennel, and tomato essence, ending with a delightful grand finale of mocha soufflé laced with crème anglaise. For dinner there is a slightly larger selection of entrées, such as squab baked in a crust of eggplant, crispy potatoes, and red wine; medaillons of lamb with oregano, potatoes, tomatoes, and basil; or sliced fillet of beef with ginger and plum wine. A four- or five-course sampling menu is also available. Brunch is served on Sunday, and an afternoon tea is offered daily. Request a table on the terrace overlooking the wooded property when weather permits. ♦ California ♦ M-Sa afternoon tea and dinner; Su brunch, afternoon tea, and dinner. Reservations recommended; jackets are suggested for weekend dinners. ♿

The Grill at Meadowood ★$$ In mild weather, this informal restaurant overlooking the golf course offers a glorious place to dine on the terrace. The breakfast buffet offers an attractive display of croissants, muffins, cereals, yogurt, fresh fruits, and beverages, or you may order French toast, eggs, or omelettes. At lunch and dinner you have a choice of a half-dozen salads and traditional sandwiches, and a few children's plates are offered. ♦ American ♦ F-Su breakfast, lunch, and dinner; M-Th breakfast and lunch ♿

149 White Sulphur Springs Resort $$
The oldest hot-springs resort in California, established in 1852, is three miles west of St. Helena on a 330-acre estate in a quiet valley. This family-owned resort offers rustic lodging in the 13-room inn (shared kitchen and shower, private toilets and sinks), a carriage house that sleeps 30 (individual rooms, and shared bath and kitchen), or eight cabins (private baths; most have kitchens).

This resort really feels like the country, and for the times when racing around the valley is too taxing, you can settle in for a soak in the outdoor mineral-spring pool or 15-person Jacuzzi, picnic in the secluded redwood grove, take on your fellow guests in a game of basketball or horseshoes, or indulge in a massage or mud or herbal wrap at the health spa (call 963.4361 for a spa reservation). It's a great spot for bicycling, too. No smoking is allowed. ♦ 3100 White Sulphur Springs Rd (off Spring St). 963.8588; fax 963.2890

150 Newton Vineyards Set on a knoll overlooking the valley, this winery was designed by owners Su Hua Newton and Peter Newton, founders of **Sterling Vineyards,** and features a spectacular formal roof garden of old roses and boxwood. Wine maker John Kongsgaard uses grapes from the steeply terraced vineyards on Spring Mountain to produce consistently good Chardonnay, Cabernet, and Merlot. The cellar is laid out along classic French lines, with the oak barrels all housed underground. ♦ Tours Friday at 11AM by appointment only. 2555 Madrona Ave (near Fir Hill Dr). 963.9000; fax 963.5408

151 Spring Mountain Vineyards Television fans the world over will recognize the exterior of this winery as the fictional mansion featured in the once-popular network TV show *Falcon Crest.* Unfortunately, however, the winery is closed to the public. ♦ 2805 Spring Mountain Rd (off Madrona Ave)

152 Philip Togni Vineyard Renowned vintner Philip Togni (who has acted as wine maker and manager for a slew of top estates, including **Mayacamas, Chalone, Chapellet,** and **Cuvaison**) now produces wine here under his own label. Most notable are a rich and intense Cabernet Sauvignon and a crisp, lean Sauvignon Blanc. He's also producing a dessert wine, Ca'Togni. ♦ Tours by appointment only. 3780 Spring Mountain Rd (near Boyson La). 963.3731; fax 963.9186

153 Robert Keenan Winery Perched on Spring Mountain where a 1904 winery used to be, this family-owned winery produces only four varieties: Chardonnay, Merlot, Cabernet Franc, and a sturdy and tannic Cabernet Sauvignon. There is a picnic area, too. ♦ Tasting and sales by appointment only. 3660 Spring Mountain Rd (near Boyson La). 963.9177; fax 963.8209 ♿

154 Smith-Madrone Winery Founded by brothers Charles and Stuart Smith in 1977, this winery on Spring Mountain produces Chardonnay, Cabernet, and Riesling. The 1978 Riesling won the top award at the French wine-and-food magazine *Gault-Millau*'s tasting in 1979. ♦ Sales and tours M-Sa by appointment only. 4022 Spring Mountain Rd (near Boyson La). 963.2283; fax 963.2219

154 Ritchie Creek Vineyards Located up a long, winding road at the very top of Spring Mountain, this tiny winery produces small quantities of Chardonnay and Cabernet Sauvignon from steeply terraced vineyards on the Sonoma border. ♦ Tasting and sales by appointment only. 4024 Spring Mountain Rd (off Madrona Ave). 963.4661

155 Beringer Vineyards The oldest continuously operating winery in Napa Valley, this place received its bond in 1876. Founder Frederick Beringer built the landmark **Rhine House** as a tribute to his former home when he emigrated from Germany in the mid-19th century. A popular tour of the vineyards includes the house and the caves excavated by Chinese laborers a century ago. The winery is now wholly owned by the Swiss food conglomerate Nestlé. Since 1977, the winery has been known for its extraordinary private reserve

Chardonnay and Cabernet. Wine maker Ed Sbragia also produces a roster of other well-made wines. The popular **Hudson House** is the home of the **Culinary Arts Center,** as well as the **School for American Chefs,** a graduate program for professional chefs that is directed by French chef and cookbook author Madeleine Kamman. ♦ Tasting, sales, and tours daily. 2000 Main St (north of Pratt Ave). 963.7115 &

156 Culinary Institute of America at Greystone For those of you who were able to tour this impressive and historic estate when it was **Christian Brothers–Greystone Cellars,** count your blessings. The last tour was given in the summer of 1993, when the new tenants moved in and were required by the city of St. Helena to shut the doors to the public. Heublein Inc. (owners of **Christian Brothers**) donated all but $1.68 million of this 282-acre estate's $14-million price tag to the Culinary Institute of America, a nonprofit culinary arts

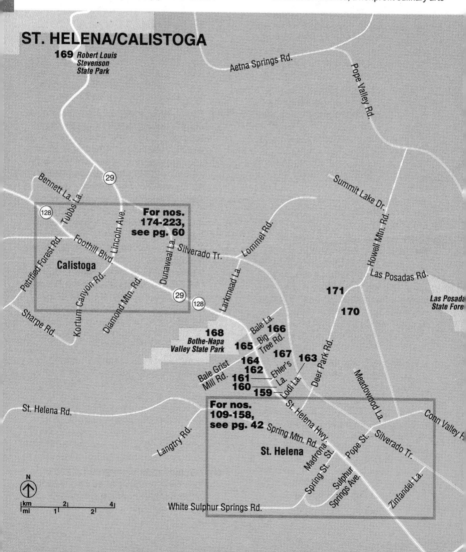

ST. HELENA/CALISTOGA

169 Robert Louis Stevenson State Park

Aetna Springs Rd.

Pope Valley Rd.

Bennett La.

(29)

Summit Lake Dr.

Tubbs La.

(128)

For nos. 174-223, see pg. 60

Lommel Rd.

Howell Mtn. Rd.

Las Posadas Rd.

Petrified Forest Rd.

Foothill Blvd

Lincoln Ave.

Dunaweal La.

Silverado Tr.

Calistoga

Larkmead La.

171

Las Posada State Fore

Kortum Canyon Rd.

Diamond Mtn. Rd.

(29)

(128)

170

Sharpe Rd.

Bale La.

Big **166**

Tree Rd.

St. Helena Rd.

168
Bothe-Napa
Valley State Park

165

167

163

Deer Park Rd.

Meadowood La.

164

162

Ehler's

La.

Conn Valley R

Bale Grist
Mill Rd.

161

160

159

Lodi La.

St. Helena Hwy.

For nos.
109-158,
see pg. 42

Langtry Rd.

Spring Mtn. Rd.

Madrona St.

Pope St.

Silverado Tr.

St. Helena

Spring St.

Sulphur
Springs Ave.

Zinfandel La.

White Sulphur Springs Rd.

N

km   2   4
mi 1   2

school based in Hyde Park, New York.

First opened in 1889, the 117,000-square-foot main building is the largest stone winery in the world. All of the buildings on the estate are undergoing major reconstruction to meet seismic requirements; because this site is on the National Register of Historic Places, however, the exteriors of the buildings cannot be touched (some exterior walls are as thick as 22 inches). This branch of **The Culinary Institute of America (CIA)**, slated to open at press time, will serve as a specialized graduate cooking school that's open to students from **CIA**'s baccalaureate program in New York as well as any professional working chef (an undergraduate degree from **CIA** is not required to enroll). A dorm for 36 chefs will be added to the site. The north wing will house the school and a restaurant that will be staffed by **CIA**'s graduate students and open to the public daily for lunch and dinner (at press time the restaurant's name had not yet been decided).

The south end of the estate will contain a small public museum of food and wine and a campus store stocked with cookbooks, culinary tools, and the students' baked goods. The **Christian Brothers Winery** relocated to Madera, California, and is no longer open to the public. ♦ 2555 Main St (north of Pratt Ave). 963.4503; fax 967.1113 ♿

157 Charles Krug Winery Pioneer wine maker **Charles Krug** founded this winery in 1861, though it's been run by a branch of the Mondavi family since 1943. It produces 15 different varietals, among them its

benchmark Vintage Select Cabernets and Carneros Reserve Chardonnays. ♦ Fee. Tasting and sales daily; tours by appointment only. 2800 St. Helena Hwy (north of Pratt Ave). 963.5057; fax 963.7913 ♿

158 St. Clement Vineyards The elegant mansion that appears on this vineyard's label was built in 1878 by San Francisco glass merchant Fritz Rosenbaum, and its stone cellar became one of the earliest bonded wineries in the valley. After years of neglect, the cellar

was restored in time for the 1975 vintage. In 1990 this lovely Victorian mansion, which is now used as the **Visitors' Center,** was opened to the public for the first time in 100 years. Napa Valley native and wine maker Dennis Johns concentrates on a limited production of flavorful Sauvignon Blanc, Chardonnay, Merlot, and a rich, complex Cabernet. ♦ Tasting and sales daily; tours by appointment only. 2867 St. Helena Hwy (north of Deer Park Rd). 967.3033, 800/331.8266; fax 963.9174 ♿

159 Wine Country Inn $$ Located off the highway in the midst of a quiet meadow, this small hotel was designed in the tradition of the inns of New England. All 24 rooms have private baths and views of the serene countryside; most have private patios or balconies and/or fireplaces. Country furniture (carved wooden beds, wicker chairs, and pine armoires) is balanced with coverlets, curtains, and carpeting in fall or spring colors. A continental breakfast with homemade bread and granola is served. ♦ 1152 Lodi La (off Hwy 29). 963.7077; fax 963.9018 ♿

160 Freemark Abbey This small complex features two restaurants, a winery, a shop, and offices. 3010-3022 St. Helena Hwy (north of Lodi La)

55

Within Freemark Abbey:

Brava Terrace ★★★$$

Several years ago, Fred Halpert, who was head chef at the highly regarded restaurant in San Francisco's Portman Hotel, pulled up his stakes to open this California/Mediterranean bistro—and it's been a success ever since. The light, spacious room has a large fieldstone fireplace, bright textiles on the seats and banquettes, and a pretty, shady outdoor terrace facing the woods for alfresco dining. Halpert's love of the vibrant, sun-drenched flavors of Provence and Italy—with a soupçon of California country thrown into the mix—is obvious: Provençal salad of wild greens and herbs with warm Sonoma goat cheese, a skewer of locally smoked sausage with vegetables and a Catalán romesco dip, and freshly made potato chips with warm blue cheese are just a few of the starters you'll find on his menu. He serves great sandwiches, too, including a burger made with naturally raised beef, topped with tomatoes and basil on a potato bun. Ask about the risotto and pasta of the day; a pasta dish made without butter or oil is always on the menu. And the minute it gets a little chilly outside, order the *cassoulet de Puy*, a hot, hearty French dish of lentils simmered slowly with pork tenderloin, turkey sausage, and chicken. Dishes vary in quality and service can be slow, but usually this restaurant serves excellent meals. Don't miss the delightful desserts; there's a well-chosen wine list, too. ♦ California/Mediterranean ♦ Daily lunch and dinner; closed for two weeks in January and on Wednesday from November through April. Reservations recommended. 3010 St. Helena Hwy (north of Lodi La). 963.9300; fax 963.9581 ⅃

Hurd Beeswax Candles Here you can see candlemakers roll, dip, and cut pure beeswax into fanciful shapes, such as treble clefs, flames, and spirals. Classic forms are decorated with leaves or wildflowers. Kids will love peering through a little window to see an actual hive with live bees at work. You can also buy natural beeswax candles here, from slender tapers and votive lights to tall, hefty candles big enough for a cathedral. ♦ Daily. 3020 St. Helena Hwy (north of Lodi La). ⅃ 963.7211

Freemark Abbey Winery A lovely room with a wood-beam ceiling and sofas placed in front of a fieldstone fireplace welcomes you to the tasting area, where you can sample not only

new releases, but an occasional older vintage. Wine making here dates from 1866, the year Josephine Tychson established the winery. She was the first woman to build a winery in California, and her successor, Antonio Forni, built the present stone structure circa 1900. After the repeal of Prohibition, it changed hands several times until the present owners bought it in 1967. Headed by third-generation Napa Valley resident Chuck Carpy and wine maker Ted Edwards, the winery is best known for its Cabernet from **Bosché Vineyard** near Rutherford, considered one of the finest vineyards in California. It also produces oaky Chardonnay, Merlot, and Johannisberg Riesling, which in certain years develops into Edelwein, a rich and extravagantly perfumed late-harvest dessert wine. ♦ Fee. Tasting and sales daily; tours daily at 2PM. 3022 St. Helena Hwy (north of Lodi La). 963.9694; fax 963.0554 ⅃

160 Ehlers Grove Winery Formerly known as **Stratford Winery,** this establishment continues to produce a nice, reasonably priced Chardonnay. The winery also makes Pinot Noir, Merlot, Cabernet Sauvignon, and Sauvignon Blanc. ♦ Tasting and sales daily. 3222 Ehlers La (off Hwy 29). 963.3200 ⅃

161 Village Outlets of Napa Valley Within a pleasant tree-lined shopping complex, you'll find clothing and shoes discounted by 30 to 60 percent at these factory outlets that include, among others, six popular designers: **Donna Karan, Brooks Brothers, London Fog, Joan & David, Coach,** and **Go Silk.** There are also rest rooms, a pay phone, and a small cafe that serves salads, sandwiches, and sodas that you enjoy on the shady, vine-laced patio in front, or in the peaceful picnic area in back. ♦ Daily (individual shop hours may vary). 3111 St. Helena Hwy (north of Lodi La). 963.7282 ⅃

162 Folie à Deux Winery The name of this winery comes from a French term used by psychiatrists in the US to describe a fantasy or delusion shared by two people—the duo in this case was Larry and Evie Dizmang (a psychiatrist

and psychiatric social worker, respectively).
Everyone told them they were crazy to start a
winery, hence the name. They contend that a
bottle of wine shared on a special occasion
provokes a spirit of folly and fantasy all its
own. Founded in 1981, the winery produces
wonderful Chenin Blanc, perfect for aperitifs,
along with Chardonnay and Cabernet. Their
dry Muscat Canelli, available only at the
winery, is called *à Deux*. They also make a
sparkling wine. Note the Rorschach-style ink-
blot (illustrated on page 56) on the winery's
label; it represents the designer of the label,
Susann Ortega, and her twin sister. The
tasting room is in the original turn-of-the-
century farmhouse. Oak-shaded picnic
grounds are available here. ♦ Tasting and
sales daily. 3070 St. Helena Hwy (north of
Lodi La). 963.1160; fax 963.9223

163 Duckhorn Vineyards Margaret and Daniel
Duckhorn founded this winery with 10 other
families, all family, in 1976; their first wines
from the 1978 vintage, a Cabernet and a
Merlot, were immediately acclaimed and
remain their best. The Merlots come from two
vineyards: The Three Palms Vineyard Merlot
needs several years to tame its tannins, while
the Napa Valley Merlot tends to be more
supple, elegant, and approachable when
young. They also make a Sauvignon Blanc.
♦ Sales M-F. 3027 Silverado Tr (north of Lodi
La). 963.7108; fax 963.7595 ♿

164 Bale Grist Mill State Historic Park Napa

Valley's economy was once based on wheat,
not grapes. This historic flour mill was
designed and built in 1846 by the young
British surgeon Edward Turner Bale, who
served under General Mariano Guadelupe
Vallejo, married Vallejo's niece, and settled
in Napa Valley. The handsome mill has been
restored to working condition, complete
with a 36-foot wooden waterwheel and huge
millstones. On weekends at 1PM and 4PM,
the immense wheel turns, and you can watch
the ranger/miller grind grain with the French
buhrstone; at times you may linger in the
granary to watch baking demonstrations.
It's an invigorating walk to the mill from
Bothe–Napa Valley State Park (see page 58)
along the well-marked, 1.2-mile **History Trail**,
which passes through a pioneer cemetery and
the site of the first church in Napa County,
built in 1853. This site may look familiar—it
was used by Walt Disney in the 1960 film
Pollyanna. ♦ Admission; children under six
free. 3369 St. Helena Hwy (at Bale Grist Mill
Rd). 963.2236

165 Stony Hill Vineyard Founded in 1951, this
small vineyard on the rocky hillside of the
western ridge of Napa Valley has a cult
following for its voluptuous Chardonnay.
Despite the high quality and the difficulty in
finding this wine, sold to a mailing list of
faithful customers, the prices remain

Small but Select Wineries

This guidebook to the wine country in Northern
California features a selective list of wineries; not
every winery is listed because many have a very
limited visiting policy or simply don't have the
facilities to receive visitors. That doesn't mean they
should be left out of your wine-country experience.
Keep the following producers in mind when you're
browsing in wineshops or encounter an extensive
California wine list in a restaurant. They are well
worth seeking out.

Napa Valley

Diamond Creek Vineyards (Cabernets from
Volcanic Hill, Red Rock, and Gravelly Meadow)

Dominus Estate Winery (Cabernet-based blend)

Dunn Vineyards (Cabernet from Howell Mountain
and Napa)

Far Niente Winery (Chardonnay)

Forman Vineyard (Cabernet and Chardonnay)

Grace Family Vineyards (Cabernet)

Livingston Wines (Cabernet)

Neyers (Chardonnay)

Pahlmeyer (Chardonnay, Cabernet, Merlot)

Spottswoode Winery (Cabernet, Sauvignon Blanc)

Steltzner Vineyards (Cabernet, Sauvignon Blanc,
and late-harvest Gewürztraminer)

Stony Hill Vineyard (Chardonnay)

Sonoma Valley

Clos du Bois (Chardonnay, Cabernet)

Kistler Vineyards (Chardonnay)

Laurel Glen Vineyard (Cabernet)

Nalle Winery (Zinfandel)

Wildcat Wines (Merlot)

Williams Selyem Winery (Pinot Noir)

Russian River Valley

Balverne Winery and Vineyards (Chardonnay,
Gewürztraminer)

Hanna Winery (Sauvignon Blanc, Chardonnay)

Joseph Swan Vineyards (Zinfandel)

La Crema (Chardonnay)

Pommeraie Winery (Cabernet)

"There is so much contained in a glass of good
wine. It is a gift of nature that tastes of man's
foibles, his sense of the beautiful, his idealism,
and virtuosity."

Kermit Lynch, *Adventures of the Wine Route*

Tomb paintings from ancient Thebes depict the
grape harvest and wine making.

uncommonly moderate. White Riesling and Gewürztraminer are also produced. The winery is difficult to find; ask for specific directions when you call to make your appointment. ♦ Sales by mail only; tours by appointment only. 3331 St. Helena Hwy (north of Bale Grist Mill Rd). Mailing address: Box 308, St. Helena, CA 94574. 963.2636

165 Bale Mill Classic Country Furniture
Owner Tom Scheibal designs about 80 percent of the handsome country pine furniture, stylish iron garden chairs, beds, and chaise longues for sale here. More portable are the rustic willow baskets and wire baskets. He also has some lovely lamps and weathered iron signs. Scheibal has a second shop, called **Palladio**, in Healdsburg (see page 130). ♦ Daily. 3431 St. Helena Hwy (between Bale Grist Mill and Big Tree Rds). 963.4595; fax 963.4128

166 Tudal Winery This winery consistently produces well-made Cabernet from a small property where two generations of the Tudal family work side by side. ♦ Tasting and tours daily by appointment only. 1015 Big Tree Rd (off the Silverado Tr). 963.3947; fax 963.9288

167 Rombauer Vineyards Founded in 1982 by Koerner Rombauer, the great-nephew of Irma Rombauer, author of *The Joy of Cooking,* and his wife Joan, this well-equipped winery custom-crushes wines for a number of aspiring wine makers and also produces a crisp Chardonnay, Cabernet Sauvignon, and proprietary red wine of Cabernet blended with Cabernet Franc and Merlot under the name Le Meilleur du Chai ("the best of the cellar"). ♦ Tasting daily; tours by appointment only. 3522 Silverado Tr (between Lodi and Bale Las). 963.5170; fax 963.5752

168 Bothe–Napa Valley State Park This 1,800-acre park has more than a hundred picnic sites, all with tables and barbecues, situated under huge maple and Douglas fir trees. After lunch, you may swim in the park's pool or work off your picnic by taking a hike. The 1.2-mile **History Trail,** rated as moderately strenuous, leads past a pioneer cemetery and the site of Napa County's first church, built in 1853, to the **Bale Grist Mill State Historic Park** (see entry No. 164).

Originally a country retreat built in the 1870s by Dr. Charles Hitchcock and his wife, the estate was bought by Reinhold Bothe after Hitchcock's daughter Lillie Coit died in 1929. Bothe deeded it to the state in 1960, and today the park is a haven for wine-country vacationers, offering the ultimate bargain in Napa Valley budget accommodations. There are 50 family campsites, including 10 remote, walk-in sites suitable for tent camping. The remaining 40 sites can accommodate tents or RVs. Campsites have flush toilets, hot showers, laundry sinks, picnic tables, barbecues, and use of the swimming pool. Evening campfire programs and talks about the stars and planets are held on Wednesday and Saturday. Fifteen-day limit. Reservations for campsites are accepted eight weeks in advance. ♦ Fee. Park: daily. Pool: daily mid-June through Labor Day. 3801 St. Helena Hwy (north of Big Tree Rd). 942.4575, 800/444.PARK (for reservations)

169 Robert Louis Stevenson State Park This largely undeveloped area at the northern end of the valley contains an abandoned silver mine where Stevenson and his wife, Fanny, spent their honeymoon in 1880, staying in a rustic, abandoned bunkhouse. He later wrote about his experiences and the area's beauty in *The Silverado Squatters*. He also modeled Spyglass Hill in *Treasure Island* after Mount St. Helena, which at 4,343 feet is the highest of the Bay Area's peaks. A rigorous five-mile trail to the top of the mountain offers unsurpassed views of the wine country below—on a *very* clear day, you can see all the way to Mount Shasta and the Sierra Nevada. Plan your hike for the cool morning hours and bring plenty of water. The park has no developed facilities, and the entrance is marked by a small sign and a gravel parking lot, which is easy to miss if you're speeding along. On your way here from the St. Helena Highway, don't miss the spectacular lookout over Calistoga on the right side of the road about one mile after the highway veers to the right and heads uphill. ♦ 5 miles north of Calistoga on Hwy 29. 942.4575

170 Deer Park Winery This small, state-of-the-art winery is housed in a venerable, two-story stone building erected in 1891. The winery, owned by the Robert Knapp and David Clark families, produces Sauvignon Blanc and Zinfandel from a rocky hillside vineyard. It also produces Chardonnay and a small amount of Petite Sirah and Cabernet. ♦ Tasting and sales by appointment only F-Su. 1000 Deer Park Rd (off the Silverado Tr). 963.5411 ♿

171 Burgess Cellars In a two-story wood-and-stone winery building on the site of a vineyard planted around 1880, former airline pilot Tom Burgess and wine maker Bill Sorenson produce big, bold wines from Burgess's Chardonnay, Cabernet, and Zinfandel vineyards. The Cabernet Vintage Selection and the barrel-fermented Chardonnay from **Triere Vineyard** both age well. ♦ Tasting and tours daily by appointment only. 1108 Deer Park Rd (off the Silverado Tr). 963.4766; fax 963.8774 ♿

172 Lake Berryessa Creek Canyon was dammed at one end to create this 26-mile-long artificial lake, the largest in Northern California. **Oak Shores Park** and resorts around the lake offer an array of recreational opportunities. Anglers will find plenty of trout, bass, catfish, and silver salmon. The lake's marinas have docks, berths, and boat launches. Most marinas rent fishing or ski boats, jet skis, and sailboards—and one even rents houseboats. Tent and RV camping, picnic areas, and barbecue facilities are available at the lake's resorts. ♦ For more information, call the Lake Berryessa Chamber of Commerce at 800/726.1256. At the end of Pope Canyon Rd

173 Rustridge Ranch, Vineyard & Winery
$$ This 442-acre vineyard, winery, and thoroughbred-horse breeding facility now

operates as a five-room bed-and-breakfast as well, with guests bunking down in the 1940s ranch house. Seemingly lost in the hills above the Silverado Trail, the site is actually an old Wappo Indian camp, and innkeepers Jim Fresquez and Susan Meyer Fresquez have a collection of arrowheads, leather-grinding bowls, and pestles they've found on the property. The ranch has become a popular getaway for San Franciscans who prefer a serene retreat. The entire ranch house can also be rented to families and groups.

All of the pleasant guest rooms have private baths. Four of them are in the left wing of the ranch house; the **Chiles Valley Room** is more private and has a sauna and hot tub just outside the door. The largest is the sunny **Rustridge Room,** which has its own fireplace and dressing room. It's flanked by the **Oaks Room,** a large room with a deck situated above ancient oak trees and a stream. The entire inn is decorated in an updated Santa Fe style. Guests have the run of the ranch house, which includes a large, comfortably furnished living room with a fireplace, pressed straw roof, and skylights. The innkeepers offer the unusual—and very welcome—option of using the professionally equipped kitchen to make a salad or even cook dinner for yourself. The ranch also has a tennis court and a swimming pool. The horses on the ranch are not available for riding, but you may bring your own and keep them in the stables here. There are miles of nearby trails for riding or hiking. ♦ 2910 Lower Chiles Valley Rd (off Hwy 128). 965.9353; fax 965.9263 ♿

Bests

Denise Lurton Moullé
Wine Broker

Restaurant: **Mustards Grill** in **Yountville**—a relaxed ambience and good wines.

Overnight accommodation: **Meadowood Resort** in **St. Helena** (on weekdays).

Winery: **Joseph Phelps** in St. Helena—bring a lunch from **Oakville Grocery Co.** and sit outside the winery with a bottle of wine and enjoy the view.

Shopping: **Napa Valley Olive Oil Mfg.** in St. Helena.

Michele Anna Jordan
Caterer/Food Columnist/Author of *A Cook's Tour of Sonoma*

An early dinner at **Tre Scalini** in **Healdsburg,** followed by a movie or live music at **The Raven Theater,** the best movie house in the North Bay.

A summer dinner on the patio of **Topolos at Russian River Vineyard** in **Forestville,** timed to witness the nightly emergence of the thousands of brown bats that live in the towers of the guest rooms bordering the patio.

Eating the world's best hamburger at **Rocco's** in **Freestone,** followed by a two-minute walk to the **Wishing Well Nursery** to watch the three black swans float around the pond with its replica of the Statue of Liberty.

Shopping at **Traverso's Gourmet Foods and Wine** in Santa Rosa and being waited on by Enrico or Louis Traverso.

The **Cabaret Theater,** followed by steak-and-kidney pie and a Newcastle Brown Ale draught at **Ma Stokeld's Old Vic** in **Santa Rosa.**

A private picnic at dawn or dusk at **Bodega Head.**

The rising of the October full moon anywhere at all as long as it overlooks the **Valley of the Moon** (**Viansa Winery** is a good location).

Browsing through the records—yes, the black vinyl kind—at the **Last Record Store,** near the **Old Vic** in Santa Rosa.

Visiting Madeleine Kamman, the director at **Beringer Vineyards' School for American Chefs** in St. Helena.

Dinner at **Chateau Souverain Cafe at the Winery** in **Geyserville.**

Calistoga

As its legacy of geysers, hot springs, and lava deposits attests, the Calistoga area began life with a bang—a volcanic bang, that is. Some of the eruptions formed the gray stone used in local landmarks such as the **Culinary Institute of America at Greystone** and various bridges. Local Indian tribes healed their sick in steam baths they constructed around the hot springs at the northern end of **Napa Valley**. And when Sam Brannan, California's first millionaire, visited the area in the mid-19th century, he immediately envisioned a first-class spa and set to work designing a lavish hotel to attract wealthy San Franciscans to the site of what is now **Indian Springs** spa and resort. Brannan also brought the first railroad to the valley and dubbed the town "Calistoga," a hybrid of the words "California" and "Saratoga" (the famous New York resort).

Set in the midst of rolling vineyards with extinct volcano **Mount St. Helena** standing guard in the distance, this small country town (with a population of less than 5,000), with its Old West–style main street, is famous for its mineral water and mud baths. The spas offer a rare bargain in wine-country lodging (although don't expect to find glamorous accommodations), and the pools and mineral baths are a welcome diversion, especially in summer.

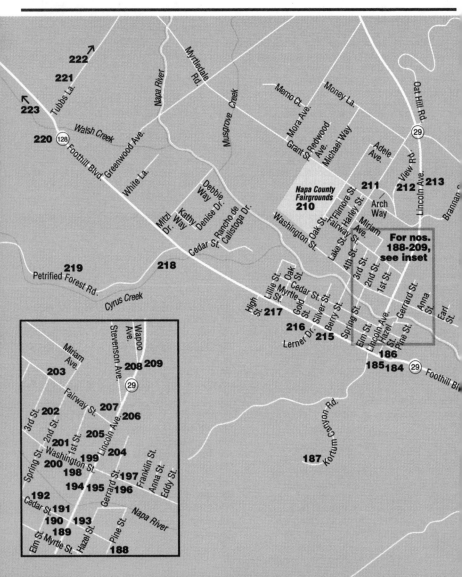

174 Schramsberg Vineyards Follow in the footsteps of Robert Louis Stevenson, who paid a visit in the late 1880s to this historic winery founded by itinerant barber Jacob Schram in 1862. The place was virtually in ruins by 1965, when Jack and Jamie Davies fell in love with it and restored it as a producer of sparkling wines. The original stone winery building stands next to the old Schram family home, and the tunneled-out hillside is now a modern wine-production cellar. In 1972 the White House served **Schramsberg** sparkling wine at the banquet President Richard Nixon gave for Premier Chou En-lai in Peking. The winery makes half-a-dozen sparkling wines in all, including Blanc de Blancs, Blanc de Noirs, and a rosé called Cuvée de Pinot. The tour of this winery is quite good and provides a thorough description of the art of making sparkling wine. ♦ Fee. Tasting and tours daily by appointment only. 1400 Schramsberg Rd (off Hwy 29). 942.4558 &

175 Larkmead Country Inn $$ This delightful country inn and the neighboring **Larkmead-Kornell Cellars** (see page 62) were once part of **Larkmead Winery,** owned in the late 1880s by the flamboyant heiress Lillie Coit. The Palladian-style farmhouse with an octagonal loggia flanked by two wings is built on two levels, with the main part of the house upstairs—the better to oversee the vineyards and catch the afternoon breezes. Four guest rooms, all with private baths and vineyard views, are in one wing of the house. The **Beaujolais Room** has a queen-size bed, vintage wicker-and-cane chairs with cushions covered in a William Morris print, and a private veranda; the airy **Chenin Blanc Room** features an antique, queen-size bed and a chaise longue covered in a flowered print; and the **Chablis Room** has its own solarium. Innkeeper Tim Garbarino serves an excellent continental breakfast (fruit plate, croissants, scones, and coffee) on Imari china and

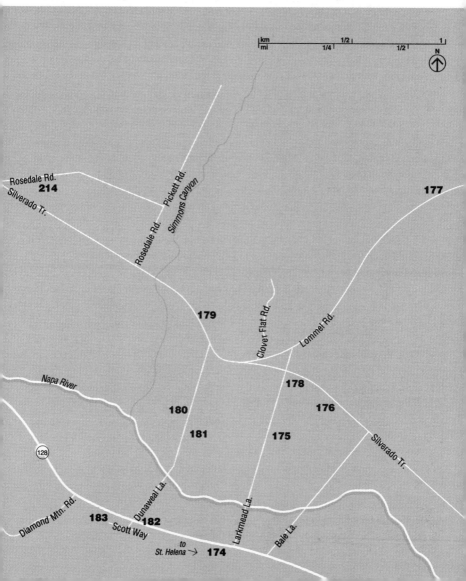

heirloom sterling. ♦ 1103 Larkmead La (between Hwy 29 and the Silverado Tr). 942.5360 &

176 Rancho Maria Louisa Seasonal organic garden produce and fresh herbs, plus wine vinegar and dried fruit, are sold at this farm stand. ♦ Daily. 3911 Silverado Tr (between Bale and Larkmead Las). 942.6941 &

177 Calistoga Ranch Campground This 168-acre park is dotted with olive trees and features 144 campsites accommodating tents, campers, and RVs (full and partial hookups). Barbecue pits, portable toilets, a nice swimming pool, a picnic area, and trails are provided, too. ♦ Daily. 580 Lommel Rd (off the Silverado Tr). 942.6565

178 Larkmead-Kornell Cellars Specializing in sparkling wines made by the traditional French *méthode champenoise,* this cellar was founded in 1958 by German immigrant Hans Kornell, who worked in Germany and Europe before settling in America. Kornell was Napa Valley's first producer of *méthode champenoise* sparkling wine. An instructive guided tour of the two-story stone winery takes you through every aspect of sparkling-wine production, and is followed by a tasting of Kornell's broad range of vintages. Among the best: the Blanc de Blancs and Blanc de Noirs Cuvée. ♦ Tasting, sales, and tours daily. 1091 Larkmead La (off the Silverado Tr). 942.0859; fax 942.0657

179 Cuvaison Winery Founded in 1969, this Spanish colonial-style winery is Swiss-owned and specializes in Chardonnay, although wine maker John Thacher's Cabernet, Merlot, and Pinot Noir are

first-rate, too. The tasting room offers an inspired collection of wine books for sale, plus insulated wine bags and picnic carriers, corkscrews, and local jams and condiments. Picnic tables are set out under moss-covered oaks for visitors to use. ♦ Fee. Tasting and sales daily; tours by appointment only. 4550 Silverado Tr (north of Dunaweal La). 942.6266; fax 942.5732 &

"Good wine is a necessity of life for me."

Thomas Jefferson

Restaurants/Clubs: Red   Hotels: Blue
Shops/♥ Outdoors: Green   Wineries/Sights: Black

180 Clos Pegase Michael Graves designed and built the winery and house here in 1986. The commission resulted from a major architectural design competition sponsored by the owner, wealthy international businessman Jan Shrem, and the San Francisco Museum of Modern Art. It was won by the architect/artist team of **Graves** and Edward Schmidt. Widely recognized for his postmodernist architecture as well as for designing household objects, **Graves** built the Shrems' house on a secluded wooded knoll overlooking the winery just south of Calistoga.

The design of the stunning earth- and russet-colored winery buildings is rooted in ancient Mediterranean architecture, with rows of tall columns (treated to look ages-old) arranged around a central courtyard. Outdoor sculptures are incorporated into the landscape; the most remarkable is an oversized bronze thumb that appears to be planted in the vineyard. The highlight of a tour of the winery building is the cylindrical room that Schmidt covered with frescoes depicting allegorical scenes of wine making. Visitors may also watch a slide show called "Wine Seen through 4,000 Years in Art," which covers images of wine making in art ranging from Egyptian reliefs and medieval illuminated manuscripts to Cubist works. The winery produces straightforward Chardonnay, Cabernet, and Merlot. ♦ Fee. Tasting, sales, and outdoor self-guided tours daily; guided tours of the winery, art collection, and caves daily 11AM and 2PM. 1060 Dunaweal La (between Hwy 29 and the Silverado Tr). 942.4982; fax 942.4993 &

181 Sterling Vineyards The flagship winery of the Seagram Corporation, this dazzling white, Mediterranean-style establishment atop a 300-foot knoll just south of Calistoga is reached via an aerial tramway that offers breathtaking views. At the end of the ride, follow the self-guided tour of the winery at your own pace and then sit at a table in the tasting room (featuring another panoramic vista) to sample the top-flight wines: Chardonnay, Merlot, and especially the Cabernet Reserve and Diamond Mountain Cabernet. In addition, wine maker Bill Dyer makes limited bottlings of Chardonnay from the **Diamond Mountain** vineyard, Pinot Noir from the legendary **Winery Lake** vineyard in the Carneros district, and a blend of Cabernet Sauvignon, Cabernet Franc, and Merlot. ◆ Fee for the aerial tramway. Tasting, sales, and self-guided tours daily. 1111 Dunaweal La (between Hwy 29 and the Silverado Tr). 942.3344; fax 942.3467 &

Within Sterling Vineyards:

Sterling Vineyards School of Service and Hospitality This professional school for training restaurant employees in the expert service of food and wine is directed by Evan Goldstein—who in 1987, at the age of 26, was the youngest person ever to pass the prestigious Master Sommelier exam, making him one of only 31 master sommeliers in the world at the time. In addition to one-, three-, and five-day seminars for professionals, the school offers "The Course for Wine Lovers" once a year, a comprehensive one-day session for non-professionals. Filled with fun and information about everything from grape growing and wine making to wine tasting and developing a personal cellar, the class includes a visit to **Sterling**'s vineyard sites and a firsthand look at what goes on in the cellar. At lunch students practice pairing a variety of wines with selected dishes. ◆ For more information, write to: Evan Goldstein, The Sterling Vineyards School of Service and Hospitality, Box 365, Calistoga, CA 94515. 942.3357, 800/955.5003; fax 942.3595

182 Stonegate Winery Founded in 1973 by Jim and Barbara Spaulding to produce wine from hillside vineyards near Diamond Mountain, this establishment makes consistently good Cabernet and Merlot, especially from the **Spaulding** vineyard. Wine maker David Spaulding also crafts both a regular and a late-harvest Sauvignon Blanc, plus a regular Sauvignon Blanc, Chardonnay, Cabernet Franc, and Meritage. ◆ Fee on weekends only. Tasting and sales daily. 1183 Dunaweal La (off Hwy 29). 942.6500 &

183 Quail Mountain $$ Nestled high above Napa Valley on a heavily forested mountain range, this comfortable, contemporary three-room bed-and-breakfast inn offers king-size beds, private baths and decks, a small lap pool next to a rose garden, and an inviting hot tub. Proprietors Don and Alma Swiers prepare a full breakfast and, aside from other guests, your only companions at this pretty site will be the deer, raccoons, squirrels, hummingbirds, and, of course, the beloved quail. No smoking is allowed. ◆ 4455 N St. Helena Hwy (between Dunaweal La and Diamond Mountain Rd). 942.0316

184 Calistoga Pottery You'll find traditional, functional stoneware here. Jeff Manfredi and his wife, Sally, specialize in ovenproof dinnerware decorated with lead-free glaze. They take custom orders, too. ◆ W-Su or by appointment. 1001 Foothill Blvd (at Pine St). 942.0216

185 Lavender Hill Spa This *très élégant* establishment is *the* couples spa, where everything is designed with partners in mind, except for the massages, which are given in complete privacy. Owner John Cashman also owns the nearby **International Spa** (see page 67), and many of his employees work in both locations. The specialties here include acupressure, foot reflexology, and Swedish massage, and this is one of the only spas in town that feature a one-time-use mud bath (the mud is not reused by other patrons) combining volcanic ash and sarvar salt, a premier bath salt widely used in Europe. Numerous aromatherapy treatments and facials are offered, as well as a relaxing biofeedback therapy known as Vibra Sound. Don't miss the terraced hillside backyard that's laced with lavender and features a picnic area—the final touch that makes this spa setting second to none in Calistoga. ◆ Daily. Reservations required. 1015 Foothill Blvd (at Hazel St). 942.4495 &

185 Wine Way Inn $ From the moment you enter this cozy bed-and-breakfast, you'll feel like innkeepers Cecile and Moye Stephens's special guests. This couple is very friendly and instantly likable, as is their dog, George. Their craftsman-style abode was built as a family home in 1915 and has been a bed-and-breakfast inn since 1979. The Stephenses set up shop in mid-1990 and have been upgrading this tidy, homey place ever since. The five small rooms upstairs come complete with old-fashioned quilts on the beds, antique decorations on the walls, and creaky floorboards—enough to make you feel like you're in Grandma's guest room. And for those seeking ultra-privacy, there's a cottage in back. Each room has its own bath and shower. An expansive multilevel wood deck juts into the inn's backyard, and a gazebo nestled on the hillside provides an ideal spot

63

for tasting wines. You may also don one of the bathrobes provided by the inn and stroll through the backyard gate directly into the spiffy spa next door (see **Lavender Hill Spa** on page 63). Unfortunately, you can hear traffic noise because the inn is located along the busy St. Helena Highway, but at night it is pretty peaceful. The great advantage of this location is that you're just a stone's throw from Calistoga's main street, so once you park your car, everything in the town is accessible on foot. A tasty full breakfast plus late-afternoon hors d'oeuvres and wine round out your stay here. ♦ 1019 Foothill Blvd (at Hazel St). 942.0680, 800/572.0679

186 Christopher's Inn $$
Laura Ashley interiors and antiques dress up the 10 rooms in this bed-and-breakfast inn. Each room has a private bath, and some have fireplaces and small patios. Although the inn is settled on the side of busy St. Helena Highway, the rooms are in the back of the building and Calistoga's main shopping street is just a few steps around the corner. A hearty breakfast featuring such homemade treats as fruit cobbler, egg soufflé, croissants, pastries, juice,

Getting Down and Dirty in Calistoga: A Guide to the Famous Mud Baths

Say "mud bath," and some people will fall into a fit of giggles at the idea of lying in a tub naked, covered in warm, gooey mud. Well, keep in mind that this is not just any mud—this is Calistoga's famous volcanic-ash mud mixed with mineral water and, in some cases, imported peat. The mud is first heated to sterilize it and then cooled to just over 100 degrees. The mud bath itself, taken in individual tubs, lasts only 10 to 12 minutes. It's usually followed by a warm, mineral-water shower and a whirlpool bath, then a steam bath. At that point, relaxation sets in as attendants swathe you in warm blankets, leaving you to rest and slowly cool down.

If soaking in a mud bath is just not your idea of a good time, the spas also offer an array of auxiliary treatments, starting with massages given in a variety of techniques. You can get a full-body massage or a neck-and-shoulder massage, which can be combined with seaweed or herbal body wraps. Or perhaps you'd prefer to be scrubbed with a loofah or to soak in a fragrant herbal bath after indulging in a facial. Every spa has its specialties and will explain them in detail. Don't plan on doing anything too rigorous immediately afterward—you'll probably feel so relaxed you won't want to move.

Calistoga Spa Hot Springs
1006 Washington St (at Gerrard St). 942.6269

Calistoga Village Inn & Spa
1880 Lincoln Ave (off Hwy 29). 942.0991

Dr. Wilkinson's Hot Springs
1507 Lincoln Ave (between Fairway St and Stevenson Ave). 942.4102

Eurospa
Pine Street Inn, 1202 Pine St (between Myrtle and Cedar Sts). 942.6829

Golden Haven Hot Springs
1713 Lake St (at Grant St). 942.6793

Indian Springs
1712 Lincoln Ave (at Wapoo Ave). 942.4913

International Spa
1300 Washington St (between First and Second Sts). 942.6122

Lavender Hill Spa
1015 Foothill Blvd (at Hazel St). 942.4495

Lincoln Avenue Spa
1339 Lincoln Ave (between Cedar and Washington Sts). 942.5296

Mount View Spa
Mount View Hotel, 1457 Lincoln Ave (between Washington and Fairway Sts). 942.5789

Nance's Hot Springs
1614 Lincoln Ave (between Fairway St and Stevenson Ave). 942.6211, 800/201.6211

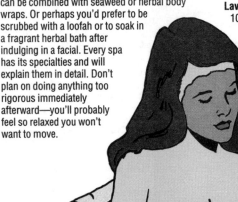

ROLANDO CARUJO

tea, and freshly ground coffee is delivered to your room in a basket. ♦ 1010 Foothill Blvd (between Pine and Hazel Sts). 942.5755

187 Falcon's Nest $$ It's only a quarter mile up steep Kortum Canyon Road from Calistoga, but you feel like you're a world away from everything at this bed-and-breakfast inn. There's a panoramic view of the valley from the three guest rooms (all with spare modern decor, private baths, and sliding glass doors), which are located on the lower floor of a spacious contemporary home. The outdoor hot tub has the same heart-stopping view. A full breakfast is served. ♦ 471 Kortum Canyon Rd (off Foothill Blvd). 942.0758

188 Pine Street Inn $$ On a quiet Calistoga side street, this 12-room inn and spa consists of several stucco bungalows with flower boxes and parking in front. The bedrooms are somewhat small, but they have pine armoires and are attractively decorated in pastels with matching curtains and drapes; some have kitchenettes with stoves. Guests can relax in the patio coffee bar, where a continental breakfast (pastries, doughnuts, and coffee) is served. To cool off, there's an outdoor kidney-shaped pool surrounded by a small, grassy, shaded area. ♦ 1202 Pine St (between Myrtle and Cedar Sts). 942.6829

At the Pine Street Inn:

Eurospa This spa specializes in a very different sort of treatment called the European fango mud bath. A private tub is filled with a dehydrated compound that is mixed with water; it has a looser consistency than a regular mud bath and is taken in a double Jacuzzi so you also get the benefits of hydrotherapy. (The tub is completely drained and cleaned between each treatment.) Herbal oils and extracts can be added to the mud if you like, and the spa also offers seaweed or herbal body wraps. Masseuses will give either a one-hour full-body massage or a half-hour massage that concentrates on the back, neck, and shoulders. The spa also has its own line of natural facial products; made from plants and herbal extracts, they contain no alcohol or abrasives. ♦ Daily. 942.6829 &

PACIFICO
COCINA MEXICANA TRADICIONAL

189 Pacifico ★$$ Terra-cotta floors, potted palms, and colorful Mexican chairs set the tone for this Mexican restaurant serving traditional regional cuisine. For breakfast, you can order *huevos rancheros,* French toast, and *machaca con huevos* (scrambled eggs with shredded beef, black beans, and fresh salsa wrapped in a flour tortilla). Marinated chicken or beef tacos, tamales, enchiladas, fajitas, grilled fresh fish with

salsa, and grilled chicken are some of the lunch and dinner offerings. A "fiesta hour" is held Monday through Friday 4:30PM-6PM, with special prices on margaritas, tacos, and *taquitos* (little tacos). Brunch is served on the weekends and the long bar makes for a pleasant watering hole. ♦ Mexican ♦ M-F lunch and dinner; Sa-Su brunch and dinner. 1237 Lincoln Ave (between Myrtle and Cedar Sts). 942.4400 &

La chaumière
a country inn

190 La Chaumière $$ This turn-of-the-century house remodeled in the 1930s in the style of a Cotswold cottage is located on a quiet residential street just steps away from the heart of town. It features two guest rooms, each with a queen-size bed and private bath. The spacious upstairs suite has its own sitting room, while the downstairs room has French doors leading to a secluded private deck with potted plants and flowers. There's also a 950-square-foot honeymoon cottage with a king-size bed, bath, and kitchen. A redwood tree that was planted in the 19th century shades a hot tub surrounded by decks. Innkeeper Gary Venturi serves a full breakfast. ♦ 1301 Cedar St (at Elm St). 942.5139, 800/474.6800; fax 942.5199

191 The Elms $$ Built in 1871 by Judge A.C. Palmer, this truly elegant three-story French Victorian house with a formal parlor and tall windows overlooking Cedar Street has been furnished with grace and style by innkeepers Stephen and Carla Wyle. The Wyles owned and operated a small hotel outside of Düsseldorf, Germany, before moving to the Napa Valley in 1994, and both they and their friendly golden retriever, Ivory, know how to make guests feel welcome. Beautiful old European-style furnishings and Oriental rugs fill each room. While some bed-and-breakfasts have just one exceptional guest room, here all seven have something special—for example, one room has a magnificent 19th-century Swedish sleigh bed converted to a king-size bed and another enjoys a splendid view of the mountains. The cottage in back is ideal for honeymooners. Each morning, a two-course gourmet breakfast is prepared by **California Culinary Academy**–trained chef Gabriele Ondine. The inn is located in a peaceful neighborhood very close to Calistoga's main street. ♦ 1300 Cedar St (at Elm St). 942.9476, 800/235.4316

192 Pioneer Park Tired of touring the town? This small, quaint park offers a peaceful place to rest your dogs. It sports a white Victorian gazebo, several benches, and a well-equipped, fenced-in playground that's frequented by the neighborhood kids. ♦ Cedar St (between Elm and Spring Sts)

193 Calistoga Inn $ For travelers on a budget, this turn-of-the-century building located on Calistoga's main street offers 18 clean, basic rooms with double beds and two bathrooms down the hall (something like a French one-star hotel). The rooms, which can be noisy until the bar below settles down at night, include portable electric fans in the summer and small heaters in the winter. A continental breakfast (juice, coffee, and fresh pastries) is included in the price. ♦ 1250 Lincoln Ave (at Cedar St). 942.4101; fax 942.4914

Within the Calistoga Inn:

Calistoga Inn Restaurant $$ California cuisine has been served in this dining room since 1986. When the sun is out and it's not too hot, the garden patio is one of the most pleasant spots in town to kick back and sip a beer made at the inn's own brewery. If you're hungry, though, stick to the simple stuff—salads, sandwiches, and items from the grill. ♦ American ♦ M-Sa lunch and dinner; Su brunch and dinner

Napa Valley Brewery Company Founded in 1987, this was the valley's first brewery since Prohibition. It's housed in an old water tower in the back of the garden, and the shady patio in front offers a great place to sit and sample the suds. Brewmaster Randy Gremp creates a good Calistoga Golden Lager, a Calistoga Red Ale, and a Calistoga Wheat Ale that won a gold medal at the prestigious 1994 Great American Beer Festival in Denver. The beer is served with the **Calistoga Inn Restaurant**'s lunch and dinner menus and is also available in 22-ounce bottles to go. ♦ Tours by appointment only

THE ARTFUL EYE

194 Artful Eye This inspiring gallery features crafts by top West Coast artists, including exquisite handblown glass, ceramics, jewelry, wooden objects, and textiles. Glass paperweights, intricately painted silk scarves, handwoven shawls, mufflers, wine goblets, and an entire case of handmade marbles are just a few of the items. The prices match the quality. ♦ Daily. 1333-A Lincoln Ave (between Cedar and Washington Sts). 942.4743 ⓧ

"Come, come; good wine is a good familiar creature if it be well used; exclaim no more against it."

William Shakespeare

"Why look you now, 'tis when men drink they thrive, grow wealthy, speed their business, win their suits, make themselves happy, benefit their friends."

Aristophanes

---

194 Lincoln Avenue Spa Relax at this spa offering herbal-mud treatments with 34 herbs imported from India, herbal blanket wraps, facials, Swedish/Esalen massages, acupressure face-lifts, and foot reflexology. Special deluxe spa packages are also available. ♦ Daily. 1339 Lincoln Ave (between Cedar and Washington Sts). 942.5296 ⓧ

194 Calistoga Bookstore Here's a comfortable place to browse through books on wine and California travel and history, with a good section of paperback mysteries, children's books, and art supplies. The inviting sofa in the back of the store is often adorned with a sleeping cat named Sara. ♦ Daily. 1343 Lincoln Ave (between Cedar and Washington Sts). 942.4123 ⓧ

194 Wexford & Woods An unusual combo of antique pine furniture imported from Ireland and quality skin-care products dominates this attractive shop. The sweet scent alone is worth stopping here. ♦ Daily. 1347 Lincoln Ave (between Cedar and Washington Sts). 942.9729, 800/919.9729; fax 942.0536 ⓧ

195 Las Brasas ★$ This restaurant, whose name is Spanish for "red-hot charcoal," dishes out good burritos as well as mesquite-grilled chicken fajitas, pork chops, steaks, and *carnitas* (Jalisco-style roast leg of pork). ♦ Mexican ♦ Daily lunch and dinner. 1350 Lincoln Ave (between Cedar and Washington Sts). 942.5790

195 Bosko's Ristorante ★$$ This casual dining spot with oilcloth-covered tables and sawdust on the floor offers a dozen fresh pasta dishes—everything from spaghetti and meatballs to fettuccine with a sauce of bay shrimp and tomatoes. You may have your pasta cooked to order here (and do speak up if you prefer it al dente). The best deal at lunch is a half order of any fresh pasta with a green salad. Other dishes include generous Italian club sandwiches (made with pancetta instead of bacon) and a variety of pizzas. Espresso drinks are available, too. Meals may also be eaten at the pleasant counter, and you may order food to go. ♦ Italian ♦ Daily lunch and dinner. 1364 Lincoln Ave (between Cedar and Washington Sts). 942.9088 ⓧ

195 Silverado Tavern ★★$$ The wine cellar here, noted for its tremendous breadth and scope, is owner Alex Dierkhising's special passion. As you pass through the entrance, note the numerous awards from *The Wine Spectator* magazine for "greatest wine list in the world." Lunch features a nice selection of sandwiches, salads, gourmet pizza, and pasta, while dinner focuses on fresh fish with creative sauces, grilled chicken, and New York steak. The bar offers its own menu of pizzas and the like. You'll find live jazz here on the weekends, too. ♦ California ♦ M-W, F-Su breakfast, lunch, and dinner; Th dinner.

Bar: M-Th, Su noon-11PM; F-Sa noon-midnight. 1374 Lincoln Ave (at Washington St). 942.6725; fax 942.9420 ♿

196 Palisades Mountain Sport Hidden behind the fire department, this bicycle shop offers mountain-bike rentals by the hour or the day, bike repairs, and rugged outdoor wear. No tours are available, but they will provide a map of suggested routes. ♦ Daily. 1330-B Gerrard St (at Washington St). 942.9687 ♿

197 Calistoga Spa Hot Springs $ This is the people's spa—relaxed, fun, unpretentious, and a great base for exploring the wine country. It has all the amenities of a resort at budget prices, including kitchenettes and cable TV. The best rooms have king-size beds, high ceilings, a muted pastel decor, and a larger kitchen. All open onto the attractive pool area that boasts four mineral pools: a giant 80-degree pool for lap swimming, a 100-degree soaking pool, a 105-degree pool with Jacuzzi jets, and a 90-degree wading pool with a fountain. Barbecues are set up near the pool area, but there is no restaurant.

Make an appointment in advance for a volcanic-ash mud bath, mineral bath, steam bath, blanket wrap, or massage. Exercise equipment and aerobics classes are also available. Families are welcome. If you plan to stay elsewhere and still want to enjoy the pool, the resort has a day-use pass; stop by early in the day to buy one, as they go fast. ♦ Spa and pools: daily. 1006 Washington St (at Gerrard St). 942.6269 ♿

198 Gloriosa Owner Valerie Beck (of the ubiquitous Beck & Taylor realty company) has fine taste, as you'll see for yourself when you browse through her small shop stuffed with gilded frames; wrought-iron furniture; vibrant hand-painted plates, bowls, and teacups; decorative herbal vinegars; and many other carefully selected works of art. Most items are pricey, but Beck always tries to keep less expensive treasures in stock, too. ♦ Daily. 1215 Washington St (between Lincoln Ave and First St). 942.4062 ♿

199 Wappo Bar Bistro ★★$$ You won't find a full bar at this popular neighborhood restaurant, but you will discover a great gazpacho, chiles rellenos (poblano chilies stuffed with cheese) with walnut pomegranate sauce,

succotash (Native American vegetable stew), and fish and pasta dishes. When the weather is mild, dine alfresco on the pretty brick patio shaded by a grapevine-laced trellis. ♦ Southwestern ♦ M, Th-Su lunch and dinner; W lunch. 1226-B Washington St (off Lincoln Ave). 942.4712 ♿

200 Sharpsteen Museum and Brannan Cottage After 30 years at Walt Disney Studios as an animator (Pinocchio, Fantasia) and Oscar-winning producer, Ben Sharpsteen retired to Calistoga and created this museum. With the help of a few friends from his Disney days, he designed and constructed elaborate dioramas re-creating the arrival of the railroad, Calistoga's former Chinatown, and more. The largest depicts Calistoga as it looked when millionaire Sam Brannan opened the town's first spa in 1860. Hailed by Brannan as the "Saratoga of the Pacific," his Calistoga included a hotel, dining hall, stables, and racetrack, plus an indoor pool, a pavilion for dancing and roller skating, a distillery, a winery, and a cooper's workshop. One of the 14 original cottages is part of the museum, furnished as it would have been in the 1860s (that is, with no kitchen; guests were expected to take meals in the hotel). Books on the history of Napa Valley are for sale, too. ♦ Free. Daily. 1311 Washington St (between First and Second Sts). 942.5911

201 Roman Spa $ You'll find motel-like accommodations at this no-frills establishment. A lounge and chairs are set out on Astro-Turf around a mineral pool. Yes, it's as ugly as it sounds, but people come here for the facilities at the adjacent **International Spa** (see below), which is one of the best in town, and the staff is quite friendly. If you'd rather take your treatment in more beautiful (and more expensive) surroundings, try **Lavender Hill Spa** (see page 63), which has the same owner as the **International Spa.** A Finnish sauna and an outdoor Jacuzzi are featured here, too. ♦ 1300 Washington St (between First and Second Sts). 942.4441 ♿

At the Roman Spa:

International Spa This spa offers mud baths for couples, plus Japanese enzyme baths, seaweed baths, Swedish/Esalen massages, foot reflexology, acupressure, herbal facials, and herbal blankets—all in an unassuming bungalow directly behind the **Roman Spa** hotel. You'll find some of the most reasonable spa rates in the city here. ♦ Daily. 942.6122

202 Scott Courtyard $$
A great wine-country find, this classy bed-and-breakfast inn will please even those folks who don't much care for the typical bed-and-breakfast experience. You'll get plenty of privacy and space here—and you won't feel as if you have to tiptoe around the premises for fear of disturbing other guests. Proprietors Lauren and Joe Scott have gone to great lengths to make their six spacious suites comfortable and attractive while remaining unpretentious; each one has a sitting room, queen-size bed, a private bath, and its own entrance (the downstairs suites and the cottages are the best choices). The common area is a large, high-ceilinged living room with a big stone fireplace, plush couch, and a library complete with picture books, magazines, and mystery novels. And every morning Lauren shows off her love of cooking with large breakfasts, which may include moist poppy-seed French toast and maple syrup, eggs, ham, fresh fruit, freshly squeezed orange juice, coffee, and tea.

The inn is lined with rows of rosebushes and terra-cotta pots bursting with flowers, and the courtyard boasts a swimming pool, a Jacuzzi, lounge chairs, and a picnic table. Tucked off to the side of the garden is a small aviary, as well as something you won't find at any other Calistoga inn: a studio where guests can try out their talents in ceramics, welding, and other arts and crafts. Best of all, it's located off the main road in a quiet neighborhood, and it's an easy walk to Calistoga's finest shops, spas, and cafes. Another plus: The Scotts are savvy about the latest wine-country offerings and can provide plenty of information on what's happening around town. ♦ 1443 Second St (between Washington and Fairway Sts). 942.0948; fax 942.5102

203 Hideaway Cottages $$ On a quiet residential street off Lincoln Avenue, this place offers overnight lodging, mostly for clients of **Dr. Wilkinson's Hot Springs** spa (see page 71) around the corner. The 15 cottages on the property have private baths and picnic tables and barbecues outside; some also have kitchenettes. The bonus here is the outdoor, mineral-water Jacuzzi and a large, heated mineral-water swimming pool with chaise longues, tables, and umbrellas in a shady lawn and garden area. The somber 1940s decor could use a little brightening up, though. No children are allowed. ♦ 1412 Fairway St (at Third St). 942.4108

Wine-Tasting Tips

1 If you're drinking a white wine, the wine should be chilled but not icy. If it's too cold, the flavors and aromas will be suppressed. Conversely, a red wine should not be too warm. Reds should be served at room temperature, but not if the room in question is hot (80 degrees F or higher). When red wine is too warm, the alcohol is accentuated and the wine tastes coarser and harsher than it should.

2 Before pouring a bottle of wine, sniff the wineglass to make sure it hasn't picked up any odors of wood from the cupboard and that there's no soap residue, which will affect the wine's taste.

3 Pour the wine into a wineglass until the glass is a quarter to a third full. Don't fill up the glass; if it's too full, the wine cannot *aerate* (mix with air) properly, and it will be difficult to swirl the wine in the glass and experience its aroma, which is part of the pleasure.

4 Hold the glass by the base or stem up to the light, and look at the *clarity* of the wine. It should be anywhere from clear to brilliant. Then note its *color*. Whites range from pale yellow to golden, rosés from pink to orange-pink, and reds from light purple to deep ruby.

5 Swirl the wine around in the glass. This aerates it, which releases the *aroma*. Hold the glass under your nose and breathe deeply. The aroma should be reminiscent of the grape from which the wine was made. Then note the *bouquet,* which results from the aging process and is stronger in older red wines and dessert wines.

6 Take a sip and swirl it around in your mouth. Keeping a sense of the wine's aroma and bouquet in mind, try to determine its *texture* and *balance.* Is it dry or sweet? Soft or tart? Full-bodied?

ROLANDO CORUJO

204 All Seasons Cafe ★ ★ $$ Completely remodeled after being damaged by a fire in 1994, this take-out deli–turned-cafe is a favorite because of its great wine list and enlightened pricing policy. Instead of doubling or tripling the retail price of the wine (which is what most restaurants do), they simply add a $7.50 corkage fee to each bottle and sell it at the retail price. Needless to say, they sell a lot of wine from a list of top-notch Burgundy, Bordeaux, and Napa Valley producers.

Wine is so much on chef/owner Mark Dierkhising's mind that he divides the menu into dishes appropriate to different styles of wines. The menu changes seasonally and is particularly strong in first courses such as fresh Dungeness crab cakes or grilled mari-nated shiitake mushrooms with smoked fresh mozzarella and a roasted-garlic vinaigrette. Complex wines are shown off with entrées such as roast chicken with whole garlic cloves and potatoes, grilled fresh rabbit with potato-pancetta hash and wild mushroom sauce, or grilled salmon with braised white beans, tomatoes, and spinach. The cafe is a wonderful spot for lunch, too, offering a menu of pasta dishes, pizzas, and excellent sandwiches. For picnics, with a morning's notice, the cafe can have a simple box lunch or a more lavish spread ready to go. It might include their terrific "Beyond BLT," made with pancetta, tomatoes, local lettuces, and mustard aioli on a home-made cheese-and-onion roll, and one or more appealing salads. ♦ California ♦ F-Su breakfast, lunch, and dinner; M, Th lunch and dinner; Tu lunch. Reservations recommended for dinner. 1400 Lincoln Ave (between Washington and Fairway Sts). 942.9111; fax 942.9420 &

Within the All Seasons Cafe:

All Seasons Wine Shop Go all the way to the back of the cafe and turn left for this wineshop, which manager David Dennis stocks with an inspired array of Burgundies and top California wines from small producers. He loves to talk wine and will put together a mixed case of hard-to-find wines at very good prices and then arrange to ship them home for you. He also produces a well-written, informative newsletter. For picnics, he offers a nice selection of chilled white wines. ♦ 942.6828 &

204 Checkers Pasta & Pizza Restaurant ★ $ This trendy, informal spot has a polished wood floor, black-and-white tile details, and bright abstract paintings, and offers more than a dozen pizzas with a thin, California-style crust. Choices include a sun-dried-tomato–and-artichoke pizza scattered with fresh thyme and pine nuts, or an unusual Thai pizza with marinated chicken, cilantro, and peanuts. The calzone (pizza turnovers) are large enough for two. Add a salad or soup for a casual lunch or dinner. At night, pasta and several chicken dishes are offered as well. For dessert, make your own frozen yogurt creation at the bar. Breakfast (eggs, French toast, waffles) is also served starting at 8AM. This is a great place to take the kids. Espresso drinks and a short wine list are offered, too. No smoking is allowed. Take-out is available and evening delivery is free within Calistoga. ♦ Italian ♦ breakfast, lunch, and dinner. 1414 Lincoln Ave (between Washington and Fairway Sts). 942.9300 &

204 Silverado Ace Hardware Here you'll find hardware, garden supplies, and used wine barrels for planters. ♦ Daily. 1450 Lincoln Ave (between Washington and Fairway Sts). 942.4396 &

204 Calistoga Depot Railroad Station Established in 1868 and restored a century later, this historic landmark is believed to be the oldest railroad depot remaining in California. The clapboard building is now a mini-shopping gallery that's home to the **Chamber of Commerce** (see below), a restau-rant, and several shops. Six restored Pull-mans are parked alongside the station and house some of the stores. ♦ Daily (some store hours vary). 1458 Lincoln Ave (between Washington and Fairway Sts)

Within the Calistoga Depot Railroad Station:

Calistoga Wine Stop Parked right in the middle of the depot, this bright yellow train car trimmed in green makes an ingenious space for a serious, small wine store with more than a thousand Napa and Sonoma wines. Some rare and older bottles are available, and the store ships out of state. ♦ Daily. 942.5556 &

Chamber of Commerce You can get all kinds of information here on Calistoga and Napa Valley. ♦ Daily. 942.6333 &

Calistoga Candy Company You'll be greeted here with an overwhelming smell of licorice as you pass through the doors, as well as a huge stuffed black bear seated in front of the loud player piano. More than 200 kinds of old-fashioned candies, from candy sticks and saltwater taffy to jelly beans and licorice drops, are sold here—all priced by the pound. ♦ Daily. 942.6838 &

Gold Treasury Some old jewelry pieces are for sale, as well as sterling silver items made by local designers. ♦ Daily. 942.6819

Adela's Yarn North This tiny cottage is crammed with European yarns, knitting books, and supplies for needlepoint and embroidery. You can even have a sweater custom-made here. ♦ Daily. 942.4872

205 Evans Ceramics Gallery Exotic handmade pottery, many pieces oversized or one-of-a-kind, are all discounted by 40 to 90 percent at this factory outlet. Notice the gaudy New Age twist on the subtle art of *raku* (an ancient Japanese method of firing pottery) from Tony Evans and company, the world's largest producer of raku ware. ♦ Daily. 1421 Lincoln Ave (between Washington and Fairway Sts). 942.0453 ♿

205 Mount View Hotel $$ Built in 1917, this hotel, which is on the National Register of Historic Places, has been restored in the Art Deco style of the 1920s and 1930s. There are eight fantasy suites, which are furnished with handsome period pieces, and three private cottages, each of which features a patio and hot tub as well as a wet bar. The 22 standard doubles, all with private baths, are less glamorous—Deco on a budget. But everybody gets to enjoy the pool and Jacuzzi out back, and there's a full-service spa that's open to the public. The **Catahoula Restaurant & Saloon** here (see below) is one of the few places in the valley with live music in the evenings. ♦ 1457 Lincoln Ave (between Washington and Fairway Sts). 942.6877; fax 942.6904

Within the Mount View Hotel:

Catahoula Restaurant & Saloon ★★★ $$$ After nearly six years as the acclaimed chef of San Francisco's chichi Campton Place Restaurant, Jan Birnbaum put away his bow tie and moved to the country, where he is now owner and chef of this far-from-pretentious spot (whose name is pronounced Cat-a-*who*-la).

According to Birnbaum, the catahoula (shown on the restaurant's logo, above) is the state dog of Louisiana, which is his home state. He chose the name because it's one-of-a-kind and it's southern—a reflection of his cuisine, which he describes as "American with southern inspiration." And make no bones about it, his menu (which changes weekly) offers many tempting creations. Appetizers may include cold oysters with salsa, spicy corn soup, and grilled hominy cakes, while the entrées vary from shrimp and andouille sausage creole with jalapeño drop biscuits to oven-baked seafood

jambalaya and grilled T-bone steak. His desserts are equally enticing: strawberry shortcake with fresh whipped cream and strawberry ice cream, chocolate truffle tart with brandied cherries, and lemonade float with lemon gelato, to name just a few.

In addition to the main dining room, there's a separate alfresco eating area around the pool in the back of the hotel that offers a smaller, less-expensive menu. The pool menu changes weekly, too, and the main courses range from fried sand dabs with spring-onion tartar sauce and sweet-potato frites to crawfish tamales. The saloon sports a zinc-topped bar, a menu of small dishes, and live music on the weekends. Don't miss the "Blues Brunch" on Saturday and Sunday, which features— what else?—live blues. ♦ California/Cajun ♦ M, W-F lunch and dinner; Sa-Su brunch and dinner. Reservations recommended. 942.BARK; fax 942.5338 ♿

Mount View Spa Time for some true R&R? Treat yourself to one of this spa's many services—a Swedish massage, a seaweed toning bath, a mud wrap, or a deep-pore cleansing facial. Or you can go whole hog and sign up for one of the full-day spa plans. Relaxation is guaranteed. ♦ Daily. Reservations recommended. 942.5789; fax 942.9165

206 Palisades Market This ranch market has good-looking produce, a small wine section, and imported chocolate bars, teas, and gourmet groceries. ♦ Daily. 1506 Lincoln Ave (near Fairway St). 942.9549; fax 942.6476 ♿

206 Tin Barn Antiques It's fun to browse through the hodgepodge of old furniture, vintage hats and clothing, costume jewelry, collector's items, and bric-a-brac at this antique dealers' collective hidden behind **Palisades Market.** ♦ Daily. 1510 Lincoln Ave (near Fairway St). 942.0618

Short of uprooting the vines, burning every trace of them, and sterilizing the soil, there was no cure for the root louse of phylloxera that devastated much of the world's vineyards in the late 19th century. Scientists finally discovered that a certain type of American rootstock, *Vitis riparia,* was resistant to the pest, whereas the European *Vitis vinifera* was not. And so the solution was to graft the European grape varieties onto the disease-resistant American rootstock. This is still the practice today.

California gray whales are born after a 13-month gestation period and have a life span of 60 to 75 years. The whales travel in pods (groups) of three to eight.

206 Calistoga Gliderport The valley's warm up-currents of air, called lifts, are perfect for gliding. Here, you can take exhilarating, 20- to 30-minute rides over Napa Valley; two people may even go together, provided their combined weight is not more than 340 pounds. Be sure to bring your camera to capture the views. There are only seven gliders, so reserve ahead in peak season (June through September). Spectators can settle into garden chairs on the side of the airfield to watch tiny planes tow the graceful gliders into the sky. Picnic tables and a Weber barbecue are available, too. ◆ Daily. 1546 Lincoln Ave (at Fairway St). 942.5000

206 Nance's Hot Springs $ Indulge in an indoor hot mineral pool and a mud or steam bath, which you can top off with a wonderful therapeutic massage. The 24 bargain motel rooms include private baths, kitchenettes, and cable TV, and some rooms have views of the **Calistoga Gliderport** runway. ◆ Spa: daily. Reservations recommended. 1614 Lincoln Ave (between Fairway St and Stevenson Ave). 942.6211, 800/201.6211

207 Dr. Wilkinson's Hot Springs $ "Doc" Wilkinson was a young chiropractor when he came to Calistoga and established this spa in 1946. His spa/resort features a wide variety of treatments, including facials, acupressure face-lifts, back and shoulder treatments, mud baths, natural whirlpool baths, mineral steam baths, blanket wraps, Swedish/Esalen massages, and special spa packages. There are 37 modern, motel-like units and five Victorian-style rooms, all with private baths, mini-refrigerators, drip-coffee makers, and color TV sets; several rooms also have full kitchens. Guests may use the three mineral-water pools (indoor whirlpool, outdoor soaking pool, and outdoor cool swimming pool). The patio area is furnished with chaise longues and tables. ◆ Spa: daily. 1507 Lincoln Ave (between Fairway St and Stevenson Ave). 942.4102 &

208 Brannan Cottage Inn $$ When Sam Brannan opened his **Calistoga Hot Springs Resort** in 1860, he built 14 cottages where the **Indian Springs** resort now stands. Of the three cottages remaining today, only the one housing this charming inn remains on its original site. Listed on the National Register of Historic Places, this bed-and-breakfast was originally owned by the Winn sisters, Brannan's cousins. Its restoration was a long labor of love for former innkeepers Jay and Dottie Richolson (they have since sold the inn, and the current owner is Peter Bach). The townspeople got interested in the project along the way. One man donated the matching porch lights, and others provided the turn-of-the-century photos that were enlarged to make templates for the intricate gingerbread gable. Each of the six rooms is stenciled with a different wildflower border and decorated with antiques and wicker furnishings. All have their own entrances, private baths, and queen-size beds with down comforters. On sunny mornings, a lavish breakfast (which might include Grand Marnier–scented French toast with chicken-and-apple sausage) is served in the courtyard under the lemon trees. No smoking is allowed. ◆ 109 Wapoo Ave (at Lincoln Ave). 942.4200 &

209 Indian Springs $$ Founded in 1860 by millionaire Sam Brannan, this spa and resort is so-named for the Wappo Indians, who built sweat lodges around the springs long ago. To the left of the spa building you can see one of the three active geysers that provide the spa with a constant supply of 212-degree mineral water, which is cooled for use in the spa and pool. Treatments include mud baths, massages, facials, and mineral-water baths in a thoroughly professional setting. This is also the home of California's oldest operating swimming pool—a huge, beautiful, hot-spring pool that was built in 1913. The pool is kept at 100 degrees in the winter and 90 degrees in the summer; it's open to nonguests daily for a fee and is available free of charge with any of the spa services.

Owners John and Patricia Merchant have decorated the 17 cottages with summery wicker furniture, and white hammocks hang all around the grounds. The cottages are studios and one-bedrooms, and the resort also offers a three-bedroom house. Other amenities include a clay tennis court, a large playground complete with slides and a tetherball, and barbecues. ◆ Spa and pool: daily. Reservations recommended for spa. 1712 Lincoln Ave (at Wapoo Ave). 942.4913 &

210 Napa County Fairgrounds Each Fourth of July weekend the Napa County Fair kicks off for five fun-packed days. Choose between live music and entertainment or auto racing at night; leave the day for touring exhibits on domestic arts and watching the homemade wine competition. ◆ Call for information on other events during the year. 1435 Oak St (at Fairway St). 942.5111; fax 942.5125

Restaurants/Clubs: Red   **Hotels:** Blue
Shops/♥ Outdoors: Green **Wineries/Sights:** Black

211 Golden Haven Hot Springs $ It's not Southern California's sybaritic Golden Door Spa, but it does have the requisite mud bath that you may take with your mate. Also offered are a deeply relaxing hot mineral Jacuzzi, herbal mineral baths, European body wraps, massages, acupressure treatments, herbal facials, and a whole slew of other treatments. The mineral pool is in a makeshift building with a fiberglass roof and is often filled with Europeans who understand the tradition of spas and don't think of it as a luxurious extra to their everyday lives.

The spa's accommodations, like most in Calistoga, are hardly glamorous and are more akin to motels. This one has 26 rooms with private baths and sliding-glass doors opening onto a minuscule patio overlooking a parking lot; some rooms have kitchenettes and/or a private Jacuzzi and sauna. Guests have use of the swimming pool, hot mineral-water pools, and sundeck. No children are allowed on weekends and holidays. ♦ Spa: daily. 1713 Lake St (at Grant St). 942.6793

212 Comfort Inn $$ This comfortable motel has its own hot mineral-water swimming pool and spa, and a sauna and steam room. The 54 rooms have modern decor, private baths, and cable TV; upstairs rooms have decks with views of the hills. A continental breakfast is provided. ♦ 1865 Lincoln Ave (off Hwy 29). 942.9400; fax 942.5262 &

213 Calistoga Village Inn & Spa $$ Another full spa/inn combo, this one offers mud baths, mineral baths, steam and blanket wraps, body massages, natural facials, and salt scrubs. The comfortable accommodations include use of the mineral-water swimming pool, spa, sauna, and steam rooms. All 41 rooms and suites have cable TV and private baths, and some of the suites have whirlpools. Spa-and-lodging deals are available. ♦ Spa: daily. Reservations recommended. 1880 Lincoln Ave (off Hwy 29). 942.0991; fax 942.5306 &

Within the Calistoga Village Inn & Spa:

Cheri's Spa Café ★$$ Formerly the **Lincoln Avenue Grill,** this pleasant restaurant with white-linen tablecloths and a polished pinewood floor offers straightforward fare that includes omelettes for breakfast and burgers and sandwiches for lunch. Dinner features grilled pork chops, New York steak, and a daily fish and pasta special. ♦ American ♦ Daily breakfast, lunch, and dinner. 942.0850 &

Pink Mansion

214 Silver Rose In Hot Springs $$$ Nine spacious rooms all with private baths, are featured at this bed-and-breakfast inn on a knoll overlooking the Silverado Trail just west of Calistoga. Four of the rooms feature fireplaces and balconies; two of them have whirlpool tubs. Sally and J-Paul Dumont have had a lot of fun decorating the rooms and suites—each has a different theme such as teddy bears, period dolls, safaris, and cats. Shoji screens, Oriental rugs, a Japanese lacquer bed, and a Jacuzzi make the **Oriental Suite** one of the most popular. The swimming pool was carved out of the natural rock hillside and has an adjoining Jacuzzi in the shade of a tremendous, 300-year-old oak tree. Mineral water from the inn's own hot springs is available for drinking and bathing. Spa services, including massages, facial treatments, and body wraps and scrubs, are offered in the privacy of the guest rooms. At breakfast time, the Dumonts offer fresh fruit and homemade bread, and during their early evening wine-and-cheese hour they serve Silver Rose Cellars Napa Valley wine. No smoking is allowed. ♦ 351 Rosedale Rd (off the Silverado Tr). 942.9581, 800/995.9381; fax 942.0841

215 Pink Mansion $$ Built in 1875 by the pioneer William F. Fisher, who founded Calistoga's first stagecoach line, this extravagant pink house (pictured on page 72) is now a five-room inn run by Leslie Sakai and Toppa Epps. Each room has its own bath and views of the valley or forest behind. The **Rose Room** has a sunken sitting room and a private redwood deck, while the **Angel Room** holds a sampling of Seyfried's aunt's treasured collection of decorative angels. There's also a heated indoor pool, a Jacuzzi, and a substantial breakfast. ♦ 1415 Foothill Blvd (between Spring and Berry Sts). 942.0558, 800/238.7465; fax 942.0558

216 Calistoga Wayside Inn $$ Set on a wooded hillside, this Spanish-style 1920s house has three guest rooms, all with private baths. Down comforters and feather pillows, a small library of reading material, and an outdoor terrace where a full breakfast is served all contribute to a feeling of well-being. Sherry and spiced teas are served in the evening. ♦ 1523 Foothill Blvd (at Silver St). 942.0645

217 Culver's Country Inn $$ Major John Oscar Culver, a Milwaukee newspaperman, built this beautifully restored Victorian house in the early 1870s. The period decor is refreshingly understated in the six guest rooms, all with shared baths and comfortable custom-made mattresses. A medium-size swimming pool and sauna are also available. Innkeepers Meg and Tony Wheatley prepare a full country breakfast. ♦ 1805 Foothill Blvd (between Oak and High Sts). 942.4535 &

218 Meadowlark $$ This 1886 farmhouse has been remodeled into a bed-and-breakfast inn set on a wooded, 20-acre estate with a swimming pool and sundeck. Innkeeper Kurt Stevens raises horses, too (though not for guests' use). The four guest rooms have queen-size beds, private baths, and contemporary furniture and art. Guests share the downstairs area, which includes a living room, a refrigerator, and a shady veranda overlooking an English garden. The continental breakfast includes orange juice, fruit, muffins, and scones, plus a more substantial dish such as quiche. No smoking is allowed. ♦ 601 Petrified Forest Rd (off Hwy 29). 942.5651; fax 942.5023

219 Petrified Forest Six miles from Calistoga are gigantic redwoods that turned to stone more than three million years ago when Mount St. Helena erupted and molten lava coursed through the valley that is now known as the **Petrified Forest.** Silicates in the ash that blanketed the area seeped into the tree fibers, replacing wood cells with crystallized silica. Highlights along the well-marked trail include "The Giant," a 60-foot-long, six-foot-in-diameter tree that was 2,000 years old when it was petrified three million years ago; the 105-foot-long, six-foot-in-diameter Monarch tunnel tree; a wishing well; a museum; and a nature store. A bronze plaque marks the meadow where Charles Evans discovered the first stump of petrified wood in 1870 while tending his cows. His meeting in 1880 with Robert Louis Stevenson is immortalized in Stevenson's book *The Silverado Squatters*. There is wheelchair access to part of the trail. ♦ Admission; children under age 10 free. Daily. Group tours are offered and picnic tables are available on a first-come, first-served basis. No smoking on the trail. 4100 Petrified Forest Rd (off Hwy 29). 942.6667

Up, Up, and Away: Where to See Napa from the Air

Whether you drift in a hot-air balloon or soar in a glider or small plane, there's nothing like an aerial view of one of the world's most scenic wine regions. Here's where you can get that high in the sky:

Hot-Air Balloons

One-hour flights in Napa Valley cost about $130 to $165 per person.

Above the West Hot-Air Ballooning Balloon flights over **Napa Valley** followed by a Champagne breakfast. Transportation from San Francisco can be arranged. ♦ Daily by reservation. Box 2290, Yountville, CA 94599. 944.8638, 800/NAPA.SKY

Adventures Aloft Balloon trips topped off with a Champagne brunch. ♦ Daily by reservation. Vintage 1870, Box 2500, Yountville, CA 94599. 944.4408

American Balloon Adventures Flights followed by a Champagne toast. ♦ Daily by reservation. Box 795, Calistoga, CA 94515. 944.8116, 800/333.4359

Balloon Aviation of Napa Valley Trips over Napa Valley with a continental breakfast before and a Champagne brunch afterward. ♦ Daily by reservation. Box 2500, Yountville, CA 94599. 800/FOR.NAPA

Balloons above the Valley Flights from **Monticello Cellars** followed by a Champagne brunch. ♦ Daily by reservation. Box 3838, Napa, CA 94558. 253.2222

Bonaventura Balloon Company Rides from the **St. Helena** area followed by a Champagne toast. Options include a continental breakfast, a full breakfast at the **Meadowood Resort,** or a picnic. ♦ Daily by reservation. 133 Wall Rd, Napa, CA 94558. 944.2822, 800/FLY.NAPA

Napa's Great Balloon Escape Flights followed by a full Champagne brunch at the **Silverado Country Club.** ♦ Daily by reservation. Box 795, Calistoga, CA 94515. 253.0860, 800/564.9399 in CA

Napa Valley Balloons, Inc. Trips from **Domaine Chandon** winery with a continental breakfast before the flight and a full Champagne breakfast afterward. Complimentary color photo of you in the balloon, too. ♦ Daily by reservation. Box 2860, Yountville, CA 94599. 253.2224, 800/253.2224 in CA

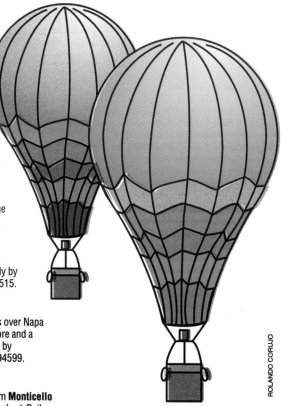

ROLANDO CORUJO

Small Planes and Gliders

For one to two people, 30- to 60-minute flights cost about $80 to $150.

Bridgeford Flying Service Fly over the wine country in a Cessna Skyhawk or Centurion; accommodates one to five passengers. ♦ Daily by reservation. Napa County Airport, 2030 Airport Rd, Napa, CA 94558. 224.0887, 644.1658

The Calistoga Gliderport One- or two-passenger glider rides over Napa Valley. ♦ Daily 9AM-dusk. 1546 Lincoln Ave, Calistoga, CA 94515. 942.5000

220 Foothill House $$

Nestled in the foothills of Calistoga, this small, turn-of-the-century farmhouse is a romantic, comfortable, and tastefully decorated hideaway. Each of the three large guest suites, featuring a private entrance and bath, takes its color scheme from the intricate handmade quilt on the antique bed. Each room has a radio/cassette player, a refrigerator, a wood-burning fireplace, and soundproof walls. The **Evergreen Suite** features a Jacuzzi and a private sundeck with a table and chairs. An even more private cottage has a fireplace and a kitchenette so you can settle in for a longer stay. Innkeepers Doris and Gus Beckert deliver a great gourmet breakfast to your room. ♦ 3037 Foothill Blvd (between Greenwood Ave and Tubbs La). 942.6933, 800/942.6933; fax 942.5692

221 Old Faithful Geyser Just two miles north of Calistoga, you'll find one of the town's prime attractions, one of three faithful geysers (so called because of their regular eruptions) in the world. Every 50 minutes, thar she blows—a column of 350-degree water and vapor comes roaring more than 60 feet into the air. The geyser became a paying attraction at the turn of the century, when people would arrive in their Model Ts, spread picnic cloths and lavish lunches on the grounds, and settle in for the show. Upon request, visitors may see a video explaining how geysers are formed. You will also find a wishing well and picnic facilities nearby. ♦ Admission. Daily. 1299 Tubbs La (off Hwy 128). 942.6463

222 Château Montelena Winery Don't miss this historic winery secluded at the foot of Mount St. Helena. It was built of local and imported stone in a grandiose French-château style in 1882 by Alfred L. Tubbs, one of California's first state senators. A Chinese engineer bought the property in the 1950s and added the five-acre lake with three islands and a floating Chinese junk (ship). In 1972 the Barrett family and partners replanted the vineyards, restored the cellars, and hired Mike Grgich (now at his own winery in Rutherford, **Grgich Hills**) as wine maker. His second vintage, the 1973 Chardonnay, brought the establishment fame and fortune in the famous 1976 Paris competition, when expert French tasters rated it first over several world-famous French White Burgundies in a blind tasting. The winery, with Bo Barrett as wine maker, continues to produce classic Napa Valley Chardonnay and Cabernet Sauvignon with plenty of aging potential, plus Zinfandel and Riesling. Only one reservation per day is taken for each of the two spectacular picnic sites under the shelter of a Chinese pagoda on Jade Lake. Don't rule out this lovely spot in fall and winter; it can be nice even on a rainy or misty day. ♦ Fee. Tasting and sales daily; tours daily 11AM and 2PM by appointment only. Picnic facilities usually require a reservation months in advance. 1429 Tubbs La (off Hwy 128). 942.5105; fax 942.4221 &

223 Storybook Mountain Vineyards This small winery is entirely devoted to producing Zinfandel—and owner Bernard Seps does a knockout job, consistently making one of the top California Zinfandels in both a regular bottling and a reserve bottling that improves with age. ♦ Tasting, sales, and tours M-Sa by appointment only. 3835 Hwy 128 (3 miles north of Petrified Forest Rd). 942.5310 &

Bests

Lauren and Joe Scott
Proprietors, Scott Courtyard, Calistoga

Catch the sunset at the bar at **Auberge du Soleil**—their special pizzas are the best!

Late dinner at the **All Seasons Cafe** in Calistoga. Walk to the **Mount View Hotel** for dancing and dessert.

Oh, and in your spare time, there's some great wine tasting.

Evan Goldstein
Director, The Sterling Vineyards School of Service and Hospitality, Calistoga

The breathtaking and awesome **Petrified Forest** (the world's largest) in **Calistoga.**

The **Anderson Valley Wine Country**—underrated compared to **Napa** and **Sonoma.**

Drinks at **Auberge du Soleil,** where you'll get the best mid-valley view of Napa.

The South Terrace at **Sterling Vineyards** for the best north and south view of **Napa Valley.**

The town of Sonoma—it has retained its sleepy charm.

Dry Creek Valley for the most European feel in the North Coast wine country.

Where to Sleep: The **Sonoma Mission Inn**—worth the price! **St. Orres** in **Gualala**—romantic, and great food, too (go in the off-season).

Where to Eat: Lunch at the **Calistoga Inn**—outside when it's sunny. **Terra** in St. Helena has the best food in Napa Valley. Brunch at **The Diner** in **Yountville.**

Wineries to See: **Napa Valley**'s **Château Montelena, Silverado Vineyards, Sterling Vineyards,** and **Stag's Leap Wine Cellars** (any that need reservations are always more personal). Sonoma's **A. Rafanelli, Robert Stemmler, Dry Creek,** and **Jordan.** Mendocino's **Navarro, Husch,** and **Roederer Estate.**

Sonoma County

The crescent-shaped **Sonoma Valley**, birthplace of the California wine industry, extends from **San Pablo Bay** through a small cluster of old hot-springs towns, past tiny, bucolic **Glen Ellen** and **Kenwood**, and stops just short of **Santa Rosa**. Bounded to the east by the **Mayacamas Mountains** and to the west by the **Sonoma Mountains**, Sonoma is an easy hour's drive from San Francisco—close enough for a one-day jaunt through the wine country. It is also ideal for a long weekend of winery visits paired with a stroll through the town of **Sonoma** and a drive through the pastoral **Valley of the Moon.**

The earliest vineyards on the North Coast were planted in 1824 by the Franciscan fathers at the **Mission San Francisco Solano de Sonoma**, which had been founded the year before. The fathers planted the Mission grape, which they used to produce sacramental wines. When Mexican *comandante* General Mariano Guadalupe Vallejo closed the mission in 1834 under orders from the Mexican government, he took over the existing vineyards, planted more vines behind the presidio barracks, and in 1841 became Sonoma's first commercial vintner. His cellar, wine presses, and sales outlet were housed in the barracks, and he bottled his wines under the **Lachryma Montis** label (the name means "tears of the mountain"). A decade later, when the flamboyant Hungarian count and political exile Agoston Haraszthy arrived in Sonoma, he quickly realized the possibilities this fertile valley held for wine making, having already tried and failed to grow grapes in Wisconsin, San Diego, and San Francisco. In 1857 he planted the first major vineyard of European grape varietals in California at his **Buena Vista** estate on the eastern outskirts of Sonoma. Today Haraszthy, who cultivated 300 varieties of grapes, is widely known as the father of California wine. Other wine-savvy immigrants soon followed, including Jacob Gundlach of **Gundlach-Bundschu Winery.** By 1870 Sonoma was already considered the center of California's burgeoning wine industry.

Today Sonoma Valley is home to more than 150 grape growers and 35 wineries, including some of the most familiar names in California wine making: **Buena Vista, Sebastiani**, and **Benziger.** Several of the smaller estates are also noteworthy, such as **Ravenswood**, which just happens to make one of the best Zinfandels in California. Together they produce about 25 types of wines, ranging from crisp Sauvignon Blancs and buttery Chardonnays to robust Cabernets and spicy Zinfandels. Some vintners are experimenting with Sangiovese from Tuscany, Italy, and with Syrah and Viognier from the Rhône Valley in southern France. This region also produces premium sparkling wines and luscious late-harvest dessert wines made from Johannisberg Riesling. Both large and small wineries here tend to be much more casual than those in Napa Valley about drop-in visits. Most may be visited without calling ahead; those who ask for an appointment do so only to make sure someone will be around when visitors arrive.

As in Napa Valley, Sonoma producers have taken special pains to provide visitors with lovely picnic spots. Many wineries have picnic supplies on hand, too; most notably, Sam and Vicki Sebastiani go all out with an upscale Italian marketplace and deli at **Viansa**, their hillside property at the gateway to Sonoma Valley. With its red-tile roof and grove of olive trees, **Viansa** seems like a slice of Italy transplanted to Sonoma—and indeed, the countryside here is reminiscent of Tuscany. Much of the valley's food, too, is Italian-influenced, a legacy from the Italian stonecutters who originally emigrated to the valley in the 19th century to quarry stone and later turned to the career of wine making. You may choose from restaurants serving hearty, old-fashioned Italian-American fare and from a newer generation of restaurants concentrating on

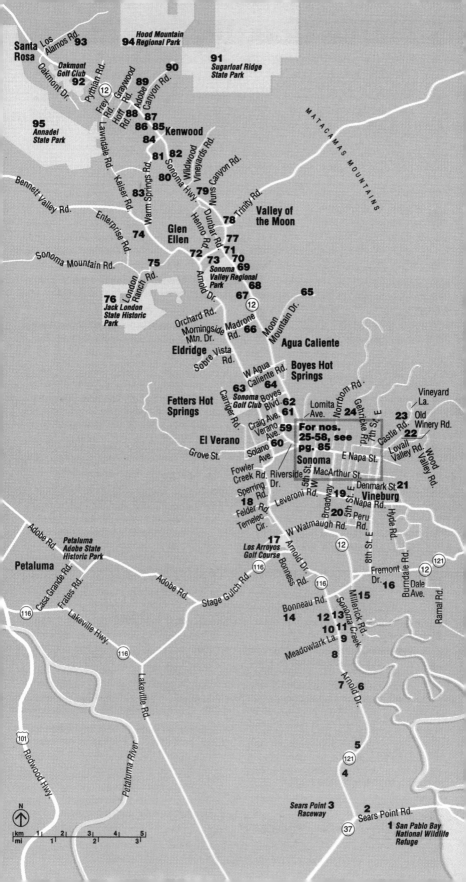

regional Italian cuisine and California wine-country cooking.

Sonoma County also has a number of state parks and nature reserves, including **Jack London State Historic Park** in Glen Ellen, **Sugarloaf Ridge State Park** in Kenwood, and **Annadel State Park** just outside of Santa Rosa. If you like, you can take a break from wine tasting and wander through fields of wildflowers and groves of redwoods, spend the afternoon basking in the sun, or go for a hike or a horseback ride. The valley is compact enough to make bicycling a great way to explore the wine country.

1 San Pablo Bay National Wildlife Refuge Birdwatchers and wildlife photographers frequent this largely undeveloped 332-acre marsh on San Pablo Bay. Park your car at the locked gate at Tolay Creek and Highway 347, then hike in two-and-three-quarters miles to the bird sanctuary on Lower Tubbs Island; from there more trails lead down to the bay and the salt marshes (where critters such as the opossum shrimp live). Bring your binoculars and a good field guide to identify canvasback ducks, the endangered California clapper rail, and the more than 280 species of other resident and migrating birds that call this preserve home. It might be a good idea to pack a few sandwiches in case you want to linger in this unspoiled spot. The best time to visit is in the winter, when the weather is cool and the birds are plentiful. From certain points along the trail you can see the San Francisco skyline and the Golden Gate Bridge. Waterfowl and pheasant hunting is permitted in specified areas during the legal hunting season (months vary; call for schedules). No rest rooms or drinking water are available. ◆ Daily. Hwy 37 (just past the Hwy 121 cutoff for Sears Point Raceway). 646.2434

2 Port Sonoma-Marin This diverse port offers a combination of open bay, tidal salt marsh, and freshwater wetlands. It also has a boat-launching facility and picnic area. ◆ Daily. 270 Sears Point Rd (off Hwy 121). 778.8055

3 Sears Point Raceway This is one of the most demanding courses in the country, offering automobile, bicycle, and motorcycle racing at its best. Pros such as Mario Andretti and Al Unser have raced frequently on the 12-turn, two-and-a-half-mile course, along with celebrities such as Tom Cruise, Paul Newman, Clint Eastwood, and Candice Bergen. Most events are held from March through October; call for schedules and more information. ◆ Hwy 37 (near the junction of Hwys 37 and 121). 938.8448, 800/870.RACE

Also at Sears Point Raceway:

Skip Barber Racing School This school specializes in one- to three-day classes in high-performance BMW driving for amateurs; it offers professional racing courses, too. Call for more information. ◆ 939.8000

4 Roche Winery Established in 1988, this winery is surrounded by 25 acres of Chardonnay and Pinot Noir vines. Owners Joseph and Genevieve Roche believe in producing estate wines at reasonable prices; their wine maker, Steve MacCrostie, also makes wines under his own label. Picnic facilities are available. ◆ Fee for tasting special or older wines. Tasting and sales daily; tours by appointment only. 28700 Arnold Dr (Hwy 121, just north of Sears Point Raceway). 935.7115; fax 935.7846 &

5 Cherry Tree The pure, unsweetened black bing cherry juice made by the Napoli family at this white clapboard stand is a Sonoma tradition. Sizes ranges from eight-ounce bottles to gallon jugs; the juice is so addictive that you may want to pick up a case on your way out of Sonoma. The family recipe, which originated in Germany more than a century ago, is a mixture of cherry juice and apple cider. The Napolis also produce unsweetened fruit butters and sell 100-percent Sonoma varietal wines under their own label, **Napoli Cellars.** ◆ Daily. Arnold Dr (Hwy 121, north of Sears Point Rd). 938.3480 &. Also at: 1901 Fremont Dr (Hwy 12, off Hwy 116). 938.3480 &

6 Viansa Winery and Italian Marketplace Sam Sebastiani, a third-generation vintner from one of Sonoma's oldest wine families and founder of **Sebastiani Vineyards,** has created a fantasy Tuscan village on the top of a Carneros-district hill. The russet-colored winery with terra-cotta roof tiles and green shutters is surrounded by a grove of olive trees, and inside the Italian theme continues

---

Restaurants/Clubs: Red   **Hotels:** Blue

Shops/ Outdoors: Green   **Wineries/Sights:** Black

with evocative frescoes of vineyard scenes by San Francisco artists Charlie Evans and Charley Brown. Sebastiani hired a wine maker from Tuscany and is experimenting with the Italian grape Sangiovese, but his flagship wines are still Chardonnay, Cabernet, and Sauvignon Blanc made from a blend of premium grapes from the Napa and Sonoma Valleys. His top wine, Obsidian, is a blend of Cabernet Franc and Cabernet Sauvignon.

Sebastiani and his wife, Vicki, an accomplished cook and gardener, offer elegant Italian picnic fare in their marketplace. The produce comes from the estate's huge kitchen garden, and the food is very classy—focaccia-bread sandwiches, country pâtés, pasta salads, imported Italian cheeses, and cold cuts. Look for the colorful *torta rustica* (a tall, layered vegetable-and-cheese pie), tasty little cookies, and fig and walnut tartlets. Enjoy the informal picnic fare at a bistro table inside, or dine alfresco in the olive grove with its sweeping view of the valley. The marketplace also features an array of local food products, such as jam, mustard, olive oil, and vinegar, all handsomely packaged, plus hand-painted terra-cotta items and books on wine and Italian food. ♦ Tasting, sales, and guided tours daily. 25200 Arnold Dr (Hwy 121, north of Sears Point Rd). 935.4700; fax 996.4632 &

Also at the Viansa Winery and Italian Marketplace:

6 Sonoma Valley Visitors' Bureau Stop here for information on wineries, lodging, restaurants, shops—you name it, they've got it. For a free copy of the **Sonoma Valley Visitors' Guide,** send a request to: Sonoma Valley Visitors Bureau, 453 First St E, Sonoma, CA 95476 (it's free if you order it by mail but costs $1.50 at the bureau). ♦ Daily. 996.1090

7 Cline Cellars California Rhône-style wines are the specialty here. Owner Fred Cline, a **University of California at Davis** graduate, makes three blends of Zinfandel with Carignane or Mourvèdre (both varietals from France's Rhône Valley), along with terrific unblended Zinfandels, a barrel-fermented Sémillon, and a lush dessert wine made from Muscat of Alexandria. Certain special varietals and reserves are only available at the tasting room inside the restored white-and-green

1850s farmhouse. The surrounding vineyards are planted with Syrah and the rare white Rhône varietals Viognier and Marsanne. The picnic area has views of Sonoma Valley. ♦ Tasting and sales daily; tours by appointment only. 24737 Arnold Dr (Hwy 121, north of Sears Point Rd). 935.4310; fax 935.4319 &

8 Fruit Basket Bins overflow with Sonoma's fresh bounty at this produce stand. Stop here for farm-fresh eggs, milk from Clover-Stornetta Farms, artichokes, asparagus, luscious strawberries, dried fruit and nuts, and other staples. There is also a selection of Sonoma Valley wines, some of them chilled. ♦ Daily. 24101 Arnold Dr (Hwy 121, north of Sears Point Rd). 938.4332 &

9 Aero-Schellville Take an exhilarating 15- to 20-minute ride over Sonoma in a 1940 Stearman biplane once used to train World War II combat pilots. Unlike balloons, which depend on wind currents, these little planes can take off anytime and head straight for the sights. Based at **Schellville Airport,** this company offers all sorts of rides (most for just one or two people), ranging from leisurely flights over Sonoma Valley or an extended scenic ride over both Napa and Sonoma Valleys to an aerobatic ride with loops, rolls, and assorted dizzying maneuvers. Another option—and one that's definitely not for the faint at heart—is the "Kamikaze," described as an "intensely aerobatic" ride. Whoopee! Or you can stay safely on the ground and hire one of the pilots to skywrite a message to your honey. ♦ Daily. 23982 Arnold Dr (Hwy 121, near Meadowlark La). 938.2444; fax 938.2453

10 Country Pine English Antiques Country kitchen pine tables and armoires (either English antiques or modern reproductions) are sold in this gracious shop, along with antique kitchen utensils, teapots, vases, and country-style dinnerware. The wooden plate racks are handy additions for any kitchen. ♦ Daily. 23999 Arnold Dr (Hwy 121, north of Meadowlark La). 938.8315; fax 938.0134 &

11 World of Birds Giant parrots, macaws, cockatiels, and smaller exotic birds warble, honk, and chirp away in this menagerie of feathered vertebrates. It's the largest indoor breeding facility of exotic birds in the country, and, somewhat incongruously, it is also home

Harvesttime in Sonoma

San Franciscans who appreciate farm-fresh foods send for the free *Sonoma County Farm Trails* map and guide every year for an updated listing of more than 125 family farms and a dozen farmers' markets that sell directly to the consumer. Many of these farms and markets are near wineries, which makes it easy to stop on your wine-country excursion to buy freshly picked apples or berries. You'll often find homemade jams, jellies, and vinegars, along with handmade dried-flower or grapevine wreaths and seasonal produce (see the chart below). The annual guide is available at chamber of commerce offices and visitor's bureaus throughout Sonoma, or send a self-addressed envelope with 55¢ postage and a request for the farm guide to: **Sonoma County Farm Trails,** Box 6032, Santa Rosa, CA 95406. For more information, call 996.2154.

What's in Season When

	May	Jun	July	Aug	Sep	Oct	Nov	Dec
Apples			✓	✓	✓	✓	✓	✓
Delicious				✓	✓	✓		
Jonathan			✓	✓	✓			
Rome						✓	✓	✓
Azaleas/Rhododendrons	✓	✓						
Blackberries	✓	✓	✓					
Blueberries	✓	✓						
Bonzai					✓	✓		
Cherries	✓	✓						
Corn			✓	✓	✓			
Figs				✓	✓	✓		
Fresh Flowers	✓	✓	✓	✓	✓	✓	✓	
Grapes				✓	✓			
Japanese Maples	✓	✓	✓	✓	✓	✓	✓	✓
Kiwi						✓	✓	
Orchids	✓							✓
Peaches		✓	✓	✓	✓			
Pears			✓	✓	✓	✓		
Persimmons						✓	✓	✓
Plums		✓	✓	✓	✓			
Prunes				✓	✓			
Pumpkins					✓	✓	✓	
Raspberries	✓	✓	✓					
Strawberries	✓	✓						
Succulents	✓	✓	✓	✓	✓			
Tomatoes			✓	✓	✓	✓	✓	
Vegetables	✓	✓	✓	✓	✓	✓	✓	

to a herd of Peruvian llamas. Kids will want to get a close-up look, and if somebody in the family happens to fall in love with these gentle creatures. . . well, they're for sale, too. Also sold are wine-country souvenirs, items with the **World of Birds** logo, bird cages, books, and all kinds of bird paraphernalia. ◆ Daily. 23570 Arnold Dr (Hwy 121, north of Meadowlark La). 996.1477

12 Gloria Ferrer Champagne Caves

By the time America won its independence in 1776, the family of José Ferrer (the vintner, not the actor) had already accumulated 15 generations of wine-making experience in Catalonia. Because *cava* (sparkling wine) from the family's well-known Spanish producing house, Freixenet, had become such a runaway success in this country, the firm decided to start its own California facility in 1976. Named for Ferrer's wife, this Carneros-district winery with a tiled roof, rows of arches, and whitewashed walls boasts extensive subterranean aging cellars. In the **Sala de Catadores** (hall of the tasters), complimentary *tapas* (appetizers) are served with glasses of the winery's appealing Brut. In the winter, settle in at the green-marble bistro tables in front of the massive fireplace; in warmer weather, sit on the terrace overlooking the vineyard. The winery's popular cellar tour gives visitors an overview of the art of making sparkling wine. Catalan oil and vinegar, olives, anchovies, and other Spanish delicacies are sold in the winery's store. Spanish cooking classes are occasionally offered, and every July the winery hosts a **Catalan Festival.** ◆ Fee. Tasting, sales, and tours daily. 23555 Arnold Dr (Hwy 121, north of Meadowlark La). 996.7256 ⴲ

13 Angelo's Wine Country Meat & Deli Pull up to this deli for generous sandwiches made with Angelo Ibleto's own roasted and smoked meats, plus 15 varieties of homemade sausages. Some are smoked and may be eaten as is; others are perfect for the grill. Hikers and campers swear by Angelo's flavored beef jerkies; he makes a half-dozen now, including a dynamite Cajun style. (Ask for a taste before you buy.) For picnics, consider the small boneless ham, about as big as two fists, or the smoked Cornish game hen. ◆ Daily. 23400 Arnold Dr (Hwy 121, north of Meadowlark La). 938.3688 ⴲ

Much of Sonoma County's highway system follows old Indian trails.

14 Schug Carneros Estate Winery Originally located in Napa, Walter Schug's winery has been re-established in Sonoma, just north of **Gloria Ferrer Champagne Caves.** The half-timbered building, which pays tribute to Schug's German heritage, includes an underground cellar dug into the hillside for aging the casks of wine. The winery concentrates on Carneros-district Chardonnay and Pinot Noir (the estate's vineyard consists of two-thirds Chardonnay and one-third Pinot Noir grapes). There are picnic facilities on a sometimes windy site. ♦ Tasting and sales daily; tours upon request. 602 Bonneau Rd (west of the junction of Hwys 116 and 121). 939.9363, 800/966.9365; fax 939.9364 ♿

SONOMA CREEK
W I N E R Y

15 Sonoma Creek Winery This family-owned, Carneros-district winery with vineyards first established in the late 19th century specializes in barrel-fermented, estate-bottled Chardonnay. Former veterinarian Bob Larson and his two sons and two daughters also produce Cabernet and Zinfandel. ♦ Tasting and sales daily; tours by appointment only. 23355 Millerick Rd (off Bonneau Rd). 938.3031; fax 938.3424 ♿

16 Cherry Tree No. 2 Every other car heading down Highway 12 seems to pull in at this larger and fancier version of the original **Cherry Tree.** This one features a deli and picnic area. Skip the sandwiches, but buy as much of the delicious, unsweetened cherry juice as you can carry. ♦ Daily. 1901 Fremont Dr (Hwy 12, off Hwy 116). 938.3480 ♿. Also at: Arnold Dr (Hwy 121, north of Sears Point Rd). 938.3480 ♿

17 Los Arroyos Golf Course This nine-hole, par 29 course is open to the public on a first-come, first-served basis. ♦ Daily. 5000 Stage Gulch Rd (Hwy 116, off Arnold Dr). 938.8835

18 Happy Haven Ranch Locals buy cases of the Adamson family's hot red-pepper and green-pepper jellies. In season, the ranch also has an old-fashioned mix of flowers, decorative wheat sheaves, and juicy strawberries, which you can pick yourself. ♦ M-Sa Apr-Dec; Sunday by appointment only. 1480 Sperring Rd (off Arnold Dr). 996.4260 ♿

19 Traintown Railroad Kids—and train buffs of all ages—will love this meticulously crafted railroad system. Every 20 minutes a scaled-down reproduction of an 1890s steam train leaves the depot, carrying passengers through

10 acres landscaped with miniature forests, tunnels, bridges, and lakes. At the halfway point, the little steam engine stops to take on water in **Lakeville,** a small replica of a mining town, where passengers may hand-feed a menagerie of farm animals. ♦ Admission. Daily in the summer; F-Su in the winter. 20264 Broadway (Hwy 12, off Leveroni Rd). 938.3912; fax 996.2559

20 Ranch House ★★$$ A real find, this restaurant serves Yucatecan cuisine in a relaxed, informal setting. Aficionados line up for the succulent *carne adobada* (beef braised with onions, tomatoes, and a mix of Yucatecan spices) or the *puchero* (chicken in a sharp tomatillo sauce). Burritos get an interesting twist with a filling of spicy prawns spiked with bay leaves and orange extract, yet you can still find well-prepared standard enchiladas and tostadas, and crisp, not soft, tortillas. ♦ Mexican ♦ Daily lunch and dinner. 20872 Broadway (Hwy 12, off Leveroni Rd). 938.0454

21 Gundlach-Bundschu Winery California's second-oldest bonded (state-licensed) winery was founded in 1858 by Bavarian-born Jacob Gundlach, who planted 400 acres of vineyards and introduced the German varietal Johannisberg Riesling to California at his **Rhinefarm** vineyards. Soon he and his son-in-law, Charles Bundschu, had created a worldwide market for their wines, sold under the Bacchus label. (Their warehouse in San Francisco covered an entire city block.) The family had to shut down their operations after the 1906 earthquake destroyed the winery and Prohibition effectively ended their business, but they still held on to the land and vineyards. The story has a happy ending, though: In 1976 Jacob's great-great-grandson, Jim Bundschu, reopened the historic winery, rebuilding the original cellar and restoring the **Rhinefarm** vineyards. The specialty is Kleinberger, a little-known white German varietal, but Bundschu also makes Chardonnay and a crisp Riesling. The Cabernet from **Rhinefarm** and **Batto Ranch** and the Rhinefarm Estate Merlot and Pinot Noir are excellent. After your visit, hike up a short trail to the landmark **Towles'**

Eucalyptus, a tree on a hill with a panoramic view of the valley. The tree was planted by 10-year-old Towles Bundschu, a fourth-generation Californian Bundschu, in 1890. Picnic tables are set out on a grassy knoll. ♦ Tasting and sales daily. 2000 Denmark St (off Eighth St E). 938.5277; fax 938.9460 ♿

22 Buena Vista Winery Founded by flamboyant Hungarian émigré Count Agoston Haraszthy, California's oldest premium winery shouldn't be missed. On a visit in the 1850s, Haraszthy happened to taste the wines from General Vallejo's Sonoma estate (and also wooed Vallejo's daughter). Realizing the region's wine-making potential, he opened his own winery and lived in a very grand style in a nearby villa. Widely acknowledged as the father of California wine, Haraszthy brought back thousands of cuttings of European grape varieties from France (for which he unsuccessfully tried to get reimbursed by the state) and turned this site into a showcase wine estate. A few years before phylloxera (a louse that attacks the roots of grapevines) ravaged the region's vineyards in 1874, Haraszthy disappeared somewhere in Nicaragua. His sons Attila and Arpad managed the estate until the 1906 earthquake forced the winery to close. It remained abandoned until 1943, when war correspondent Frank Bartholomew revived the historic property. He sold it 25 years later and in 1973 founded **Hacienda Wine Cellars** (now **Bartholomew Park Winery**—see below) on the site of Haraszthy's former villa. The winery's present owner, Marcus Moller-Racke, has continued the restoration of the huge, forested estate and massive stone cellars.

From the parking lot, follow the nature trail past rambling roses and wild blackberry bushes to the winery grounds. Picnic tables are set up in front of the cellars and in the shady grove just beside them. The original press house now serves as the tasting room, where visitors can sample most of the winery's current releases, including a good Chardonnay and a graceful Sauvignon Blanc produced by wine maker Judy Matulich-Weitz. The new releases of Grand Reserve and Estate Cabernets are consistently top-notch. For a small fee, visitors can taste older vintages of the Private Reserves along with Bricourt Champagne and Maison Thorin Burgundies, both from the owner's French wineries. The winery also stocks picnic supplies: Sonoma jack and cheddar, local goat cheese, salami, pâtés, and even Muscovy duck breast. The wine is not processed here, but you can take a self-guided or guided historical tour of the stone winery. ♦ Fee for older vintages. Tasting, sales, and self-guided tours daily. Guided tours daily at 2PM. 18000 Old Winery Rd (off Lovall Valley Rd). 938.1266, 800/926.1266; fax 939.916 ♿

Within the Buena Vista Winery:

Presshouse Gallery This upstairs gallery in the tasting room, once the winery press house, mounts monthly shows of local artists. ♦ Daily.

23 Bartholomew Park Winery Buena Vista Winery's founder, Agoston Haraszthy, really knew how to pick a site. The first building at the end of the grand drive is not the winery, but a reconstruction of the Pompeian-style villa Haraszthy built here in 1857. A plaque commemorates a masked ball held on this site at the original building (which was destroyed by fire) on 23 October 1864, the first formal vintage celebration in California history— General and Señora Vallejo were guests of honor. Farther along is the winery, a Spanish-colonial building originally intended as a community hospital. The building was the home of **Hacienda Wine Cellars** (founded in 1973 by Frank Bartholomew) until 1994, when the label was sold to a large Central Valley wine company. The interior of the building has been extensively renovated; an airy, light-filled tasting room, a museum filled with wine memorabilia from the days of Haraszthy in the 1850s to the present, and a photo gallery of Sonoma Valley grape growers have been added. Under wine maker Antoine Favero (formerly of **Gundlach-Bundschu**), the winery completed its first crush in 1994. Visitors can sample 1990 to 1994 vintages of Chardonnay, Zinfandel, Merlot, and Cabernet Sauvignon in the tasting room or in the picnic area outside in the wine garden. ♦ Tasting, sales, and self-guided tours daily. 1000 Vineyard La (off Castle Rd). 935.9511 ♿

The last decade has seen the emergence of a number of small wineries in California. In 1979, there were just 400 bonded wineries; by 1994, there were more than 800.

The favorite grape of bootleggers during Prohibition was Alicante Bouschet because its thick skin could well withstand transportation.

24 Ravenswood A stone building with a sod roof is the headquarters of this winery specializing in Zinfandel. The tidy tasting room with a wood-burning stove and a cat cozying up to the fire has a sign that reads "No Wimpy Wines Allowed." Wine maker Joel Peterson, formerly an immu-nologist, started the

winery in 1976 with W. Reed Foster, president of the **San Francisco Vintners Club.** Its name came from two ravens who scolded Peterson during his first day of harvesting—and from the opera *Lucia de Lammermoor.* The winery has established a reputation as one of California's leading Zinfandel producers. Grapes come from several very old, dry-farmed vineyards, yielding rich, concentrated wines. The winery also produces Cabernet Sauvignon, Merlot, and a small amount of Chardonnay, Gewürztraminer, and Claret. The distinctive label (shown above) was designed by the renowned Bay Area poster artist David Lance Goines. ♦ Tasting and sales daily; tours by appointment only. 18701 Gehricke Rd (off Lovall Valley Rd). 938.1960; fax 938.9459 &

Bests

Allan Temko
Architecture Critic, *San Francisco Chronicle*

Beringer Vineyards in **St. Helena**—the Rhineland of California.

The Culinary Institute of America at Greystone in St. Helena—stone architecture of monumental dignity and power.

The Hess Collection Winery in **Napa**—exquisite restoration and expansion of a historic winery with an adventurous art collection.

Jack London State Historic Park in **Glen Ellen**—ruins of what had been a magnificent house.

Sonoma Plaza—a wonderful public space and town hall; stone mementos of early California, especially the Bear Flag Revolt, surround the square.

The Salvador Vallejo Adobe, west of Sonoma—the greatest and truest ranch house in Northern California.

Lisa Jang
Owner, Bay Bottom Beds, oyster farm, Santa Rosa

David Auerbach's "Carols in the Caves" concerts in **St. Helena.** Auerbach uses folk instruments from all over the world to play Christmas carols and other holiday music in the storage caves of several wineries. It's a really special way to get the annual dose of Christmas music.

Beautiful routes to travel: **Santa Rosa** to **Calistoga** via **Mark West Springs Road,** and **Sonoma** to Santa Rosa via the **Sonoma Highway (Highway 12),** especially in the early fall.

The noisy and fun **Ma Stokeld's Old Vic** (a pub) in Santa Rosa, which serves good food and great English pastries at very reasonable prices.

The miniature horse ranch in **Petaluma** for the miniature horses.

Jeremiah Tower
Restaurateur, Stars and Stars Cafe in San Francisco and Stars Oakville Cafe in Oakville

After dinner, the steam room at **Auberge du Soleil,** with a bottle of Krug Rosé in an ice bucket. The only way to recover after a long day in **Napa.**

An early-fall lunch at **Mondavi Winery** during the **Great Chefs'** program. They do it all (wine, food, flowers) the best.

Madeleine Kamman's week-long classes at **Beringer Vineyards**—only Madeleine knows that much and would work you that hard.

Any event at **Jordan Winery** in the **Alexander Valley,** especially if you try their "*J*" sparkling wine.

Joseph Phelps's birthday-party barbecues and any of the small lunches serving French and California wines.

Sonoma and Environs

The wine-country town of Sonoma, whose name is said to come from a Suisun Indian word meaning "valley of many moons," began as **Mission San Francisco Solano de Sonoma**, founded by Franciscan Padre José Altimira in 1823. In 1834 the Mexican government sent the young General Mariano Guadalupe Vallejo to oversee the secularization of the mission and to establish a Mexican pueblo and presidio. It was Vallejo who laid out Sonoma's lovely Spanish-style plaza and the cluster of rustic adobe buildings that grew up around it. By 1845 the little town had 45 houses and a population of more than 300 people. Sonoma was incorporated as a city in 1850.

This was also the site of the short-lived Bear Flag Revolt, in which disgruntled American settlers, who had been lured to the area by rumors of free land, rebelled against the Mexican government when they discovered noncitizens were prohibited from owning property. For 25 days in 1846, a ragtag band of immigrants who called themselves the Bear Flag Party seized control of Sonoma, jailed Vallejo, and raised their flag (the grizzly bear–emblazoned banner later adopted by the state of California) over the plaza, declaring the independent Republic of California. The revolt ended less than a month later when the American government stepped in and took over.

Today, this city at the very end of **El Camino Real** (the royal Spanish road that connected the missions of California) offers visitors a glimpse into California's past, as well as a chance to visit several interesting vineyards, browse through antiques shops, galleries, and country stores, and dine at some of the best restaurants in Sonoma Valley.

There's plenty to see beyond Sonoma, too. The stretch of the **Sonoma Highway (Hwy 12)** that heads north toward **Santa Rosa** is a state-designated scenic route, marked with signs depicting an orange poppy (California's state flower) on a blue background. The half-hour drive runs along an old stage-coach and railroad route, past rolling hills, neatly manicured vines, and old barns and farmsteads. Along the way, you'll come to several noteworthy places, including the hot-springs resorts of **Fetters Hot Springs, Boyes Hot Springs, El Verano**, and **Agua Caliente**; as well as **Glen Ellen**, writer Jack London's old stomping grounds; and the bucolic little town of **Kenwood**.

Sonoma

The center of this small, quiet town (pop. 8,200) is its eight-acre, parklike plaza surrounded by historic adobe buildings that house boutiques, antiques stores, restaurants, food shops, and several renovated Gold Rush–era hotels. The **Sonoma State Historic Park** comprises a half-dozen sites in and around the plaza, including the old mission; the Indian barracks; the **Toscano Hotel**, a restored mining hotel; and General Vallejo's Gothic Victorian–Revival home at his estate, **Lachryma Montis**. There's plenty for wine-lovers to see here, too—such as **Sebastiani Vineyards**, perhaps Sonoma's best-known winery, the 19th-century **Carmenet Vineyards**, and **Hanzell Vineyards**, where the practice of aging wines in French oak barrels began in California. And after a long day of sightseeing, nothing tops a great dinner at **Della Santina's** or the **East Side Oyster Bar & Grill**.

25 Magliulo's Restaurant ★$$ Specialties at this family restaurant in a spiffed-up Victorian include homemade minestrone and a wide variety of pasta dishes (such as angel-hair pasta with a basil, tomato, and pine-nut sauce and spaghetti and meatballs). Other familiar Italian-American dishes on the menu include chicken marsala and several versions of veal scallopini; there's also a good New York sirloin steak. For dessert, you can enjoy such succulent sweets as spumoni or frothy zabaglione. On summer evenings, ask to be seated outside in the brick-paved courtyard. There's also a full bar. ◆ Italian ◆ M-Sa lunch and dinner; Su brunch and dinner. 691 Broadway (at France St). 996.1031 ⬧

25 Magliulo's Pensione $ The proprietors of **Magliulo's Restaurant** have turned the adjacent cornflower-blue Victorian house into a bed-and-breakfast inn. They decorated the four guest rooms with brass beds, armoires, and ceiling fans, and antique quilts are hung

Restaurants/Clubs: Red	Hotels: Blue
Shops/ ⬧ Outdoors: Green	Wineries/Sights: Black

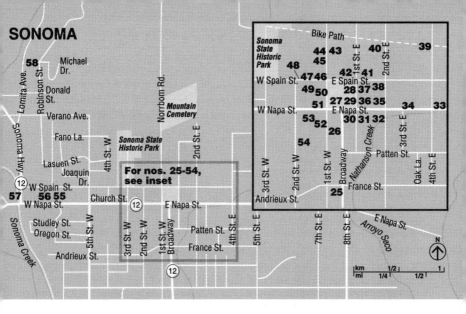

SONOMA

on the walls. Rooms have either private or shared baths. The parlor features a pink sofa and a fireplace framed in copper with cozy chairs pulled up in front. A continental breakfast is served in the inn's dining room. No smoking is allowed. ♦ 681 Broadway (at France St). 996.1031 &

26 Bear Moon Trading Company In an 1880s building with an Italianate false front, this shop carries a good selection of natural-fiber sweaters, socks, and comfortable hot-weather clothing. Consider one of the handsome Panama hats to ward off the summer sun. ♦ Daily. 523 Broadway (between Patten and W Napa Sts). 935.3392

DRAWING BY E. ROSS PARKERSON

27 Sonoma City Hall To avoid slighting any of the merchants on the plaza, when San Francisco architect **A.C. Lutgens** drew the plans for Sonoma's new city hall in 1906, he designed the square Mission-Revival building (pictured above) to be identical on all four sides. Built of locally quarried basalt, the eccentric golden-stone building is the subject of Sonoma schoolchildren's drawings at the annual art show. If the building looks familiar, it might be because you saw it as the **Tuscany County Courthouse** on TV's long-running

wine-country soap opera, *Falcon Crest*. City hall is on the Napa Street edge of Sonoma Plaza at the head of Broadway, the grand boulevard that marks the entrance to Sonoma. ♦ Broadway and E Napa St.

28 Sonoma Plaza The real heart of Old Sonoma is this eight-acre Spanish-style plaza, a state and national landmark. General Mariano Vallejo, the Mexican *comandante,* laid it out with a pocket compass in 1835 as the nucleus of a square-mile town. At first it was a bare, dusty place where Vallejo drilled his troops. Later it was used to graze livestock and provide soil to make adobe bricks. Then at the turn of the century the **Ladies' Improvement Club** took it over and turned it into the verdant park it is today, with more than 200 trees and an intriguing mix of native and exotic plants, including a salmon-colored rose that became known as the Sonoma rose. With its shady areas, playground, duck pond, and wooden tables and benches, the plaza is an appealing spot for a picnic. Parking spots on the sides of the plaza have a two-hour limit; a lot behind the Sonoma barracks building permits longer stays. ♦ Bounded by Napa and Spain Sts, and First St E and First St W

In Sonoma Plaza:

Bear Flag Monument This bronze statue of a figure raising the Bear Flag commemorates 14 June 1846, when a band of American immigrants rode into Sonoma, imprisoned General Mariano Vallejo, and proclaimed California an independent republic. Bear Flagger John Sears contributed the white cloth for the banner's background; the flag's red stripe came from a petticoat; and Abraham Lincoln's nephew, William Todd, painted a large bear, a single star, and the name "California Republic" on the flag. The audacious band's new republic lasted just 25 days, when the US government stepped in to halt the rebellion. In 1911 the California state legislature voted to adopt the design as the official state flag. ♦ Sonoma Plaza, directly across from the Sonoma Barracks

29 Sonoma Valley Visitors' Bureau The Neo-Classical brick building that once housed the town library is now the headquarters of the visitors' bureau. Everyone on the staff here is knowledgeable about the area and will help visitors plan their itinerary as well as advise them on lodging availability. Be sure to pick up a copy of the self-guided walking tour of Old Sonoma. For a copy of the *Sonoma Valley Visitors' Guide,* send your request to: Sonoma Valley Visitors' Bureau, 453 First St E, Sonoma, CA 95476 (it's free by mail order but costs $1.50 at the bureau). A bulletin board out front lists current events and activities. The visitors' bureau also contains the offices of the **Sonoma Valley Vintners' Association** and sells its official Sonoma Valley blue-stemmed wineglasses. ♦ Daily. 453 First St E (between E Napa and E Spain Sts). 996.1090; fax 996.9212 &

GOOD DAY SUNSHINE

30 Good Day Sunshine Browse through this spacious shop if you are in the market for contemporary crafts from California. The selection runs the gamut from ceramics and hand-crafted jewelry to handblown glass goblets and beautiful hardwood wine coasters. ♦ Daily. 29 E Napa St (between First St E and Broadway). 938.4001 &

31 Della Santina's ★★★$$ It's a trattoria, a *rosticceria,* and a *pasticceria* all in one, run by cousins of the same family that operate the Joe's restaurant dynasty of San Francisco's North Beach. In the window, chickens coated with herbs turn on the Italian-style *rosticceria.* The kitchen prepares a good minestrone and Caesar salad, and the handmade pastas are delicious. Plump, tender gnocchi come with an Italian tomato, basil, garlic, and olive oil sauce; tortellini are tossed in a fragrant pesto; and wide ribbon noodles are served with a duck sauce, just as in Tuscany. But the real stars here are the meats from the *rosticceria*—half chickens, Sonoma rabbit, pork loin, roast veal, and turkey breast. The plate of mixed roasted meats will go with just about any wine. At lunch try that savory meat tucked into a roll brushed with olive oil and fresh herbs and served with grilled radicchio and sautéed onions. Offerings from the *pasticceria* include a wonderful tiramisù and tarts made with

fresh fruit. There is a limited list of Italian and Sonoma wines. Takeout and catering are available. ♦ Italian ♦ Daily lunch and dinner. 101 E Napa St (at First St E). 935.0576 &

32 East Side Oyster Bar & Grill ★★★$$ Former **Sonoma Mission Inn & Spa** chef Charles Saunders runs this very welcome addition to the Sonoma restaurant scene. The place is tiny but mighty in its great lineup of seafood specialties and dishes inspired by the wine country's seasonal bounty. Lunch offers quite a variety of entrées, such as Liberty duck burritos, Cape Cod fried clams, rock shrimp and vegetable tempura, and penne pasta tossed with fava beans, baby peas, herbs, and goat cheese. It's even more difficult to decide what to select from the dinner menu, which might include tuna tamales with spicy mango salsa wrapped in banana husks, pan-seared Atlantic salmon with mashed potatoes and asparagus, or Sonoma lamb parfait served on a mound of chick-pea mash, onion confit, roasted plum tomatoes, and crispy leeks. The garden courtyard tucked in back is the best place to sit in warm weather. As you walk through the long, narrow, outdoor entryway, don't be surprised if you have to squeeze behind the prep chefs chopping chilies and tapping their toes to the beat of Latin tunes—it all adds to the ambience of this charming, casual cafe. ♦ California ♦ M-Sa lunch and dinner; Su brunch and dinner. Reservations recommended. 133 E Napa St (between Second and First Sts E). 939.1266 &

32 Pasta Nostra ★$$ This restaurant in a white Victorian gingerbread cottage features hearty Italian-American fare. Start with prosciutto and melon, calamari salad, or garlic bread. Homemade pastas include fettuccine carbonara, spaghetti with clams, and, yes, spaghetti and meatballs. Free-range veal and chicken are prepared several ways. The portions are generous. Sit outside in the courtyard decorated with old wine barrels planted with olive trees. ♦ Italian ♦ M-F lunch and dinner; Sa-Su dinner. 139 E Napa St (between Second and First Sts E). 938.4166

When Jack London bought his Beauty Ranch in Glen Ellen, improvements to the property and agricultural experiments became a passion. In the early 1900s, he devoted two hours a day to writing and 10 hours to farming.

33 Sebastiani Vineyards When Samuele Sebastiani arrived in the area from his native Tuscany in 1895, he worked in the local stone quarries for a while before turning to wine making. Within a few years, he had produced his debut wine, a Zinfandel. The winery that continues to bear his name, today the largest premium-varietal winery in Sonoma, still has the equipment that was used to make that first batch. The third generation of the family runs the huge winery now. Sam Sebastiani opened his own winery, **Viansa,** in the Carneros district a few years ago, leaving his brother Don in charge here. The tour takes visitors through the fermentation room and the aging cellar, with its extensive collection of ornate carved cask heads, all crafted by local artist Earle Brown. The tasting room offers samples of the producer's full line of wines, from Cabernet to Merlot and more. There's a row of picnic tables set along the edge of a nearby vineyard. ♦ Tasting, sales, and tours daily. 389 Fourth St E (at E Napa St). 938.5532, 800/888.5532; fax 996.3349 ♿

34 Victorian Garden Inn $$ The white picket fence and posies in front of the inn only hint at the carefully tended garden beyond. Donna Lewis has spent years cultivating her Victorian-style garden, with its sweet-scented violets, peonies, and heritage roses and ornate wrought-iron garden benches.

Her bed-and-breakfast inn, located on a quiet residential street, has four guest rooms; one is in the main house and the rest are in a 19th-century water tower. She's left the architecture as it was, only adding private baths and decorating the rooms in period decor (guests in the main house may occasionally have to share the bathroom with the owner's personal visitors). The **Garden Room,** decorated in Laura Ashley rose-colored prints, has white wicker furniture and a claw-foot tub. Her most requested room is the **Woodcutter's Cottage,** which has a sofa and armchairs set in front of the fireplace, and a private entrance. For breakfast she serves cherry or apple juice, farm-fresh eggs, a

special granola or muffins, and fresh fruit from the garden. ♦ 316 E Napa St (at Third St E). 996.5339; fax 996.1689

35 Sunnyside Coffee Club and Blues Bar ★★$  Fans of the popular **East Side Oyster Bar & Grill** across the street (see page 86) were delighted when owner Charles Saunders opened this casual breakfast and lunch cafe in 1994 on the former site of **Peterberry's.** Signature morning dishes include hangtown scramble (fried oysters with bacon, roasted peppers, and barbecue sauce) and Pancho Villa (corn biscuits topped with smoked pork loin, poached eggs, and chili sauce), while lunch leans toward soup, salads, pasta, and sandwiches, all prepared in the open kitchen. ♦ Eclectic ♦ Daily breakfast and lunch. 140 E Napa St (between Second and First Sts E). 996.5559 ♿

36 Robin's Nest A paradise for serious cooks, this shop features an ever-changing array of cookware at discount prices. Proprietors Debra and Larry Friedman were in the restaurant business for years and can advise on how to use everything they sell. Sort through seconds of Spanish hardwood spoons, baking pans, and gadgets galore. Also stop here for acrylic wineglasses (perfect for picnics). ♦ Daily. 116 E Napa St (at First St E). 996.4169

37 Sonoma French Bakery This bakery makes delicious sourdough French bread, as well as sour French baguettes, torpedoes (short loaves), and sandwich rolls. Mornings bring plain and almond croissants warm from the oven. The Italian *panettone,* made year-round in one-pound loaves, makes excellent toast. ♦ Tu-Su. 470 First St E (between E Napa and E Spain Sts). 996.2691 ♿

37 Place des Pyrenees Inside this peaceful courtyard you'll find several shops, a great French restaurant, an Irish pub, and a coffee roaster. ♦ 464 First St E (between E Napa and E Spain Sts).

According to William F. Heintz, author of *Wine Country—A History of Napa Valley,* when the 1906 San Francisco earthquake hit, an estimated 45 to 50 million gallons of wine were stored in San Francisco warehouses, which easily could have been used to put out the fire that devastated nearly 500 city blocks.

Building a Better Corkscrew

The humble corkscrew seems to be one common household utensil designers are always attempting to improve. There are dozens of models in use today, ranging from the simple and functional to the whimsical and elaborate. Most corkscrews will pull that cork out just fine, but some are harder to use than others. Here's a sampling of some of the most popular models:

The simplest corkscrew is this old standby, the type featured on the Swiss army knife. Center the tip of the corkscrew over the cork, and screw it in clockwise, trying as much as possible to drive it in at a vertical angle. Get a good hold on the bottle and pull. The cork comes out with a resounding pop—a joyful sound to wine lovers.

This model features movable wings that look a little like flying buttresses. As you screw down through the cork, the wings slowly rise. Push down on the wings simultaneously and the cork rises straight out of the bottle.

The handy waiter's pocket corkscrew is small and compact—perfect for picnics. The lever attached to the end of the corkscrew is used to help ease out the cork.

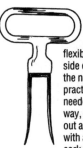

In this clever and eminently portable version, no screw is involved. Instead, two narrow, flexible blades are inserted on either side of the cork (between the cork and the neck of the bottle). It takes some practice to master the rocking motion needed to insert the blades all the way, but this type is better for easing out a damaged, crumbled cork. Pull with a slight twisting motion and the cork comes right out.

The Screwpull is an ingenious design that features a long Teflon-coated screw that slips easily through the dense cork. As you turn it clockwise, the cork slowly rises; no exertion is needed. This is the one foolproof corkscrew. Widely available at wineshops, it comes in both a waiter's version and a tabletop model.

Within Place des Pyrenees:

Sugar Bears Jars of old-fashioned candies priced by the pound fill this tiny shop. ♦ Daily. 996.6177

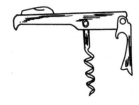

Babette's Restaurant & Wine Bar
★★★★$$$$ Beautifully prepared modern French cuisine takes center stage at this 1994 addition to the Sonoma restaurant scene, already a favorite with locals and critics alike. Owners Daniel Patterson and Elizabeth Ramsey have created quite a gem, thanks in part to years of experience at other top wine-country restaurants (**Domaine Chandon, Mustards Grill**). Chef Patterson spent childhood summers in France, where his mother taught school, and this place is infused with authentic French soul, from the elegant, seductive atmosphere to the high quality of ingredients and classic French cooking techniques. Served in a romantic dining room decorated with velvets, brocades, white table linen, and fine silver and china, dinner is truly an evening-long event, meant to be savored course by course. The restaurant features both three- and five-course menus with a choice of entreés (usually fish, fowl, meat, and a vegetarian selection) that change nightly. Starters may include Patterson's silky Sonoma foie gras, Hama Hama oysters, and exquisite tarts, perhaps filled with blue cheese, caramelized onions, green apples, and sage flowers. Entreés may range from grilled

breast of Muscovy duck with potato puree; salmon with portobello mushrooms, celery root puree, peas, and baby leeks; and ragout of spring vegetables with handmade ravioli stuffed with morel mushrooms. Desserts are equally stunning: bing cherries in an almond phyllo basket with lavender ice cream, walnut-chèvre cheesecake, and rhubarb soufflé gratin with crème fraîche ice cream. Wines are offered by the glass or even half-glass so you can try different types with each course. There's also a casual wine bar that offers a separate, less expensive bistro-style menu of soups, salads, and sandwiches, as well as a list of more than 30 vintages. ♦ French ♦ Tu-Sa dinner. 939.8921 &

Jeanine's Coffee & Tea Company Enjoy a cappuccino or espresso at tables outside in the cobblestoned courtyard. Proprietors Jeanine and Bruce Masonek buy the beans and roast their own coffees in an old-fashioned drum roaster to get the slow-roasted flavor they prefer. To compensate for flavor lost in the decaffeination process, they roast their decaf coffees a bit darker. ♦ Daily. 996.7573 &

Briar Patch Tobacconist The other half of **Jeanine's Coffee & Tea Company** is devoted to hand-crafted cigars and custom-blended tobaccos (some with affectionate local names: Glen Ellen, Jack London, Sonoma, etc.). ♦ Daily. 996.7573 &

37 **Basque Boulangerie Cafe** ★$ Fresh-baked breads and pastries fill the shelves of this bustling bakery and cafe with a few tables and a marble bar. Locals gather for coffee and fresh-baked sourdough Basque bread, walnut-studded sticky buns in the morning, or a bowl of oatmeal or granola, and for homemade soups, salads, sandwiches, or tasty Basque potato omelettes at lunch. A rack behind the bar holds a large selection of Sonoma County wines, available by the glass. ♦ Eclectic ♦ Daily breakfast, lunch, and early dinner. 460 First St E (between E Napa and E Spain Sts). 935.7687 &

37 **The Mercato** *Mercato* is Italian for "market," and this postmodernist building bathed in stylish pastels contains a number of interesting shops. Note the 16-by-13-foot mural on the side of the building depicting a bird's-eye view of Sonoma Valley; it was painted by local artist Claudia Wagar. ♦ 452 First St E (between E Napa and E Spain Sts). &

Within The Mercato:

Artifax Proprietors Candace Tisch and Tom Rubel travel all over the world buying crafts for this elegant gallery with a special emphasis on offerings from Asia and Africa. Japanese flower-arranging tools, African musical instruments, handsome woven platters from the Philippines, tribal dolls from Kenya, Tibetan singing bell bowls, and bamboo trays from Japan all make special gifts. ♦ Daily. 996.9494 &

Papyrus This stationery store has a collection of appealing cards, writing materials, and ornate wrapping papers, many from museums around the world. ♦ Daily. 935.6707 &

HandWorks

Handiworks A welcome change from tourist-oriented bric-a-brac stores, this gallery concentrates on fine examples of contemporary crafts. You'll find intricately crafted jewelry, handwoven clothing, and hand-painted silk scarves. And for the practical at heart: masterful bowls created on a wood turner's lathe, shimmering ceramics, and hardwood cutting boards. ♦ Daily. 996.2255 &

Wine Exchange of Sonoma This spacious, well-organized shop offers a dynamite array of more than 500 California wines selected by the knowledgeable staff. This is the place to go for some serious wine talk—or beer talk, for that matter, as the shop also features a superb collection of more than 250 brews from around the world. And—this is the best part—there is a comfortable, informal wine bar at the back where you can sample a dozen top wines by the taste or glass, as well as several draft beers. The store gives case discounts and will ship your orders. ♦ Daily. 938.1794, 800/938.1794

37 **Zino's on the Plaza** ★$$ The tried-and-true Italian-American fare here keeps the regulars coming back. The menu features fresh pasta dishes, chicken parmesan, turkey scaloppine, and osso buco (braised veal shanks), among other items. The wine list is perfunctory. ♦ Italian ♦ Daily lunch and dinner. 420 First St E (between E Napa and E Spain Sts). 996.4466 &

Restaurants/Clubs: Red   **Hotels:** Blue
Shops/ ♥ Outdoors: Green   **Wineries/Sights:** Black

37 El Paseo After passing under an archway of plum stone from local quarries, you'll discover a series of small shops off a charming courtyard. Rents have increased dramatically in recent years, forcing many of the longtime tenants to find other quarters. ♦ 414 First St E (between E Napa and E Spain Sts). &

Within El Paseo:

Vasquez House Built in 1855 by the Civil War hero "Fighting" Joe Hooker, who later sold it to early settlers Catherine and Pedro Vasquez, this small steep-gabled house (pictured below) is now the headquarters for the **Sonoma League for Historic Preservation.** It contains a library that is devoted to the town's history and a changing exhibit of historical photos gleaned from the town archives. The diminutive tea room is staffed by league volunteers who serve homemade desserts and tea at modest prices. In the summer, sit at an umbrella-shaded table outside. For eight to 10 people, walking tours can be arranged; reservations should be made one month in advance. You can also pick up books on Sonoma's history and copies of the guide, *Sonoma Walking Tour.* ♦ W-Su 1:30-4:30PM. 938.0510

37 Sonoma Wine Shop Come here for one-stop shopping for wine-related paraphernalia from many of the valley's wineries, plus cork-screws, wine carriers, picnic baskets outfitted with wineglasses—and a modest selection of wine. On weekends you can taste several different vintages by the glass at the little wine bar in back. ♦ Daily. 412 First St E (between E Napa and E Spain Sts). 996.1230; fax 944.2710 &

37 Alberigi's Old Sonoma Creamery ★$ This is a shop with a split personality. One side is an old-fashioned ice-cream parlor with a row of booths where you can create your own sundae fantasy from the 40 flavors made here at the height of summer. Next door is an informal wine-tasting bar and deli featuring cheeses, cold cuts, salads, and sandwiches to take out or eat inside. For dessert, try the Toscano, a fudge brownie topped with vanilla ice cream and hot fudge sauce. ♦ Eclectic ♦ Daily breakfast, lunch, and early dinner. 400 First St E (between E Napa and E Spain Sts). 938.2938 &

38 La Casa ★★$$ Tradition-al Mexican cuisine is served in this restaurant tucked in **El Paseo** courtyard off East Spain Street. Start with one of the excellent margaritas (try the Horni Rita) and an appetizer or two, such as *seviche* (fresh marinated fish, cilantro, and salsa) and *chimichanguitas* (deep-fried tortillas filled with spicy shredded beef). Entreés include enchiladas, tamales, and other classic Mexican dishes; you can end your meal with a simple flan. Ask to sit on the lovely back patio in warm weather. ♦ Mexican ♦ Daily lunch and dinner. 121 E Spain St (between Second and First Sts E). 996.3406 &

Vasquez House

DRAWING BY E. ROSS PARKERSON

38 Blue Wing Inn This two-story Monterey-Colonial adobe was built by General Vallejo to lodge troops and travelers. During the Gold Rush, the inn became an infamous saloon where Ulysses S. Grant, Kit Carson, and the bandit Joaquin Murrietta stopped to hoist a few. In the spring, cascades of wisteria blossoms hang from the hand-hewn balconies. ♦ 125-139 E Spain St (between Second and First Sts E)

39 Sonoma Bike Path No cars are allowed on this path, making it ideal for bicyclists and pedestrians. The bicycle trail takes you past the **Vella Cheese Company,** the **Sonoma Depot Museum** and **Depot Park,** and General Vallejo's Victorian home, **Lachryma Montis.** ♦ The trail starts at Sebastiani Vineyards and ends at Maxwell Farms Park in El Verano

40 Vella Cheese Company When Tom Vella arrived in California from his native Sicily in 1916, he sold butter, eggs, and cheese in San Francisco until he saved enough to open his own cheese-making business in Sonoma in 1931. His Monterey Jack cheese and the "Bear Flag" dry Monterey Jack (a grating cheese popular with local Italians) have long been wine-country favorites. Under the direction of Tom's son Ig, the company now makes at least half-a-dozen cheddars, an Oregon blue, and several flavored jacks at its headquarters in an old stone building. Sample pesto-flavored jack or the jalapeño version made from fresh New Mexico peppers. And if you live nearby, pick up some of Vella's sweet butter. Call ahead to arrange to watch the entire artisanal cheese-making process; Ig often conducts the tours himself. A mail-order catalog is available. ♦ Daily. 315 Second St E (north of E Spain St). 938.3232, 800/848.0505; fax 938.4307 ♦

41 Mission San Francisco Solano de Sonoma One of the five sites that comprise the **Sonoma State Historic Park,** this is the northernmost and the last of the 21 Franciscan missions built along the length of California (see the illustration at right). Named after a Peruvian saint, it was constructed on a site chosen by Padre José Altimira in 1823, when California was under Mexican rule. Construction of the original church began in 1823, but all that survives of those times is the adobe building that served as the padre's quarters. (The present church was built under the direction of General Vallejo in 1840.) You can walk through the mission fathers' former rooms and tour blacksmith, weaving,

and bread-baking workshops to get a sense of what life was like in this mission outpost. ♦ One ticket entitles you to same-day admission to this site as well as to the **Sonoma Barracks, Toscano Hotel, Lachryma Montis,** and the **Casa Grande Indian Servants' Quarters.** 114 E Spain St (at First St E). 938.1519 ♦

42 Casa Grande Indian Servants' Quarters Part of the **Sonoma State Historic Park,** this two-story Monterey-Colonial structure, once used as servants' quarters, is all that's left of General Vallejo's early Sonoma home. The imposing **Casa Grande,** built circa 1835, featured a three-story tower from which the general could survey the surrounding countryside. Eleven of his 14 children were born in the sprawling adobe house, but in 1853 he moved his family to **Lachryma Montis** (see page 93), a new home he built on a secluded site north of Sonoma. In 1867 a fire destroyed **Casa Grande**'s main buildings, leaving only these servants' quarters, where a small Native American exhibit is now housed. ♦ One ticket entitles you to same-day admission to this site as well as to the **Mission San Francisco Solano de Sonoma, Toscano Hotel, Lachryma Montis,** and the **Sonoma Barracks.** 20 E Spain St (between First St E and First St W). 938.1519

42 Sonoma Barracks Between 1836 and 1840, Native American laborers built this two-story Monterey-Colonial adobe to serve as General Vallejo's Mexican troop headquarters. Seized by the Bear Flag Party when they set up a short-lived independent republic in 1846, it was a US military post until the 1850s. A century later, the state bought and restored it as part of the **Sonoma State Historic Park.** ♦ One ticket entitles you to same-day admission to this site as well as to the **Mission San Francisco Solano de Sonoma, Toscano Hotel, Lachryma Montis,** and the **Casa Grande Indian Servants' Quarters.** At the intersection of First St E and E Spain St. 938.1519

Mission San Francisco Solano de Sonoma

DRAWING BY E. ROSS PARKERSON

42 Toscano Hotel Originally built as a general store and lending library in the 1850s, this early California wood-frame building became a hotel in 1886, its name a tribute to the proprietors' Tuscan heritage. In 1957 a descendant of the hotel's original owners sold it to the state, and now it's part of the **Sonoma State Historic Park**. The **Sonoma League for Historic Preservation** stepped in to help restore the old mining hotel, endowing it with a certain raffish charm. Whiskey glasses and hands of cards sit on the tables, as if the players had just slipped out for a minute or two, and ragtime music plays in the background. Upstairs, the six bedrooms are furnished with period antiques and authentic touches. The turn-of-the-century kitchen in back displays a quirky collection of cookware and gadgets. ◆ One ticket entitles you to same-day admission to this site as well as to the **Mission San Francisco Solano de Sonoma, Sonoma Barracks, Lachryma Montis,** and the **Casa Grande Indian Servants' Quarters.** M, Sa-Su. 20 E Spain St (between First St E and First St W). 938.1519

43 Depot Park A few old train cars are pulled up alongside the replica of an old train station, which is now a museum (see below). The park includes a playground area, a gazebo, picnic tables, and barbecue pits. ◆ 200 block of First St W (north of E Spain St)

Within Depot Park:

Sonoma Depot Museum A replica of the old **Northwestern Pacific Railroad** station now houses Sonoma's impromptu historical museum. The volunteer docents are eager to show off the restored stationmaster's office, where the big clock still ticks away. Show an interest and they'll conduct you around the museum, pointing out a map and a collection of memorabilia that trace the coming of the railroads in this part of the West. A re-creation of the kitchen and other rooms in a typical Victorian household and photos of local historical figures (including members of the infamous Bear Flag Party) complete the display. The museum has a good selection of historical books and monographs on Sonoma, plus coloring books for kids on California history. ◆ Free. W-Su. 270 First St W. 938.1762

The 1915 Panama Pacific International Exposition held in San Francisco was the first major American wine competition in which Cabernet Sauvignon wines were judged as a separate category.

"A meal without wine is like a day without sunshine."

Anthelme Brillat-Savarin,
Physiologie du Goût, 1825

Restaurants/Clubs: Red   **Hotels:** Blue
Shops/ 🌳 Outdoors: Green   **Wineries/Sights:** Black

Sonoma Farmers' Market Don't miss this vibrant outdoor market, which is held twice a week for much of the year. Where better to shop for a picnic? ◆ Tu May-Nov; F 9AM-noon year-round. Arnold Field parking lot

44 Depot Hotel, Restaurant and Garden ★★$$ Built in 1870 with stone from nearby quarries, this restaurant (pictured above) was originally a three-bedroom home with a saloon operating out of the living room. Once the railroad was extended and a station was built across the street, the railroad purchased the house and saloon to accommodate travelers. Now it's been transformed into a spacious, airy, casual northern Italian restaurant. The severe stone facade gives no hint of the surprises inside. The dining room is dressed in blue and white; outside, a glassed-in garden room and terrace look out to a pool and formal garden. At lunch soups, salads, and sandwiches are offered; more elaborate dishes are served at dinner. For main courses, try one of the pasta dishes, Tuscan-style *bistecca alla fiorentina* (prime rib grilled over mesquite), sautéed chicken with mushrooms, or prawns sautéed with white wine, garlic, and lemon. Dessert often features tiramisù (espresso-soaked ladyfingers layered with mascarpone and cream), along with chocolate decadence (a dense, dark-chocolate cake served with raspberry puree). Wine is also served in the fireside parlor. ◆ Italian ◆ W-F lunch and dinner; Sa-Su dinner. 241 First St W (north of W Spain St). 938.2980; fax 938.5103 &

CHAIRHOUSE~SONOMA

45 Chairhouse-Sonoma This is the place to find baskets, textiles, toys, hand-crafted ethnic arts, pottery, and more—but not one chair. The gallery takes its name from the owners' original San Francisco shop (which sold chairs in the 1950s). ◆ F-Su and holidays. 383 First St W (north of W Spain St). 938.0298

Flights of Fancy: Sonoma Valley from the Air

Most flights based in **Sonoma County** travel over the **Russian River Valley,** and the farther north you go, the more scenic your trip will become. Here's where you can get that stunning aerial view:

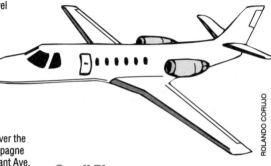

ROLANDO CORUJO

Hot-Air Balloons

One-hour tours in Sonoma County cost about $140 per person.

Air Flambuoyant Hot-air balloon flights over the Sonoma wine country followed by a Champagne brunch. ♦ Daily by reservation. 250 Pleasant Ave, Santa Rosa, CA 95403. 838.8500, 800/456.4711

Aerostat Adventures Rides above the **Healdsburg** area with a continental breakfast before and a Champagne brunch afterward. ♦ Daily by reservation. 2414 Erickson Ct, Santa Rosa, CA 95401. 579.0183, 800/579.0183

Sonoma Thunder Wine Country Balloon Safaris Flights followed by a Champagne celebration. ♦ Daily by reservation. 6984 McKinley St, Sebastopol, CA 95472. 538.7359, 800/759.5638

Small Planes

For one to two people, 30- to 60-minute flights cost about $80 to $120.

Aero-Schellville Rides in a Stearman plane once used to train World War II combat pilots. ♦ Daily by reservation. Schellville Airport, 23982 Arnold Dr, Sonoma, CA 95476. 938.2444

Petaluma Aeroventure Scenic flights in one- or three-passenger planes. ♦ Daily by reservation. 561 Sky Ranch Dr, Petaluma, CA 94954. 778.6767

46 Sonoma Cheese Factory The plate-glass windows at the back of this crowded shop offer a good view of workers in white hard hats and yellow aprons making cheese (a schedule is posted here listing the cheese-making days and hours). Famous for its Sonoma Jack, the factory has developed a growing line of cheeses, including jack spiked with pepper, garlic, or caraway seeds; a mild cheddar; and a tender cheese called Teleme. Many of them are cut up for free tasting. Founder Celso Viviani's son Pete and grandson David now run the family business. The store is filled with all sorts of picnic fare, not only cheeses (already wrapped), but also slices of pâté and cold cuts sliced to order; the prepared salads are less tempting. You can have the staff make you a sandwich and then retire to the shady patio or the plaza out front for lunch. Crackers, local mustards, jams, and Sonoma wines are also offered, some arranged in gift baskets. ♦ Daily. 2 W Spain St (at First St W). 996.1931 ₺

46 Marioni's Restaurant ★$$ Built in 1951, this building used to be a post office: Now this wood-lined canteen is for die-hard surf 'n' turf fans—the place to get a variety of steaks and seafood. The teriyaki chicken is about as exotic as it gets. ♦ American ♦ M bar service only; Tu-Sa lunch and dinner; Su brunch and dinner. 8 W Spain St (between First and Second Sts W). 996.6866 ₺

46 Swiss Hotel $$ Small and full of authentic charm, this property has five antiques-filled guest rooms with views of the plaza or garden patio and access to the balcony. The building, now a **California Historical Landmark,** was originally constructed in 1850 for General Vallejo and has been an inn since 1909. ♦ 18 W Spain St (between First and Second Sts W). 938.2884

46 Plaza Books This is a welcome refuge from the tourist fray. Just the smell of the old leather- and cloth-bound books transports you to a bygone era. There are no current best-sellers here, just high-quality used and rare books. ♦ Daily. 40 W Spain St (between First and Second Sts W). 996.8474

47 Sonoma Hotel $ Completed in 1880, this corner building (pictured at right has had a checkered past. As in many buildings of the era, the downstairs was used as the site for a series of shops and

saloons. Upstairs, it featured a hall and a stage for social occasions. When Samuele Sebastiani bought it in the 1920s, he added a third floor and a balcony encircling the second floor and made himself a hotel, which he dubbed the **Plaza.** There are now 17 rooms here, and the upstairs rooms, with shared baths in the European tradition, are wine-country bargains. Maya Angelou wrote *Gather together in My Name* in **No. 21,** a small, cozy room with a pitched ceiling, a floral comforter, and lace curtains. Rooms with private baths on the first two floors have deep claw-foot tubs. The grandest is **The Bear Flag Room,** which has a private bath and is furnished with a bedroom suite of carved mahogany from the Bear Flag era. ♦ 110 W Spain St (between First and Second Sts W). 996.2996, 800/468.6016; fax 996.7014

48 Lachryma Montis A visit to General Vallejo's Victorian home and gardens is well worth the price of the museum ticket. Set in the shelter of a hillside, the steep-gabled, yellow-and-white wood house (see drawing below) designed in the Gothic Revival style is twined with rambling roses. One yellow variety has climbed a 30-foot tree and is considered the oldest rosebush in Sonoma. Inside, the curators have tried to create the illusion that the family is only out for the afternoon. The table is set and a bottle of the general's wine decanted; his wife seems to have laid out her shawl on one of the beds upstairs. The former wine-and-olive storehouse has been turned into a little Vallejo museum, with the general's silver epaulets,

books, cattle brand, and photos on display, along with examples of his wine label, also called Lachryma Montis. It means "tears of the mountain"—a reference to a mineral spring on the property. You may picnic at shaded tables on the terraced hillside and spend the afternoon at the 20-acre estate, which has been incorporated into the **Sonoma State Historic Park.** ♦ One ticket entitles you to same-day admission to this site as well as to the **Mission San Francisco Solano de Sonoma, Toscano Hotel, Sonoma Barracks,** and the **Casa Grande Indian Servants' Quarters.** Daily. W Spain St (at Second St W). 938.1519

49 Thistle Dew Inn $$ This 1910 California Arts and Crafts house offers six guest rooms (two rooms in the main house, four in the cottage out back), all with private baths. The **Rose Garden Room** is furnished with antique oak furniture and a fan-patterned Amish quilt; the smaller **Cornflower Room** is, of course, blue with a matching Star of Texas quilt. Most of the original Arts and Crafts furniture is by Gustav Stickley or Charles Limbert; lamps, textiles, and rugs were made during the same period. Guests may use the cozy parlor

Lachryma Montis

complete with a wood-burning stove and plump, pale green sofas. Innkeepers Norma and Larry Barnett cook a full breakfast (including a special entrée such as fluffy soufflé pancakes, scrambled eggs with salmon, pancakes with fruit, or French toast with cinnamon). The inn has bicycles and picnic baskets for guests and also offers access to the best local health club, which features aerobics, Nautilus, and pool facilities. No smoking is allowed. ♦ 171 W Spain St (between First and Second Sts W). 938.2909 ♿

50 Batto Building This three-section, glazed-brick building designed in the Classic Revival style dates from about 1912. ♦ 453-461 First St W (between W Napa and W Spain Sts)

Within the Batto Building:

Sonoma Spa The owners of two Calistoga spas have set up shop on Sonoma's plaza, allowing you to pamper your body with a wide range of treatments—from full-body massages and foot reflexology to facials and mud baths. ♦ Daily. Reservations recommended. 457 First St W (between W Napa and W Spain Sts). 939.8770

Kaboodle Designer/owner Beth Labelle's charming shop is stuffed to the rafters with gift items. She sits at a table right in the shop putting together her exquisite dried-flower wreaths and also decorates romantic straw hats with silk ribbon from France. Her choice selection of children's books and stuffed animals from Germany will tempt the child in anyone. The old-fashioned topiaries and graceful birdcages make wonderful gifts. ♦ Daily. 453 First St W (between W Napa and W Spain Sts). 996.9500

50 Sign of the Bear
You'll find crocks for making pickles, pressed-glass bottles for steeping vinegar with herbs, good cookbooks, and all sorts of kitchen utensils and gadgets on the shelves of this unpretentious, friendly cookware

shop. ♦ Daily. 435 First St W (between W Napa and W Spain Sts). 996.3722

50 Salvador Vallejo Adobe Under the direction of General Vallejo's brother Don Salvador Vallejo, Native Americans completed construction of this historic adobe in 1846. The second story was probably added when it was converted to a boarding school during the late 1850s. ♦ 405, 415, 421, and 427 First St W (at W Spain St).

Within the Salvador Vallejo Adobe:

El Dorado Hotel $$
Goose-down comforters, terry robes, and the use of a heated, outdoor swimming pool are just a few of the perks at this small hotel

that opened during the Gold Rush. It has been modernized and decorated by a team led by Claude Rouas (of the posh **Auberge du Soleil** resort in Napa Valley). Instead of full-tilt luxury, they've gone for simple comfort at moderate prices. The 27 rooms, each with a private bath, are fairly small, and the designers have wisely left them uncluttered, adding terra-cotta tile floors, hand-crafted furniture, and textiles in pale, soothing colors. French doors lead to small balconies overlooking either the plaza or the courtyard and pool in back; cable TV and AM/FM radios are standard equipment. The heated lap pool is located in the hotel's private courtyard, and an Italian continental breakfast (coffee, fruit, and freshly baked breads and Italian pastries) is served on the brick patio beneath an ancient fig tree. The strong suit here is the thoroughly professional concierge service; use it to arrange dinner reservations, a massage, horseback rides, picnics, or wine tours. ♦ 996.3030, 800/289.3031; fax 996.3148 ♿

Piatti ★★★$$$ Like its sister restaurant in Napa Valley, this popular dining spot offers regional Italian cuisine. Rustic bruschetta (grilled country bread topped with tomatoes, garlic, basil, oregano, and olive oil), carpaccio, or *verdure alla griglia* (grilled seasonal vegetables with whole-roasted garlic cloves and lemon) are top choices for antipasti. The wood-burning oven turns out classic pizzas such as *margherita* (fresh tomatoes, mozzarella, and basil) or marinara (fresh tomatoes, oregano, and garlic). The numerous pasta dishes can be very good, and the main courses from the grill are always an excellent choice—particularly the marinated free-range chicken and the grilled sausage served with creamy polenta and wilted greens. *Sorbetti* and gelati put a chill on Sonoma's summer heat; save the richer desserts for cooler weather. But try the *affogato al caffè* (white chocolate and Amaretto ice cream drenched with espresso) anytime. The menu, which changes seasonally, is the same for lunch and dinner. When the weather is pleasant, ask for a table on the outdoor patio. A well-chosen wine list is also a highlight here. ♦ Italian ♦ Reservations recommended. Daily lunch and dinner. 996.2351; fax 996.3148 ♿. Also at: 6480 Washington St (between Mission and Oak Sts), Yountville. 944.2070; fax 944.9317 ♿

Wine Country Gifts Stop here to pick up ceramic and terra-cotta serving platters, bowls, jugs, and pitchers with a grape-design motif. Most items are imported from Italy and Portugal. Ceramic wine coolers from a local Sonoma potter are also sold here. ◆ Daily. 996.3453

Coffee Garden ★$ This is a pleasant place on the plaza to pick up inexpensive sandwiches, soups, salads, pastries, and, of course, an assortment of well-brewed java. Hidden behind the deli is a pretty vine-laced patio where you can settle in with your fare when the weather is fair. ◆ Eclectic ◆ Daily breakfast, lunch, and dinner. 996.6645 ৬

51 **Homegrown Baking** ★$ Order a bagel with a cream-cheese schmear or a made-to-order sandwich to eat at the counter or at any of the half-dozen tables squeezed into this small shop. Takeout is available, too. ◆ Eclectic ◆ Daily breakfast and lunch. 122 W Napa St (between First and Second Sts W). 996.0166. ৬ Also at: Maxwell Village, 19161 Sonoma Hwy (between W Spain St and Verano Ave). 996.0177 ৬

51 **Mary Stage Jewelry** It's fun to browse through the collection of antique silver and gemstone jewelry from the Edwardian era up to the 1940s. Flatware and silver serving pieces are also sold here. ◆ Tu-Sa. 126 W Napa St (between First and Second Sts W). 938.1818

51 **Chevy's** ★$$ Fare at this "Fresh-Mex" chain includes nachos, quesadillas, and slushy margaritas made with freshly squeezed lime juice. For heartier appetites, try the fajitas *al carbon* (marinated grilled beef or chicken served with flour tortillas, guacamole, hot sauce, and rice and beans), and for four people, the giant *plato gordo* (which adds mesquite-broiled quail and jumbo shrimp to the platter). Roll it all up in the tender fresh tortillas baked on the premises. Forget about drinking wine for the moment, and have an ice-cold Mexican beer. ◆ Mexican ◆ Daily lunch and dinner. 136 W Napa St (between First and Second Sts W). 938.8009 ৬

52 **Feed Store Cafe & Bakery** ★★$ One side of this enormous former feed store (built in 1921) is a bakery with dainty cafe tables. Everything is homemade, from the oversized croissants and poppy-seed muffins to the pumpkin cheesecake and peaches-and-cream pie, sold whole or by the slice. For a quick snack, order Champagne biscotti, great oatmeal cookies, or raspberry brownies with a

FEED STORE *Cafe & Bakery*

cappuccino made from Mr. Espresso beans (a superior blend roasted over an oakwood fire)—but ask the staff to make it a double or it won't be strong enough. Next door, the popular cafe (with a sunny garden terrace in back) serves build-your-own omelettes at breakfast, as well as creative egg dishes such as the "Mission Solano Scramble" (three eggs with local jack and cheddar cheeses, chilies, and tomato). Lunch here comprises burgers, hot dogs, salads, and several inventive sandwiches. ◆ Eclectic ◆ Daily breakfast and lunch. 529 First St W (south of W Napa St). 938.2122 ৬

53 **Cat & the Fiddle** This is a store for romantics and subscribers to *Victoria* or *Country Life*. It's filled with English and French country antiques, sentimental children's books and toys, hand-painted furniture, and lots of trinkets decorated with bows and lace. ◆ Daily. 153 W Napa St (between First and Second Sts W). 996.5651 ৬

53 **Sonoma Country Store** Suffused with the scent of lavender and dried flowers, this large, airy shop stocks majolica dinnerware, handblown glass, decorative frames, terra-cotta figurines, country linens and tablemats, beeswax candles—in short, everything to turn your house into Sonoma's version of Provence or Tuscany. ◆ Daily. 165 W Napa St (between First and Second Sts W). 996.0900 ৬

SONOMA VALLEY INN

54 **Sonoma Valley Inn** $$ On a busy street one block from Sonoma Plaza, this Best Western property has 75 comfortable rooms and suites, all with private baths and no-nonsense modern decor; some have wood-burning fireplaces, Jacuzzis, or kitchenettes. There's a pool and spa, and a continental breakfast is provided. ◆ 550 Second St W (south of W Napa St). 938.9200, 800/334.KRUG (in CA); 800-528-1234 (elsewhere in the US); fax 938.0935 ৬

55 **Lainie's Cuisine to Go** ★★★$ Stop at this take-out place for the full-service **Elaine Bell Catering Company** (Bell is the culinary director at **Sterling Vineyards** in Napa Valley) on your way up the valley for delectable morning pastries: honeybran muffins, banana-nut muffins, cappuccino

brownies, chocolate-chip cookies. Everything looks (and tastes) fresh and good, from chicken tabbouleh salad and special red-skinned potato salad to vegetarian lasagna and meaty pork ribs glazed with Lainie's barbecue sauce. The menu changes every Tuesday. The shop will concoct a special box lunch with 48 hours' notice (choose from half-a-dozen appealing menus), or come in and select the lunch yourself. ♦ Eclectic take-out ♦ Tu-Sa breakfast, lunch, and early dinner. 682 W Napa St (between Fifth St W and Hwy 12). 996.5226; fax 996.5773 ♿

56 Artisan Bakers Tear into a crusty loaf of dry jack and garlic sourdough or one of the other award-winning loaves of bread at this bakery. The Ponsford and Jones families bake more than a dozen types of fresh bread daily, including potato rosemary, multigrain, and pugliese, all of which have won gold medals at the Sonoma County Fair. Pastries, pizza by the slice, and cold drinks are also sold. ♦ Daily. 750 W Napa St (between Fifth St W and Hwy 12). 939.1765 ♿

57 Trojan Horse Inn $$ Innkeepers Susan and Brian Scott redecorated their blue, wood-frame bed-and-breakfast inn, which was built in 1880 as the home of a Sonoma pioneer family. They did all the plasterwork, wallpapering, and painting themselves and have made each of the six light and airy rooms, all with a private bath, quite different in character.

The spacious first-floor **Bridal Veil Room** has a wood-burning stove and a canopy bed decked out in white Battenberg lace. On the second story, the **Walden Pond Room** is painted a deep shade of green and has a lovely, carved hardwood bed. The **Grape Arbor Room**, in shades of silver, lavender, and rose, has a border of stenciled grapes and its own two-person Jacuzzi. The inn has bicycles for guests' use, an outdoor Jacuzzi on the patio beside the creek, and a large garden hidden from the street. ♦ 19455 Sonoma Hwy (north of W Napa St). 996.2430 ♿

58 Hanzell Vineyards When former ambassador to Italy James D. Zellerbach established this boutique winery in the late 1950s, he set out to emulate the wines he admired in Burgundy. He modeled the two-story winery's stone facade after Clos de Vougeot, a famous Burgundian property, and finished off his idea by ordering a shipment of French oak barrels to age his Chardonnay. In 1975, the winery was purchased by Australian heiress Barbara de Brye, and today it is owned

and run by her family. The winery still produces an intense, full-bodied Chardonnay, along with Burgundian-style Pinot Noir. The wine maker, Bob Sessions, previously worked at **Mayacamas Winery.** ♦ Tasting, sales, and tours by appointment only. 18596 Lomita Ave (between Robinson St and Hwy 12). 996.3860; fax 996.3862

Hot Springs Resorts

At the northwest end of Sonoma are the old resort towns of **Boyes Hot Springs, Fetters Hot Springs, Agua Caliente** (Spanish for "hot water"), and **El Verano** (see the map on page 77). Local Indians discovered the hot springs and brought their sick to bathe in the healing waters, but it was the young British naval officer Captain Henry Boyes, urged on by General Mariano Vallejo, who developed the sites as resort areas. By the turn of the century, San Franciscans were taking their families north by train—and later in their private cars—to spend summers at the popular resorts. These vacation destinations became less family-oriented during Prohibition; speakeasies served bootleg liquor, the atmosphere was rowdy, and madams such as Spaniard Kitty Lombardi set the tone. Today only a few vestiges of the hot springs' heyday remain, notably the **Sonoma Mission Inn & Spa** in Boyes Hot Springs.

59 Maxwell Farms Park Picnic spots, hiking trails, and a playground for kids are just minutes from downtown Sonoma in this regional park with about 85 acres of woods and meadows along Sonoma Creek. The farm once belonged to turn-of-the-century conservationist George Maxwell, an advocate for small farmers. A footpath runs along the creek; the **Sonoma Bike Path** (see page 91), which runs from **Sebastiani Vineyards** past **Depot Park** and **Lachryma Montis,** is a scenic route into the park for bikers and pedestrians. Shady picnic facilities are available. ♦ Parking fee. Day-use only. Entrance at Verano Ave and Riverside Dr, El Verano. 938.2794

60 Little Switzerland Kick up your heels to the live polka, tango, and waltz music at this popular weekend dance hall. All the fun people are here—they'll even tell you so on the phone. A menu of beer sausages and dumplings adds to the European atmosphere. ♦ Cover. Sa-Su. Reservations recommended. Grove St and Riverside Dr, El Verano. 938.9990 ♿

61 Fruit Basket Stop here for a veritable cornucopia representing the best of Sonoma County produce at good prices, plus dried fruits and nuts, bulk foods, farm-fresh eggs, cherry juice from the **Cherry Tree,** and an array of Sonoma wines. ♦ Daily. 18474 Sonoma Hwy (south of Boyes Blvd), Boyes Hot Springs. 996.7433

61 Good Time Bicycle Company Owner Doug McKesson will deliver his well-maintained rental bikes to your hotel or bed-and-breakfast inn by prior arrangement. Back at the shop, he sells bicycles, racing gear, accessories, and books on local biking routes. If you're pedaling his way, stop in for updated route advice and information on guided tours. ♦ Daily. 18503 Sonoma Hwy (south of Boyes Blvd), Boyes Hot Springs. 938.0453; fax 939.1505

62 Sonoma Mission Inn & Spa $$$$ Native Americans were the first to appreciate this Boyes Hot Springs site. They were attracted to its underground mineral springs and used the area as a sacred healing ground for many years. Then in the mid-1800s, an eccentric San Francisco physician, Dr. T.M. Leavenworth, built a water-storage tank and a small bathhouse here, creating a small spa of sorts. It's rumored that right after the doc built his little spa, he promptly burned it down, all due to a tiff with his wife. It wasn't until 1883 that English adventurer Captain Henry Boyes built a posh hot-water spa at this site, which became a fashionable summer retreat for San Francisco's wealthy Nob Hill set. About 40 years later, the spa was hit by another devastating fire, and the present California Mission–style inn wasn't built until 1927. It was completely renovated in the 1980s, and more rooms were added in 1986. Today it's Sonoma's premier luxury retreat, drawing such stars as Barbra Streisand, Harrison Ford, Oprah Winfrey, Tom Cruise, and Billy Crystal, to name a few. The 170 guest rooms and suites are decorated in soft shades of peach and pink; each has ceiling fans, plantation-style shutters, a TV set and VCR, and down comforters on the beds. The newer rooms have grand, granite bathrooms, some have fireplaces and terraces, and most overlook the eucalyptus-shaded grounds.

The primary draw here, however, is the state-of-the-art European-style spa (see below). The eight-acre site also includes a spring-fed stream (the source of the inn's privately bottled water); two pools (the pool by the spa is heated to a toasty 92 degrees year-round); two lighted, championship tennis courts; a fitness room equipped with treadmills, stationary bikes, and other exercise machines; and two restaurants. The resort pipes naturally hot artesian mineral water from 1,100 feet underground into its pools and whirlpools. The water was discovered after a two-year search for a source of hot, mineral-rich water on the property (the springs used by local Native Americans and subsequent residents became dormant in the early 1960s). The inn's guests have access to the nearby 18-hole **Sonoma Golf Club,** too (see page 99). The estab-

lishment is a member of the prestigious Preferred Hotels & Resorts Worldwide organization. ♦ 18140 Sonoma Hwy (at Boyes Blvd), Boyes Hot Springs. 938.9000, 800/862.4945 (for reservations made in CA), 800/358.9022 (for reservations made elsewhere in the US) &

Within the Sonoma Mission Inn & Spa:

The Spa Reserve well ahead, especially on weekends, for a wide range of spa treatments in a glamorous, pristine, coed setting, complete with soft lights and soothing music. The possibilities here range from individual body treatments and aerobic and yoga classes to custom-designed one- to five-day packages of diet and exercise programs. Choose from several types of massages (including Swedish/Esalen, reflexology, shiatsu, aromatherapy, and sports massages), body scrubs, body wraps, various facials, or a go-for-broke, all-in-one treatment. Also available are full salon services, fitness and nutrition evaluations, a small weight room with exercise machines and TV sets, and even tarot-card readings and personal meditation consultations. One favorite therapy is a relaxing body massage topped off with a purifying wrap of steaming Irish linens infused with fragrant herbs. Afterward, become even more relaxed (if that's possible) in the bathhouse sauna, steam room, whirlpool bath, or outdoor swimming pool. The pool and both the indoor and outdoor whirlpools are filled with the inn's hot artesian mineral water. The large roster of famous and not-so-famous guests swear by the spa's restorative powers. ♦ Must be at least 18 years old to use the spa facilities. Reservations required for body treatments. Hotel guests: daily; nonguests: M-F, Su &

The Grille ★★★$$$ Chef Mark Vann emphasizes fresh local produce and naturally raised meats in his menus, which change seasonally, and his wine list is extensive—more than 200 Napa and Sonoma selections. For lunch, he offers sandwiches, salads, pasta, fish, and other light fare, as well as a classic cheeseburger. Dinner entrées include good pasta and fish dishes, along with his signature dish, grilled Sonoma double-cut lamb chops served with whole roasted garlic, red-wine sauce, and potato gratin. A good selection of dishes low in fat, sodium, and cholesterol are always available on the "spa" menu. And for those not counting calories, don't miss the crème brûlée for dessert. The elegant peaches-and-cream dining room has tables overlooking the pool and garden area, and when the weather is mild, ask for a seat on the terrace. A full bar is located next to the restaurant. ♦ California ♦ M-Sa lunch and dinner; Su brunch and dinner. Reservations recommended &

The Cafe ★★$$ Famous for its generous breakfasts and Italian-inspired lunch fare, this handsomely remodeled cafe includes a wine bar and market. At the height of summer, it's a refreshing spot for lunch, with its open kitchen, green-and-white decor, and old-fashioned ceiling fans. And this is one restaurant where everyone in the family can find something to like, from a nice selection of salads to burgers (the Sonoma burger is topped with Swiss cheese, sautéed onions, mushrooms, and sour cream), savvy pasta dishes, and hip California pizzas from the wood-burning oven. Smoothies and shakes are served, too, and the wine bar features more than a dozen Sonoma wines by the glass. A "spa" menu featuring low-fat, low-cholesterol meals is available as well. Take home **Sonoma Mission Inn & Spa** sweatshirts from the marketplace, along with books and all the appurtenances of country life in the Italian-Californian style. ♦ California-Italian ♦ Daily breakfast, lunch, and dinner. Reservations recommended ♿

63 Sonoma Golf Club Originally designed in 1926 by Sam Whiting and Willie Watson (who also designed the Lakeside Course at San Francisco's Olympic Club), this 18-hole championship course has been completely restored by the renowned golf-course architect Robert Muir Graves. It has a spectacular setting: more than 177 acres and three lakes bordered with centuries-old oak and redwood trees with the majestic Mayacamas Mountains in the background. The Japanese owners offer both a Californian and a Japanese menu in the clubhouse restaurant. ♦ Daily. 17700 Arnold Dr (off Boyes Blvd), Sonoma. 996.4852; fax 996.5750

64 Agua Caliente Mineral Springs Cool off at this family swimming spot, which has a warm-water mineral pool and a cool-water diving pool, plus a special kids' pool and a picnic area with barbecue pits. ♦ M-Th, Sa-Su mid-May to Sept; Sa-Su Oct to mid-May. 17350 Vailetti Dr (off the Sonoma Hwy), Agua Caliente. 996.6822

65 Carmenet Vineyard This estate's steep, terraced vineyards near the crown of the Mayacamas Mountains date from the 19th century. They were reworked in 1981 when Chalone, a small premium-wine company that also owns top-rated **Chalone Vineyard, Edna Valley Vineyard,** and **Acacia,** bought the property. Chalone replanted the vineyard to Bordeaux varietals and began making the kind of blends the Bordelaise refer to as *carmenet,* hence the name. Cool, underground aging cellars hold French oak barrels of **Carmenet** estate red, a Bordeaux-style wine made from a blend of Cabernet Sauvignon, Merlot, and Cabernet Franc that consistently earns high marks. Wine maker Jeffrey Baker's white reserve is mostly Sauvignon Blanc blended with a small amount of Sémillon; the inexpensive, well-made Colombard comes from old vines just off the Silverado Trail in Napa Valley. ♦ Tours by appointment only. 1700 Moon Mountain Dr (off the Sonoma Hwy just outside of Agua Caliente), Sonoma. 996.5870; fax 996.5302

Glen Ellen

The nucleus of early Glen Ellen was the sawmill General Vallejo built on **Sonoma Creek** in the mid-19th century. Before long, wine makers from all over Europe had followed pioneering vintner Joshua Chauvet to the area, planting vineyards and establishing landmark wineries in the heart of the **Valley of the Moon.** When the narrow-gauge railroad tracks reached the town of Glen Ellen in 1879, the rural community was invaded by scores of San Franciscans, and the saloons, dance halls, and brothels that opened to serve the city slickers turned Glen Ellen into a country cousin of the Barbary Coast. Author Jack London came to have a look and stayed to write at the place he dubbed **Beauty Ranch** (now known as **Jack London State Historic Park**). The diminutive town, which for many years was home to the late food writer and novelist M.F.K. Fisher, is a quiet backwater now, its bawdy days left far behind.

66 Valley of the Moon Winery In 1941 San Francisco salami king Enrico Parducci bought a defunct winery with 500 acres of vineyards laid out in 1851 by the Civil War hero "Fighting" Joe Hooker. The property was owned at one time by newspaper tycoon William Randolph Hearst's father, Senator George Hearst, who introduced varietals from France and enjoyed pouring his own wines at his home in the nation's capital. The original structure, a low-slung stone building with a galvanized tin roof, is still used today. The enormous California bay laurel in front (featured on the wines' label) is at least 400 years old and is protected by a special city ordinance. For years this winery was known for its jug wines, but the Parducci family began making affordable estate-bottled premium wines in the early 1980s. Taste them all here—Chardonnay, Sémillon, and Cabernet—or take a bottle over to the grassy picnic area beside the creek. ♦ Tasting and sales daily. 777 Madrone Rd (off the Sonoma Hwy). 996.6941; fax 996.5809 ♿

Restaurants/Clubs: Red   Hotels: Blue
Shops/♟ Outdoors: Green   Wineries/Sights: Black

99

67 B.R. Cohn Winery As manager of the rock 'n' roll band the Doobie Brothers, Bruce R. Cohn guided the group to fame and fortune. He used his share of the fortune to buy this beautiful property, then known as **Olive Hill Vineyards,** in 1974. He sold the grapes in the beginning, but in 1984 he released his first wines. Every year the winery makes a highly rated Cabernet with grapes from the **Olive Hill Vineyard** on the slopes of a rounded hill planted with gnarled olive trees. Cohn also produces two Chardonnays, plus Merlot and Pinot Noir, and continues to manage both his music enterprises and the winery from an office in Sonoma. ♦ Tasting and sales daily by appointment only. 15140 Sonoma Hwy (north of Madrone Rd). 938.4064; fax 938.4585 &

68 Oak Hill Farm Stop here for organic summer fruits and vegetables, including vine-ripened tomatoes and fresh garlic, plus bouquets of flowers. ♦ Th-Sa mid-June to Oct. 15101 Sonoma Hwy (north of Madrone Rd). 996.6643

69 Garden Court Cafe ★$ Hearty country breakfasts at this simple roadside cafe feature three eggs, home fries, toast or biscuits, and fresh fruit. At lunchtime stop in for straightforward burgers, sandwiches, and salads. ♦ American ♦ W-Su breakfast and lunch. 13875 Sonoma Hwy (north of Madrone Rd). 935.1565 &

70 Sonoma Valley Regional Park In the springtime, the wildflower preserve in this park six miles north of Sonoma is a carpet of California poppies, lupines, wild irises, and other native flowers. You'll also find a picnic area and hiking and bike paths. ♦ Entrance on the east side of Sonoma Hwy, north of Madrone Rd

71 Three Springs Ranch $$ It's easy to imagine staying for a week at this cottage in the Valley of the Moon. Amenities include a large living room with a wood-burning stove and a fully equipped kitchen. Two bedrooms, one with a queen-size bed, the other with twin beds, make it ideal for two couples or a group of friends. The quilts are handmade, and owners Jerry and Bettylou Hutton have installed baseboard heaters, air conditioners, and a TV set with a VCR. A flagstone patio next to the lawn is furnished with Victorian garden furniture and an umbrella, while the front porch boasts white wicker furniture and an unbeatable view of the Sonoma Mountains. No smoking is allowed. ♦ 12851 Sonoma Hwy (near Arnold Dr). 996.1777

GAIGE HOUSE INN

72 Gaige House $$ Built in 1890 for the town butcher, A.E Gaige, this brown-and-beige Italianate Queen Anne Victorian home is now a comfortable bed-and-breakfast inn in the heart of old Glen Ellen. Innkeeper Ardath Rouas, one of the original partners in Napa Valley's acclaimed **Auberge du Soleil,** has furnished the interior with large canvases of abstract art, a Balinese armoire, and oversized lounge chairs. The nine bedrooms all have private baths, queen- or king-size beds, and cozy quilts folded over quilt racks. The largest is the **Gaige Suite,** the old master bedroom, furnished with handsome antiques, its own Jacuzzi, and a private deck. A full country breakfast is served in the formal dining room or outside on the terrace on summer mornings. (Bay Area locals will enjoy the freshly ground Peet's coffee.) The large lawn with a brick-edged swimming pool along Calabazas Creek is an ideal spot for an afternoon of relaxation. ♦ 13540 Arnold Dr (off the Sonoma Hwy). 935.0237, 800/935.0237; fax 935.6411

72 Glen Ellen Inn ★$$ Christian and Karen Bertrand prepare a variety of cuisines in their romantic restaurant using the freshest local produce and ingredients available. Lunch entrées might include warm duck salad with pomegranate-Zinfandel dressing and cold poached salmon salad with caper-dill vinaigrette; dinners may feature grilled prawns served on fettucine with saffron cream sauce, grill pork tenderloin with a Cabernet-honey sauce, and vegetarian cannelloni with wild mushrooms, scallions, and roasted tomatoes. Call in advance for a synopsis of the latest offerings on the changing menu. ♦ Eclectic ♦ Tu-Su lunch and dinner. Reservations required. 13670 Arnold Dr (off the Sonoma Hwy). 996.6409

72 Jack London Lodge $ Set beside a creek and the entrance to **Jack London State Historic Park,** this two-story motel has 22 fairly large guest rooms, all with private baths and functional decor brightened with country prints; ask for one of the upstairs rooms. It's hardly luxury, but it's just fine for the budget traveler, and it even has a creekside swimming pool. ♦ 13740 Arnold Dr (off the Sonoma Hwy). 938.8510 ♿

Adjacent to the Jack London Lodge:

Jack London Grill ★$$ This is the spot to get hardwood-smoked country pork ribs, garlic-herb–roasted chicken, steaks, fish specials, and large quantities of vegetables served family-style. ♦ American ♦ W-Su lunch and dinner; winter hours vary. 935.1071; fax 939.8085 ♿

Jack London Saloon Plaid shirts, hiking boots, and the lumberjack look are de rigueur at this historic saloon. The bar has been pouring drinks to locals and city slickers alike since Jack London's days, and the saloon seems to have saved every bit of memorabilia from those rowdy years. On warm summer evenings, it's fun to linger over drinks outside on the patio beside the creek. ♦ Daily. 996.3100 ♿

72 Jack London Bookstore
Established by Winifred Kingman and her late husband, Russ, this bookstore is filled with works by and about Glen Ellen's famous writer. Russ Kingman was one of the country's leading experts on Jack London, and some of his large collection of memorabilia about the writer is displayed in the store. It is a resource much used by London scholars and aficionados. Here you can find first editions by London, rare and out-of-print works, and other books not relating to London. It's a cozy, unintimidating place to spend an afternoon and is one of an endangered species: a serious small bookstore. ♦ M, W-Su. 14300 Arnold Dr (off the Sonoma Hwy). 996.2888

72 Jack London Village Almost hidden in the hoary oaks along Sonoma Creek, this complex of ramshackle redwood buildings is home to a series of small shops and artisan's workshops. ♦ 14301 Arnold Dr (off the Sonoma Hwy)

Within the Jack London Village:

Spinner's Web This shop crammed with exotic fleece, weaving supplies, and spinning wheels just may inspire you to try your hand at traditional crafts. Occasional classes are offered, and books on weaving are sold along with concentrated, natural extracts that can dye cottons, wools, and other fibers. If you're interested in textiles, pick up a copy of "Sonoma County Fiber Trails," a map that lists spinners, weavers, felters, knitters, and

sources for fleeces and fibers. ♦ Daily. 935.7006 ♿

73 Village Mercantile An ever-changing selection of teapots and cups, plus other items collected by owner Raegene Africa, can be found in this shop. Some are choice pieces from the 1930s and 1940s; others are reproductions of antique pieces. Specialty teas are available, too. ♦ Tu-Sa. 13647 Arnold Dr (off the Sonoma Hwy). 938.1330

73 Glen Ellen Village Market Now an all-purpose grocery market, this store dates back to Glen Ellen's pioneer days. You'll find all the basics here, plus a bakery, wine section, meat department, and catering services. ♦ Daily. 13751 Arnold Dr (off the Sonoma Hwy). 996.6728

74 Glenelly Inn $$ Originally built as an inn for train travelers in 1916, this charming place on a rural road retains the ambience of another era with its long verandas furnished with wicker chairs. The inn consists of two peach-and-cream buildings set on a hillside, with a terrace garden shaded by old oaks in back. A hot tub is sheltered by an arbor twined with grapevines and old roses. All eight rooms have private baths and private entrances. Pine armoires, ceiling fans, and claw-foot tubs add to the country feel; some rooms also have wood-burning stoves. Innkeeper Kristi Hallamore pays attention to details such as reading lights, down comforters, and firm mattresses. Breakfast includes a hot dish, fruit, and fresh-baked muffins. ♦ 5131 Warm Springs Rd (off Bennett Valley Rd). 996.6720

BENZIGER

75 Benziger Family Winery Young wine maker Mike Benziger was scouting vineyard properties in Sonoma Valley when he came across this historic estate, established by the carpenter Julius Wegener, who received the land as payment from General Vallejo for constructing his Sonoma home. Benziger was so taken with the steep, terraced vineyard site that he convinced his father, Bruno Benziger, to buy it. **Glen Ellen Winery,** as it was originally called (the name was changed in 1994), flourished under the inspired marketing of the elder Benziger, the founder of a wine-and-spirits distributorship; in little more than a decade, it grew from a small family operation to Sonoma Valley's second-largest winery. The straightforward wines, especially the ready-to-drink, modestly priced Proprietor's Reserve Chardonnay and Cabernet Sauvignon, have won an unassailable place on the market; the best wines are those made from grapes grown on the steep, terraced **Home Ranch Vineyard.** Sauvignon Blanc, Merlot, and Zinfandel are also made here. The property includes a folksy tasting room, a classic California-barn winery building, and a picnic grove. ♦ Tasting, sales, and tours daily. 1883 London Ranch Rd (off Arnold Dr). 935.3000 ♿

76 Jack London State Historic Park Just as Robert Louis Stevenson is associated with Napa Valley, Sonoma Valley is Jack London territory. It was London who, in his 1913 novel *The Valley of the Moon,* recounted an Indian legend that says Sonoma means "valley of many moons." This 800-acre park, a memorial to the adventurer and writer, is located on what was once London's beloved **Beauty Ranch.** The highest-paid author of his time, with *Call of the Wild* (1903) and *The Sea Wolf* (1904) under his belt by the age of 28, London settled permanently on his Glen Ellen ranch in 1909. Here visitors can experience the unspoiled landscape much the way it was during London's time.

Just off the Sonoma Highway on the east side of the valley, the well-maintained park is a paradise for hikers and horseback riders, with nine miles of trails. You can visit the restored white-frame cottage where London and his wife, Charmian, lived and where he wrote many of his books, as well as the log cabin and artificial lake he constructed in tribute to his Klondike days. And don't forget to visit the remarkable **Pig Palace** with its two 40-foot-high silos.

You'll also see the eerie remains of **Wolf House,** the dream home built by London and his wife, which mysteriously burned down days before they were to move in. Charmian later built a scaled-down version of **Wolf House,** which she dubbed the **House of Happy Walls.** Now a touching museum of London memorabilia, it is filled with the furniture, art, and personal photographs the Londons had planned to keep in **Wolf House**—it even includes a collection of the successful author's rejection slips. Nearby is the tranquil grove of oaks where London is buried. In the 40 years of his life, London managed to write 51 books and 193 short stories (and somehow he also fit in two lifetimes of travel and adventure in exotic locales).

Bring a picnic, because you'll want to roam this magnificent park for hours. A rigorous three-mile trail leads to the summit of Sonoma Mountain and a breathtaking view of the Valley of the Moon. ♦ Admission fee per car. 2400 London Ranch Rd (off Arnold Dr and the Sonoma Hwy). 938.5216

Within the Jack London State Historic Park:

Sonoma Cattle Company One of the best ways to see the park is on horseback, riding down trails Jack London once used to survey his Valley of the Moon domain, past lush meadows, redwood groves, and vineyards now owned by London's descendants. The stone barn London built to house his English shire horses now stables the horses used for guided rides through the park. The company provides horses for riders of all levels and takes them out in groups of two to 20. You may sign on for a two-hour horseback ride followed by a personal tour and a picnic at **Benziger Family Winery.** Children must be at least eight years old; no previous riding experience is required. This outfit also offers rides in nearby **Sugarloaf Ridge State Park** (see page 105). ♦ Jack London State Historic Park rides: 1 Apr to 31 Oct, weather and trails permitting. Sugarloaf Ridge State Park rides: year-round. Reservations required. 996.8566

77 JVB Vineyards $ The pair of adobe cottages with terra-cotta roofs and tile floors looks right at home on this grape-growing estate. Both have decks and patios, queen-size beds, full baths, and a small kitchen areas with a coffeemaker and toaster oven (but no real stove). One of the cottages is on top of a hillside overlooking the valley; the other lies at the bottom of the hill. A full breakfast is served at the farmhouse or on the patio. Jack and Beverly Babb or their daughter Mary, the vineyard manager, will take guests through the vineyard to explain how grapes are grown. They also have a Christmas tree farm and raise ostriches. No ostrich-egg omelettes for breakfast, though—one egg would be the equivalent of 24 chicken eggs! ♦ 14335 Sonoma Hwy (north of Arnold Dr). 996.4533

77 Arrowood Vineyards and Winery When **Chateau St. Jean**'s longtime wine maker Richard Arrowood founded his own small winery in 1987, he decided to make just one Chardonnay and one Cabernet Sauvignon, using a blend of grapes from different regions. He feels he can make better wines by blending

---

Restaurants/Clubs: Red   **Hotels:** Blue
Shops/ ♟ Outdoors: Green   **Wineries/Sights:** Black

grapes from several Sonoma Valley regions, rather than by focusing on single-vineyard wines as he did at **Chateau St. Jean.** He might be onto something, as you'll see when you taste both of these consistently excellent wines at his New England–style winery's tasting room. The Maple Leaf flag flies out front right next to the American flag because Arrowood's wife, Alis, who manages the winery, was born in Canada. ♦ Tasting and sales daily; tours by appointment only. 14347 Sonoma Hwy (north of Arnold Dr). 938.5170

78 Trinity Road—Oakville Grade Buckle up for this 12-mile scenic drive from the Sonoma Highway near Glen Ellen over the Mayacamas Mountains to Highway 29 in Napa Valley at Oakville. The twists and turns, along with the panoramic views of the valley and mountains, make for an exciting ride. Be sure your brakes—and stomach—are up to the task before you set off. ♦ Off the Sonoma Hwy

79 Beltane Ranch Bed & Breakfast $$ This restored 1892 bunkhouse painted buttercup-yellow and white once belonged to the former slave and abolitionist Mammy Pleasant—who, at one time or another, was also a madam, a cook, and the mistress of British millionaire Thomas Bell. (When Bell was murdered in their posh San Francisco home, Pleasant was suspected but never indicted.) Innkeeper Rosemary Wood inherited the place from her aunt and uncle, who had raised turkeys here since the 1930s, and reopened the house as a bed-and-breakfast inn in 1981. She has four guest rooms: two simply decorated suites, another guest room upstairs, and one bedroom downstairs. (Try to get the suite with a king-size bed and wood-burning stove.) All have private baths. Wood keeps a library of books on local history, fauna, and flora, and sets up chairs in the shade of a venerable old oak. There's a tennis court and, for the less active, a hammock perfect for snoozing. Guests have the run of the 1,600-acre estate, which extends to the Napa County line and includes eight miles of hiking trails. A brisk early-morning walk should work up your appetite for the full country breakfast. ♦ 11775 Sonoma Hwy (north of Nuns Canyon Rd). 996.6501

Kenwood

The town of Kenwood, the surrounding valley, and what is now **Annadel State Park** were once part of the vast **Rancho Los Guilicos.** The name was a Spanish corruption of Wilikos, the name the Wappo Indians had given their village. In 1834, just after General Vallejo established the Sonoma presidio, smallpox and cholera epidemics reduced the local Native American population by thousands. Those who survived were later driven away or relocated to the Mendocino reservation. Juan Alvarado, the Mexican governor of California, ceded the 18,883-acre ranch to Captain John Wilson, a Scottish sea

captain who had married General Vallejo's sister-in-law, Romona Carrillo. Wilson sold the vast holding shortly after the 1846 Bear Flag uprising in Sonoma; the buyer was William Hood, another Scotsman, who had fallen in love with the valley as a young man. Hood was a shipwright, carpenter, and cabinetmaker who made his fortune in real estate in Australia, South America, Canada, and California. The old Indian settlement was soon renamed Kenwood. Laid out in the 1880s, Kenwood is built around a small central plaza where the Gothic **Kenwood Community Church** still stands. On Warm Springs Road, you can see the valley's only stone railroad depot, built in 1887 of basalt quarried in the surrounding hills. Another appealing option is to take the horse-drawn wagon tour of Kenwood's vineyards and wine caves offered by **Wine Country Wagons** (Box 1069, Kenwood, CA 95452; 833.2724).

THE KENWOOD INN & SPA

80 Kenwood Inn & Spa $$$ Former San Francisco contractor Terry Grimm and his wife, Roseann, a restaurateur who owns the Anchor Oyster Bar in San Francisco, have transformed an old antiques store into this posh pension with 12 rooms and suites. The living room and kitchen area are defined with Italianate colors—rusts and ambers—and the full breakfast continues the Italian theme, with Mediterranean egg dishes, polenta, and freshly baked fruit tarts and pastries. Outside, the Grimms have dabbed the stucco with pale washes of color and planted a romantic garden of old roses and wisteria. Each of the suites is very different in size, decor, and feeling, though all have fireplaces and private baths. Sensualists will appreciate the down comforters and Egyptian cotton sheets. One suite features faux-marble walls in yellow and amber, a yellow comforter on the bed, and a high window that looks out on a bank of green foliage. Another is drenched in burgundy, peach, and rose tones and furnished with two tapestry-covered sofas. The honeymoon suite upstairs is the most private, featuring a small stone balcony overlooking the swimming pool, a separate living room, and a dramatically canopied bed decorated in somber autumn colors. A potpourri of spa treatments have now been added, including Swedish massage, mud and enzyme wraps, manicures, and pedicures. ♦ 10400 Sonoma Hwy (south of Warm Springs Rd). 833.1293; fax 833.1247 ♿

81 Kenwood Restaurant and Bar ★★$$ The view is all vineyards from the outdoor terrace here, where you can eat in the shade of large canvas umbrellas. Inside, this California roadhouse with polished wood floors and a natural pine ceiling is simply furnished with white linens and bamboo chairs. Chef Max Schacher features the same appealing California wine-country menu at both lunch and dinner—and serves all through the afternoon. You may want to check the large, reasonably priced wine list first, and then choose dishes to go with the wine. For whites, Schacher offers sautéed oysters, clam chowder, or grilled swordfish with a fresh tomato salsa, plus an excellent Caesar salad. Red-wine aficionados can select from lamb, Petaluma duck in orange sauce, a Kenwood burger with a tall pile of thick-cut fries, and braised Sonoma rabbit with mushrooms and polenta. ♦ California ♦ Tu-Su lunch and dinner. 9900 Sonoma Hwy (south of Warm Springs Rd). 833.6326; fax 833.2238 ♿

82 Kunde Estate Winery Now famous as the site of Oscar-winning actress Geena Davis's wedding to movie director Renny Harlin *(Nightmare on Elm Street Part IV, Die Hard)* in September 1993, this winery has been around for more than a hundred years. The beauty of the winery's 2,000 acres of rolling hills covered with grapevines, oak trees, and grazing pastures attracted Davis and Harlin to this location. They exchanged their wedding vows next to stone ruins of a winery that was built here in 1882.

The Kunde family has been one of the largest grape growers in Sonoma County for many years, supplying grapes to several other wineries. Their first crush was in 1990, and the Kundes are now producing numerous wines, primarily Chardonnay, Sauvignon Blanc, Cabernet Sauvignon, Merlot, and Zinfandel. All the winery's vintages can be sampled in its tasting room. ♦ Tasting and sales daily; tours by appointment only. 10155 Sonoma Hwy (south of Warm Springs Rd). 833.5501 ♿

83 Morton's Warm Springs This spot provides the setting for a local family tradition in Kenwood for summer swimming and picnics. It has been open since 1887, and has three swimming pools heated by the naturally warm springs. Indians used to bring their sick to bathe in its waters, and early pioneers created an impromptu bathhouse by putting up a burlap sack around a wooden tub. At the turn of the century, **Warm Springs** (then called **Los Guilicos Warm Springs**) was a popular resort. The water still bubbles out of the ground at 87 degrees (about a hundred degrees too cool to be classified as a hot spring), and actually has to be cooled a bit for use in the swimming pool. Plan on spending the day here; there are 25 or so barbecues and picnic tables, plus a baseball diamond, volleyball and basketball courts, and a snack bar. ♦ Fee. Sa-Su May-Sept. 1651 Warm Springs Rd (off the Sonoma Hwy). 833.5511

84 Smothers Brothers Wine Store Comedian Tom Smothers, a Kenwood resident, makes wines from grapes grown on his Sonoma Valley ranch. The old country store that is now the tasting room pours his wines and a few of his neighbors', too— **Coturri & Sons, Van Der Kamp Champagne Cellars,** and **Pat Paulsen Vineyards** (yes, it's owned by the comedian who declared a mock candidacy for president in the 1960s). This is also the headquarters for wine-country condiments, gadgets, and paraphernalia. There's a picnic area, too. ♦ Daily. 9575 Sonoma Hwy (north of Warm Springs Rd). 833.1010; fax 833.2313 ♿

85 Kenwood Vineyards Originally built in 1906 by the Italian Pagani brothers, who peddled their jug wines from door to door, the property's name changed from **Pagani** to **Kenwood** when the Martin Lee family, newcomers to the business, bought it in 1970. They promptly restored and modernized the wood barns that still serve as the cellars, and with Michael Lee as wine maker they launched a series of excellent Cabernets and Zinfandels. His top wines are the Artist Series Cabernets, with labels based on a painting by a different artist every year. Artists have included David Lance Goines, Joseph Neary, and James Harrill. The winery also makes Chardonnay from Beltane Ranch grapes and an outstanding Sauvignon Blanc, a blend of grapes from 17 vineyards from Geyserville to Carneros. ♦ Tasting and sales daily; tours by appointment only. 9592 Sonoma Hwy (north of Warm Springs Rd). 833.5891

86 Iron Rose Art for the home and garden created by local artists using local materials is the specialty of this shop along Kenwood's main street. Look for hand-painted birdhouses, whimsical iron sculpture, iron bells, candle holders, and other distinctive pieces. ♦ M, W-Su. 9212 Sonoma Hwy (north of Warm Springs Rd). 833.1153

Cafe Citti

86 Cafe Citti ★★$$ Luca and Linda Citti cook their hearts out at this small, casual Italian takeout and trattoria. Lunch features sandwiches on homemade focaccia bread along with pasta dishes with a choice of sauces. For picnics, try one of the spit-roasted chickens. Add a few salads and biscotti or a slice of ricotta cheese torte and you'll have a veritable feast. Table service may be slow when it's busy, but the food tastes authentically Italian. Italian groceries are available, too, and the espresso is good and strong. ♦ Italian ♦ Daily lunch and dinner. 9049 Sonoma Hwy (north of Warm Springs Rd). 833.2690 ઙ

Chateau St. Jean

87 Chateau St. Jean One of the best-known boutique wineries of the late 1970s, this establishment now produces well over 150,000 cases per year. Wine maker Don Van Staaveren (who replaced Richard Arrowood when he moved on to open **Arrowood Vineyards and Winery,** just up the road) concentrates on single-vineyard wines, notably those from five designated vineyards: **Robert Young, Belle Terre, Frank Johnson, McCrea,** and the estate's 70-acre **St. Jean Vineyard.** The 250-acre estate in the shelter of Sugarloaf Ridge was once the preserve of a wealthy businessman; his former living room is used as the tasting room, and visitors may picnic on the lawn in front of the country mansion. The view of Sonoma Valley from the mock medieval tower is one of the highlights of a visit here. ♦ Tasting, sales, and self-guided tours daily. 8555 Sonoma Hwy (near Adobe Canyon Rd). 833.4134 ઙ

88 St. Francis Winery and Vineyards The original vineyard, planted in 1910, was part of a wedding gift to Alice Kunde (of the prominent grape-growing family) and her husband, Will Behler. The hundred-acre estate is now owned by Lloyd Canton and former San Francisco furniture dealer Joe Martin and his wife, Emma. Top wines include their fine Merlot (regular and reserve), the Barrel Select Reserve Chardonnay, and the Sonoma Mountain Cabernet. They also make Gewürztraminer. The oak tasting room with burgundy awnings features chilled white wines to purchase for a picnic and cold Calistoga water for the kids. From the patio area equipped with picnic tables, you can enjoy views of the surrounding vineyards. ♦ Tasting and sales daily. 8450 Sonoma Hwy (near Adobe Canyon Rd). 833.4666; fax 833.6534 ઙ

89 Landmark Vineyards The whitewashed California Mission–style complex houses one of the first wineries in the state that concentrated primarily on Chardonnay. The owner is now Damaris Deere Ethridge, the great-granddaughter of John Deere (famous for his tractor company). There's a picnic area near the winery's pond. ♦ Tasting and sales daily; tours by appointment only. 101 Adobe Canyon Rd (off the Sonoma Hwy). 833.0053

90 Buckley Lodge ★★$$$; Since its opening in 1994, this pleasant dining spot (on the former site of **Oreste's Golden Bear Restauranté**) has received rave reviews for its excellent wine country cuisine. Nestled in an out-of-the-way spot two miles off the Sonoma Highway at the foot of Mount Hood, it serves tasty dishes prepared with fresh local ingredients such as Sonoma field greens, vine-ripened tomatoes, smoked Delta sturgeon, lamb, duck, and chicken. A fireplace in the bar and lovely views of a nearby creek add warmth, charm, and romance, making a meal here a special experience. ♦ California ♦ M-Sa lunch and dinner; Su brunch and dinner. Reservations recommended. 1717 Adobe Canyon Rd (off the Sonoma Hwy). 833.5562 ઙ

91 Sugarloaf Ridge State Park The conical ridge that rises behind **Chateau St. Jean** in the heart of the Mayacamas mountain range is known as Sugarloaf Ridge. Follow Adobe Canyon Road as it winds into the hills, past **Buckley Lodge,** to the entrance of this spectacular state park. Archaeologists now believe Sugarloaf Ridge was first inhabited 7,000 years ago. The steep hills of the 2,700-acre park, covered in redwood, fir, oak, and chaparral, offer more than 25 miles of hiking and riding trails. From the park's highest elevations, views extend to Sonoma and Napa Valley. You can even spot San Francisco Bay and the Sierra Nevada from certain sites. Near the entrance to the park, look for the remains of old charcoal-burning areas that Congressman John King Luttrell used for the production of charcoal in the late 1890s.

The park includes 50 family campsites, each with a tent space, barbecue, and picnic table. There are corrals for horses, too. A rigorous foot trail (Goodspeed Trail) leads to the adjacent **Hood Mountain Regional Park** (see page 107), but "good speed" here means several hours of hiking. ♦ Admission. 2605 Adobe Canyon Rd (3 miles off the Sonoma Hwy). For camping reservations, call 800/444.7275

Within the Sugarloaf Ridge State Park:

Sonoma Cattle Company It's fun to tour the park on horseback with knowledgeable guides here who can identify the local flora and fauna. And the trails along the Mayacamas Mountains offer great panoramic views of the valleys and ocean. There are

Making the Most of Your Winery Visits

The number of wineries in **Napa** and **Sonoma** can be daunting to the first-time visitor. From the highway, the names of famous wineries whiz by, and it's natural to want to stop at all of them, but too many visits in one day—particularly too many tours—can leave you exhausted and ready to head for the nearest beer. You should take one or two tours just to get the gist of how wine is made. But after that, the rows of stainless-steel fermentation tanks, presses, and bottling lines quickly become redundant.

In choosing an itinerary, keep in mind that some wineries present information better than others. For example, **Robert Mondavi**'s tours always include well-thought-out educational components, and the winery offers several tours, depending on your interests. **St. Supéry** has a good self-guided tour that presents information on soil types and pruning methods. And it's definitely worth visiting a historic winery, such as **Beringer** or **Buena Vista,** to get a glimpse of 19th-century wine-making practices.

However, the focus of most visits should be tasting the wines. The general procedure is to start with the simplest white wines (such as Chenin Blanc and Colombard) and move up the ladder through the more complex Sauvignon Blanc and Chardonnay to the red wines, finishing with a dessert wine. Most wineries do not offer food along with their wines, although some provide crackers to clear the palate. However, many are now stocking limited picnic supplies so you may purchase cheese, crackers, packaged cold cuts, and more, without having to drive back to town.

Sampling all of the offered vintages may be too much for one set of taste buds; your palate can quickly become fatigued and you may not be able to distinguish the differences. And if you're driving, you risk becoming a potential hazard on the highway. The best strategy is to limit your winery visits to only a few per day and choose the wines you'd like to taste rather than opting to sample the winery's entire lineup. Another essential is to spit out the wine after you've had a chance to let it register on your palate, or pour out the remaining sample after you've taken a sip (special buckets are usually provided for this purpose). These are practices the professionals engage in all the time, so be assured, no one will be offended by such actions.

If you're hoping to find bargain prices at the wineries, you'll most likely be disappointed. Wineries don't want to compete against the shops that sell their products, so prices at the wineries are generally higher than in the stores. The only time it's worth buying wines from the source is if the winery is offering selections from its "library"—that is, older vintages that are no longer available in wineshops—or if the wines are made

in such limited quantities that they are sold only at the tasting room.

There is absolutely no obligation to buy a bottle of wine when you visit a tasting room. The rooms are there to promote brand recognition, not push bottles; this is evident from the number of non-wine-related objects bearing the name and logo of the winery that are for sale in many tasting rooms: T-shirts, baseball hats, umbrellas, refrigerator magnets, pasta sauces—you name it.

A good tactic for visiting the wine country is to include a mix of large and small wineries in your itinerary and set an easy pace (you're here to relax, remember?). If you like Chardonnay, for example, you might want to organize your itinerary around top Chardonnay estates. Your hotel concierge or innkeeper should be able to advise you, but you'll have to carefully assess any suggestions because not everybody living in the wine country is well informed about wine. Before you begin planning your trip, ask a wine merchant you know and trust which wineries and estates he or she suggests visiting. Read up on the latest new wineries in wine magazines such as *The Wine Spectator,* study the wine column in your local newspaper, and start buying the Wednesday edition of *The New York Times* for Frank J. Prial's informative column written with the layperson in mind.

If you really have a strong interest in wine, a visit to a small premium winery that requires an appointment may be the highlight of your tour, since you'll get the winery's story straight from the source, often from the wine maker who has created the wine. Understandably, small wineries that have no tasting-room staff or even formal tasting rooms have a limited amount of time to receive visitors, but it doesn't hurt to ask.

Finally, keep in mind that you don't have to do all your tastings at the wineries. You can take a bottle on a picnic or visit one of the local restaurants to try a fine wine with food—which, after all, is the way wine is supposed to be enjoyed.

horses for riders of all levels available, but children must be at least eight years old. The stables are located on the valley floor. Full-moon and sunset trips may also be scheduled, and rides are offered at nearby **Jack London State Historic Park** (see page 102). ♦ Daily (weather and trails permitting). Reservations required. 996.8566

92 Oakmont Golf Club This club offers two 18-hole championship courses, both designed by Ted Robinson. The east course is considered challenging; the west course is for more casual golfers. ♦ Daily. 7025 Oakmont Dr (off the Sonoma Hwy), Santa Rosa. 538.2454, 539.0415

93 Adler Fels Founded in 1980 by Dave Coleman and his wife, Ayn Ryan, whose family had a hand in starting **Chateau St. Jean,** this tiny winery sits high atop a 26-foot-wide ridge, very near the outcropping of rock that locals have dubbed Eagle Rock (in German, that name translates to *adler fels*—hence the winery's name). The half-timbered building looks a bit like something from the Rhine or Alsace. White wine is the focus here—Chardonnay, Fumé Blanc, and Gewürztraminer. ♦ Tasting, sales, and tours daily by appointment only. 5325 Corrick La (off Los Alamos Rd), Santa Rosa. 539.3123 &

94 Hood Mountain Regional Park This 1,300-acre park in the Mayacamas Mountains offers hiking and riding trails, campgrounds, and shaded picnic sites. Clamber up Gunsight Rock Lookout for heart-stopping views of Sonoma Valley all the way to San Francisco Bay and, on occasion, the Sierra Nevada. To get to the park, follow Los Alamos Road about five miles up to the steep ridge that marks the park boundaries. ♦ Day-use fee. Weekends and holidays Oct-May. Los Alamos Rd (off the Sonoma Hwy), Santa Rosa. 527.2041

95 Annadel State Park The Pomo and Wappo Indian tribes gathered food and obsidian in the wilderness here 3,000 years before Europeans arrived in the area. In 1837 Scottish sea captain John Wilson (who was also General Vallejo's brother-in-law) received a land grant of 18,883 acres from the Mexican government; that parcel included what is now this state park. From the 1870s until the 1920s Italian stoneworkers cut paving stones from the basalt rock quarried here; production stepped up dramatically just after the 1906 earthquake, when the rebuilding of San Francisco was under way. Today this 5,000-acre park bordering the city of Santa Rosa offers nearly 40 miles of trails for hikers, horseback riders, and mountain bikers. Most of the trails interconnect and include a wide range of terrain and landscape, from rigorous mountain hiking to leisurely walks through meadows of wildflowers. You can head to Lake Ilsanjo for fishing or go bird-watching in Ledson Marsh. Camping is available in nearby **Sugarloaf Ridge State Park** (see page 105). ♦ Day-use fee. Off the Sonoma Hwy, between Kenwood and Santa Rosa. 539.3911

Bests

Jon Beckmann
Publisher, Sierra Club Books, San Francisco

After a hard day at the wineries in **Sonoma,** relax at **Piatti,** especially on the patio in good weather. The hottest restaurant in town.

For a touch of history, try Sonoma's **Swiss Hotel,** built in the mid-19th century. There are no tourists at the bar, and the restaurant is a local favorite. The food's good, and every Wednesday features pot roast and garlic mashed potatoes.

To enjoy Sonoma sans automobile, stay at the **Thistle Dew Inn,** just off the square. Owner Larry Barnett will make blueberry pancakes for breakfast.

Sonoma Plaza is almost a movie set for the wholesomeness of a small town's good old days—duck ponds, picnic tables, the early-summer ox roast (beef really), and a great selection of trees. The missions are worth visiting—this is where California began with the Bear Flag Revolt.

Chris Phelps
Wine Maker, Dominus Estate Winery, Yountville

Waking up at the **White Sulphur Springs Resort** in **St. Helena** with the birds and the deer, followed by a quick walk through the surrounding redwoods. Best when the waterfalls are full!

A piping hot bowl of café mocha crème at the **Napa Valley Coffee Roasting Company,** a great place to read the paper and meet people.

A leisurely bicycle ride with a good friend through **Pope Valley** (stopping to see the rattlesnakes at the **Pope Valley Garage**), on up to **Middletown,** looping back over **Mount St. Helena.**

Three hours with a good book in the pools at the **Calistoga Spa.**

Hiking through the vineyards in St. Helena to a dinner at **Brava Terrace** with a bottle of Cabernet, followed by a movie at **Liberty Theatre.**

Santa Rosa

In 1875 Luther Burbank took his older brother's enthusiastic advice to leave the East Coast and move to Santa Rosa. Burbank immediately liked the place. "I firmly believe, from what I have seen, that this is the chosen spot of all this earth as far as nature is concerned," he wrote. For more than 50 years the world-renowned horticulturist labored here in his greenhouse and gardens, producing more than 800 new varieties of fruits, vegetables, and plants.

Santa Rosa was once part of an immense Spanish land grant held by Doña Maria Ignacia Lopez Carrillo, the mother-in-law of General Mariano

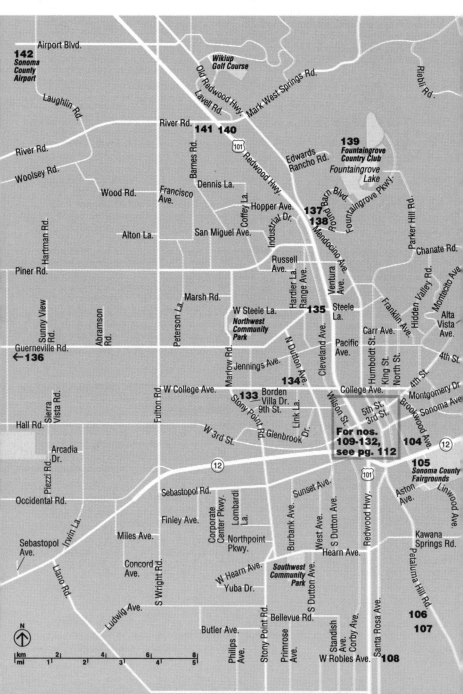

For nos. 109-132, see pg. 112

Guadalupe Vallejo. Americans first came to Santa Rosa to establish a trading post in 1846, and it was incorporated as a town eight years later.

Santa Rosa, which is Sonoma's county seat, is home to more than 100,000 people and is just minutes from the **Valley of the Moon** and about a half hour from the town of Healdsburg, in the heart of the Russian River Valley. The city is considered the hub of **Sonoma County** because most of the main roads cross here.

A quiet town that recalls another era, Santa Rosa offers a respite for those who find the country a little too quiet, but don't want San Francisco–style nightlife. **Railroad Square**, just west of the freeway in downtown Santa Rosa, is a six-square-block area of restored turn-of-the-century buildings filled with antiques shops, stores, and restaurants. And **Fourth Street**, the main artery of Santa Rosa's restored downtown area, comes alive every Thursday night from May to September with an exuberant farmers' market featuring music, street food, and entertainment that attracts folks from miles around.

History buffs will want to visit the **Sonoma County Museum** and the **Luther Burbank Home and Gardens.** Across the street from Burbank's home is the **Church Built from One Tree** in **Juilliard Park,** which was entirely constructed from the lumber provided by one enormous redwood, and now, believe it or not, is a museum devoted to Santa Rosa resident Robert L. Ripley, connoisseur of the strange and wonderful. Santa Rosa is surrounded by 5,000 acres of city, county, and state parks offering everything from walking, hiking, and horseback-riding trails to campgrounds and lakes for fishing, swimming, and boating. One of Sonoma County's top restaurants, **John Ash & Co.,** is in Santa Rosa, and bed-and-breakfasts and several comfortable inns lie on the northern outskirts of town, including the deluxe **Vintners Inn.**

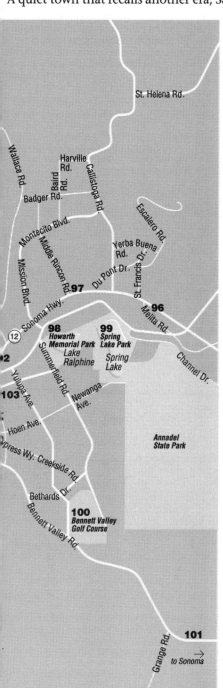

96 Melita Station Inn $ Near **Annadel State Park** on the winding country road that served as the old Sonoma Highway is a six-room bed-and-breakfast in a restored turn-of-the-century train station. This comfortable inn is filled with American folk art and antiques. Five of the six rooms have private baths, and a full country breakfast (juice, fruit, muffins or bread, and an omelette or another main course) is included. The location, at the head of the Valley of the Moon, is ideal for winery touring by bike or car. ♦ 5850 Melita Rd (off the Sonoma Hwy). 538.7712

97 Rincon Cyclery You can rent bikes by the hour, by the day, or by the week here. Take one of the 18-speed mountain bikes up to a trail in nearby **Annadel, Sugar Loaf Ridge,** or **Jack London State Parks.** Helmets and bike racks are also available. ♦ Daily. 4927-H Sonoma Hwy (at Middle Rincon Rd). 538.0868, 800/965.BIKE; fax 538.0879

98 Howarth Memorial Park Pack up that fishing pole and cooking gear and head for Lake Ralphine in this city-owned and -operated park to catch some lunch—catfish, black bass, trout, and bluegill. The park has picnic and barbecue facilities so you can cook your catch right here. After-lunch activities include a hiking trail and, for the kids, a playground, a merry-go-round, pony rides, a miniature train ride, and an animal farm. Canoes, paddleboats, rowboats, and sailboats are available to rent, too. ♦ Fee for each ride. Summerfield Rd, via Sonoma Ave or Montgomery Dr. 524.5115

99 Spring Lake Park This state park is on the east side of Santa Rosa, between Howarth Memorial Park and Annadel State Park; it has campsites, rest rooms, shower facilities, hiking and equestrian trails, and a 72-acre lake. It is open for swimming and boating during the summer and stocked with catfish, black bass, trout, and bluegill for year-round fishing. Launch your own boat or rent a sailboat, canoe, or rowboat for a modest hourly charge; the lake is a popular spot for windsurfing, too. Access to the camping area is available via Newanga Ave; the campsites are available on a first-come, first-served basis. ♦ Park: daily. Campsites: daily between Memorial Day and Labor Day; F-Su the rest of the year. 5390 Montgomery Dr (off the Sonoma Hwy). 539.8092 (general park information), 539.8082 (campground information)

100 Bennett Valley Golf Course This 18-hole municipal golf course (par 72) is shaded by trees and surrounded by mountain views. It's open to the public for individual, club, and tournament play. ♦ Daily. 3330 Yulupa Ave (off Channel Dr). 528.3673

MATANZAS CREEK WINERY

101 Matanzas Creek Winery For a particularly scenic drive, take Warm Springs Road and Enterprise Drive to Bennett Valley Road to get to this showcase winery overlooking Bennett Valley and the Sonoma Mountains. Owned by Bill and Sandra McIver, it is an inviting place, with a loggia leading up to the tasting room and tables on a deck sheltered by a centuries-old oak. Since the beginning, when Merry Edwards made the wines, the winery's Chardonnays have appeared on the most discerning wine lists in the country; and current wine makers Bill Parker and Susan Reed continue this tradition. The Chardonnays remain among the best in California, and the Sauvignon Blanc is also top-grade. The Merlot is so much in demand that it sells out every year a few weeks after it's released. You'll also find the Matanzas Creek poster by painter Mary Silverwood on sale here. ♦ Tasting, sales, and guided tours daily. 6097 Bennett Valley Rd (at Grange Rd). 528.6464; fax 571.0156

102 Petrini's Market This upscale supermarket features real butchers (how often do you see them anymore?) and a good produce section, and its extensive deli runs along an entire wall—a veritable picnic-supply emporium with barbecued chicken and ribs to go, local and imported cheeses, cold cuts, custom-made sandwiches, and breads from **Costeaux French Bakery** in Healdsburg. There's also a fair selection of Sonoma County wines. ♦ Daily. 2751 Fourth St (at Farmers La). 526.2080; fax 526.2192

102 Flamingo Resort Hotel $ Formerly called just the **Flamingo Hotel,** this landmark 1957 property on the outskirts of Santa Rosa was overhauled and renamed in the early 1990s. They couldn't do much about the architecture (call it 1950s nostalgia), but the 137 rooms and suites have been spruced up, and the heated Olympic-size pool is now surrounded by lawns and five tennis courts. Ask about special getaway packages that include dinner in the hotel restaurant and golf, ballooning, or horseback riding. The resort is unique in offering comfortable accommodations at moderate prices; guests have access to the **Montecito Heights Health and Racquet Club** (see page 111) at reduced rates. ♦ 2777 Fourth St (at Farmers La). 545.8530, 800/848.8300; fax 528.1404 &

Restaurants/Clubs: Red   **Hotels:** Blue
Shops/ Outdoors: Green   **Wineries/Sights:** Black

At the Flamingo Resort Hotel:

Montecito Heights Health and Racquet Club This state-of-the-art fitness center offers a weight room, aerobics studio, sauna, steam room, and whirlpool facilities. The club has five tennis courts, basketball and volleyball courts, and a lighted jogging path. Massages are also available. ♦ Daily. 526.0529; fax 528.1404

103 Lisa Hemenway's ★★★ $$ A graduate of **John Ash & Co.** (see page 119), one of Santa Rosa's top restaurants, chef/owner Lisa Hemenway features items from the mesquite grill, including burgers, fresh fish, and daily specialties such as grilled halibut or pan-seared ono with pickled vegetables and a ginger beurre blanc. This light, airy restaurant looks very European with its sidewalk seating area, and it's definitely a surprise to find such a savvy restaurant in the midst of the **Montgomery Village** shopping center. Dinner emphasizes dishes such as duck in cherry sauce and daily pasta specials such as pumpkin ravioli. And as for dessert, Hemenway's California nut torte is always a winner. ♦ California ♦ M-Sa lunch and dinner; Su brunch and dinner. 714 Village Ct (Sonoma Ave and Farmers La). 526.5111; fax 578.5736 ♦

103 Lisa Hemenway's Tote Cuisine Put together a wine-country picnic at this Santa Rosa deli, a spin-off of Lisa Hemenway's more formal restaurant next door. You can order from a set box-lunch menu or create your own as you browse. It's all eclectic fare—and a very welcome change from the standard deli menu. Fill your picnic basket with chili-spiked smoked chicken empanadas, Cajun chicken wings, and Greek dolmas. ♦ Daily. 710 Village Ct (Sonoma Ave and Farmers La). 578.0898; fax 578.5736 ♦

104 Farmers' Market The parking lot of the **Veterans Memorial Building** is the site of a lively open-air market. Bring your own shopping bag and stock up on farm-fresh eggs, flowers, produce, and herb and vegetable starts for the garden. ♦ W, Sa 9AM-noon year-round. Brookwood Ave (off Hwy 12). 538.7023

105 Sonoma County Fairgrounds Summer brings the annual three-week **Sonoma County Fair** here, with hundreds of crafts and homemaking exhibits, plants, flowers, livestock, and wool—and blue ribbons galore. It runs from the latter half of July to early August, and is a great way to sample Sonoma's bounty. Other events are held here year-round, including horse shows and harvest fairs. ♦ 1350 Bennett Valley Rd (off Hwy 12). 545.4200

Also at the Sonoma County Fairgrounds:

Sonoma County Fairgrounds Golf Course This nine-hole public golf course is a par 29. During the fair, the course is filled with exhibits. ♦ Daily. 577.0755

106 The Gables $$ A historic landmark, this imposing 113-year-old Victorian (see drawing above) with 15 (count 'em) gables sits in front of a weathered barn on three-and-a-half acres. The seven guest rooms, most with a private bath, have Victorian claw-foot tubs and, of course, period decor. The most sought-after accommodation is the two-story cottage in back with a wood-burning stove, a double Jacuzzi, and a kitchenette where you can prepare produce from the local farmers' market. At sunset guests like to congregate on the deck and take in the view. Innkeepers Michael and Judy Ogne cook a full country breakfast, which may include French toast and fruit compote with coconut cream. ♦ 4257 Petaluma Hill Rd (off Kawana Springs Rd). 585.7777 ♦

107 Crane Melon Barn This farm stand specializes in Crane melons, luscious, sweet melons first developed by proprietor Jackie Crane's grandfather in the early 1920s. String beans, apples, and dried fruit are also sold here. ♦ Daily Aug-Oct. 4947 Petaluma Hill Rd (off Kawana Springs Rd). 584.5141

108 Friedman Bros. A Sonoma County fixture, this giant hardware store sells everything from ice chests and portable barbecues to galvanized farm and ranch gates, rural mailboxes, and livestock watering troughs. ♦ Daily. 4055 Santa Rosa Ave (south of Kawana Springs Rd). 584.7811, 795.4546

American wine is made in more than 30 states, and California's share is about 72 percent.

109 Pygmalion House $ This restored two-and-a-half-story Queen Anne cottage is tucked away at the end of a quiet residential street a short walk from the **Railroad Square Historic District** (see below), though it's close to the freeway. There are five rooms, all with private baths featuring old-fashioned claw-foot tubs and furnished with antiques and reproductions. The full breakfast, which includes fruit and freshly baked muffins and croissants, is served in the large country kitchen. ♦ 331 Orange St (at Laurel St). 526.3407

110 Days Inn $ Part of the dependable chain, this property has 140 rooms and suites furnished in contemporary style, each with either two double beds or one queen-size bed, cable TV, and a private bath. Guests have use of the pool and outdoor Jacuzzi. The hotel is a block from **Railroad Square** and bordered by the freeway and a residential area. Nonsmoking rooms are available. ♦ 175 Railroad St (at Third St). 573.9000; fax 573.0272 &

111 Railroad Square Historic District In 1870 the first Santa Rosa–North Pacific train chugged into town, bringing San Franciscans to the countryside. The old depot is now part of a restored historic district called **Railroad Square**. The surrounding turn-of-the-century stone and brick buildings have been spruced up to house antiques shops, restaurants, and cafes; the depot is on the National Register of Historic Places. ♦ Bounded by Third and Sixth Sts, Hwy 101, and Santa Rosa Creek. 578.8478

112 La Gare ★★$$$ At this family-owned restaurant in a charming stone building on **Railroad Square,** you'll find the type of old-style French dishes that have virtually disappeared from trendier menus—standbys such as quiche lorraine, onion soup au gratin, veal medaillon cordon bleu, duck *à l'orange,* and *filet de boeuf Wellington.* Yet the proprietors are savvy enough to include a vegetarian special, and they offer chocolate decadence (that divine combo of dark chocolate and raspberries) alongside that old favorite, cherries jubilee. ♦ French ♦ Tu-Su dinner. 208 Wilson St (at Third St). 528.4355; fax 528.2519 &

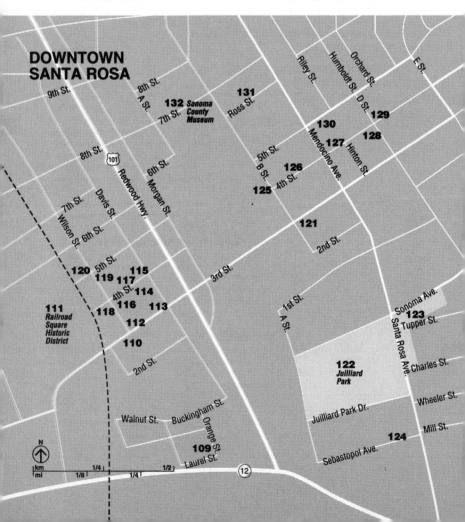

112 Hot Couture

Hot Couture

Inveterate vintage clotheshounds are sure to get derailed for an hour or two in this emporium stocked with sequined sweaters, 1940s coats, and glamorous 1950s cocktail dresses. For men, the store offers old-fashioned tuxedo shirts (which look great on women, too) and classic jackets and coats à la Bogie. ◆ Daily. 101 Third St (between Davis and Wilson Sts). 528.7247; fax 528.7615

112 Antiques, Apples & Art This is a great place for browsing—it's full of small objets d'art, glassware, textiles, lamps, and much more. ◆ M, F, Sa. 105 Third St (between Davis and Wilson Sts). 578.1414

112 Cole Silver Shop This is the place to shop for antique silver, including sterling silver flatware. Silver plating, polishing, repairs, and appraisals are also available. ◆ M-F; Sa morning by appointment only. 107 Third St (between Davis and Wilson Sts). 546.7515

112 Marianne's Antiques Handsome tables, sideboards, armoires, and other large pieces of furniture are the specialty at this spacious antiques store. ◆ Daily. 111 Third St (between Davis and Wilson Sts). 579.5749

113 Sonoma Outfitters This large store in **Railroad Square** features a friendly, knowledgeable staff and a terrific selection of outdoor gear and apparel, including boots, tents, sleeping bags, and packs. If you're heading for the Russian River, take a look at the bright canoes. And if you're into in-line skating, you can even test out a pair of skates on the oval ring that winds through the middle of the store. On weekends, a vertical climbing wall is set up. The staff is well versed on all of the equipment and gear. ◆ Daily. 145 Third St (between Davis and Wilson Sts). 528.1920

114 Whistlestop Antiques Pack rats will have a ball prowling through this two-story antiques collective for old furniture, kitchenware, costume jewelry, and knickknacks. Some stalls specialize in Art Deco plastic jewelry, 1950s cocktail shakers, sleek chrome furniture, and stylish vintage radios. Collectors can also find Russell Wright dinnerware (1939-59). ◆ Daily. 130 Fourth St (between Davis and Wilson Sts). 542.9474

115 Mixx ★★★$$$ **California Culinary Academy**–trained owners/chefs Dan and Kathleen Berman create inventive yet homey California-style fare for lunch and dinner. Chicken pot pie, freshly ground hamburgers with red potato fries, and a wonderful bouillabaisse are just some of the lunch selections. At dinner the Bermans focus on the freshest of fish and pasta dishes, plus Sonoma County chicken roasted with lemon, thyme, and sherry and plump pork chops stuffed with chorizo sausage. End the meal with one of Kathleen's homemade desserts, such as frozen white chocolate mousse torte and hazelnut biscotti dipped in chocolate. The menu is considerately labeled "small dishes" and "large dishes" and heart symbols guide those watching their fat intake. The excellent wine list features vintages that have won gold medals at the **Sonoma County Harvest Fair.** No smoking is allowed. ◆ California ◆ M-F lunch and dinner; Sa-Su dinner. 135 Fourth St (at Davis St). 573.1344 &

116 Omelette Express ★$ Santa Rosa's casual breakfast spot offers about 50 types of omelettes, from standard combos to vegetarian and seafood, all served with cottage fries. From 11AM on, they serve charbroiled sirloin burgers and classic sandwiches, including roast beef, grilled cheddar cheese, and tuna salad. There's a kids' menu, too. ◆ American ◆ Daily breakfast and lunch. 112 Fourth St (between Davis and Wilson Sts). 525.1690 &

117 Las Manos This store's appealing collection of ethnic clothing, much of it handwoven cotton or silk, is perfectly suited to the wine-country climate. You'll find summer frocks, Panama hats, and an interesting selection of accessories such as hand-crocheted wallets from Guatemala and jeweled baseball caps from Thailand. Check the racks upstairs for discounted items and handwoven Guatemalan fabrics. ◆ Daily. 125 Fourth St (between Davis and Wilson Sts). 578.1649; fax 433.9363

117 Consuming Passions At this tiny shop, you'll find a variety of handmade chocolates, including truffles, deep chocolate fudge, rich caramels, chocolate-covered cherries, molded chocolate roses—even sugar-free chocolates sweetened with a corn derivative. Mail order is available, too. ◆ Tu-Su. 115 Fourth St (between Davis and Wilson Sts). 571.8380

118 Chevy's ★$$ Part of a highly successful chain, this restaurant has an appealing menu of Mexican specialties. If you can handle the summer heat, there's a large deck out back.

♦ Mexican ♦ Daily lunch and dinner. 24 Fourth St (at Wilson St), Suite 100. 571.1082 ♿

119 Hotel La Rose $ Located in a turn-of-the-century stone building (illustrated above) in **Railroad Square,** this establishment offers 20 rooms with private baths and country-on-a-budget decor: flower wallpaper, rose comforters, carpeting, and period reproductions. Most of the bathrooms are on the small side and some rooms overlook the freeway. But the hotel has a sundeck with a Jacuzzi, air-conditioning, a restaurant that serves California cuisine, and a pleasant bar downstairs with a fireplace and decorative grape motif. They serve high tea on weekday afternoons. Ask about midweek specials. ♦ 308 Wilson St (at Fifth St). 579.3200, 800/527.6738; fax 579.3247 ♿

120 A'Roma Roasters & Coffeehouse This is the best coffeehouse/club in town, with great espresso, cappuccino, *caffè latte,* and house specialties. When it's sweltering outside, come in for a refreshing Italian soda, an iced coffee, or one of the frappés of the day. The bright red French roaster trimmed in brass sits right in the middle of the store, filling the air with the heady scent of fresh-roasted coffee; owners Dayna McCutchen and Sandra Young offer 18 types to choose from. They'll also tempt you with organic fruit pies and other locally made desserts. Thursday through Saturday they feature live music (with no cover charge), ranging from flamenco guitar and chamber music to jazz and blues. ♦ Daily. 95 Fifth St (at Wilson St). 576.7765; fax 577.7711 ♿

121 Traverso's Gourmet Foods and Wine Since 1929 this Italian deli, opened by Louis and Enrico Traverso, two brothers from Genoa, has been a treasure trove of local and Italian foodstuffs. It has a decent selection of local cheese and cold cuts already sliced for fast service, plus all the standard fixin's. To stock the pantry, shop for Californian and Italian olive oils, vinegars, Sonoma County dried tomatoes, and jams. In the well-stocked wine section, vintage photos give a glimpse of Santa Rosa in the 1930s and 1940s. Ask about the used wine-shipment boxes for mailing from two to 12 bottles. ♦ M-Sa. 106 B St (at Third St). 542.2530; fax 542.0736

122 Juilliard Park These nine acres in the center of the city were once home to wine-and-fruit broker C.F. Juilliard, a Santa Rosa pioneer. The site is now a park with a self-guided tour of 42 varieties of trees. ♦ Off Santa Rosa Ave (at Juilliard Park Dr and A St)

Within Juilliard Park:

Robert L. Ripley Memorial Museum This unusual museum, housed in the historic **Church Built from One Tree,** was made famous by the phenomenally successful cartoonist Robert L. Ripley. The entire church was built in 1873 from a single giant redwood from Guerneville. The tree, 275 feet high and 18 feet in diameter, provided 78,000 board feet of wood. Inside is a collection of memorabilia from the archives of the Santa Rosa cartoonist, whose newspaper strip, "Ripley's Believe It or Not!" (see above), is read by millions of people in 38 countries. You'll find some of his original cartoons, photos of Ripley in outlandish situations and places, his battered old suitcase covered with stickers from his travels, and a lifelike wax figure of the cartoonist sculpted by a blind man. ♦ Nominal admission. W-Su Apr-Oct. 492 Sonoma Ave (between Santa Rosa Ave and A St). 524.5233 or 543.3737 ♿

123 Luther Burbank Home & Gardens Visit the home where world-famous horticulturist Luther Burbank worked from 1875 to 1926. The gardens where he conducted his experiments have been completely renovated and feature demonstration garden beds of Burbank's work, extensive labeling of his projects, and a huge pictorial wall constructed with porcelain tiles illustrating the history of his life and accomplishments. Brochures are also now available for self-guided tours through the gardens. The docent-guided tour that starts on the half hour is an enjoyable ramble through part of the garden, the greenhouse, and the modified Greek-Revival house where his wife, Elizabeth, lived until her death. The carriage house is a mini-museum with photographs of notables who visited Burbank and drawings of his creations, such as the shasta daisy, the russet potato, and the Santa Rosa plum. This brilliant, self-educated man introduced more than 800 new varieties of plants to the world (including over 200 varieties of fruits alone). His objective was to improve the quality of plants and thereby increase the world's food supply. After his death, Congress inducted him into the Hall of Inventors. An annual holiday open house and gift sale is held here the first weekend of December. ◆ Nominal fee for tours. Home: W-Su Apr-Oct; tours every half hour. Memorial gardens: daily. Extensive, guided garden tours available for groups by appointment. 204 Santa Rosa Ave (at Sonoma Ave). 524.5445

124 Brother Juniper's Bakery Like its justly famous Forestville counterpart, this shop run by Ron and Lorene Colvin makes and sells wonderful, fresh-baked loaves of bread, coffee, and tea, as well as fiery hot home-made barbecue sauce. ◆ M-Sa. 463 Sebastopol Ave (off Santa Rosa Ave). 542.9012; fax 542.6682. Also at: 6544 Front St (Hwy 116), Forestville. 887.7908

125 Thursday Night Farmers' Market From Memorial Day through Labor Day, downtown Santa Rosa's Fourth Street is closed to traffic on Thursday nights, when it becomes the site of a remarkably successful farmers' market. With live music, jugglers, magicians, and plenty of food, it's a nonstop party that attracts people from miles around. Get down with everything from grilled sausages and beer to fresh pastries and breads. And take home some of the Holy Smokes barbecue sauce and jams from **Kozlowski Farms** in Forestville. The farmers set up their stalls along B Street, touting their luscious strawberries, goat cheese, spring onions, Santa Rosa plums, and whatever else the season has to offer. Bring a big shopping bag because it's impossible not to get into the spirit of things. ◆ Th 5:30-7:30PM May-Sept. Fourth St (at B St). 544.4980

126 Sonoma Coffee Co. The toasty scent of whole-bean coffees pervades this long, narrow shop, where a sandblasted brick wall stands in as an informal photography and print gallery. A collection of Thermoses sits atop an old Wedgewood stove for the serve-it-yourself house coffee; they also offer espresso drinks and an array of morning pastries. ◆ Daily. 521 Fourth St (between Mendocino Ave and B St). 573.8022

126 Caffè Portofino Ristorante & Bar ★★ $$$ The bar at the front of this cafe is a popular spot for wine tasting. Best bets on the menu are the classic bruschetta (toasted bread rubbed with garlic and doused with virgin olive oil), Caesar salad prepared at the table, and slices of fresh buffalo-milk mozzarella and tomatoes drizzled with olive oil and topped with fresh basil. The linguine with fresh clams is decent, and the pasta tossed with potato and pesto is an authentic Genoese preparation. You can't go wrong with simply prepared grilled items such as fresh tuna or lamb chops served Roman-style with a mint sauce. At lunch you might try the special *panini* (sandwiches), but they're really more American than Italian. In good weather, you can either eat inside or on the sidewalk at umbrella-shaded tables. ◆ Italian ◆ M-Sa lunch and dinner. 535 Fourth St (between Mendocino Ave and B St). 523.1171; fax 522.8190 ♿

in a Bottle?

The standard bottle of wine in this country is designed to hold 750 milliliters (that's three-quarters of a liter or four-fifths of a quart). The half bottle (or "split") is half of the standard bottle; it's ideal for someone dining alone or for a couple who wants to drink a white wine with the first course and a red with the main course. Most wineries also bottle a limited number of magnums—handsome, oversized bottles that hold the equivalent of two bottles of wine (these are often preferred by connoisseurs because the wine ages more slowly in the larger bottles). A series of even larger bottles are occasionally used for red wines, Champagnes, and sparkling wines.

Half Bottle Holds 375 milliliters (half the quantity of a standard wine bottle).

Bottle Whether it has the sloping shoulders of a Burgundy-style bottle, the high, rounded shoulders of a Bordeaux-style bottle, or the tall, elongated shape of an Alsace- or German-style bottle, the typical American wine bottle holds 750 milliliters.

Magnum Holds the equivalent of two bottles of wine.

Double Magnum (or **Jeroboam**) Holds the equivalent of four bottles of wine.

Rehoboam Holds the equivalent of six bottles of wine.

Imperial (or **Methusaleh**) Holds the equivalent of eight bottles of wine.

Salmanazar Holds the equivalent of 12 bottles of wine.

Balthazar Holds the equivalent of 16 bottles of wine.

Nebuchadnezzar The granddaddy of them all holds the equivalent of 20 bottles of wine (or a little less, depending on where the bottle was made).

Glass Menagerie

There's more to the wineglass than meets the eye. For example, do you know why the long, slender stem of the wineglass was developed? To allow you to hold the glass without cupping your hand around the wine, which would affect the temperature of this sensitive liquid. And why are wineglasses made of clear glass? So you can see the color of the wine, which, to the practiced eye, gives an indication of the wine's age. In general, the bigger (or more full-bodied) the wine, the larger the glass should be; this is to ensure there's enough air and space for the wine to develop its bouquet or aroma. Many other wineglass features have been developed to suit certain wine varieties and to enhance your appreciation of the wine. Here are some of the basic shapes:

Champagne Flute

The familiar saucer-shaped Champagne glass is, in fact, the worst vessel for serving sparkling wines because the bubbles escape too fast. Champagne should be served in a narrow wineglass; the ideal shape is the slender flute pictured at left.

White Wineglass

This simple shape, which narrows slightly at the top to focus the bouquet of the wine, is perfect for serving white wines. It's also a good choice for aperitif wines, rosés, and blush wines, as well as light, young red wines.

Bordeaux Glass

This glass is taller than the white wine model but also narrows slightly at the top. It has enough room for a full-bodied, complex red wine to develop a bouquet.

Burgundy Glass

Even larger than the Bordeaux glass, this version has a modified balloon shape so that a robust red has room to aerate and develop a full bouquet.

Brandy Snifter

This is the classic shape for serving brandies and Cognacs and often comes in several sizes. However large the glass, only a small amount of brandy should be poured at a time so you can warm the spirit by cupping the bowl with your hands.

127 Treehorn Books This bookstore has a good cookbook section, including the complete works of the late, great Glen Ellen food writer M.F.K. Fisher; Michele Anna Jordan's affectionate *A Cook's Tour of Sonoma;* and books on California wine-country cooking. ♦ Daily. 625 Fourth St (between D St and Mendocino Ave). 525.1782

128 Copperfield's Annex You'll find lots of reduced-price books here, including cookbooks, wine books, and works on travel, gardening, and art. Browse through the big mystery section. ♦ Daily. 650 Fourth St (at D St). 545.5326

129 Ma Stokeld's Old Vic ★★$ Locals come here for live music in the evenings (folk, jazz, rock, and more), plus hearty pub grub and good beer and ale. ♦ Pub ♦ Daily. 731 Fourth St (between E and D Sts). 571.7555

129 Last Record Store Rock, blues, reggae, classical, and world music have all found a home in this exceptional store. Both new and used recordings are available, much of it on old-fashioned vinyl. ♦ Daily. 739 Fourth St (between E and D Sts). 525.1963

130 Cafe Lolo ★★★$$$ Talented chef Michael Quigley and his wife Lori Darling work together to make this intimate eatery one of the best in wine country. The decor is chic and elegant, with crisp white table linen and colorful flowers everywhere. The menu changes based on what fresh ingredients are available each day. The list of appetizers may include salad tossed with balsamic vinaigrette dressing and warm goat cheese flan with sweet-and-sour onion relish. Sample entrées include poached fillet of salmon with basil mashed potatoes; osso buco (veal shanks) with white beans, tomatoes, and olives; and oven-roasted breast of chicken. ♦ California ♦ M-F lunch and dinner; Sa dinner. 620 Fifth St (between D St and Mendocino Ave). 576.7822 &

131 Taj Mahal ★★$$ At last—an Indian restaurant worth recommending in the wine country. Sadananb Charka has created a lovely ambience here, with white walls, pastel tablecloths, and outdoor dining on the broad sidewalk area in front. You'll find a variety of seafood dishes, including king prawns cooked with paprika, tomatoes, onions, and herbs and grilled fillet of salmon with Indian spices. Charka has four fixed menus in addition to the à la carte items. Strict vegetarians may order an entire menu cooked without oil or dairy products, and you may request brown rice instead of white. ♦ Indian ♦ M-Sa lunch and dinner; Su dinner. 53 Ross St (between Mendocino Ave and B St). 579.8471 &

DRAWING BY E. ROSS PARKERSON

Sonoma County Museum

132 Sonoma County Museum Housed in the old **Post Office and Federal Building** (built in 1909 by **James Knox Taylor**), the county museum (see drawing at top) has a permanent collection of 19th-century landscape paintings and a permanent display on the history of Sonoma County. Other exhibits change frequently, but all relate to Sonoma County and the North Bay. On one visit, you may find an exhibit of Pomo Indian basketry with fine black-and-white photos of the basket-making process, a show of local woodwork, or an exhibit with a Victorian theme. Check the museum gift shop for books on Sonoma history and architecture, work from local craftspeople, and souvenirs of Sonoma County. ◆ Nominal admission. W-Su. 425 Seventh St (between B and A Sts). 579.1500 ♿

133 Bay Bottom Beds Have oyster knife, will travel. If you and a few hungry friends can handle a minimum of 50 oysters, order ahead and pick them up at this Santa Rosa supplier. Lisa Jang and her husband, Jorge Rebagliati, cultivate their Miyagi oysters (a variety of Pacific oysters originally from Asia) at Preston Point in Tomales Bay. Harvested to order, the oysters are always pristinely fresh. Call

Monday to place an order and make an appointment to pick it up later in the week. They will send your order via overnight mail, too. ◆ 966 Borden Villa Dr, No 103 (off W College Ave). 578.6049

134 Ristorante Siena ★★★$$$ This Italian restaurant is the brainchild of Michael Hirschberg, the founder of what used to be Santa Rosa's best French restaurant, the now-defunct **Matisse.** Here Hirschberg concentrates on homemade pasta and seafood dishes. Start with bruschetta (grilled bread with assorted toppings) or mussels prepared Roman-style with white wine, garlic, and parsley. Then try the supple fettuccine with pesto, pine nuts, and asiago or the penne with rosemary-scented white beans and tomatoes. Ravioli might be stuffed with smoked salmon or goat cheese and served with a dill and caper sauce or with a southern Italian caponatina (pickled eggplant and onion). The simply grilled fish dishes are always a good bet, as is the *calamari fritti* (fried calamari) with a garlic-infused lemon sauce. You might also find more familiar dishes, such as veal scaloppine cooked with Marsala and mushrooms, a grilled rib eye steak, or Petaluma duck breast in fresh cherry sauce. All the breads come from Hirschberg's popular bakery down the street, **Mezzaluna.** The lunch menu includes interesting sandwiches, burgers, and salads (such as roast chicken, pears, and gorgonzola cheese), a half-dozen moderately priced pasta dishes, and individual pizzas. If the weather is pleasant, ask for an outdoor table when you make your reservation. A good selection of California and Italian wines is offered. ◆ Italian ◆ M lunch; Tu-F lunch and

117

dinner; Sa-Su dinner. Reservations recommended. 1229 N Dutton Ave (north of W College Ave). 578.4511; fax 578.0703 &

135 Redwood Empire Ice Arena "Peanuts" cartoonist Charles Schultz, one of Santa Rosa's most eminent citizens, came up with the idea for this Olympic-size ice-skating rink, which opened in 1969. You can rent skates here or bring your own. The arena includes a coffee shop and ice-cream parlor. An ice show is staged every year. The flexible design permits the arena to be converted in just a few hours into a concert theater seating 3,000; headliners such as Bill Cosby and Helen Reddy have appeared here in the past. Fans of Schultz's long-running comic strip will want to visit the gallery next door (see below). ◆ Daily. 1667 W Steele La (between Cleveland and Range Aves). 546.7147

135 Snoopy's Gallery & Gift Shop The world's largest collection of Snoopy memorabilia and merchandise is housed here—and Schultz generously permits Charlie Brown, Lucy, Linus, and the rest of the "Peanuts" gang to hawk their likenesses here, too. Don't miss the collection of Schultz's original drawings and personal photos. ◆ Daily. 1665 W Steele La (between Cleveland and Range Aves). 546.3385; fax 546.3764

136 De Loach Vineyards Noted for their Russian River Chardonnay, Cecil and Christine De Loach make wines in an easy, accessible style. Their top-of-the-line O.F.S. ("our finest selection") is a rich, barrel-fermented Chardonnay. They also make Sauvignon Blanc, Fumé Blanc, Gewürztraminer, and White Zinfandel, along with the original Zinfandel, red, and Pinot Noir. A few picnic tables are set out with views of the vineyard. ◆ Tasting and sales daily; tours by appointment only. 1791 Olivet Rd (at the Guerneville Hwy). 526.9111 &

137 Doubletree Hotel Santa Rosa $$ Part of a large chain, this hotel offers 252 spacious and pleasantly decorated guest rooms and suites, a terrace bar, and an Olympic-size pool. The hotel also houses a restaurant that serves lunch and dinner. ◆ 3555 Round Barn Blvd (off Fountaingrove Pkwy). 523.7555; 800/222.8733; fax 545.2807 &

Brother Timothy, a member of the Christian Brothers order and an avid corkscrew collector, credits Samuel Hensall, an English parson, with designing the first patented corkscrew in 1795.

In the wine trade, it is said, "buy on bread, sell on cheese," because cheese flatters the wine.

FOUNTAINGROVE INN

138 Fountaingrove Inn $$ Understated luxury is the theme at this contemporary inn on the old **Fountaingrove Ranch**. All of the 85 rooms and suites are decorated with simplicity and taste, featuring custom-designed furniture and attention to details such as soundproofing, separate dressing alcoves, double closets, and work spaces with modem jacks. Suites feature a Jacuzzi and a dining area. There is also a beautifully landscaped pool with a waterfall and an outdoor Jacuzzi. Special weekend wine-country packages bring a double room here into the price range of most of the area's bed-and-breakfast inns. ◆ 101 Fountaingrove Pkwy (off Mendocino Ave). 578.6101

Within the Fountaingrove Inn:

Equus Restaurant & Lounge ★★$$$ The hotel restaurant offers an eclectic seasonal menu encompassing men's club standbys such as oysters Rockefeller and lobster bisque, along with a Sonoma Valley salad prepared with fresh local greens, a raspberry vinaigrette, and baked brie. The rack of local spring lamb or the mixed grill (lamb chop, veal medallion, and beef fillet served with cottage fries and vegetables) is perfect to show off a hearty red vintage chosen from their extensive list of Sonoma County wines. ◆ California ◆ M-Sa lunch and dinner; Su brunch and dinner. 578.0149

139 Fountaingrove Country Club This par-72, Ted Robinson championship golf course opened in 1985. It was once owned by the pioneering Japanese wine maker Kanaye Nagasawa, who added an Asian touch to the landscape with bonsai trees and stone lanterns. Reserve ahead, as it's very popular. ◆ Daily. 1525 Fountaingrove Pkwy (off Mendocino Ave). 579.4653

140 Luther Burbank Center for the Arts The three theaters here are used for guest lectures, concerts, and performances by big-name artists such as Ray Charles, Johnny Mathis, and Barbara Mandrell. Call for a schedule of events. ◆ Hwy 101 (at River Rd). 546.3600 &

141 Vintners Inn $$$ Set amid vineyards, this 44-room luxury inn blends European style with a California-wine-country ambience. Rooms are furnished with pine antiques and quilts, but unlike most bed-and-breakfast inns, there's also first-class room service, a concierge, TV sets, and in-room phones. The four Spanish-style, two-story buildings with a red-tile roof face an inner courtyard with a fountain. All of the rooms are spacious, but those on the upper floor get a great view as well. Suites boast a fireplace and a wet bar, plus a refrigerator for chilling wine. The inn also features a sundeck and an outdoor whirlpool bath and serves a good-size breakfast that includes fresh fruit and homemade waffles and muffins. ♦ 4350 Barnes Rd (off River Rd at Hwy 101). 575.7350; fax 575.1426 ♿

Within Vintners Inn:

John Ash & Co. ★★★★$$$$ Save up for a meal at this casual-yet-chic wine-country enclave that has Southwestern-inspired decor, entrancing vineyard views, and an exciting menu. Founder John Ash (who is also culinary director of the **Fetzer Food & Wine Center at Valley Oaks** in Hopland) pioneered wine-country cooking, bringing a diversity of influences—French, Italian, Asian, and Southwestern—to bear on Sonoma's bounty of local ingredients. With Ash's top chef, Jeff Madura, at the helm, the restaurant turns out dishes with both imagination and flair. Start with Hog Island oysters on the half shell, king salmon cured in fresh herbs, lemon, and Buena Vista sherry, or rillette (a country-style pâté made with Petaluma duck instead of the pork or goose more commonly used in France). Main courses are well conceived, ranging from rabbit braised in wild honey and balsamic vinegar to marinated and grilled tenderloin of pork served in a raspberry-vinegar and shallot sauce. The dry-aged sirloin steak in Jack Daniels sauce studded with wild mushrooms is highly recommended. The desserts, listed on a separate menu along with coffees, teas, and spirits, command as much attention as the main courses; highlights include lemon and white chocolate cheesecake, macadamia nut, caramel, and chocolate tarts, and peaches and vanilla cream. The wine list offers a broad range of Sonoma County vintages, as well as a select few from the rest of Northern California. A special reserve list includes older vintages of California wines, plus Bordeaux and Burgundies. ♦ California ♦ Tu-Sa lunch and dinner; Su dinner. Reservations recommended. 527.7687

142 Sonoma County Airport You can fly from San Francisco or San Jose to this county airport served by **Reno Air Express** and **United Express.** Rental cars are available from **Avis, Hertz,** and **Thrifty.** ♦ 2200 Airport Blvd (off Hwy 101). 524.7240 ♿

Bests

Patrick Campbell
Wine Maker/Owner, Laurel Glen Vineyard

A 40-acre vineyard on **Sonoma Mountain,** dedicated to the exclusive production of an estate-grown, traditionally made, blended Cabernet Sauvignon.

What other county in the US produces such a range of wines, vegetables, meats, and seafoods as **Sonoma County?** Not one. From spicy Russian River Gewürztraminer to rich Sonoma Mountain Cabernet; from Jenner's smoky salmon to Jim Reichardt's fabulous ducks; from Laura Chenel's tangy goat cheese and Bellwether Farm's lovely sheep cheeses to robust Sonoma foie gras; from Hog Island oysters to Bruce Campbell's upland lamb; from Bob Cannard's mountain-grown organic produce to Dry Creek Peach and Produce's superlative fruits. . . .

Where can you eat all this bounty?

Want it elegant?—**John Ash & Co. (Santa Rosa)** and **The Grille** at the **Sonoma Mission Inn & Spa (Sonoma).**

Want it casual?—**Lisa Hemenway's** (Santa Rosa).

Want it on the cutting edge?—**Charles Saunders' East Side Oyster Bar & Grill** (Sonoma).

Best bread: **Brother Juniper's, Mezzaluna, Artisan.**

Best magazine: *Sonoma Style.*

Best wine appellation: **Sonoma Valley** from **Carneros** through the **Valley of the Moon** to **Kenwood.**

Laura Chenel
Cheesemaker/Owner, Laura Chenel's Chèvre, Sonoma

The Thursday-night farmers' market in downtown **Santa Rosa.**

Cantinetta Tra Vigne in **St. Helena.**

A horseback ride at **Annadel State Park** or on the **Bodega Dunes.**

A bicycle ride in the **Dry Creek** and **Alexander Valleys.**

A lazy summer afternoon on the square in **Healdsburg Plaza,** including a visit to the **Downtown Bakery & Creamery**.

John Ash & Co. in Santa Rosa for lunch or dinner.

A drive through western **Petaluma** and **Bodega Bay,** taking **Coleman Valley Road** to **Occidental,** then over to **Freestone**—a west-county tour.

Russian River Valley

Northwest of **Santa Rosa** is Sonoma **County**'s fastest-growing wine region, the Russian River Valley, a remarkably diverse landscape of gently rolling hillsides, apple orchards, sandy river beaches, and prime redwood country. This region is so large that it is divided into several subvalleys, each with its own microclimate and appellation, by the **Russian River** and its tributaries.

Explored by the Russians based at Fort Ross in the 1840s, the Russian River Valley is much less compact than either Sonoma or Napa Valley. More than 50 wineries are spread out in many directions, and there is no one wine route to follow. A network of small country roads connects the smaller valleys and appellations here, and much of the area is uncongested, so you can make your trip somewhat impromptu.

Alexander Valley extends from **Cloverdale** south to **Healdsburg** along the Russian River, which takes a more or less parallel course here with **Highway 101** to the west. This stretch of river offers some of the best canoeing in the area, where you can drift past prime vineyards of Chardonnay and Cabernet.

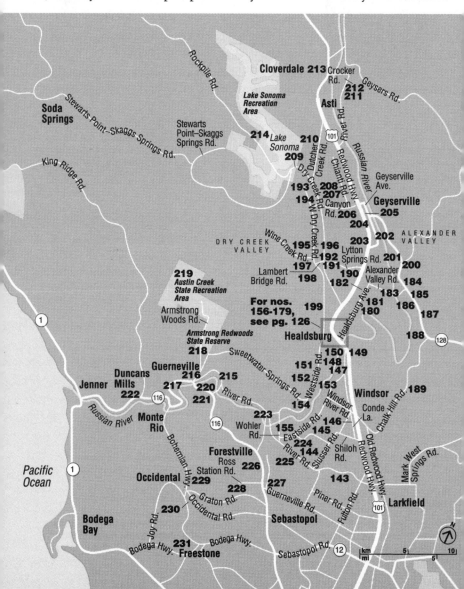

The valley is named for Cyrus Alexander, an early settler from Pennsylvania who cultivated grapes and other crops here in the mid-19th century. In the past three decades, several top-notch wineries have been built in this scenic valley.

To the west is **Dry Creek Valley**, bracketed by serpentine **Lake Sonoma** to the north and the Russian River to the south. Scattered along the valley are a number of small wine producers (many of them require appointments to visit—and it's well worth taking the time to make them). Dry Creek Valley is primarily Zinfandel country, producing some of California's finest. You'll also encounter excellent Sauvignon Blanc here.

Just past the southern tip of Dry Creek Valley, the river heads west to the sea and the Russian River appellation, prime territory for Pinot Noir and Burgundian-style wines. **Westside Road**, which runs south from Healdsburg to meet **River Road**, is an entrancing country drive dotted with small family wineries, old hop-drying kilns, and a few farms where you can buy home-grown fruit, vegetables, and freshly laid eggs. River Road cuts through the redwoods to **Guerneville,** and just before arriving at the town, you'll encounter **Korbel Champagne Cellars** and its heritage rose garden with more than 300 varieties of old-fashioned roses.

The Russian River Valley also includes two smaller wine appellations within its boundaries: the **Chalk Hill** area to the east, which produces wonderful Chardonnay and Merlot, and the cooler **Green Valley** toward **Sebastopol** to the southwest, which boasts ideal growing conditions for Pinot Noir and Chardonnay.

The diminutive town of Healdsburg is the hub of the Russian River Valley, with the three major subvalleys fanning out from its boundaries. At its heart is **Healdsburg Plaza**, a Spanish-style square that resembles Sonoma's famous plaza in miniature. You can swim in the Russian River at **Healdsburg Memorial Beach**, rent a bicycle, or go kayaking on the river. Pack a picnic lunch, because once you're on the wine trail, there are few places to eat and it can be a long way back into town. Healdsburg offers the most accommodations in the area, but you can also stay in Victorian bed-and-breakfast inns in **Geyserville** and Cloverdale to the north.

You could also make the Russian River resort area near Guerneville your base. It offers a number of family resorts and comfortable bed-and-breakfast inns, near sunny river beaches and virgin redwood forests. **Armstrong Redwoods State Reserve** is one of the largest reserves of ancient trees in California, and the rugged Sonoma Coast is just a short drive away, making the Russian River Valley one of the most dramatic and appealing wine regions in California.

Windsor

Early settler Hiram Lewis thought the landscape in this area resembled the countryside around Windsor Castle in England, hence the name of this sleepy little township that was established in 1855. For wine-country visitors, Windsor offers a country bed-and-breakfast inn, a waterslide park, golfing, and kayaking.

MARTINELLI

143 Martinelli Winery Located on the scenic road to Guerneville and the Russian River, this family-owned winery housed in a rustic hop-drying barn produces Chardonnay, Sauvignon Blanc, Gewürztraminer, Zinfandel, Pinot Noir,

and more, all of which can be tasted here. It also stocks a good selection of picnic supplies and local food products. A second barn across the way is home to an art gallery showcasing Sonoma County artists. There's a picnic area, too. ♦ Tasting and sales daily; tours by appointment only. Art gallery: Th-Su. 3360 River Rd (off Hwy 101). 525.0570, 800/346.1627; fax 525.WINE &

143 Z Moore Winery You can sample Chardonnay, Gewürztraminer, and Zinfandel from a wine maker with experience at the **Milano** and **Hop Kiln** wineries. Those are the serious wines. Wine maker Daniel Moore breaks out a different label for his less expensive but still excellent table wines—

it's called Quaff. ♦ Tasting and sales daily; tours by appointment only. 3364 River Rd (off Hwy 101). 544.3555; fax 544.3563 ঙ

144 Sonoma-Cutrer Site of the **US Open** and the **World Championship Croquet Tournaments** every year, **Sonoma-Cutrer** is just as serious about croquet as it is about wine. The winery's three vineyard-designated Chardonnays created by wine maker Terry Adams are found on the best wine lists worldwide. Les Pierres is its top wine. ♦ Tasting and tours M-Sa by appointment only. 4401 Slusser Rd (off River Rd). 528.1181 ঙ

145 Windsor Golf Club This 18-hole, par 72 golf course sits on 120 acres in a country setting of gentle hills. ♦ Daily. 6555 Skylane Blvd (off Shiloh Rd). 838.PUTT

146 Windsor Waterworks and Slides There's no turning back once you've started down the 42-foot drop through 400 feet of tunnels, slopes, and hairpin curves to the pool at the very bottom. That's the thrill of the **Doom Flume** and three other ingenious waterslides. Don't worry; pint-size aficionados will offer lots of advice on how to get the maximum effect. If you'd rather just swim, **Waterworks** also has a large pool and a children's wading pool, plus horseshoe pits, Ping-Pong tables, an electronic game arcade, and a snack bar. Bring your own supplies for a picnic or barbecue. ♦ Special weekday rates are offered from 4 to 7PM. Daily May-Sept. 8225 Conde La (near Windsor River Rd). 838.7760, 838.7360

147 California Rivers When veteran canoeist Ann Dwyer took up kayaking, she quickly became frustrated with the kayak designs then available. No problem—this silver-haired grandmother simply designed and manu-factured her own. Dwyer's Kiwi kayaks are small, light, and versatile enough to be safe in all sorts of waters. At her store in Windsor you can rent a kayak by the day or by the weekend (she offers a discount on weekdays). In addition, Dwyer sells accessories such as waterproof gear bags, sailing rigs, knee pads, and coveralls (look for her own Dragonfly Designs). The store also takes reservations for kayaks. ♦ Daily mid-May through mid-Oct; W-Sa mid-Oct through mid-May. 10070 Old Redwood Hwy (near Starr Rd). 838.8919 ঙ

148 Country Meadow Inn $$ Only a few minutes from downtown Healdsburg, this two-story, brown-shingle Victorian farmhouse, now a country bed-and-breakfast inn, was once part of a large farm that stretched to the Russian River. The remaining six-and-a-half-acre estate is surrounded by meadows and rolling hills. The inn has five guest rooms, all with private

baths, and some have fireplaces and/or whirlpool baths. The pleasant Victorian-era decor features antique furniture and period fabrics. Most romantic is the garden suite, with a king-size bed, a separate sitting area with a fireplace, a sunny atrium, a double Jacuzzi, a private entrance, and a deck. Guests can cool off in the 16-by-30-foot pool at the edge of a vineyard. A full country breakfast is served by innkeeper Susan Hardesty. No smoking is allowed. ♦ 11360 Old Redwood Hwy (near Eastside Rd). 431.1276 ঙ

Healdsburg

This town lies at the convergence of three famous viticultural regions—the **Alexander, Dry Creek,** and **Russian River Valleys**—and there is something here to please every wine-country visitor. Many come for a lazy trek down the **Russian River** in a canoe rented from **W.C. "Bob" Trowbridge Canoe Trips.** Others prefer to cap off a string of visits to local wineries with dinner at one of the town's very good restaurants (such as **Tre Scalini**) or a snack at the **Downtown Bakery & Creamery.** And for history buffs, a stop at the restored Spanish-style **Healdsburg Plaza** and the town's museum is a must.

149 Christopher Creek Winery At this small winery perched on a knoll in the Chalk Hill appellation, owners John and Susan Mitchell primarily concentrate on red wines made from grapes grown on their 10-acre estate. They make Petite Sirah, Syrah, and a Chardonnay. ♦ Tasting M, F-Su; tours daily by appointment only. 641 Limerick La (off Old Redwood Hwy). 433.2001; fax 433.9315 ঙ

PIPER SONOMA

150 Piper Sonoma Founded in the early 1980s, this California sparkling-wine house is owned by the French champagne firm Piper-Hiedsieck, which has chalked up almost two centuries in the bubbly business. The modern winery building is notable for the broad terrace in front surrounded by fountains and a moat with floating water lilies. The beautifully landscaped gardens, which have been featured in home-and-garden magazines, make this a popular spot to meet friends for a glass of Brut or a walk through the vineyards. Tours of the facility end with a complimentary tasting. The tasting room also sells the firm's Sonoma County Brut by the glass or by the bottle. For a small fee, the tasting-room staff will take you through a technical tasting of each sparkling wine: the Brut (a blend of Pinot Noir and Chardonnay), the Blanc de Noirs (made entirely from Pinot Noir), and the Brut Rosé. Top-of-the-line is the Tête de Cuvée, a vintage sparkling wine made in limited quantities from the best Chardonnay and Pinot Noir cuvées each harvest. ◆ Tasting and sales daily. 11447 Old Redwood Hwy (north of Eastside Rd). 433.8843; fax 433.6314 ♿

150 Rodney Strong Vineyards The vineyards come right up to the base of this monolithic structure built in buff concrete finished with massive wood beams. Rodney Strong, previously a Broadway choreographer, pioneered direct-mail wine marketing with his first venture, **Windsor Vineyards,** in the early 1960s, then went on to found this big operation. The current wine maker is Rick Sayre, who produces a wide spectrum of wines: Chardonnay, Fumé Blanc, late-harvest Riesling, Cabernet Sauvignon, Merlot, Pinot Noir, and Zinfandel—all available at the tasting room. The picnic lawn is the site of summer concerts. ◆ Tasting and sales daily; tours daily at 11AM, 1PM, and 3PM. 11455 Old Redwood Hwy (north of Eastside Rd). 433.6511, 431.1533; fax 433.8635

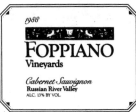

150 Foppiano Vineyards Founder John Foppiano, an immigrant from Genoa, began making wine from Russian River Valley grapes as early as 1896. Today, this establishment remains a family-run winery, with the third and fourth generations now in charge. The tasting room is a modest bungalow with an old red-and-white train car sitting behind it. While it's one of California's oldest wineries, the firm began producing varietal wines under its own label only in 1970. Its best may be the Petite Sirah, closely followed by the Sonoma Cabernet. The Riverside Vineyards Zinfandel is a good everyday wine for the money. ◆ Tasting and sales daily; tours by appointment only. 12707 Old Redwood Hwy (north of Eastside Rd). 433.7272 ♿

151 Madrona Manor $$$ Built in 1881 by John Alexander Patton, a wealthy entrepreneur and state legislator, this grand, gabled Victorian inn on the outskirts of Healdsburg includes a first-class restaurant acclaimed for its eclectic wine-country cuisine. The three-story manor boasted 17 rooms, three-and-a-half baths, and seven fireplaces. John and Carol Muir bought the mansion in 1981 and after a yearlong restoration, they opened it as a country inn. It now includes the main house and several other buildings (with a total of 18 rooms and three suites). The elegant guest rooms on the mansion's second floor are the best—particularly **No. 204,** which has a tall, carved

wooden bed, a chaise longue, a fireplace, a Victorian claw-foot tub, and French doors opening onto a balcony. Rooms in the carriage house, which dates from 1881, are furnished in a more contemporary (and less attractive) style with hand-carved rosewood from Nepal; one of the suites features a king-size bed, a marble-tiled bath, and a double Jacuzzi. The most secluded unit is the **Garden Suite,** furnished in rattan, with a fireplace, a private garden, and a deck area. Guests can relax in the manor's gracious parlor and music rooms, explore the extensive gardens, or use the swimming pool. A buffet breakfast is served in the dining room or on the outdoor deck. This is also one of the few inns that allow children (the staff will even baby-sit if parents want to dine in the restaurant). The front desk offers full concierge services. ◆ 1001 Westside Rd (north of Sweetwater Springs Rd). 433.4231; fax 433.0703 ♿

Within Madrona Manor:

Madrona Manor Restaurant ★★$$$$ Directed by the owners' son Todd Muir, who trained at the famous Chez Panisse restaurant in Berkeley, this restaurant serves produce that comes primarily from the inn's extensive kitchen garden. Muir also smokes his fish and meats and makes the breads and some desserts himself. The three dining rooms are decorated in elegant style with Persian rugs, damask tablecloths and napkins, silver candelabras, and fresh flowers. Choose either the five-course prix-fixe menu or order à la carte. First courses may include potato blinis with delicate smoked salmon, caviar, and dill beurre blanc, or marinated, grilled blue prawns on a bed of tricolored pappardelle (wide ribbon noodles). For a main course, he offers a half-dozen choices, ranging from Peking duck served with almond-coconut rice, stuffed chilies, and a rhubarb-honey sauce to salmon steak with sorrel cream sauce and vegetable strudel. Muir never stints on his ingredients and he has a flair for combining unusual flavors. The pastry chef holds to the same high standards, turning out skillful desserts—try the chocolate menagerie, the banana-coconut napoleon, or the sumptuous sorbets and ice creams. On Sundays Muir prepares a special prix-fixe brunch with a choice of entrées and desserts. ◆ California ◆ M-Sa dinner; Su brunch and dinner ♿

The Geysers power plant 18 miles east of Cloverdale is the largest geothermal plant in the world. It can generate enough power to meet the needs of a million people.

Restaurants/Clubs: Red   **Hotels:** Blue

Shops/ 🍴 Outdoors: Green   **Wineries/Sights:** Black

151 Mill Creek Vineyards This family-owned winery (pictured above), perched on a knoll overlooking its vineyards in Dry Creek Valley, was founded in 1965. The two-story redwood tasting room sits beside the creek, where a wooden mill wheel turns. You can sample the Kreck family's full range of varietal wines: Chardonnay, Sauvignon Blanc, Cabernet Blush, Cabernet, Merlot, and Gewürztraminer. Up a steep path at the back of the property is a large tree-shaded picnic deck with a panoramic view of Dry Creek Valley. ♦ Daily. 1401 Westside Rd (north of Sweetwater Springs Rd). 433.5098; fax 431.1714 ♿

151 Middleton Gardens Nancy and Malcolm Skall sell superb organic fruits and vegetables here, many of them grown from European heirloom seeds. Drive past the perfect white farmhouse surrounded by a mass of old-fashioned flowers. Ring the bell in front of the barn behind the house and one of the Skalls will arrive shortly to weigh out garlic braids, French pumpkins, 15 kinds of sweet and hot peppers, seven types of potatoes, true sun-dried tomatoes (as well as 40 types of fresh tomatoes), figs, peaches, pears, sweet corn, and seven kinds of eggplants. And don't miss Nancy's luscious strawberries (you may have to call ahead to secure a basket or two). Look for Malcolm at the Healdsburg, Santa Rosa, and Sebastopol farmers' markets, too. ♦ Daily Apr-Nov; call for Dec, Feb, and March schedule. 2651 Westside Rd (north of Sweetwater Springs Rd). 433.4755

Rabbit Ridge
Winery & Vineyards

152 Rabbit Ridge Winery & Vineyards Recently opened to the public for the first time since it was established in 1979, this winery produces impressively rich wines made from grapes grown on its 45-acre vineyard. Sauvignon Blanc, Zinfandel, Carignane, Cabernet Sauvignon, Cabernet Franc, Barbera, and a Port are among the varieties fashioned by owners/wine makers Darryl Simmons and Erich Russell. Sample them in the sunny tasting room, with its view of rolling hills. ♦ Tasting and sales daily; tours by appointment only. 3291 Westside Rd (north of Sweetwater Springs Rd). 431.7128 ♿

152 Belvedere Winery Here, the top-of-the-line wines are Chardonnay, Zinfandel, Merlot, and Cabernet Sauvignon. The winery also produces a late-harvest Moscato de Canelli. ♦ Tasting and sales daily. 4035 Westside Rd (north of Sweetwater Springs Rd). 433.8236

152 Sonoma Antique Apple Nursery Terry and Carolyn Harrison grow more than a hundred types of antique or heritage apple trees (varieties no longer commercially grown but that offer a spectrum of delicate and very different flavors), more than 30 kinds of pear trees, and peach trees. They have a mail-order catalog, too. ♦ Tu-Sa mid-Jan to Mar; phone orders only Apr-Dec. 4395 Westside Rd (north of Sweetwater Springs Rd). 433.6420; fax 433.6479

153 Hop Kiln Winery A brass plaque just outside this immense old building with three towers (pictured above) reads: "This structure served the important hop industry of California's North Coast region, once the major hop-growing area in the West." Built in 1905 by a crew of Italian stonemasons, it represents the finest existing example of its type, consisting of three stone kilns for drying the hops, a wooden cooler, and a two-story press for baling hops for shipment. Listed on the National Register of Historic Places, the hop-kiln barn was restored and converted to a winery in 1974 by Dr. Martin Griffin, who is still the owner. The tasting room pours the winery's Chardonnay along with its robust reds, among them Zinfandel, Primitivo Red, and Marty's Big Red (made from four unidentified grape varieties found growing on a remote corner of the property). With its picnic grounds beside a duck pond, this is a popular stop for bicyclists heading to or from the Russian River on Westside Road. ♦ Tasting and sales daily. 6050 Westside Rd (north of Sweetwater Springs Rd). 433.6491; fax 433.8162

153 J. Rochioli Vineyards & Winery The Rochioli family has been growing premium grapes since the 1930s. They make good Sauvignon Blanc and Pinot Noir as well as Chardonnay and Cabernet Sauvignon. A small gallery offers a changing art show. Bring your lunch, and picnic at the tables on an outdoor deck. ♦ Tasting and sales daily. 6192 Westside Rd (north of Sweetwater Springs Rd). 433.2305

On the fertile banks of the Russian River

154 Westside Farms Stop at this restored 1869 farmhouse for wreaths and homegrown popcorn, and to stroll through the herb and flower garden. During the summer Pam and Ron Kaiser also sell several kinds of corn, tomatoes, onions, and potatoes. In addition to farming 40 acres of Chardonnay and Pinot Noir grapes, the Kaisers raise sheep and Angora goats for wool, along with the miniature donkeys that are always a big hit with kids. During their October **Farm Pumpkin Fest,** the public is invited to visit their family farm with 20 acres of pumpkins, free hayrides, and Indian and decorative corns. ♦ F-Su June-4 July; M, W-Su 5 July-Sept, Nov; daily Oct. 7097 Westside Rd (south of Sweetwater Springs Rd). 431.1432

154 Davis Bynum Many of the wines available for tasting here are sold only at the winery. Chardonnay, Sauvignon Blanc, and Cabernet are good bets. Occasionally visitors may be treated to a special "future wines" barrel tasting. There is a shady picnic area with tables set up at the edge of a cool ravine. ♦ Daily. 8075 Westside Rd (south of Sweetwater Springs Rd). 433.5852; fax 433.4309 &

155 Raford House $$ When Raford W. Peterson built this two-story farmhouse northwest of Santa Rosa in the 1880s, it was intended to shelter both his family and his ranch hands. Called the **Wohler Ranch** at the time, the property was surrounded by more than 400 acres of hops, which Peterson processed and shipped to the flourishing beer-brewing industry. In 1981, after a year of restoration, the house, which now sits on four-and-a-half acres in the midst of vineyards and orchards, was converted to a bed-and-breakfast inn. Flanked by stately palms, the **Raford House,** a Sonoma County Historical Landmark, has seven guest rooms. All of them are decorated with period decor; five rooms have a private bath and two share a bath. Two of the guest rooms also have

fireplaces; the bridal suite is the most private, featuring a fireplace and its own patio. Innkeepers Carole and Jack Vore provide a full breakfast. ♦ 10630 Wohler Rd (off River Rd). 887.9573; fax 887.9597

156 Healdsburg Memorial Beach Park At this popular park on the Russian River, a beach and swimming lagoon are created by a dam that is erected every Memorial Day and taken down just after Labor Day weekend. Fishing and canoeing are available year-round, as are several riverside picnic sites. ♦ Nominal fee. Swimming: daily Memorial Day through Labor Day. Park: daily. 13839 Old Redwood Hwy (near Healdsburg Ave). 433.1625

157 W.C. "Bob" Trowbridge Canoe Trips Since the 1960s, this company has been renting silver metal canoes for unguided trips along the Russian River. According to veteran canoeists, this is the most popular canoeing river in the world—and on summer weekends it certainly appears to be. Sign up for any of five reasonably priced, one-day canoe trips. You can drop off your car at your final destination point and catch a shuttle to the starting area for a minimal fee. Canoe all the way from Cloverdale to the company's **Alexander Valley Campground** or to the town of Guerneville, or choose shorter segments in between. One of the most scenic routes starts at the **Alexander Valley Campground** and winds back to Healdsburg through the heart of the valley and its vineyards, past blue heron rookeries, secret picnic spots, and swimming holes. You don't need to know much about canoeing to set off down the river safely, but bring plenty of sunblock and a hat (sunburns are the biggest hazard).

Sign up for the inexpensive chicken- and steak-buffet barbecues, which are held on Saturday and Sunday from 4 to 7PM. And if camping along the river sounds appealing, the campground to one side of the Alexander Valley Bridge is an idyllic location. It's highly recommended that you reserve a campsite and a canoe in advance, especially on the weekends. Check in between 8:30 and 11:30AM, and plan to be on the river by noon. Children must be at least six years old. No dogs are allowed on the campgrounds or in the canoes. For a free brochure listing all the launch sites and locations of the two campgrounds, stop by or write to: Trowbridge Canoe Trips, 20 Healdsburg Ave (near the river), Healdsburg, CA 95448. ♦ Registration daily 8:30-11:30AM 1 Apr to mid-Oct. 20 Healdsburg Ave (between the river and Mill St). 433.7247, 800/640.1386

158 Alderbrook Winery Award-winning Chardonnay, Sauvignon Blanc, Sémillon, Gewürztraminer, Petite Sirah, and Zinfandel are produced at this winery west of Highway

101 and downtown Healdsburg. The 1993 vintages of Dry Creek Valley Chardonnay, Dry Creek Valley Sauvignon Blanc, and Muscat de Frontignan won gold medals at the Sonoma County Harvest Fair in 1994. Bring a picnic to enjoy on the veranda. ♦ Tasting and sales daily. 2306 Magnolia Dr (off Kinley Dr). 433.9154 ♿

159 Healdsburg Chamber of Commerce The staff here is happy to provide information on lodging, restaurants, and events in the greater Healdsburg area, plus maps of Healdsburg and the Russian River Wine Road, Sonoma Farm Trails, and more. ♦ Daily. 217

Healdsburg Ave (between Mill and Matheson Sts). 433.6935; fax 433.7562

159 Antique Harvest There's plenty of good stuff in this shop, including Irish pine furniture, handsome old ceramic bowls, cookware for your country kitchen, handmade quilts and crocheted bedspreads, vintage hats, and old jewelry. ♦ Daily. 225 Healdsburg Ave (between Mill and Matheson Sts). 433.0223

159 Tre Scalini ★★$$$ This small, sleek Italian restaurant offers *nuova cucina*—that's new Italian cooking prepared with choice local ingredients. The ambience is casual,

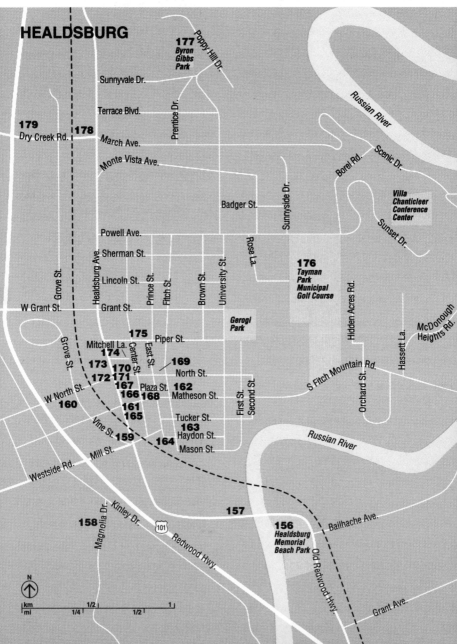

reservations are a must, and the service is exemplary. Cynthia and Fernando Urroz present a fat list of Sonoma County wines, but you may bring in one of your recent discoveries, and they'll open and pour it for a modest corkage fee. ♦ Italian ♦ M-Sa dinner. Reservations required. 241 Healdsburg Ave (between Mill and Matheson Sts). 433.1772 ♿

159 Vintage Plaza Antiques This is the largest antiques collective in Sonoma County, with more than 50 dealers showing their wares in Healdsburg's "Big Blue Building." Browsers will find everything from china and quilts to antique tools, rare buttons, and fancy old hats. Two booths carry only 1950s nostalgia items; another specializes in goods with Coca-Cola logos. Jewelry repair experts, upholsterers, furniture restorers, and clock specialists will fix your own precious items. From spring through fall, the parking lot is the site of a Saturday flea market, open to any dealer who wants to participate. Head for the picnic tables at the east end of the building to rest your weary legs. ♦ Mall: daily. Flea market: Sa 8AM-4PM Apr-Nov (weather permitting). 44 Mill St (at Healdsburg Ave). 433.8409 ♿

160 Farmers' Market You'll find all the makings for a sumptuous wine-country picnic right here. It's a marvelous, sociable event, and a vibrant showcase for all the countryside's bounty. ♦ Tu 4-7PM June-Oct; Sa 9AM-noon May-Dec. City Parking Lot (at W North and Vine Sts). 431.1956 ♿

161 Toyon Books Visit this plaza bookstore for bedside reading and a nice selection of books on wine and travel with an emphasis on Sonoma County and the North Coast. ♦ M-Sa. 104 Matheson St (at Healdsburg Ave). 433.9270

161 Robinson & Co. This well-stocked cookware store has a small collection of great cookbooks, whole-bean coffees, and imaginative gifts for cooks. It also often sells true bay-laurel leaves that come from a flourishing bay tree a local woman, now in her 80s, smuggled in as a seedling from France years ago. ♦ Daily. 108 Matheson St (at Healdsburg Ave). 433.7116 ♿

161 Healdsburg Inn on the Plaza $$ This Victorian, built as a Wells Fargo bank at the turn of the century, is now a nine-room bed-and-breakfast inn. Most attractive are the large rooms that have sunny bay windows and fireplaces and overlook the plaza. All guest rooms have private baths, queen-size brass beds, and the requisite romantic Victorian decor. Early risers will find a continental breakfast laid out on the breezy veranda at

7:30 every morning; guests can sit down to a hot breakfast at 9AM. No smoking is allowed. ♦ 110 Matheson St (at Healdsburg Ave). 433.6991 ♿

Within the Healdsburg Inn on the Plaza:

Innpressions Gallery Fine arts and crafts by North Coast artists are for sale at this compact gallery, which also carries jewelry. A special gift show runs every year from October until Christmas. ♦ Daily. 433.7510 ♿

161 Friends in the Country Jane Oriel has filled her shop with an enchanting collection of hand-painted dinnerware, porcelain tea sets, sumptuous cushions, and throws—all the niceties of life in the countryside of France and Italy displayed with an artist's flair. ♦ Daily. 114 Matheson St (between Center St and Healdsburg Ave). 433.1615 ♿

161 Fabrications
This small shop is crammed from floor to ceiling with bright cottons and natural-fiber fabrics for summer frocks or quilt making. You'll find supplies for textile arts, too: needles and quilting

templates for patchwork, embroidery hoops and floss, and ribbons and trims for Victorian ribbon-work. The staff is knowledgeable and ready to answer any questions. ♦ M-Sa. 118 Matheson St (between Center St and Healdsburg Ave). 433.6243

162 Healdsburg Museum Housed in the former 1910 **Healdsburg Carnegie Library** building, the museum displays the town's historical collection, much of it donated by local families. Permanent displays showcase the culture of the area's Pomo Indians, the Mexican land-grant era, the town's founding, and the notorious Westside squatters' wars. There is even an 1892 people-drawn fire engine. Special exhibits highlighting 19th-century tools, weapons, costumes, and other treasures of the collection change several times a year. At Christmastime, the focus is the annual antique toy and doll exhibit. Check the museum gift shop for reproductions of old-time toys, replicas of Indian crafts, and books on local history and lore. ♦ Free. Tu-Su. 221 Matheson St (at Fitch St). 431.3325 ♿

163 Haydon Street Inn $$ It seems like another era when you walk up to the white picket fence and find guests chatting on the wraparound veranda of this 1912 Queen Anne Victorian (pictured above). The eight rooms have a tranquil ambience, with lace curtains, gleaming wood floors, and pastel country prints. Six of the rooms are in the main house; the two least expensive are upstairs and share a hall bath, while the others have private baths. The **Rose Room** has a half-canopied bed covered with an antique crocheted coverlet. The two largest rooms, both in the two-story, Victorian-style cottage behind the house, feature vaulted ceilings and private baths with whirlpool tubs: the **Pine Room** has a four-poster bed with a Battenberg-lace canopy, while the **Victorian Room** is decorated with wicker and Ralph Lauren prints. The full country breakfast may include fresh fruit, homemade muffins, and strawberry crepes. ♦ 321 Haydon St (at Fitch St). 433.5228

164 White Oak Vineyards Former Alaskan fisherman Bill Myers pulled up stakes and opened this winery in 1981. From this functional building in downtown Healdsburg, Myers and wine maker Paul Brasset produce Chardonnay, Sauvignon Blanc, Alexander Valley Cabernet, Cabernet Franc, Chenin Blanc, and Dry Creek Valley Zinfandel. ♦ Tasting and sales F-Su. 208 Haydon St (at East St). 433.8429; fax 433.8446

165 Windsor Vineyards A pioneer in the direct marketing of wines, this establishment sells wines only from its tasting room and by mail order. The winery produces a wide range of vintages, from sparkling wines, Fumé Blanc, and several Chardonnays to Cabernet, Merlot, and Zinfandel, plus late-harvest dessert wines. You can also get personalized wine labels (for three or more bottles); order 10 days to two weeks in advance. ♦ Daily. 239-A Center St (between Mill and Matheson Sts). 433.2822; fax 433.7302 ♿

Restaurants/Clubs: Red   Hotels: Blue
Shops/♥ Outdoors: Green   Wineries/Sights: Black

165 Spoke Folks Cyclery Rent 12-speed touring bikes by the day or half-day; helmets are extra. No guided trips are available, but the store has biking maps and workers will advise on the best route for your interest and fitness level. The Alexander Valley route and Westside Road are both easy rides and favorites with local cyclists. ♦ M, W-Su. 249 Center St (between Mill and Matheson Sts). 433.7171

166 Healdsburg Plaza Crisscrossed with walkways and shaded by redwood and palm trees, this lovely plaza that was laid out in 1856 features a gazebo at one end and is the focus of special events throughout the year, including summer concerts, a May wine-tasting festival, and an annual Christmas-tree-lighting ceremony. Like Sonoma's historic Spanish-style square, the plaza is bordered by shops and restaurants. ♦ Bounded by Center St and Healdsburg Ave, and Matheson and Plaza Sts

166 Salame Tree Deli Step up to the counter to order sandwiches to go, or order items by the pound and make your own creation on bread from the **Downtown Bakery & Creamery.** For more substantial picnic fare, try the barbecued chicken (while supplies last). Wine and beer are sold here, too. ♦ Daily. 304 Center St (between Matheson and Plaza Sts). 433.7224

166 Levin & Company
Bibliophiles will want to make time to browse the aisles of this used-book store; hardbound copies of the classics share shelves with an eclectic collection of paperbacks in many categories, including travel and gardening. History and architecture buffs may want to pick up a copy of *Historic Homes of Healdsburg,* which provides a self-guided tour of 70 houses representative of local architecture and history. ♦ Daily. 306 Center St (between Matheson and Plaza Sts). 433.1118

166 Jimtown Intown ★★$ John H. Werner and Carrie Brown have been so successful with their **Jimtown Store** on Highway 28 (see page 131) that they decided to open a second branch on Healdsburg Plaza in 1994. You can stop in for a quick muffin and coffee at the espresso bar, order a box lunch to go, or have a full sit-down meal in the cheery cafe decorated with brightly painted wooden chairs and vinyl tablecloths with a fruit design. The menu features homemade, hearty dishes, including chicken noodle soup, pot pie, stews, and sandwiches made with roast turkey, ham, and spicy seasonings. There are also daily specials such as Tuscan white bean soup and ravioli. Local wines are served by the glass. ♦ American ♦ Daily breakfast, lunch, and dinner. 306 Center St (between Matheson and Plaza Sts). 433.0770 ♿

166 Downtown Bakery & Creamery Lindsey
Shere, the longtime pastry chef at Berkeley's
famous Chez Panisse restaurant and author
of *Chez Panisse Desserts,* and co-owner
Kathleen Stewart have graced the plaza with
this evocation of an old-fashioned bakery.
Everything is top-notch—from the yeasty
pecan rolls sticky with caramel to the fruit-
drenched sorbets and ice creams. You won't
be disappointed by the wonderful flour-dusted
loaves of bread, fragile tarts, eccentric but
irresistible cookies, skillfully baked cakes,
and whatever else inspires the chefs that day.
Don't miss dipping the crunchy biscotti in
cappuccino, and nothing beats the old-
fashioned milk shakes or sundaes after a
canoe ride. There isn't a chair in the place,
only a little stand-up marble bar to one side
and a single garden bench out front, but the
plaza's ample benches and inviting lawn
are right nearby. ♦ Daily. 308-A Center St
(between Matheson and Plaza Sts). 431.2719;
fax 431.1579 &

166 Wild Rose This gift shop is filled with
scented soaps, lavish wrapping papers,
whimsical ceramics, and furniture. To take
the chill off a damp fall day, wrap yourself in a
handwoven wool-and-mohair throw. ♦ Daily.
308-B Center St (between Matheson and Plaza
Sts). 433.7869

166 Healdsburg Coffee Company Cafe ★$
Sit down with a muffin and a cup of house
coffee or a *latte macchiato* (graduated layers
of espresso, hot milk, and foam topped with
chocolate) at this pleasant little cafe. You can
also buy any of a dozen whole-bean coffees
from Mountanos Bros., the master San
Francisco roasters. At lunch choose from a
casual menu of salads, soups, and sandwiches, along with Sonoma wines by the glass
and juices from **The Cherry Tree** in Sonoma.
Savor your purchase on the plaza, if you like.
♦ Eclectic ♦ Daily. 312 Center St (between
Matheson and Plaza Sts). 431.7941 &

167 Samba Java ★★$$$ Chef Colleen
McGlynn, who used to work at the popular
Stars restaurant in San Francisco, brings a
breath of fresh air to the sometimes staid
wine country with her menus based on
Caribbean flavors. The decor picks up
the same theme with vibrant paintings,
galvanized metal tables, and brightly colored
tile accents. Her small yet imaginative menu
changes daily and features dishes such as
chilled mango and avocado salad, fried

plantains, Cuban chicken in citrus and roast
garlic, and curried pork loin. McGlynn and
co-owner Jim Neeley also offer an array of
interesting lunchtime antipasto dishes and
great burgers and sandwiches served on
Downtown Bakery & Creamery buns and
breads. At breakfast—and this is a must—
you can delve into freshly baked pastries
such as the divine coconut–sour cream
coffee cake or fresh berry muffins.
♦ Caribbean ♦ Tu-W lunch; Th-F lunch and
dinner; Sa breakfast, lunch, and dinner; Su
breakfast and lunch. 109-A Plaza St (between
Center St and Healdsburg Ave). 433.5282 &

168 El Farolito ★$ The standard Mexican
menu offers no surprises, but everything
from the tamales and enchiladas to the
burritos and vegetarian tacos is well prepared
and reasonably priced. And there is a good
list of Mexican beers. Takeout is available,
too. ♦ Mexican ♦ Daily breakfast, lunch,
and dinner. 128 Plaza St (between East and
Center Sts). 433.2807

169 Camellia Inn $$ Del Lewand and her
husband, Ray, have been running this
elegant bed-and-breakfast inn in the center
of town since the early 1980s. Horticulturist
Luther Burbank was a family friend of the
former owner's, and the camellias (more
than 50 varieties) surrounding the house are
attributed to him. The Lewands have painted
the 1869 Italianate Victorian a lovely pale
pink trimmed in cream and a deeper rose;
two tall pines flank the entryway, and the low
stone wall in front is bordered with roses.
The house features a double parlor with a
fireplace framed in Minton tiles depicting the
seven ages of man from Shakespeare's *As
You Like It.* The nine rooms are named after
camellia varieties and are furnished with
quality antiques and Oriental carpets. All of
the rooms have a private bath, and a favorite
of many guests is the **Tiffany Room,** papered
in Bradbury & Bradbury hand-silkscreened
wallpaper in a pattern of scallop shells, with
a queen-size four-poster bed, a gas fireplace,
and a whirlpool tub for two. Out back, the
swimming pool is surrounded with shade
trees and a grape arbor. A full buffet
breakfast is served. ♦ 211 North St (at
Fitch St). 433.8182; fax 433.8130

170 Raven Theater and Film Center
Current releases dominate the marquee at
Healdsburg's main movie theater. You can eat
before the show at the cafe next door, the
Ravenous Raven (see below). ♦ Daily. 115
North St (between Center St and Healdsburg
Ave). 433.5448

170 Ravenous Raven ★$ This great little cafe
has an appealing mix of salads, sandwiches,
and light entrées. ♦ Eclectic ♦ W-Su lunch and
dinner. 117 North St (between Center St and
Healdsburg Ave). 431.1770

PALLADIO

171 Palladio Behind the postmodernist facade lies a stylish design shop specializing in country and garden furniture, including wicker chairs, weathered armoires, and stone and iron tables designed by the owners. Smaller pieces are sold, too, including interesting lamps, willow baskets, and ornate étagères for plants. ◆ Daily. 324 Healdsburg Ave (at North St). 433.4343 &

171 Vintage Antiques Browse for flower vases, cut-crystal, silver-back mirrors, and other remembrances of times past. This is a good place to score a fabulous find. ◆ Daily. 328 Healdsburg Ave (at North St). 433.7461

172 Healdsburg Charcuterie & Delicatessen ★$ In this contemporary deli decorated with bay wreaths and fruit-crate labels, order sandwiches to go or settle in at one of the wooden tables along the big picture window. The turkey and beef are roasted here; the homemade meat loaf and the chicken salad are also good bets. A few daily specials are offered, and on Tuesday through Friday nights the supper menu includes a couple of soups and half-a-dozen entrées, such as beef Zinfandel, pork chop *charcutière*, sautéed salmon with lemon butter, gnocchi with pesto, and pasta *bolognese*. Frozen sausages from **Sonoma Sausage Company** are sold to take home. ◆ Eclectic ◆ M, Tu-Sa breakfast and lunch; Tu-F dinner. 335 Healdsburg Ave (at W North St). 431.7213 &

172 Evans Designs Gallery This is the world's largest producer of *raku*, a type of ceramic ware invented by the Japanese potter Chojiro in the 16th century. In this process, the fired pot is removed from a red-hot kiln and heavily smoked, producing a one-of-a-kind glaze. Founder Tony Evans and his team of potters have managed to turn *raku* into production pottery, no mean feat. The decorative pieces are glazed in extravagant colors and metallics; some verge on the gaudy. At any rate, this shop in **Willow Creek Plaza** is actually **Evans Ceramics'** outlet, selling prototypes, seconds, and discontinued stock at reduced prices. ◆ M, W-Su. 355 Healdsburg Ave (at W North St). 433.2502

172 Kendall-Jackson Wine Country Store This is the tasting outpost for Lake County's **Kendall-Jackson Winery** and **La Crema, Stonestreet, Cambria, Robert Pepi, Edmeads, and Lakewood Vineyards.** The roster of wines includes several barrel-fermented Chardonnays, a Johannisberg Riesling, and an excellent

Sauvignon Blanc. Reds run the gamut from Cabernet and Zinfandel (including several fine vineyard-designated wines from old mountain vineyards) to a great Syrah. In addition to wine, the store stocks glasses, cookbooks, wine books, and a slew of tempting California gourmet products. ◆ Daily. 337 Healdsburg Ave (at W North St). 433.7102; fax 433.6215 &

173 Costeaux French Bakery This bakery stacks the display counters with its signature latticed fruit tarts, lemon-curd tarts, and dainty pecan tartlets. But sourdough bread, strawberry-rhubarb pie, and tall bittersweet-chocolate mocha cake are the real stars, drawing raves from loyal fans. The sandwiches on homemade bread are fairly standard, but handy for a picnic. On weekend evenings in the summer, simple dinner fare, such as salads, chili, and pizza, is offered at tables set out along the sidewalk. You'll take your chances with the espresso, though; the servers just can't seem to get it right. ◆ Daily. 417 Healdsburg Ave (between W North and Piper Sts). 433.1913 &

174 Western Boot ★$$ You can order down-home portions of steak, ribs, chicken, and seafood at this family-owned restaurant. ◆ American ◆ Daily lunch and dinner. 9 Mitchell La (off Healdsburg Ave). 433.6362 &

175 Sonoma County Wine Library This special collection at the Healdsburg branch of the **Sonoma County Library** brings together a wide range of materials on wine-related subjects. The library subscribes to more than 70 periodicals and numbers well over 2,500 books in its collection, ranging from technical works on viticulture and enology to books on wine appreciation and cooking. There's a file containing current information on county wineries, too. ◆ M-Sa. 139 Piper St (at Center St). 433.3772; fax 433.7946 &

176 Tayman Park Municipal Golf Course This nine-hole, par 35, public golf course set on 60 acres overlooks the town. It was founded in 1922 as the private **Healdsburg Country Club** by US Army colonel C.E. Tayman. ◆ Daily. 927 S Fitch Mountain Rd (off Matheson St). 433.4275

177 Byron Gibbs Park This two-and-a-half-acre park offers tables for picnicking and a children's play-ground. ◆ 1520 Prentice Dr (off Sunnyvale Dr)

178 Tip Top Liquor Warehouse There's a great selection of Sonoma County wines here. Shipping is available, too. ◆ Daily. 90 Dry Creek Rd (between Healdsburg Ave and Hwy 101). 431.0841; fax 800/413.WINE

179 Best Western Dry Creek Inn $ This contemporary inn has 102 rooms (choose between a king-size or two queen-size beds) and a vaguely Spanish-style decor on a busy street not far from the freeway. If standard comforts such as cable TV and a heated pool are more important than wine-country ambience, this is the place for you. A continental breakfast is included. Ask about special midweek rates. ◆ 198 Dry Creek Rd (between Healdsburg Ave and Hwy 101). 433.0300, 800/222.KRUG; fax 433.1129 ♿

180 Jordan Vineyard & Winery When Denver oilman Tom Jordan and his wife, Sally, opened their winery in the Alexander Valley, they created quite a stir in the wine world. Everybody hurried to see the grandiose French-style stone château (pictured above) and to taste their first release, a 1976 Alexander Valley Cabernet, which was full-bodied, lush, and eminently ready to drink— Jordan had the time and capital to age the wine in his own cellars before releasing it. Later wines have kept to the same high standard set by that first release. Jordan also makes fine estate-bottled Chardonnay. ◆ Tours by appointment only. 1474 Alexander Valley Rd (2 miles from Healdsburg Ave). 431.5250

181 Belle de Jour Inn $$$ This serene retreat is set on a hill overlooking the rolling green landscape of the Russian River Valley. Innkeepers Tom and Brenda Hearn live in the 1873 Italianate Victorian in front. They've turned the caretaker's cottage into a very private suite with a king-size bed swathed in Battenberg lace, a Franklin stove, a whirlpool bath for two, and hotel conveniences such as hair dryers and a refrigerator. Three other cottages are nestled alongside, each with a private entrance and view. The **Terrace Room** offers a king-size bed, a double whirlpool tub, hardwood floors, and a spare, contemporary decor. The snug **Morning Room,** the smallest of the four cottages, has a queen-size bed, paneled walls, green shutters opening onto a serene country view, a wood-burning stove, and a shower/steam bath. There is a telephone in each room, too. A full breakfast is served on the deck of the main house, or you can have a

breakfast basket set outside your door. The fresh, unfussy decor and the privacy make a welcome alternative to Victorian orthodoxy. ◆ 16276 Healdsburg Ave (a mile north of Dry Creek Rd). 431.9777

Within the Belle de Jour Inn:

Belle de Jour Vintage Car Tours Sign up for guided trips in a 1925 Star touring car through the Alexander, Dry Creek, or Russian River Valley. Itineraries can be custom-tailored to your interests. The chauffeured Star can also be reserved on an hourly basis (two-hour minimum) for private trips.

182 Simi Winery Wine maker Nick Goldschmidt produces regular and reserve wines that are well worth seeking out, and you can sample most of them in the tasting room of this winery (pictured above), across from the **Belle de Jour Inn.** Reserve offerings of older vintages of Chardonnay and Cabernet are for sale, too, including a collection of five different bottles in a specially designed wooden box. The tours are well run and informative. Picnic facilities are available, too. ◆ Tasting and sales daily; tours daily 11AM, 1PM, and 3PM. 16275 Healdsburg Ave (a mile north of Dry Creek Rd). 433.6981; fax 433.6253 ♿

183 Alexander Valley Campground This family campground by a beautiful stretch of the Russian River features 400 sites that are suitable for either two tents or a trailer (under 30 feet long). There are canoe rentals and free use of acres of sandy swimming beaches. ◆ Fee. Alexander Valley Rd (at the Alexander Valley Bridge). 431.1453

184 Jimtown Store This place is named for James Patrick, who settled here in the 1860s and ran a country store first at Soda Rock and then here in the heart of Alexander Valley. When New Yorkers John H. Werner and Carrie Brown came across the old country store for sale, they decided to move to the wine country and revive the historic building. First they hired the Berkeley architecture firm **Fernau & Hartman** to restore the large, lofty space, then they painted it an eye-popping yellow and green. Stop in for well-made espresso drinks and coffee cake in the morning; on Saturday mornings, look for dried-cherry scones, and on Sunday, cinnamon-caramel buns. The deli counter stocks top-quality cold cuts and homemade salads, including a notable buttermilk cole slaw. The mile-high sandwich includes baked ham, salami, mortadella, provolone, and the store's own olive salad on a baguette. Try the refreshing sports tea (an iced ginseng tea) and the old-fashioned chocolate cake. For kids there is a special lunch (a peanut-butter and Jimtown-jam sandwich, celery and carrot sticks, and a cowboy cookie). There's a patio eating area in back, where suppers are served throughout the summer, and part of the store is stocked with locally made jams, honey, and crafts. Call in advance to get a brown-bag picnic lunch. ♦ Daily; closed for two weeks in January. 6706 Hwy 128 (north of Alexander Valley Rd). 433.1212; fax 433.1252 ♿ Also at: 306 Center St (between Matheson and Plaza Sts), Healdsburg. 433.0770 ♿

185 Sausal Winery The Demostene family purchased the 125-acre **Sausal Ranch** in 1956 and began replanting prune and apple orchards with vineyards. In 1973 they turned a building formerly used to dehydrate prunes into a full-fledged winery, which wine maker Dave Demostene initiated with the 1974 vintage, a Zinfandel. Demostene continues to make good Zinfandel, especially an intense, rich private reserve. He also makes a very fine Cabernet, along with Chardonnay, Sausal Blanc, and White Zinfandel. Older vintages are for sale, too, rereleased for collectors. The tasting room has a shady picnic area on the veranda. ♦ Daily. 7370 Hwy 128 (south of Alexander Valley Rd). 433.2285; fax 433.5163 ♿

186 Johnson's Alexander Valley Wines This small, family-owned winery features Ellen Johnson as wine maker. Cabernet Sauvignon and Zinfandel are her main wines. ♦ Tasting and sales daily. 8333 Hwy 128 (south of Alexander Valley Rd). 433.2319

ALEXANDER VALLEY
MERLOT
ESTATE BOTTLED
1989

ALEXANDER VALLEY VINEYARDS

187 Alexander Valley Vineyards Once owned by Cyrus Alexander, for whom the Alexander Valley is named, this 250-acre ranch with the original 1841 homestead now belongs to the Wetzel family, who produce varietals from grapes grown on their estate. Most of the wines are available only at the tasting room (the age-worthy Cabernet is the one most seen in wineshops). They also make a good

Chardonnay and Gewürztraminer, plus small quantities of Pinot Noir and Merlot. There is a small, shady picnic area beside the parking lot. ♦ Tasting and sales daily; tours by appointment only. 8644 Hwy 128 (south of Alexander Valley Rd). 433.7209, 800/888.7209; fax 431.2556 ♿

188 Field Stone Winery & Vineyards This family-owned and -operated winery tunneled into the hillside takes its name from the excavated stones used to construct the rustic facade. Known primarily for its Cabernet and Petite Sirah, this high-quality act also produces Gewürztraminer, Sauvignon Blanc, and a barrel-fermented Chardonnay. ♦ Tasting and sales daily; tours by appointment only. 10075 Hwy 128 (at Chalk Hill Rd). 433.7266, 800/54.GRAPE; fax 433.2231 ♿

CHALK HILL WINERY

189 Chalk Hill Winery When Frederick Furth purchased the **Donna Maria Ranch** in the Chalk Hill area in 1980, he replanted the vineyards and constructed a barnlike winery building. Thomas Cottrell was the first wine maker; today David Ramey (formerly of **Matanzas Creek**), one of the county's most talented wine makers, is in charge. He produces Chardonnay, Cabernet, and a regular and late-harvest Sauvignon Blanc. ♦ Tasting, sales, and tours by appointment only. 10300 Chalk Hill Rd (south of Hwy 128). 838.4306 ♿

RIDGE / Lytton Springs

190 Ridge-Lytton Springs Winery This winery has one of the best Zinfandel vineyards in California. Originally planted by Italian immigrants at the turn of the century on a dry-farmed (nonirrigated) hillside, it produces grapes with a rich concentration of fruit and flavor. One corner of the functional winery acts as an impromptu tasting room, with a bar constructed just in front of a stack of wine barrels; if something is going on in the cellar, you're right there to see it. Try the Sonoma Zinfandel, especially the private reserve and the Zinfandel made from old vines with even more concentration. ♦ Tasting and sales daily, weather permitting. 650 Lytton Springs Rd (between Hwy 101 and Dry Creek Rd). 433.7721; fax 433.7751 ♿

190 Mazzocco Vineyards The first vintage at this family-owned winery was the 1985 Chardonnay. Today Tom Mazzocco and family produce two barrel-fermented Chardonnays (the best comes from their own **River Lane** vineyard) and a firmly structured Cabernet

Sauvignon. The Zinfandel comes from a vineyard planted in the early 1900s in nearby Dry Creek Valley. Wine maker Phyllis Zouzounis worked at **Dry Creek Vineyard** up the road (see below) before coming here. ♦ Tasting and sales daily. 1400 Lytton Springs Rd (between Hwy 101 and Dry Creek Rd). 431.8159; fax 431.2369 ♿

191 Dry Creek General Store Pick up picnic supplies and sandwiches to go, plus cold drinks and snacks here. ♦ Daily. 3495 Dry Creek Rd (off Lytton Springs Rd). 433.4171

192 Dry Creek Vineyard Founded in 1972 by Bostonian David Stare, who studied enology and viticulture at the **University of California at Davis,** this winery is a good, steady performer producing first-rate Fumé Blanc and Zinfandel. Picnic tables are set out on an enclosed lawn in the midst of an old-fashioned flower garden. ♦ Tasting and sales daily. 3770 Lambert Bridge Rd (at Dry Creek Rd). 433.1000; fax 433.5329 ♿

192 Robert Stemmler Vineyards Founded in 1977 by Robert Stemmler, who had worked at **Charles Krug** and **Inglenook** in Napa Valley, and partner Trumbull Webb Kelly, this small winery specializes in Pinot Noir and also produces Chardonnay and Cabernet Sauvignon. ♦ Tasting and sales F-Su by appointment only. 3805 Lambert Bridge Rd (at Dry Creek Rd). 433.6334; fax 433.1531 ♿

193 Ferrari-Carano Vineyards and Winery
Founded in 1981 by Reno attorney and hotelier Don Carano and his wife, Rhonda, this establishment is housed in a state-of-the-art complex at the head of Dry Creek Valley. Under wine maker George Bursick, the winery has been gaining a reputation for its whites, especially the oaky Chardonnay and a well-made Fumé Blanc. It also produces Cabernet, Merlot, and Eldorado Gold (a luscious late-harvest Sauvignon Blanc). All can be sampled in the tasting room, which has windows looking into the winery. There's also a spectacular underground barrel-aging cellar, which houses 1,500 French oak *barriques* (a type of wooden barrel). Next door is the winery's most recent addition, **Villa Fiore,** which serves as headquarters for an ambitious food and wine program (a series of events offering classes and tastings); it also includes a second public tasting room. ♦ Tasting and sales daily; tours by appointment only. 8761 Dry Creek Rd (at Dutcher Creek Rd). 433.6700; fax 431.1742 ♿

194 Preston Vineyards Lou Preston first entered the wine scene as a grape grower, and the quality of the grapes coming from his 125-acre Dry Creek Valley estate convinced him to become a wine maker in the late 1970s. The winery specializes in Sauvignon Blanc and Zinfandel, producing both a regular and a reserve Zinfandel. It also makes great Syrah, Barbera, and Muscat Canelli dessert wine (which sells out quickly). ♦ Tasting and sales daily; tours by appointment only. 9282 W Dry Creek Rd (beyond Yoakim Bridge Rd). 433.3372; fax 433.5307 ♿

Wine Varieties

Table Wines
Varietals

Red	White
Barbera	Chardonnay
Cabernet Franc	Chenin Blanc
Cabernet Sauvignon	French Colombard
Gamay	Gewürztraminer
Gamay Beaujolais	Johannisberg Riesling
Merlot	Moscato de Canelli
Pinot Noir	Pinot Blanc
Ruby Cabernet	Sauvignon Blanc
Syrah	Sémillon
Zinfandel	White Riesling

Generics

Red	White
Burgundy	Chablis
Chianti	Moselle
Claret	Rhine
Red Table Wine	Sauterne
Rosé	White Table Wine

Aperitif Wines
Madeira
Sherry
White Vermouth

Dessert Wines

Angelica
Cream Sherry
Marsala
Muscat de Frontigan
Muscatel
Port
Tokay

Sparkling Wines

Brut (Driest)
Extra-Sec (Extra Dry)
Sec (Dry)
Demi-Sec (Semidry)
Doux (Sweet)

195 Michel-Schlumberger This mission-style estate, which is run by chairman Jacques Schlumberger and honorary chairman/Swiss banker Jean-Jacques Michel, is surrounded by a hundred-acre vineyard. They produce estate-grown-and-bottled Chardonnay and Cabernet Sauvignon under the **Domaine Michel** label. ♦ Tours daily by appointment only. 4155 Wine Creek Rd (off W Dry Creek Rd). 433.7427, 800/447.3060; fax 433.0444 &

196 Quivira Winery Owners Henry and Holly Wendt took the name of this stark, modern winery from a legendary wealthy kingdom, which early explorers believed was situated somewhere in the Sonoma County area. It is known primarily for its Zinfandel and Sauvignon Blanc. The wine maker is Grady Wann. ♦ Tasting and sales daily; tours by appointment only. 4900 W Dry Creek Rd (at Wine Creek Rd). 431.8333, 800/292.8339 in CA; fax 431.1664 &

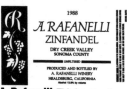

A. RAFANELLI
ZINFANDEL
DRY CREEK VALLEY
SONOMA COUNTY
1988
PRODUCED AND BOTTLED BY
A. RAFANELLI WINERY
HEALDSBURG, CALIFORNIA

197 A. Rafanelli Third-generation vintner Dave Rafanelli still has two of the vineyards his grandfather planted when he first came to this country. The winery is in the redwood barn where Dave Rafanelli's father, Amerigo, made wines with little help from modern-day technology. Dave will take you through the winery, explaining how he makes his beautifully balanced Dry Creek Valley Zinfandels and letting you taste the new vintages from the barrel and from the bottle. His Zinfandels and Cabernets just keep getting better every year. ♦ Tasting, sales, and tours by appointment only. 4685 W Dry Creek Rd (between Lambert Bridge and Wine Creek Rds). 433.1385 &

198 Lambert Bridge Winery When Jerry Lambert first bought this property, he replaced the existing prune orchards with 76 acres of prime vineyards. The tasting room is a rustic wooden building twined with wisteria in a serene wooded setting. On damp mornings a big stone fireplace takes off the chill. Sample the Fumé Blanc and Chardonnay, along with the best wines, the Merlot and the Crane Creek Cabernet. Reservations are required for the picnic gazebo. ♦ Tasting and sales daily. 4085 W Dry Creek Rd (south of Lambert Bridge Rd). 433.5855; fax 433.3215 &

199 Bellerose Vineyard Grapes were first planted on this Dry Creek Valley estate as early as 1887. Today's winery, founded by Charles Richard in 1979, specializes in three Bordeaux-style wines. The flagship is Cuvée Bellerose (a blend of Cabernet Sauvignon with Cabernet Franc and Petit Verdot). This small but very good producer also makes a Merlot and a Sauvignon Blanc. ♦ Tasting and sales daily; tours by appointment only. 435 W Dry Creek Rd (north of Westside Rd). 433.1637; fax 433.7024 &

Geyserville

The little town of Geyserville was founded in 1851 as **Clairville Station,** a stage stop for visitors on their way to see the famous Devil's Canyon geysers on **Geyser Peak,** the world's largest geothermal field, 16 miles to the east. Discovered by William B. Elliott in 1846, they are not true geysers, but smoking hot springs and hissing steam vents. From the 1860s to the early 1880s the "geysers" were a prime tourist attraction, and it's remarkable how many people made the difficult journey north to see them—some 3,500 people ventured here in 1875 alone. Ulysses S. Grant, Teddy Roosevelt, and William Jennings Bryan were among the notables who visited. But after 1885, when the more spectacular Yosemite and Yellowstone areas became more accessible, the geysers lost much of their allure. Today PG&E and other companies have several large plants up there and the geysers are closed to the public, although you can see their steam in the distance.

The town of Geyserville offers two lovely Victorian bed-and-breakfast inns, an old-time Italian restaurant, and several wineries, including **Chateau Souverain.** At the **Geyserville Bridge,** you can slip your canoe into the **Russian River** and paddle through the pastoral **Alexander Valley** all the way to Healdsburg.

200 Alexander Valley Fruit & Trading Company This small, family-owned winery has been forging a reputation for its honest, reasonably priced wines and its innovative gift packages, which combine bottles of wine with the firm's own dried fruits, mustards, jams, and sauces. On summer weekends you can sample most of these wines and food products in the frontier-style tasting room. Owners Steve and Candace Sommer also sell picnic supplies, including bread, cheese, soft drinks, and their own trail mix. Instead of the usual cellar tour, Steve will take you on a vineyard walk. ♦ Tasting and sales daily; tours by appointment only. 5110 Hwy 128 (north of Alexander Valley Rd). 433.1944, 800/433.1944; fax 433.1948 &

201 Murphy-Goode Estate Winery In 1979 Tim Murphy and Dale Goode, with more than two decades of grape-growing experience in

---

Restaurants/Clubs: Red   **Hotels:** Blue
Shops/ ♦ Outdoors: Green   **Wineries/Sights:** Black

the Alexander Valley, founded their own winery. They made only Fumé Blanc and Chardonnay for their first vintage (1985); Merlot and Cabernet were added to the lineup the following year. Try the lush Fumé Blanc Reserve—wine maker Christina Benz barrel-ferments certain lots of Sauvignon Blanc and leaves the wine on the lees to develop a rich aroma and flavor. The tasting-room manager, Karen Demostene, is well informed and will answer questions as she pours the wines. Some, such as the Fumé Blanc Reserve and a late-harvest Muscat, are available only at the winery. Tours include a walk through the vineyards with a discussion of the grapes, along with a visit to the fermentation and aging rooms. ◆ Tasting and sales daily. 4001 Hwy 128 (north of Alexander Valley Rd). 431.7644; fax 431.8640 ఈ

202 Trentadue Winery At this facility with massive red barn doors, the Trentadue family, grape growers in the valley since the early 1960s, produce a slew of wines: Zinfandel, Carignane, Merlot, sparkling wine, Old Patch Red (which comes from a patch of century-old vines), dessert wines, and a few Port-style wines. In the tasting room pick up picnic supplies, cut-crystal wineglasses, and baskets to tote it all to the shady picnic area sheltered by a latticed grape arbor. ◆ Tasting and sales daily. 19170 Geyserville Ave (off Hwy 101). 433.3104; fax 433.5825

203 Chateau Souverain This architectural complex (illustrated above), with a distinctive bluish slate roof meant to evoke a French château, started out as **Villa Fontaine** in 1972, owned by Pillsbury Flour. Since then, it has changed names and owners a number of times, and it is now owned by Wine World Inc. and Nestlé. Their roster of wines includes a Carneros reserve and regular Chardonnay, along with Pinot Noir, Sauvignon Blanc, Cabernet, Merlot, and Zinfandel. The winery also has a very good cafe (see below). ◆ Tasting and sales M, W-Su. 400 Souverain Rd (at Independence La). 433.8281 (weekdays), 433.3141 (weekends); fax 433.5174 ఈ

Also at Chateau Souverain:

Chateau Souverain Cafe at the Winery ★★$$ The owners really have the right idea with this contemporary cafe with bright paintings on the walls and jazz playing in the background. There used to be a separate restaurant next door, but now the cafe and restaurant have merged, offering deftly prepared dishes by chef Martin Courtman. Enjoy a glass of **Chateau Souverain**'s wine with oysters on the half shell, a fruit-and-cheese plate, or a slice of homemade duck pâté at one of the little bistro tables upstairs or down. Or do a little California-style grazing with more substantial dishes such as leg of lamb, grilled salmon, or a bowl of steamed mussels and clams. This is a great place to eat when you get hungry on the wine trail. ◆ California ◆ F-Su lunch and dinner. Reservations recommended ఈ

204 Isis Oasis Lodge $ To get here, follow the signs past Goddess Way to a fanciful Egyptian-style frieze (with mauve and purple accents, no less) and the retreat's main lodge. The **Society for Inspirational Studies** offers a wide variety of funky accommodations. You can sign up for the lodge (which sleeps 24), a tepee, a yurt (a Tibetan tent), the tower room, or a little house in the midst of the vineyard. The most private are the yurts and the tower, but midweek you may find yourself the only guest in one of the larger cottages. Some of the guest rooms have shared baths. This 10-acre retreat might be a good choice for a family or a small group on a budget—the vineyard house can sleep eight to 10, and the retreat house can fit up to 15 and includes a private hot tub, kitchen, and three baths. The complex also includes a theater and a ragtag menagerie (ocelots, llamas, black sheep, and pygmy goats); animal tours are held daily at 11AM. Take a look before you make reservations; this is definitely not to everyone's taste. Bodywork and massages are available by appointment. ◆ 20889 Geyserville Ave (off Hwy 101). 857.3524, 800/679.7387 ఈ

205 Rex ★★$$ The Catelli family has been serving hearty Italian-American fare for more than half a century. They make all their pastas and age and cut their meats themselves, including an excellent New York steak. In addition to the large set menu, they offer daily specials such as fettuccine Alfredo, pork roast with sage stuffing, beef short ribs, and leg of lamb with rosemary and sage dressing, all served in trencherman's portions. The herbs come from their own kitchen garden, and the wine list is long on Alexander Valley creations.

When the weather is warm, you can also dine outdoors. ♦ Italian-American ♦ M-F lunch and dinner; Sa-Su dinner. 21047 Geyserville Ave (off Hwy 101). 857.3935; fax 433.6066 &

205 Hope-Bosworth House and Hope-Merrill House $$ Bob and Rosalie Hope spent more than four years restoring the **Hope-Merrill House,** the handsome 1870 Eastlake-style Victorian on Geyserville's main street, doing much of the exterior and all of the interior labor themselves. It's fascinating to flip through the photo album detailing their meticulous work, which was rewarded with a first-place award for bed-and-breakfasts from the National Trust for Historic Preservation. The stunning hand-silkscreened wallpapers and the carefully chosen antique furnishings make this place very special. Each of the eight guest rooms has a private bath and a different decor. The largest are the **Victorian** and **Briar Rose** rooms upstairs, with antique queen-size beds, bay windows, private baths, and chaise longues. Another favorite is the **Bradbury,** with a queen-size bed, a fireplace, a shower for two, and a coffered ceiling papered in an intricate patchwork of patterns. Rosalie and her daughter, Kim, who manages the place, are real country cooks. In the handsome formal dining room they serve breakfast, which might include a platter of sausages from the **Sonoma Sausage Company,** fluffy buttermilk pancakes, and a light, flaky apple tart, still warm from the oven. With advance notice, they will put together a gourmet picnic lunch; the menu changes every week and always includes a bottle of wine the Hopes make from their tiny vineyard beside the house.

The **Hope-Bosworth House** across the street is a 1904 Queen Anne–style Victorian that is furnished in a less formal style; the four guest rooms are smaller and less expensive (all have private baths). Guests at both houses have use of the large swimming pool and gardens at the **Hope-Merrill House.** The Hopes know a lot about the wine country, and will sit down with you to outline a personal tour of small wineries. Also ask them about their "Pick and Press" package, which provides you with an opportunity to stay at the inn in the summer and pick and press grapes, and then return to the inn in the spring to taste, bottle, and

personally label your own wine. ♦ 21253 and 21238 Geyserville Ave (off Hwy 101). 857.3356, 800/825.4BED; fax 857.HOPE

206 Campbell Ranch Inn $$ Drive up to this 35-acre ranch and you're likely to find innkeepers Jerry and Mary Jane Campbell working in the exuberant flower garden planted around the swimming pool in front of the suburban-ranch-style inn. They have a greenhouse on the property and start many of the plants as seedlings. They're also avid bakers; the breakfast here, served outside on the brick terrace with a view of Geyser Peak, is one of the inn's main attractions. The pampered guests also get homemade pie or cake as a bedtime snack. The inn has four guest rooms, all with private baths and king-size beds; most have private balconies. The Campbells also rent the old bunkhouse as a private cottage with its own deck and fireplace. Guests have use of the tennis court, hot tub, and bicycles. And for those who don't want to miss their favorite TV shows, there's a satellite dish and a large-screen television set. ♦ 1475 Canyon Rd (off Hwy 101). 857.3476

207 J. Pedroncelli Winery Just down the road from the **Campbell Ranch Inn** is this winery. The original winery and buildings were bought in 1927 by Giovanni Pedroncelli; his sons John and Jim are still running the show. Along with the jug wines of their father's day, the Pedroncellis produce a range of Sonoma County varietals. Try the Zinfandel, especially the reserve, and the Cabernet—both good values. They also make Fumé Blanc and Chardonnay, and one of their latest wines is a Brut Rosé. ♦ Tasting and sales daily; tours by appointment only. 1220 Canyon Rd (off Hwy 101). 857.3531; fax 857.3812 &

208 Geyser Peak Winery You can't miss this ivy-covered stone building with flags flying overhead. The winery is owned by Santa Rosa businessman Henry Trione, and the once-staid wines are improving, particularly the 1989 and later vintages of the Reserve Cabernet. Fans of Gewürztraminer made in a softer style should try the winery's version, along with the Riesling, both easy on the wallet. The Estate Reserve Chardonnay is definitely a good buy, as is the Semchard (a blend of Sémillon and Chardonnay). Among the cellar selections (featured only at the winery) there is some-times a late-harvest Riesling. ♦ Tasting and sales daily. 22281 Chianti Rd (off Canyon Rd). 857.9463, 800/255.WINE; fax 857.9402 &

209 Lake Sonoma Winery The Polson family, who have more than three decades of experience growing grapes in Sonoma, established this winery in 1977 at the very end of Dry Creek Valley. The tasting room built over the underground cellar is 140 feet above the valley floor and affords a view of Warm Springs Dam and the valley. Sample their full range of wines, which includes Chardonnay and Zinfandel, at the bar or on the veranda. ♦ Tasting, sales, and tours daily. 9990 Dry Creek Rd (between Dutcher Creek and Rockpile Rds). 431.1550, 800/750.WINE (in CA); fax 431.8356 ♿

Cloverdale

An agricultural community just 20 miles north of Healdsburg, Cloverdale was settled in the mid-1800s and is home to one of California's oldest newspapers, *The Cloverdale Reveille,* founded in 1879. From Cloverdale, it is only one-and-a-half hours to the Mendocino Coast by way of the Anderson Valley.

210 J. Fritz Winery Known for its Chardonnay, this small establishment named for owner Arthur J. Fritz also makes Sauvignon Blanc and Zinfandel; many of the vintages are available only at the winery, which is built partly underground for maximum energy efficiency. Visitors can use the picnic area overlooking the creek. ♦ Tasting and sales daily. 24691 Dutcher Creek Rd (between Dry Creek Rd and Hwy 101). 894.3389; fax 894.4781 ♿

211 KOA Kampground One hundred and fifty campsites (55 of them are tent sites) are offered at this well-maintained family campground on 60 acres that includes a 60-foot-long swimming pool, a mini-golf course, a couple of fishing ponds, and a completely stocked store. Horses may come along with the family, too. ♦ Fee. 26460 River Rd (off Hwy 101). 894.3337, 800/368.4558

212 Ye Olde' Shelford House $ Built in 1885 by Eurasthus M. Shelford on part of a large ranch acquired by his family in 1863, this charming Victorian bed-and-breakfast inn (pictured above) is just a short walk from the Russian River. The long porch in front looks west across a sea of vines. The inn offers six guest rooms, three in the main house and three in the carriage house. The two upstairs bedrooms in the main house share a bath, but guests have

the entire floor to themselves. All the rooms are furnished with antiques and handmade quilts, giving the inn a cozy, country feel. Guests can use the gazebo for wine tasting and picnic lunches, and inn-keeper Ina Sauder has a few 10-speed bikes and a bicycle-built-for-two available. She also cooks a full breakfast every morning. And if you're interested in touring the wine country in a 1929 Model A, she can arrange that, too. The inn provides tours to five wineries in the antique car, followed by a picnic lunch at the inn (reservations are required). No smoking is allowed. ♦ 29955 River Rd (off Hwy 101). 894.5956, 800/833.6479

213 Vintage Towers Bed & Breakfast Inn $ This renovated blue-and-white Queen Anne Victorian sits on a quiet residential street in downtown Cloverdale. Listed on the National Register of Historic Places, the handsome house has a big side veranda overlooking a rose garden and a lawn where guests sometimes play a game of croquet. The inn features a library furnished with chaise longues, a parlor with a TV set, a stereo, and a phone for guests' use. The four guest rooms and three upstairs tower suites are beautifully furnished with quality antiques and lavish period fabrics; two rooms share a bath, and the rest have their own. The largest is the **Vintage Tower** suite, with a sitting room in the five-sided tower, a queen-size bed, a Victorian claw-foot tub, and Eastlake Victorian furniture. Innkeeper Jane Patton prepares a full breakfast. ♦ 302 N Main St (at Third St). 894.4535

213 Dutcher Creek RV Park and Campground This rustic campground with seasonal and native-plant gardens is about a half mile west of Highway 101 and a 10-minute drive or 30-minute bike ride from Lake Sonoma. It has 30 campsites, 15 suitable for tents and another 15 for RVs or trailers, with water and electric hookups, a laundry room, and a picnic area. Call for directions. ♦ Fee. 230 Theresa Dr (off Hwy 101). 894.4829

214 Lake Sonoma and Warm Springs Dam This serpentine lake, created by the US Army Corps of Engineers to protect Dry Creek Valley from flooding, was opened in 1985 as a recreational area. The lake and surrounding park total 17,600 acres with 53 miles of shoreline. Just 10 miles from Healdsburg, the area offers wonderful picnic spots, miles of hiking trails, and, in the summer, swimming, camping, and fishing. At the visitors' center you can pick up trail guides and learn about the region's wildlife and the Pomo Indians who originally settled the area. During the spawning season (generally November through March), salmon return to the adjoining Lake Sonoma fish hatchery to lay their eggs; from the second-floor **Interpretive Center,** visitors can watch as eggs are removed from females and incubated for about 20 days. The hatchery's rearing ponds are home to the fish until they become six- or seven-inches long and are released into Dry Creek. ♦ 3333 Skaggs Springs Rd, Geyserville (9 miles west of Cloverdale). 433.9483

Within the Lake Sonoma area:

 Liberty Glen Campground This campground offers 113 campsites for tents or RVs, as well as 15 environmental lakeside sites that can be reached only by hiking or boating on a first-come, first-served basis. ♦ 433.9483

 Lake Sonoma Marina Open to the public, this privately owned marina has boats (including houseboats) and 250 boat slips for rent, a boat launch, a picnic area, and parking. ♦ 433.2200

Guerneville

This unpretentious little town sits squarely on the site of the logging camp and sawmill George Guerne set up in 1865 to cash in on the redwood logging boom. So many trees were felled that the area around what is now Guerneville was referred to as **Stumptown;** in fact, the center of Guerneville is built on top of the stumps of centuries-old redwoods. Things stepped up when the **San Francisco–North Western Pacific Railroad** chugged into town for the first time in 1877. Soon tremendous trainloads of logs and lumber were heading south, and Guerneville became one of the busiest logging centers in this part of the West. When the area was nearly logged out, entrepreneur A.W. Foster decided to transform the old logging camps into vacation resorts. And so a tradition was born. Guerneville and the **Russian River** remain a popular weekend getaway for San Franciscans bent on fishing, camping, and tramping in the redwoods.

Guerneville offers cafes and restaurants, picnic supplies, canoe and boat rentals, and accommodations ranging from family camping sites to resorts oriented to a gay clientele and Victorian bed-and-breakfasts. Reservations should be made early, especially from August through October. Annual events include the wildly successful Russian River Jazz Festival in September and the Russian River Rodeo and Stumptown Days in June.

215 Ridenhour Ranch House Inn $$ Built in 1906 by Louis E. Ridenhour, this turn-of-the-century redwood house (pictured above) was once part of the famed **Ridenhour Ranch,** which extended for 940 acres on both sides of the Russian River. Now an eight-room bed-and-breakfast inn, the ranch stands on two-and-a-quarter forested acres just next door to **Korbel Champagne Cellars** (see page 139). Innkeepers Diane Rechberger and her Austrian husband, Fritz, had a restaurant in Orange County before moving up to the Russian River in 1988. Fritz, who trained as a chef in Europe, cooks quite a breakfast in the large kitchen. Most mornings he bakes at least three pastries and serves them with his own homemade jam, yogurt, and granola. For the main course, he might prepare an omelette filled with duck-apple sausage or scrambled eggs with Bodega Bay smoked salmon. He leaves out a big tray of cookies in the afternoon, and guests may also arrange for him to cook a five-course dinner. The large living room features a 1913 Steinway grand piano, a fireplace, and forest views. The most private accommodation is the **Hawthorne Cottage;** it has a queen-size bed, a fireplace, and a window seat for curling up with a good book. In the main house, the cozy **Spruce Room,** with a queen-size brass bed and an antique English armoire and dresser, has a forest view. The rooms are more like the guest bedrooms you'd find in a friend's house than the fussy theme rooms whipped up by some bed-and-breakfast owners, and they all have private baths. There's a hot tub outside. ♦ 12850 River Rd (at Odd Fellows Park Rd). 887.1033; fax 869.2967 ¿

KORBEL CHAMPAGNE CELLARS

215 Korbel Champagne Cellars Nestled among the redwoods, this gabled brick building covered with ivy overlooks gentle, vine-carpeted hills and the Russian River. The winery was founded in 1886 by the three Korbel brothers, Czech immigrants who had first gone into the logging business along the Russian River felling huge redwood trees, cutting them into timber, and crafting them into cigar boxes. They decided to plant vineyards among the redwood stumps on some of the land they had cleared, first concentrating on still wines and distilling some of them into brandy. Soon, however, they decided to produce sparkling wines from European grape varieties. The first shipment of their champagne was made in the spring of 1882, and the business remained in the family until 1954, when it was purchased by Adolf Heck, a descendant of a wine-making family from the Alsace area in France.

The Heck family has since extended their vineyards and now produces nine vintage and nonvintage sparkling wines, which range from a vintage 1991 Blanc de Blancs, a vintage 1990 Blanc de Noirs, a Rouge (a medium-dry dark red champagne), a medium-dry Brut, a nonvintage Blanc de Noirs, a Brut Rosé, and the original champagne Sec, first produced in 1882. Korbel Natural was the sparkling wine poured at the 51st Presidential Inauguration in January 1989, and it won a gold medal at the Sonoma County Harvest Fair in 1994. The Hecks also make the original brandy (first produced in 1889), a new spiced brandy, Grappa, and a selection of still wines available only at the winery. Tours here guide visitors through the complicated process of making *méthode champenoise* wines from start to finish and end with a tasting of the firm's wines. From May through September, you can also opt for a tour of the glorious hillside rose garden, planted with more than 300 varieties of antique roses and a wealth of other old-fashioned flowers and bulbs. ♦ Tasting and sales daily; tours daily at 10AM, 11AM, noon, 12:45PM, 1:30PM, 2:15PM, and 3PM. 13250 River Rd (near Odd Fellows Park Rd). 887.2294; fax 869.2981 &

216 King's Sport and Tackle Shop Serious fishers will enjoy trolling here for all sorts of gear and diving equipment. Owner Steve Jackson keeps customers up to date with information on river and fishing conditions. He will also arrange sportfishing trips with knowledgeable guides. During the fishing season (which runs generally from mid-August through February), he opens as early as 5AM. Whether you fish or not, you can still find beach gear and attire at this friendly shop. ♦ Daily. 16258 Main St (at Armstrong Woods Rd). 869.2156 &

216 Mike's Bikes This shop carries a full range of bikes and accessories. Sign up for bike rentals by the hour, half day, or full day. No guided tours are offered, but you can get plenty of good advice on favorite spots to bike

either along the river or through the redwood groves. ♦ Daily May-Sept; M, Th-Su Oct-Apr; closed the first three weeks of January. 16442 Main St (at Mill St). 869.1106

216 Johnson's Beach Every summer a temporary dam goes up to create this swimming lagoon located along a sandy stretch of beach. It may be foggy and dreary only an hour away in San Francisco, but it is definitely summer here. When you tire of swimming or sunbathing, you can always rent one of the silver aluminum canoes and paddle off into the afternoon. This is also the site of the annual **Russian River Jazz Festival** in September. ♦ First and Church Sts

On Johnson's Beach:

Johnson's Beach Resort $ This family resort sits right on the beach, from which it's only a short walk into town. More than 50 camping spaces are suitable for either tents or RVs; they also have 10 inexpensive, simple rooms with private baths. The campground has hot showers, a laundromat, a picnic area, and access to the river for swimming or fishing. Boats are also available for rent. Daily and weekly rates. ♦ Daily May-Sept. 16241 First St (at Church St). 869.2022

216 Russian River Region Information Center Pick up details on Russian River and other Sonoma County area restaurants, lodgings, wineries, recreation, and events. You can also get tickets for some activities here. ♦ Daily; hours vary in the winter. 14034 Armstrong Woods Rd (off Hwy 116). You can write for information to: Box 255, Guerneville, CA 95446. 869.9212, 800/253.8800 &

217 Sweet's River Grill ★★$$ In the morning stop in to this eatery for Belgian waffles, omelettes, and their own freshly baked pastries and croissants, plus espresso and a special coffee made from beans roasted on the premises. At lunch the kitchen turns out homemade soups, salads, roast chicken, and sandwiches, as well as eclectic fare such as

SWEET'S RIVER GRILL

Thai chicken burritos and a cold salad of cheese tortellini with a blue-cheese and basil sauce. Desserts are all homemade, including the fruit pies and cheesecake. At night choose from special dishes such as phyllo-dough triangles stuffed with goat cheese and vegetables, fresh fish, or sliced pork tenderloin in ginger sauce. There's a good list of top-notch beers and Sonoma County wines at reasonable prices. On warm days you can eat outside on the patio. ♦ Eclectic ♦ M-Tu, Th-Su breakfast, lunch, and dinner. 16521 Main St (at Mill St). 869.3383

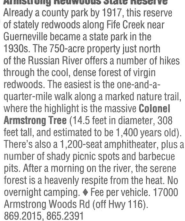

218 Ring Canyon Campground Just two blocks from the entrance to Armstrong Woods, this family campground has 35 tent sites under the redwoods and some trailer sites. All have picnic tables and fire rings; a bathhouse provides hot showers. ♦ 1747 Armstrong Woods Rd (off Hwy 116). 869.2746

218 Armstrong Redwoods State Reserve Already a county park by 1917, this reserve of stately redwoods along Fife Creek near Guerneville became a state park in the 1930s. The 750-acre property just north of the Russian River offers a number of hikes through the cool, dense forest of virgin redwoods. The easiest is the one-and-a-quarter-mile walk along a marked nature trail, where the highlight is the massive **Colonel Armstrong Tree** (14.5 feet in diameter, 308 feet tall, and estimated to be 1,400 years old). There's also a 1,200-seat amphitheater, plus a number of shady picnic spots and barbecue pits. After a morning on the river, the serene forest is a heavenly respite from the heat. No overnight camping. ♦ Fee per vehicle. 17000 Armstrong Woods Rd (off Hwy 116). 869.2015, 865.2391

Within Armstrong Redwoods State Reserve:

Armstrong Woods Pack Station Laura and Jonathan Ayers organize guided horseback rides in the redwood country. Sign up for half-day or full-day rides with a picnic lunch. You can also opt for two- or three-day pack trips by horseback into the wilderness of adjoining **Austin Creek State Recreation Area** (see below). Brochures are available with more information. ♦ Reservations required. 887.2939

219 Austin Creek State Recreation Area This 4,200-acre wilderness of oak forests, canyons, and sunny glades surrounds Austin Creek and its tributaries. You can camp at Redwood Lake or hike or ride your horse into one of the three remote, primitive campsites. The park is sometimes closed in the summer because of fire hazards. ♦ Fee per vehicle. 17000 Armstrong Woods Rd (off Hwy 116). 869.2015, 865.2391

APPLEWOOD
INN & RESTAURANT

220 Applewood $$$ Surrounded by redwood country, this elegant inn, once the country home of a wealthy banker, offers first-class service in the more personal setting of a bed-and-breakfast inn. Owners Jim Caron and A. Darryl Notter have furnished the 10 guest rooms in the Mission-Revival mansion and six newer rooms in an adjacent building with discriminating taste and all the comforts of home. The rooms, traditional yet not fussy, are decorated with antiques, queen-size beds, down comforters, reading lights, and armloads of flowers. Each room has a private bath, a telephone, and cable TV, and most have serene forest views; several also have fireplaces, verandas or balconies, and Jacuzzis. A lavish breakfast is included. The inn also has a swimming pool, and the Russian River is only a few minutes away. ♦ 13555 Hwy 116 (near River Rd). 869.9093 ⅋

Within Applewood:

Applewood Restaurant ★★$$$ Innkeeper Jim Caron doubles as chef in the dining room, where he prepares a prix-fixe four- to six-course dinner five nights a week. Caron gives fresh local ingredients a Mediterranean touch. You can choose to sit either in the solarium (where inn guests eat breakfast), with tall windows on three walls, forest views, a massive rock fireplace, and marble-topped tables; or the formal, dusty rose–colored dining room, with linen napkins and tablecloths and a chandelier hanging from

---

Restaurants/Clubs: Red **Hotels:** Blue
Shops/♥ Outdoors: Green **Wineries/Sights:** Black

the arched ceiling. The menu changes nightly, but dishes might include potato, leek, and roquefort soup, figs stuffed with prosciutto and goat cheese, rack of lamb with an Asian-style peanut sauce, and, for dessert, a heavenly Tuscan cream cake. Guests can bring their own wine or choose from a list of primarily Sonoma County wines. ♦ California ♦ Tu-Sa dinner; one seating nightly at 7:15PM. Reservations required. ♿

221 Santa Nella House $ Just across the river from the **Ridenhour Ranch House Inn** (see page 138) is this hotel, once the wine maker's residence at the historic **Santa Nella Winery.** Surrounded by lush redwoods and only a short walk from the Russian River and **Korbel Champagne Cellars,** the 1870 Victorian features a wraparound veranda where guests can relax after a day's touring. The inn has four guest rooms, all with queen-size beds, private baths, and fireplaces. Innkeepers Ed and Joyce Ferrington serve a full breakfast. ♦ 12130 Hwy 116 (near River Rd), Guerneville. 869.9488

Duncans Mills

As soon as the railroad reached Guerneville in 1877, brothers Alexander and Samuel Duncan took apart the sawmill they had been running at the tiny coastal community of Bridgehaven, loaded it on a barge, and headed upriver to meet the railroad at this bucolic spot. Today the Victorian Revival village that sprang up around Duncans Mills and the old 1880s depot has been refurbished to attract travelers on their way to or from the coast. This charming hamlet (located just off **Highway 116**) with about 20 residents is filled with shops, delis, restaurants, and the old general store.

222 Duncans Mills General Store This old-time general store dates from the sawmill days in the late-19th century. It still offers everything from picnic supplies, coffee, and pastries to fishing tackle, cookware, and beef jerky for the trail. Campers come in for newspapers and magazines—and to get fishing licenses before heading off for that secret fishing hole. ♦ Daily. 25200 Hwy 116 (near King Ridge Rd). 865.1240

222 Gold Coast Espresso Bar ★$ Pull into this delightful pit stop along the road to the coast to find well-made espresso drinks and morning pastries. The eatery roasts its own whole-bean coffees, and on sunny days you can take your coffee outside to the garden. On the weekends, try the grilled, freshly harvested Tomales Bay oysters. ♦ Coffeehouse ♦ M-F breakfast and lunch; Sa-Su breakfast, lunch, and dinner. Steelhead Blvd (off Hwy 116). 865.1441 ♿

222 Casini Ranch Family Campground This huge 125-acre site surrounded on three sides by the Russian River offers great family camping. Each of the 225 campsites (suitable for either tents or RVs) has picnic tables and a barbecue pit. George Casini and family have turned the old 1862 horse barn into a recreation hall, now used for parties. There are one-and-a-half miles of beach here with plenty of fishing holes, so you can catch trout, silver salmon, or catfish for supper. RV hookups include cable TV. The Casinis have a store, a laundromat, and hot showers, and will rent you a rowboat or canoe. Other highlights include an arcade, volleyball games, and free hayrides on Saturday nights. Weekly and monthly rates are available. ♦ 22855 Moscow Rd (off Hwy 116). Reservations recommended. 865.2255, 800/451.8400 ♿

Forestville/Sebastopol

Deep in the heart of redwood country is Forestville, a tiny hamlet that's primarily known for its wines, produced in the nearby **Green Valley** appellation, and for its many berry farms. Everybody stops at **Kozlowski Farms** on the way home from the **Russian River** to pick up baskets of raspberries and other homegrown products. Just south of Forestville is Sebastopol, another small town which is best known for producing a bumper crop of apples each year (particularly the Gravenstein variety). On the outskirts of town are several wineries, including **Iron Horse Vineyards.**

223 Burke's Canoe Trips Canoe down the Russian River for 10 miles through the majestic redwood forests from Forestville to Guerneville. The unguided trip takes from three to three-and-a-half hours from start to finish, but most people dawdle along the way, turning it into an all-day affair. Bring an ice chest, pack a picnic, and don't forget the sunscreen and sun hats—it can get blistering hot out there. When you arrive in Guerneville, a shuttle takes you back upriver to your car. There's also a campground in the redwoods with river views, plus a beach for swimming and a picnic and barbecue area. No dogs allowed. ♦ Daily May-Sept; Oct by appointment only. 8600 River Rd (off Hwy 116), Forestville. 887.1222

224 Mark West Vineyards Founded in 1976 by pilot Bob Ellis and his wife, Joan, and named for one of the valley's original settlers, the winery is housed in a converted dairy building. Visitors can sample their full-flavored Gewürztraminer, Pinot Noir, and Chardonnay, as well as wines produced under their **Marion** label, which includes Cabernet, Sauvignon Blanc, and White Zinfandel. You can also picnic on one of three separate lawns (one or more may be reserved for a private group). Along with the usual wine paraphernalia, they also sell impromptu picnic supplies for those who arrive unprepared: cheeses, crackers, salami, and more. ◆ Tasting and sales daily; tours by appointment only. 7010 Trenton-Healdsburg Rd (near River Rd), Forestville. 544.4813; fax 836.0147 ♿

Also at Mark West Vineyards:

California Carnivores This unusual nursery specializes in carnivorous plants from all over the world. Proprietors Marilee Maertz and Peter d'Amato's collection includes more than 200 species of Venus flytraps and other bug-chomping plants. They claim you can find more species here than at London's Kew Gardens. ◆ Daily. 838.1630

225 Farmhouse Inn $$$ This bed-and-breakfast inn lies just off River Road and is nearly hidden in a grove of trees. Designed in the style of English-country row cottages, the inn consists of a turn-of-the-century farmhouse and guest cottages built in the 1920s. There are six guest rooms and two suites decorated in restful sand and mauve color schemes, each with a private entrance, private bath, hot tub, sauna, and fireplace. Unlike at most bed-and-breakfasts, rooms here boast phones, refrigerators, and terry cloth robes. And in the common living room, guests can watch satellite TV or choose a film from the movie library to view on the VCR. With all these comforts, you needn't venture very far. Spend the day sunbathing around the swimming pool surrounded with formal English gardens or playing croquet. Innkeeper Rebecca Smith's herb and vegetable garden provides ingredients for her full country breakfast. She is also flexible enough to provide a special low-cholesterol or vegetarian breakfast on request and will put together two- or three-day itineraries for guests. ◆ 7871 River Rd (between Slusser and Wohler Rds), Forestville. 887.3300, 800/464.6642; fax 887.3311 ♿

Within the Farmhouse Inn:

Farmhouse Inn Restaurant ★★$$$ Decorated in a pink and green color scheme, this light and airy hotel dining room opens to the public for dinner. The ambience is informal and rustic without being unsophisticated. Chef Rick Jewell, who owned a restaurant in St. Thomas before moving to Sonoma, prepares regional cuisine with a Cajun twist. The menu changes nightly, but signature dishes include shrimp creole with jambalaya rice and blackened fish or beef fillet. The menu may also include ravioli stuffed with roasted garlic, peppers, sun-dried tomatoes, basil, and feta and asiago cheese or linguine with chicken, pine nuts, and fresh vegetables in a garlic and basil cream sauce. ◆ California ◆ M, Th-Su dinner in summer; Th-Su dinner in winter. Reservations required. ♿

226 Topolos at Russian River Vineyard There's no mistaking this winery with its eccentric wooden towers. Wine maker

Michael Topolos produces Chardonnay, Sauvignon Blanc, Zinfandel, Cabernet Sauvignon, Pinot Noir, and Petite Sirah. Sample them in the tasting room or at the Topolos family's Greek restaurant on the property (see below). ◆ Tasting daily; tours by appointment only. 5700 Hwy 116 (north of Guerneville Rd), Forestville. 887.1575; fax 887.1399 ♿

Within Topolos at Russian River Vineyard:

Topolos at Russian River Vineyard Restaurant ★$$ If California cuisine shares certain affinities with French or Italian cuisine, why not Greek? After all, they come from the same Mediterranean roots, and the flavors of olive oil, garlic, tomatoes, and fresh herbs are certainly familiar and heartwarming. Enjoy hearty Greek food at tables set out on a brick patio area. Begin with the *meze,* a platter of Greek appetizers, or the *saganaki,* imported kasseri cheese flamed right at the table. The Greek salad with crumbled feta cheese and Kalamata olives is always refreshing. Main courses include *spanakopita* (a spinach and feta cheese phyllo-dough pie), prawns Santorini (prepared with tomato, feta, and fresh dill), and roast baby rack of lamb in a tarragon and port sauce. Desserts include a honey-drenched baklava, chocolate mousse, and berry pies. ◆ Greek ◆ M-Sa lunch and dinner; Su brunch and dinner. The restaurant occasionally closes on Monday and/or Tuesday; winter hours vary. 887.1562

226 Kozlowski Farms Famous for their wonderful jams, vinegars, and condiments, the Kozlowski family, in business since 1949, runs this shop on the highway between Sebastopol and Guerneville. In season, you can buy apples by the barrelful and fabulous berries—raspberries, boysenberries, blackberries, loganberries, and blueberries. They also have homemade berry and apple pies (including their special no-sugar pies), individual berry tartlets, and all sorts of cookies. In all, they make 65 food items—every one of them worth taking home (especially the raspberry white-fudge sauce, which comes in a dark-chocolate version, too). They'll put together a gift basket of Sonoma County products or ship your purchases anywhere in the continental US. A mail-order catalog is available. ◆ Daily. 5566 Hwy 116 (north of Guerneville Rd), Forestville. 887.1587; 887.9650 ♿

227 Dehlinger Winery Owner/wine maker Thomas Dehlinger produces top-notch Pinot Noir and Chardonnay loaded with flavor from a small, functional winery in the Russian River area. ♦ Tasting and sales F-Su. 6300 Guerneville Rd (at Vine Hill Rd), Sebastopol. 823.2378 ♿

228 Iron Horse Vineyards
This winery is responsible for some of California's top sparkling wines, produced exclusively by the *méthode champenoise*. One of the

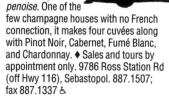

few champagne houses with no French connection, it makes four cuvées along with Pinot Noir, Cabernet, Fumé Blanc, and Chardonnay. ♦ Sales and tours by appointment only. 9786 Ross Station Rd (off Hwy 116), Sebastopol. 887.1507; fax 887.1337 ♿

Occidental/Freestone

Tucked into the beautiful coastal valley along the **Bohemian Highway** west of **Forestville** are the quaint villages of Occidental and Freestone. Both towns were important stops on the **North Pacific Coast Railroad** in the mid-19th century; today, they retain an intimate charm, with historic buildings that house a few antiques shops, restaurants, a winery, the popular **Osmosis** spa, and the European-style **Inn at Occidental**.

229 Sea Ridge Winery Pinot Noir, Merlot, and a lusty Zinfandel are the specialties of this small winery owned by Dan and Dee Wickham. A winery has existed on this site since 1903, and the wine-making methods employed here reflect that history: The grapes are hand-picked and the vintages individually bottled on an antique bottling line. ♦ Tastings and tours Saturday or by appointment. 1304 Dupont Rd (off the Bohemian Hwy), Occidental. 874.1707

THE INN AT OCCIDENTAL

230 Inn at Occidental $$ In the few short years since this lovely place opened its doors, it has established a reputation as one of the best bed-and-breakfasts in the wine country. Gracious innkeeper Jack Bullard has decorated this 1877 Victorian in a delightfully old-fashioned style, with antique furnishings, warm Persian rugs, fireplaces, and fresh

flowers. Each of the eight guest rooms has a private bath, double beds with cozy down comforters, and a view of either the redwood forest or the English country garden. In the mornings, a full breakfast is served in the dining room or on the covered porch, and an elegant five-course dinner is offered on Saturday nights (reservations required). Many guests combine a stay here with a visit to the **Osmosis** spa (see below), which is only a few minutes away. ♦ 3657 Church St (off the Bohemian Hwy), Occidental. 874.1047, 800/522.6324; fax 874.1079 ♿

231 Osmosis Enzyme Bath and Massage The only spa in the country that features enzyme bath treatments, this is the ideal spot to pamper yourself. The enzyme bath is supposed to improve circulation and metabolism, break down toxins and cleanse the skin. Start by enjoying a cup of herbal tea in the Japanese-style garden; then move on to a 10- to 20-minute soak in a hot tub filled with a mixture of cedar fiber, rice bran, and more than 600 active plant enzymes. Afterwards, you can choose from either a warm, relaxing blanket wrap or a 75-minute massage. The feeling is heavenly. ♦ Daily by appointment only. 209 Bohemian Hwy (off Hwy 12), Freestone. 823.8231 ♿

Bests

Patricia Unterman
Restaurant Critic, *San Francisco Chronicle*
Chef-Owner, Hayes Street Grill in San Francisco

Beaulieu Vineyard in **Rutherford**—one of the oldest wineries in California and a maker of elegant and long-lived Cabernets.

The caves of **Carmenet Vineyards** in **Sonoma**.

Clos Pegase winery near **Calistoga**, which was designed by architect **Michael Graves** and has an art collection.

A snack under the trees at **Cantinetta Tra Vigne** in **St. Helena**.

A prix-fixe dinner at **The French Laundry** in **Yountville**.

Stopping at **Oakville Grocery Co.** to get supplies for a picnic at the **Conn Dam Reservoir**.

Visiting the **Downtown Bakery & Creamery** on **Healdsburg Plaza** for fabulous homemade ice creams and cookies.

Renting a canoe from **W.C. "Bob" Trowbridge** in **Healdsburg** for a trip down the **Russian River**.

Riding in a glider from Calistoga over **Napa Valley**.

A dinner and overnight stay at the Victorian **Madrona Manor** outside of Healdsburg.

Sonoma Coast

Just an hour's drive north of San Francisco and a half-hour west of Santa Rosa lies **Bodega Bay** and the start of **Sonoma**'s rugged and dramatic coastline—55 miles of pristine beaches, hidden coves, and grassy headlands covered with wildflowers. Home to the Pomo and Coastal Miwok Indians, this section of the coast was largely ignored by the Spanish for two centuries until Juan Francisco de la Bodega y Cuadro set anchor here on his way to Alaska and "discovered" the bay that bears his name. The Russians actually established the first white settlements on the coast, building outposts at **Fort Ross** and **Salmon Creek Valley** to supply their starving settlers in Alaska with food. But after they had killed off the sea otter population and could no longer support their colonies, they pulled up stakes in 1841. Today this gorgeous area remains sparsely populated, leaving stretches of uninhabited coastline between small resort towns such as **Jenner** and **Timber Cove.** Most of these hamlets sprang up around lumber mills in the mid-19th century as dog-hole ports, in which lumber was loaded down a chute on the bluffs to ships in the cove below.

More than 5,000 acres and 13 miles of coastline make up the **Sonoma Coast State Beach** system, which encompasses sandy beaches, salt marshes, underwater reserves and parks, and myriad tide pools. There are more than 20 distinct beaches, separated by rocky outcroppings; the most popular include **Doran Beach Regional Park at Bodega Bay**, **Salmon Creek Beach** at the mouth of **Salmon Creek, Goat Rock Beach** at the mouth of the **Russian River**, and **Salt Point State Park** just north of Timber Cove. You can camp at some of the beaches or find lodging in seaside inns. Wherever you stay, the emphasis is on quiet and relaxation, making the Sonoma Coast an ideal weekend retreat. Bring binoculars for bird-watching and spotting wildlife such as harbor seals, California sea lions, and, depending on the season, migrating gray whales. The state park system also includes protected underwater areas for diving. Watch for the brown "Coastal Access" signs with an illustration of bare feet superimposed on a wave to indicate where it's possible to get down to the beach. For more information on this area's parks and campgrounds, call the state park office at 875.3483 or 865.2391.

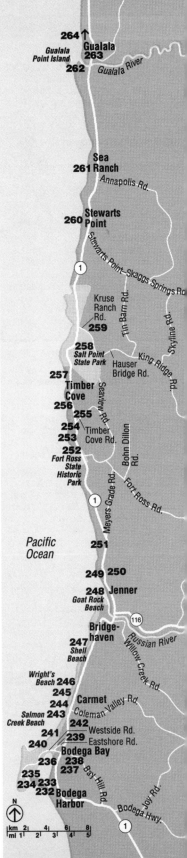

Bodega Bay

This town (just 68 miles north of San Francisco) is a popular weekend destination for those who enjoy exploring the dunes and beaches, and it has become one of the busiest commercial fishing ports between San Francisco and Eureka. The bay was discovered on 3 October 1775 by the Spanish explorer Juan Francisco de la Bodega y Cuadro, for whom it is named. Eighteen years after its discovery, the naturalist Archibald Menzies, a member of an expedition led by Captain George Vancouver, disembarked here to collect botanical specimens. The area is still rich in flora and fauna, and during the annual whale migration from November through March, **Bodega Head** draws many visitors to watch the whales as they pass on their way to or from Baja California.

232 Bodega Harbour Golf Links Robert Trent Jones Jr. designed this privately owned, 18-hole, par 70 golf course. Jones laid it out so there would be ocean views from every hole. From the champion-ship tee, the course is 6,200 yards; it is 5,630 yards from the regular tee. ♦ Daily. Reservations taken up to 60 days in advance. 21301 Heron Dr (off Harbour Way). 875.3538; fax 875.3256

232 Bodega Bay Lodge
$$$ This Best Western inn adjacent to the golf links consists of a series of two-story, brown-shingled buildings on a secluded, terraced site sheltered by pines and over-looking the salt

marshes of Bodega Bay. The showpieces of the main lobby are the massive fieldstone fireplace and two stunning, 500-gallon saltwater aquariums filled with tropical fish, starfish, and coral. All 78 of the inn's rooms have patios or balconies, coffeemakers, and cable TV. They afford views of the salt marsh and the ocean beyond, and most have tiled fireplaces. The decor is clean-cut contemporary, with carpeting, matching comforters, and tiled bathrooms. There's a modest-size swimming pool here and a whirlpool spa that stands in a roofless fieldstone-and-redwood gazebo. Guests also have use of a redwood sauna and a fitness room equipped with Lifecycles and Nautilus equipment. Bicycle down to Doran Beach on one of the inn's complimentary bikes. They'll also put together a basket lunch, and a complimentary continental breakfast is served to guests in the dining room (see below). ♦ 103 Hwy 1 (near Heron Dr). 875.3525; 800-528-1234; fax 875.2428 &

Within the Bodega Bay Lodge:

Ocean Club Restaurant ★$$$ This hotel dining room offers a nightly prix-fixe menu as well as an à la carte menu that changes monthly. Executive chef Dean Minkel concentrates on Sonoma County ingredients in the preparation of dishes such as Bodega Harbor seafood chowder, boned chicken stuffed with homemade sausage and wild rice, and grilled Petaluma duck quesadilla with pepper jack cheese and avocado chili salsa. Follow that with a fresh salad tossed with raspberry vinaigrette and the crème brûlée or poached pears and local berries served with crème anglaise. ♦ California ♦ Daily breakfast and dinner. Reservations recommended. &

233 Lucas Wharf Fish Market and Delicatessen The boats unload their catches right at the wharf, where the fish are cleaned and placed in the market for sale. Picnickers will find smoked salmon, cooked shrimp, pickled herring, and crab meat, along with fresh fish fillets and beautiful fresh whole salmon for the grill. You'll also find an array of cold cuts, cheeses, giant pickles, pig's feet, and other fare, and the deli will make any of two dozen sandwiches to go. Pick up a jar of the Peloponnese pickled baby eggplant as an appetizer. ♦ Daily. 595 Hwy 1 (on the bay). 875.3562; fax 875.3032 &

Also at the Lucas Wharf Fish Market and Delicatessen:

Lucas Wharf Seafood Bar $ To one side of the fish market and deli is a bar with oysters and hot seafood to go. The simple menu offers fish, shrimp, calamari, or oysters, all accompanied by french fries. Spicy Cajun-style shrimp and onion rings are also specialties. Get a cold beer or soft drink, and relax at one of the picnic tables beside the take-out window. ♦ Seafood ♦ F-Su lunch and early dinner. &

Lucas Wharf Restaurant and Bar ★$$ This is a pleasant spot for a beer or a quick bite. The broad, wooden-plank floorboards and old-fashioned wooden chairs give the restaurant a vaguely nautical theme, but the real decor is just outside the windows: a nonstop view of the busy harbor. A bowl of Boston clam chowder will take the chill off, or try the mussels steamed in white wine, shallots, and garlic, or the standard Dungeness crab Louis. Entrées might include grilled red snapper fillet with lemon butter, king salmon with hollandaise sauce, and a deep-fried seafood mix of calamari, prawns, and oysters. Surf 'n' turf combos and half-pound burgers are also available. Watch for daily specials such as pan-braised sea bass or garlic fettuccine with smoked salmon, scallops, and mussels. ♦ Seafood ♦ Daily

Restaurants/Clubs: Red   **Hotels:** Blue
Shops/♥ Outdoors: Green   **Wineries/Sights:** Black

lunch and dinner. 875.3522 &

233 Tides Wharf Fresh Fish Market The same folks who own the **Inn at the Tides** (see page 147) developed this uninspiring, touristy complex across the road. It's set in a great spot with a long stretch of wharf in front, but plunking down buildings better suited to a shopping mall was an unfortunate choice. However, you can pick up a cooked whole crab or oysters for a picnic, fresh fish for the grill, packaged cheeses, and chilled white Sonoma wines. The fish market also has bait and tackle, and there's a gift shop. ◆ Daily. 835 Hwy 1 (on the bay). 875.3554; fax 875.3285 &

Within the Tides Wharf Fresh Fish Market:

Tides Wharf Restaurant ★$$ This sea-food restaurant features everything from fish-and-chips and grilled or pan-fried fillets to crab cioppino (seafood stew) and deep-fried oysters. There's a great view of the harbor, but the decor is coffee-shop mundane. At breakfast, you get the usual egg dishes, hotcakes, and side orders. ◆ Seafood ◆ Daily breakfast, lunch, and dinner. 875.3652 &

234 Doran Beach Regional Park at Bodega Bay Just down the road from the **Bodega Bay Lodge** (see page 145) is a regional park perched on the narrow, two-mile-long spit of sand that separates Bodega Harbor from Bodega Bay. Bird-watchers haunt the salt marshes and the low sand dunes to gaze at sanderlings, willets, snowy plovers, and other shorebirds. The park has ocean and bay access and is a popular spot for swimming and surfing. It's also a good place for clam digging; razor and horseneck clams are just two of the varieties found here. There's an ocean-fishing pier, a public boat launch, and a fish-cleaning station, along with picnic tables and rest rooms. The park has 134 campsites with space for a car or RV, plus 10 suitable for tents only. ◆ Fee per vehicle. Doran Park Rd (off Hwy 1). 875.3540

234 Bodega Head The southernmost tip of the peninsula that extends south from Bodega Dunes, this site is characterized by high bluffs and steep, craggy cliffs. Bodega Rock, a half-mile offshore, is a breeding ground for Brandt's cormorants and western gulls; harbor seals and California sea lions can also

be spotted. During the annual whale migrations, this is a prime spot for watching the giant mammals, and talks about the whales are given to the public here on Sundays from mid-December through mid-April. On clear days the rugged area offers fine views of the Marin and Sonoma Coasts. ◆ End of Westside Rd (off Westshore Rd and Hwy 1). 875.3483

235 Bodega Marine Laboratory Part of the 356-acre **Bodega Marine Reserve** is dedicated to the **University of California**'s marine research facility. Docent-guided tours are given once a week, taking visitors through the research lab, which features aquariums (the public is not allowed on the reserve). ◆ Tours F 2-4PM (don't arrive later than 3:15PM for a complete tour). Westside Rd (off Westshore Rd and Hwy 1). 875.2211; fax 875.2089 &

236 Bodega Harbor Inn $ This very basic motel offers 16 rooms in slate-blue bungalows on a hillside overlooking **Porto Bodega Marina**. All have small private baths and cable TV. The inn also rents cottages and houses in the area. ◆ 1345 Bodega Ave (off Hwy 1). 875.3594 &

236 Candy & Kites/Harbor Kites When the wind is good, stop here to pick up dual-control stunt kites, beginners' kites, and colorful dragon kites. A series of baskets overflow with saltwater taffy in flavors such as red cinnamon, black licorice, and peanut butter. Believe it or not, the taffy comes in sugar-free versions, too. ◆ M, Tu, F-Su. 1415 Hwy 1 (near Bodega Ave). 875.3777 &

236 The Boathouse $ This seafood snack bar offers fish-and-chips, clam strips, fried calamari, oysters, prawns, and scallops. Landlubbers can also get cheeseburgers and turkey or roast beef sandwiches. Take away your food or grab a table on the large deck outside. ◆ Seafood ◆ Daily lunch and dinner. 1445 Hwy 1 (near Bodega Ave). 875.3495 &

Also at The Boathouse:

New Sea Angler & Jaws Sportfishing
The Boathouse offers sportfishing trips on the 65-foot *New Sea Angler* or the 55-foot *Jaws*, which carry 49 and 38 passengers, respectively. The larger ship heads out to Cordell Bank, Fanny Shoals, and the Farallon Islands, while *Jaws* specializes in light-tackle rock cod trips. Bait and tackle, breakfast, and box

lunches will be provided if desired. ♦ Daily. Reservations required, plus 50 percent deposit

236 Challenger Sportfishing This firm specializes in sportfishing and deep-sea fishing for salmon, rock cod, and ling cod in its 55-foot *Challenger* boat. They also give three-hour whale-watching expeditions from January through April. ♦ Daily. Reservations required. 617 Gold Dr (off Hwy 1). 875.2474

The Inn at the Tides
B O D E G A   B A Y

237 Inn at the Tides $$$ Seen from the road, the brown-shingled guest lodges scattered over the hillside to the east of Highway 1 look more like condominiums than an inn. There are 86 guest rooms altogether, every one with a view of the harbor below. Most have tiled fireplaces and all have small refrigerators, coffeemakers, cable TV, and terry robes. The decor is somewhat dated, featuring plush carpeting and print comforters. Guests have use of the outdoor lap pool, whirlpool spa, and Finnish sauna. A complimentary continental breakfast is served every morning. ♦ 800 Hwy 1 (south of Bay Hill Rd). 875.2751, 800/541.7788; fax 875.2669 ♿

Also at the Inn at the Tides:

Bay View Room ★$$$ This intimate restaurant, serving a limited California menu five nights a week, looks out on the bay and a terraced flower garden. Choose from half-a-dozen main courses (all served with soup or salad) such as poached king salmon with lemon-chive butter, seared breast of Petaluma duck in gooseberry-orange sauce, and fettuccine lavished with lobster, scallops, and parmesan cheese. Guests at the inn are served their continental breakfast here, too. ♦ California ♦ W-Su dinner. Reservations recommended. ♿

237 Crab Pot ★$ Billie and Lynn Douglas have been smoking fish and seafood at their bright orange shack with flowers planted all around since 1970. Stop by and most likely you'll find aromatic smoke seeping from the door; they use applewood to smoke salmon, tuna, swordfish, sturgeon, and peppered salmon. They'll make shrimp and crab sandwiches, too, and offer a few wines, mostly from Pedroncelli and Geyser Peak. In season, they also have whole cooked Dungeness crabs. ♦ Seafood ♦ Daily lunch and early dinner. 1750 Hwy 1 (south of Bay Hill Rd). 875.9970

238 Bay Hill Mansion $$ This three-story inn sits high on a hill overlooking the bay and is meant to be a contemporary version of a Queen Anne Victorian. The inn has six guest rooms, each with queen-size beds, down comforters, and a view; most have shared baths. Innkeeper Fran Miller serves a full breakfast each morning in the dining room, which has a view of the bay. ♦ 3919 Bay Hill Rd (off Hwy 1). 875.3577, 800/526.5927

239 Vacation Rentals International $$$ This agency rents more than a hundred private beach houses, ranging from cabins on Salmon Creek to five-bedroom places in a country-club setting. Rentals in the **Bodega Harbour** development include guest privileges at the **Bodega Harbour Country Club.** Rent for two to three nights or by the week or month. ♦ Daily. 1580 Eastshore Rd (off Hwy 1). 875.4000, 800/548.7631; fax 875.2204

239 Bodega Bay Baking Company Half-a-dozen different types of cookies are baked here. (And unlike the cookies from most similar shops, they're not too sweet!) Try the oatmeal coconut walnut cookie, the chocolate-chip macadamia nut, or the classic chocolate chip with walnuts. Other bakery treats include muffins, French bread, and pastries. You can also buy espresso drinks, cookie dough to take home and bake yourself, Thanksgiving coffee beans from Mendocino, and jams and jellies from **Kozlowski Farms** in Forestville. ♦ Daily. 1580 Eastshore Rd (off Hwy 1). 875.2280 ♿

239 Branscomb Gallery This three-level gallery exhibits works by local artists as well as by artists from around the country. Note the wildlife etchings by Mendocino artist James J.D. Mayhew, watercolors of Sonoma County landscapes by El Meyer, and colored etchings of vineyards and other rural scenes by Gail Packer. ♦ Daily. 1588 Eastshore Rd (off Hwy 1). 875.3388; fax 875.2905 ♿

240 Sandpiper Dockside Cafe & Restaurant ★★$$$ Stop in for breakfast at this casual cafe, where the service couldn't be friendlier and the bonus is a view of the harbor and bay. For breakfast try eggs served with home fries or hash browns and patty sausage, *huevos rancheros,* or a dynamite Spanish omelette loaded with salsa, avocado, and sour cream. Another favorite: the omelette made with Dungeness crab and jack cheese. At lunch try their exceptionally thick clam chowder, or their salads, fish-and-chips, burgers, and fresh fish sandwiches. The dinner menu includes several more ambitious dishes, including snapper Vera Cruz smothered in a cilantro-spiked fresh tomato sauce, linguine with clam sauce, and a New York steak served with tempura prawns. ♦ Eclectic ♦ Daily breakfast, lunch, and dinner. 1410 Bay Flat Rd (off Westshore Rd). 875.2278 &

241 **Bodega Dunes State Park & Camping** More than 900 acres of gently rolling sand dunes lie covered with soft mounds of dune grasses here. Monarch butterflies winter in the eucalyptus trees, and you can spot alligator lizards, black-tailed deer, jackrabbits, owls, foxes, and badgers throughout the year. Trails include a five-mile loop for hiking and horseback riding; another trail leads to Bodega Head. The park features a campground with 98 campsites and numerous picnic areas. ♦ Fee per vehicle. Hwy 1 (a half mile north of Bodega Bay). 875.3483, 800/444.PARK (for camping reservations)

Chanslor
GUEST RANCH
& HORSE STABLES

242 **Chanslor Ranch** $ If you're planning on horseback riding, why not bunk at the bed-and-breakfast inn on this 700-acre working ranch bordered by Salmon Creek? The suburban ranch-style main house has six guest rooms with private baths and color TV sets (two of the bedrooms can be connected to make an impromptu suite). A full breakfast is included. ♦ 2660 Hwy 1 (about 1 mile north of Bodega Bay). 875.2721; fax 875.2785 &

Within the Chanslor Ranch:

Chanslor Stables Sign up for guided trail rides through the hills and dunes surrounding Bodega Bay. The one-hour hill ride winds past Salmon Creek and returns along a hilly route with views of the coastline. The two-hour dune ride crosses over to the sand dunes on the other side of Highway 1 and provides a look at the harbor and marinas. Beginners are welcome. Guests at the bed-and-breakfast inn get a 10 percent discount on rides. ♦ Daily. Reservations recommended

243 **Salmon Creek Beach** This popular sandy beach at the mouth of Salmon Creek is about two miles long and includes a shallow swimming area. The creek is a good spot to fish for steelhead trout, and the saltwater and freshwater marshes are filled with wildlife. A trail leads south to Bodega Head. ♦ Day-use only. Hwy 1 (about 1.5 miles north of Bodega Bay). 875.3483

244 **Portuguese Beach** A steep trail leads to this beach. Rest rooms are available. ♦ Day-use only. Off Hwy 1 (about 2 miles north of Bodega Bay). 875.3483

245 **Duncans Landing** In the mid-19th century, this was where the lumber from Duncans Sawmill in Bridgehaven was loaded onto ships waiting below. (The lumber was transported by carts from the sawmill.) The small beach here is accessible via a steep trail. ♦ Hwy 1 (about 4.5 miles north of Bodega Bay)

246 **Wright's Beach** Thirty campsites with fire pits are available here; sites 0-8 are on the beach, and the rest are set back from the ocean. ♦ Fee per vehicle. Hwy 1 (about 5 miles north of Bodega Bay). 800/444.PARK (for camping reservations)

247 **Shell Beach** This beach is a good spot for observing wildlife. It's directly across from Gull Rock—a nesting area for Brandt's cormorants, Western gulls, and pigeon guillemots—and black-tailed deer, rabbits, and gray foxes can be sighted on the grassy headlands. There's a trail to the beach, too. ♦ Day-use only. Hwy 1 (about 5.5 miles north of Bodega Bay). 875.3483

248 **Goat Rock Beach** This state beach situated at the mouth of the Russian River is one of the most popular along the Sonoma Coast. The sand spit that is formed as the river empties into the sea is a haven for seals and is rich in birdlife. In the summer, fish for ocean smelt; in the winter, try the Russian River for steelhead trout. While there is access to the beach on both the river side and the ocean side, swimming is allowed only in the river; sleeper waves, which can surprise the unsuspecting swimmer by suddenly bursting forth, make it too dangerous on the ocean side. Picnic areas with fire pits are available. ♦ Day-use only. Off Hwy 1 (about 9 miles north of Bodega Bay). 875.3483

Jenner

The town of Jenner is perched on a high bluff overlooking the spot where the **Russian River** ends its journey to the sea. It was a bustling logging town in the latter half of the 19th century, and it started a new life as a summer resort at the turn of the century. Today Jenner remains a small resort area, popular for its laid-back ambience and the rugged beauty of the cove, where birds and wildlife abound. The **Penny Island Bird Sanctuary** is home to ospreys, blue herons, and other shorebirds. Another noteworthy attraction in the area is the **Fort Ross State Historic Park**, centered around the fort that served as the hub of a Russian community in the 19th century. Farther up the coast, a few miles south of Gualala, the **Sea Ranch** reserve offers 5,000 acres of mostly unspoiled wilderness, with walking trails, golf, tennis, swimming, and other recreational activities. The 20-room **Sea Ranch Lodge** is the only hotel in the development, but private vacation homes can be rented through several agencies (see page 153).

249 Seagull Gifts & Deli $ Along with espresso drinks, frozen yogurt, and ice cream, this stand-up snack bar dishes out clam chowder, chili, and sandwiches ranging from peanut butter and jelly to local Willie Bird roasted turkey. You can sit at the nearby picnic tables and watch the kayakers go by on the river. The gift shop looks touristy, but actually carries some good wines—from **Dry Creek Vineyards, Dehlinger, Kenwood, Roederer Estate,** and **Sea Ridge.** You can also pick up maps and nature books on whales here. ♦ Deli ♦ Daily. 10439 Hwy 1 (south of Meyers Grade Rd). 865.2594 &

Jenner Inn

Bed & Breakfast

250 Jenner Inn & Cottages $$ This comfortable, unpretentious inn invites you to relax on maroon velvet couches in front of a woodburning stove, with books and games available for whiling away the afternoon. Most of the 13 guest rooms, suites, and cottages are furnished with antiques and quilts and have a warm, lived-in feel. The accommodations range from simple, inexpensive rooms with river views in the **Captain's House** to suites with a private entrance or deck, a fireplace, and a full kitchen. In addition, the inn has a dozen private homes for rent, most with dramatic ocean views and fireplaces. The most romantic? The **Rosewater,** a one-bedroom cottage with a stone fireplace, which is located at the water's edge, and the **Hideaway,** a two-bedroom cottage with a hot tub, at the top of Jenner Canyon. A breakfast buffet is included. ♦ 10400 Hwy 1 (south of Meyers Grade Rd). 865.2377, 800/732.2377 (outside CA); fax 865.0829

251 River's End ★★$$ This small, popular restaurant sits atop a cliff where the Russian River empties into the sea, and the many windows afford a terrific view of the scenery. The wood-paneled dining room is decorated with photographs of the Sonoma area, and there's a bar in the solarium. Owner Wolfgang Gramatzki has attracted a loyal local following for his eclectic cooking, which includes German, Indonesian, Asian, French, and American dishes. His specialties include *Bahmie Goreng,* a mix of poultry, seafood, and beef satay served with Indonesian vegetable noodles and his own peach chutney; stuffed boneless quail; and veal medaillons with the unlikely combination of wild mushrooms and crayfish. For dessert, Gramatzki turns out chocolate mousse spiked with rum and an Old-English trifle composed of sherry-soaked sponge cake layered with Bavarian cream and wild berries. The ambience is fairly informal at lunchtime, but it becomes more elegant in the evening, when the restaurant breaks out linen tablecloths and napkins. The list of local wines is good, too. ♦ Eclectic ♦ Daily lunch and dinner; closed in December and January. Hwy 1 (at Meyers Grade Rd). 865.2484, 869.3252 &

Within River's End:

River's End Resort $$ There are three rooms underneath the restaurant, four pint-size cabins, and a separate little house that has a full-size kitchen and sleeps up to four people. The wood-paneled cabins set in a row beside the restaurant are very private and consist of a room with either one or two queen-size beds, a small shower/bath, and a coffeemaker. Sliding glass doors open onto balconies overlooking the river and the ocean beyond. There also are several campsites (no hookups) and a boat-launching facility.

252 Fort Ross State Historic Park In 1741, thirteen years after he discovered the strait that bears his name, Russian admiral Vitus Bering sailed to the Aleutian Islands and the Alaskan mainland. The Russians were soon exploiting the region for its sea otters. They established outposts on the Aleutian Islands and eventually ventured south along the California coast with the idea of founding a colony to supply the Alaskan settlers with food. In 1812 Ivan Alexandrovich Kuskov, an agent of the Russian-American Fur Company, founded Fort Ross on a high, windswept bluff overlooking the sea. Today, the fort (which was abandoned in the mid-19th century) provides a fascinating look at the life and times of the Russian settlers.

You should first stop at the **Visitors' Center** for a copy of the walking tour of the fort (see drawing on page 150). Then follow the well-marked path down to the old fort, situated on a dramatic bluff above the sea; little kids will probably be making cannon noises inside the blockhouse as you pass. The small redwood chapel with its cupolas topped with crosses is actually a reconstruction of the original chapel, which was built in 1812 and partially destroyed in the earthquake of 1906. The **Officials' Quarters** bring the era back to life with Russian furnishings and carpentry and metal workshops. Peek into the kitchen, where the silver samovar for making tea is stored. Guided tours are often available on Saturday and Sunday; call ahead to confirm. **Fort Ross Living History Day,** held annually on the last Saturday in July, re-creates a typical day at the fort in 1836. If you walk out the west gate of the compound and head north along the road, you'll pass the Call ranch house (George W. Call purchased the fort in

149

1873) and a secluded picnic area in a grove of trees. Adjacent to the park is an offshore underwater park for divers. ◆ Fee per vehicle. Hwy 1 (near Seaview Rd). 847.3286; fax 847.3602

253 Fort Ross Lodge $$ This gray, wood-framed lodge set on a hillside overlooking the ocean has been designed to give most rooms ocean views. Each of its 22 modern units has a color TV set, private patio with a barbecue, private bath, small refrigerator, and coffeemaker. ◆ 20705 Hwy 1 (between Seaview and Timber Cove Rds). 847.3333; fax 847.3330 க்

254 Timber Cove Boat Landing On the weekends, this is one busy place, with divers in wetsuits unloading their gear in front and sailors arriving to sling-launch their boats into the cove below. You can obtain a fishing license here, buy bait and tackle, or rent scuba-diving gear or boats. The nominal day-use fee includes transportation to and from the cove and use of the hot tub. There's a campground (some sites have hookups), and campers have use of the hot showers, a hot tub, and the laundry facilities. You can also sign up for guided boat tours and fishing or sight-seeing trips. ◆ Day-use fee. Daily. 21350 Hwy 1 (at Timber Cove Rd). 847.3278

Within the Timber Cove Boat Landing:

Sea Coast Hideaways $$$ The proprietors of the boat landing also rent about 15 private homes in and around Timber Cove, ranging from a rustic redwood cabin overlooking the boat landing with beach access to a two-bedroom hillside home with a view of Stillwater Cove. ◆ 847.3278 க்

255 Timber Cove Inn $$$ Outside the massive timbered lobby, a Japanese pond where swans and ducks float sets the tone of serenity and contemplation. Everything is very well designed, from the sophis-ticated simplicity of the rooms decorated with Ansel Adams photographs to the large balconies facing the wild, scenic cove. There are no TV sets or phones to disturb you. All of the 47 rooms have private baths, and a number have built-in hot tubs. Just over half have fireplaces or wood-burning stoves. True romantics will like the large ocean-view units with a hot tub either in the room or on the deck—and a shower with a glass wall facing the ocean. ◆ 21780 Hwy 1 (3 miles north of the Fort Ross State Historic Park). 847.3231; fax 847.3704

Within the Timber Cove Inn:

Timber Cove Inn Restaurant ★★$$ A few steps down from the bar is the inn's dining room. With its expansive views of the sea, lofty ceiling, and stone walls, it's a dramatic spot for a meal. Eggs, sandwiches, and the like are served for breakfast and lunch, while dinner features classic French specialties, including broiled salmon in red wine, shallots, and butter; filet mignon broiled with mushroom caps and served with Bordelaise sauce; and roasted loin of lamb rubbed with fresh herbs and carved at the table. Soup and salad are served with each entrée. ◆ French ◆ Daily breakfast, lunch, and dinner

Fort Ross Compound

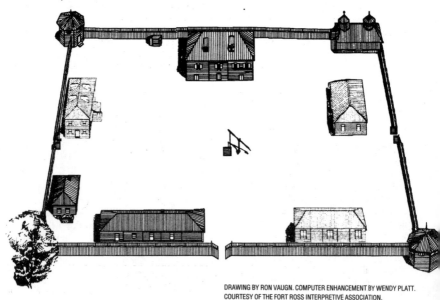

DRAWING BY RON VAUGN. COMPUTER ENHANCEMENT BY WENDY PLATT. COURTESY OF THE FORT ROSS INTERPRETIVE ASSOCIATION.

256 Stillwater Cove Regional Park You'll find a wealth of wildflowers in this park, not to mention ospreys nesting between the cove and Salt Point in the tops of redwood and fir trees. If you take the hiking trail, which runs along Stockhoff Creek, keep an eye out for the Fort Ross schoolhouse, built in Greek Revival style in 1885. There are many good picnic areas, as well as a campground with 23 sites that are available on a first-come, first-served basis. A stairway provides access to the beach. ♦ Fee per vehicle. Hwy 1 (4 miles north of the Fort Ross State Historic Park). 847.3245, 524.7175

Stillwater Cove Ranch

256 Stillwater Cove Ranch $ A former boys' school, this inn offers modestly priced accommodations on a ranch where peacocks, sheep, and deer wander the grounds. One building houses the spacious east and west rooms, both with fireplaces, kitchenettes, private baths, and two double beds. Rustic wooden chairs sit in front of the fireplace, and there's a broad veranda in front. The two white cottages are smaller, but both have private baths, fireplaces, and two double beds. Two other rooms feature king-size beds and private baths; one has a fireplace. Groups of fishermen or divers often rent the **Dairy Barn,** furnished with eight bunks, a full kitchen, and two showers (bring your own linen for this bargain accommodation). ♦ 22555 Hwy 1 (3 miles north of the Fort Ross State Historic Park). 847.3227

256 Salt Point Lodge $ The name sounds fancy, but this is really a 16-room motel with moderately priced accommodations, not easy to find along the Sonoma Coast. Rooms have a standard contemporary decor and distant ocean views; all have private baths and one has a private hot tub, while another has a fireplace. There is also an outdoor hot tub and sauna. ♦ 23255 Hwy 1 (3 miles north of the Fort Ross State Historic Park). 847.3234, 800/956.3437; fax 847.3354

Within Salt Point Lodge:

Salt Point Bar & Grill ★$$ This family restaurant features a solarium/bar with an ocean view. The breakfast includes omelettes and other egg dishes, while at lunch the kitchen staff concentrates on burgers, sandwiches, and fish-and-chips. The dinner menu offers seafood dishes and meats barbecued over mesquite: prime rib, half-chickens, and country ribs, all served with the house barbecue sauce. You can also get a grilled steak or a burger, or try the salad bar. ♦ American ♦ Daily breakfast, lunch, and dinner. 847.3238

257 Ocean Cove Store & Campground This campground has a hundred sites with fire pits; 30 are along the ocean with great views. At the store you can get all your basic groceries, as well as liquor and gas. ♦ Store: daily Mar-Nov; F-M Dec-Feb. 23125 Hwy 1 (south of Kruse Ranch Rd). 847.3422

258 Salt Point State Park In the past, the Kashaya Pomo and Coast Yuki Indians would take up summer residence here to gather the salt they used to preserve fish—hence the name. The 4,300-acre park offers a wide variety of terrains, from redwood groves and a pygmy forest of stunted cypresses to craggy bluffs and tide pools. The park has trails for hiking and horseback riding, too. It is also an underwater reserve, and diving is permitted offshore. Guided whale-watching walks are offered in the winter. ♦ 25050 Hwy 1 (south of Kruse Ranch Rd). 847.3221, 865.2391

Within Salt Point State Park:

Gerstle Cove Campground This campground has 30 family campsites with picnic tables and fire pits. Gerstle Cove is an underwater reserve; no form of marine life within its boundaries may be removed or disturbed. The rangers are trying to allow the depleted abalone population to recover.

Woodside Campground Also a part of **Salt Point State Park,** this campground has 79 campsites, plus 20 walk-in sites and 10 environmental sites accessible only by hiking. Check in at **Gerstle Cove Campground.**

Stump Beach This is a good spot to observe the breeding of cormorants. No camping is allowed on this beach, but there are picnic facilities with fire pits.

Fisk Mill Cove This beach has picnic facilities with fire pits and several trails along the bluffs that lead to the beach below.

259 Kruse Rhododendron Reserve Spectacular in the spring, this 317-acre reserve shelters a second-growth redwood forest and a large stand of native California rhododendrons. Some of the shrubs are 20 feet high, and when in bloom, mid-April to mid-June, they are quite a sight. There are a few picnic facilities and five miles of hiking trails. ♦ Day-use only. East of Hwy 1, off Kruse Ranch Rd. 847.3221, 865.2391

260 Stewarts Point This was an important doghole lumber port in the mid-19th century. Cut lumber was loaded down a chute here to the ships waiting below. Stewarts Point–Skagg's Springs Road is a scenic but very slow way to get to Dry Creek Valley near Healdsburg and the surrounding wine country. ♦ Hwy 1 (at Stewarts Point–Skaggs Springs Rd)

Restaurants/Clubs: Red **Hotels:** Blue
Shops/ ♥ Outdoors: Green **Wineries/Sights:** Black

261 **Sea Ranch Lodge** $$$ In 1964 the magnificent 5,000-acre **Sea Ranch** development was acquired by Hawaii-based Castle & Cook, which did extensive environmental studies before developing the site as a second-home community. The first condominiums were designed by the architectural firm of **MTLW (Charles Moore, William Turnbull, Donylyn Lyndon,** and **Richard Whitaker),** and their simple, elegant designs, with shed roofs and natural wood interiors, set the tone for much of the other building that followed.

Fortunately, the **Sea Ranch Lodge,** a 20-room inn, was included in the plans so that visitors can also enjoy the serenity and beauty of this unspoiled landscape. All the rooms have private baths; all except one have views of the sea. Most have natural-wood paneling and a rustic, modern decor, with patchwork quilts, bentwood rockers, and window seats. Guests have access to the **Sea Ranch Golf Links** (see page 153), as well as the **Sea Ranch** recreation center (about three miles north of the lodge), which includes tennis courts, a heated swimming pool, and a sauna. Even if you're not planning to stay here, stop by the bar and sit for a while in front of this unsurpassed view of the headlands and the sea beyond.

Within this enormous private reserve are five trails to the beach below, with parking areas west of Highway 1. Look for the brown Coastal Access signs to Walk-On Beach, Shell Beach, Stengel Beach, Pebble Beach, and Black Point Beach. In addition, there is a trail into the **Sea Ranch** development from **Gualala Point Regional Park** and another that runs along the bluffs from the same park. ♦ 60 Sea Walk Dr (off Hwy 1). 785.2371, 800/SEA.RANCH &

Good Reads on Wine, Wine Making, and the California Wine Country

American Wine: A Comprehensive Guide by Anthony Dias Blue (1988; Harper & Row). Here is an exhaustive reference volume devoted to wines, their characteristics, and the top American vintners.

Backroad Wineries of Northern California: A Scenic Tour of California's Country Wineries by Bill Gleeson (1994; Chronicle Books). This volume lists 60 lesser-known wineries throughout northern California wine country. Areas covered include **Napa, Mendocino, Sonoma,** and **Lake Counties.**

California's Great Cabernets: The Wine Spectator's Ultimate Guide for Consumers, Collectors, and Investors by James Laube (1989; M. Shanken Comm.). Cabernet Sauvignon made in California is the focus of this well-written guide. Laube, a leading wine authority, comments on how to judge this type of wine, offers a history of California Cabernets, and rates more than 1,200 vintages.

Making Sense of California Wine by Matt Kramer (1992; Morrow). Kramer, who also wrote *Making Sense of Wine* (see below), here describes the innovative wine-making techniques of California vintners, lists the best grapes and wine makers in each region of the state, and notes the specific varieties that can be found.

Making Sense of Wine by Matt Kramer (1992; Morrow). A general guide to wine and wine tasting, this book discusses the process of wine making, the standards for choosing and judging the quality of a vintage, and the proper way to serve it. Also included are recipes for dishes that go particularly well with specific wine varieties.

Napa by James Conaway (1990; Houghton Mifflin). Written in a lively, interesting style, this is a history of the people who settled in the Napa Valley and began producing wine, as well as the intense competition between vintners that helped Napa wines earn their excellent reputation.

The New Frank Schoonmaker Encyclopedia of Wine by Alexis Bespaloff (1988; Morrow). Here is an encyclopedic listing of wine terms, including explanations of the different varieties and the history of wine making in general. There's also a handy chapter about how wine drinking can complement meals.

Parker's Wine Buyer's Guide 1992-1993 by Robert M. Parker Jr. (1993; Simon & Schuster). This detailed manual is an up-to-date, worldwide guide to wines produced in a given year. Organized by region, each chapter describes and rates the current vintages being made, lists the area's best producers and growers, and gives retail prices.

Vintage: The Story of Wine by Hugh Johnson (1992; Simon & Schuster). Everything you might want to know about wine or wine history can be found in this fascinating book. Topics covered include technological breakthroughs such as the evolution of the wine bottle, the development of the different varieties, and biographical information about such important figures as Dom Pérignon and Baron Rothschild.

The Wine Atlas of California and the Pacific Northwest: A Traveler's Guide to the Vineyards by Bob Thompson (1993; Simon & Schuster). Thompson, a renowned wine expert, provides a comprehensive guide to the wine districts of California, Oregon, and Washington, including history, climatic information, and the leading vintners in each area.

Within the Sea Ranch Lodge:

Sea Ranch Lodge Restaurant ★$$ The beautiful dining room, which has views of the bluffs and the sea, is simply and elegantly furnished. There are no surprises on the breakfast menu, and lunch features such standard fare as a chef's salad, seafood pasta, burgers, and several sandwiches. The dinner menu changes seasonally but sticks to the straight and narrow: grilled New York steak, veal scaloppine, and chicken cordon bleu. ♦ Continental ♦ Daily breakfast, lunch, and dinner. ♿

Ram's Head Realty Vacation Rentals

Sea Ranch home rentals are available for two days to a week or more. They range from small redwood cabins to large luxury homes. ♦ Annapolis Rd (off Hwy 1). 785.2427

Sea Ranch Escapes This company rents **Sea Ranch** properties for the weekend, week, or month. ♦ 60 Sea Walk Dr (off Hwy 1). 785.2426

Sea Ranch Vacation Rentals More private homes at **Sea Ranch** can be rented here; write for further information. ♦ Box 88, Sea Ranch, CA, 95497. 785.2579

262 Sea Ranch Golf Links Just south of the Gualala River is this privately owned, nine-hole, par 72 championship golf course designed by Robert Muir Graves. It boasts an ocean view from every hole. ♦ Daily. Off Hwy 1 (south of the Gualala River). 785.2467, 800/SEA.RANCH

Gualala

The local Indians used to call this area **Walali,** meaning "where the river meets [the sea]," until the Spanish started calling it Gualala. Nowadays, you might hear some of the locals call it "Walala" (a combination of the two names), but don't let that confuse you. Gualala is still the town's official name.

Like most of the cities along this coast, Gualala was once a thriving lumber port where schooners were loaded with timber bound for San Francisco. With its river beaches and good fishing spots, Gualala is a haven for anglers and nature lovers. Travelers who want to spend time exploring the local beaches can find very reasonably priced lodging at the old-time **Gualala Hotel.** The town is also home to **St. Orres,** one of the best restaurants along the North Coast and definitely worth a detour.

263 Gualala Point Regional Park This park is another prime spot for winter whale-watching, and for bird-watching and wildlife spotting throughout the year. Look for great blue herons, pygmy owls, shorebirds, deer, jackrabbits, and gray foxes. Cormorants can be seen offshore on Gualala Point Island. The 75-acre park has river and ocean access, and includes 19 campsites with picnic facilities and fire pits, available on a first-come, first-served basis. ♦ Park: daily. Visitors' center: M, F-Su. Hwy 1 (1 mile south of Gualala). 785.2377; fax 785.3741

263 Breakers Inn $$ Perched on a bluff overlooking the mouth of the Gualala River and the Pacific Ocean, this recently opened luxury inn offers 27 individually decorated rooms and a one-bedroom suite with a kitchen. All rooms have fireplaces, two-person whirlpool spas, king-size beds with down comforters, private baths, and private balconies with truly spectacular ocean views. Each room is decorated in a national or regional theme, from the deluxe corner **Japan** room, with a spa tub made of warm Hinoki cypress wood, to the Early American–style **Connecticut** room, with a patchwork quilt on the four-poster bed. Innkeeper Heidi Price offers tips on wine tasting, whale watching, abalone diving, and other activities in the Gualala area. ♦ Hwy 1 (west of the Gualala River). 884.3200, 800/BREAKER; fax 884.3400 ♿

263 Gualala Hotel $ The year 1903 is proudly inscribed on the front of this historic two-story hotel that resembles an Old West movie set. It was actually built to house lumber-mill workers and stagecoach travelers. Most of the 19 rooms upstairs share a bath, just as they did in the old days. Call ahead to reserve one of the five rooms with private baths and ocean views. The unfussy period decor—patterned wallpaper, old-fashioned water basins, bouquets of fresh flowers—is charming. ♦ Hwy 1 (west of the Gualala River). 884.3441 ♿

Within the Gualala Hotel:

Gualala Hotel Restaurant ★$$ Here at this gold-hued dining room, breakfast includes omelettes, French toast, and hotcakes, and the lunch menu offers mostly sandwiches. The large Italian-American dinners are served family-style; entrées range from fresh salmon and deep-fried oysters or scallops to chicken cacciatore, meat-stuffed ravioli, and rib eye steak. A children's menu is available, and Saturday is prime-rib night. There's also a lively bar. ♦ Italian-American ♦ Daily breakfast, lunch, and dinner. Reservations recommended on weekends. ♿

263 Food Company $ Stop here for a take-out picnic that's prepared on the spot. Choices include salads, sandwiches, and pastries baked fresh daily, plus hot entrées. Patio seating is also available. ♦ Eclectic ♦ Daily breakfast, lunch, and dinner. Hwy 1 (west of the Gualala River). 884.1800 ♿

263 Old Milano Hotel $$ Overlooking the sea at Castle Rock, this two-story white Victorian trimmed in green was built in 1905 and is on the National Register of Historic Places. The nine rooms have been furnished with antiques and most have ocean views. The original owners, Bert and Maria Luccinetti, who built the hotel and named it after their hometown in Italy, lived in the master suite, which features a sitting room and a separate bedroom. Guests have use of the lovely music room and the parlor and its stone fireplace; there's also a hot tub that has a view of the ocean. You can have the full breakfast served in your room or in the parlor. ◆ 38300 Hwy 1 (west of the Gualala River). 884.3256

Within the Old Milano Hotel:

Old Milano Hotel Restaurant ★$$$
Here, dinner is served in a wood-paneled Victorian-era dining room decorated in shades of rose. The menu changes seasonally, but starters may include house-cured gravlax (salmon), steamed mussels, or a salad of local greens. All entrées come with grilled vegetables. Choose from dishes such as grilled pork tenderloin served with homemade plum chutney, rack of lamb, and roast breast of duck. A vegetarian entrée, such as green chilies stuffed with cheese or black beans, is usually available, too. ◆ Eclectic ◆ Dinner. Closed Monday in the winter. Reservations required

263 St. Orres $$ This is one of the few inns on the North Coast that combine appealing accommodations with a first-class restaurant. The Russian-influenced architecture—marked by elaborately carved wooden balustrades, stained-glass windows, and ornate towers capped with copper domes—is the four-year project of craftsmen **Ted** and **Eric Black.** The hotel, built in 1976, has eight guest rooms upstairs, all with shared baths; two have ocean views and French doors opening onto the balcony, while the less expensive side rooms overlook the gardens or trees. Scattered over the large property are also 10 unique and secluded cottages, some along a creek and others at the edge of a redwood forest; all have private baths. One favorite is the modest **Wildflower,** a rustic cabin with a double bed nestled in a loft, a wood-burning stove, a cookstove, and an outdoor hot-water shower. The **Sequoia** cottage features a carved balustrade, a queen-size bed, a fireplace, and an ocean view. The largest, **Pine Haven,** is a mini-domed building with two redwood decks, an ocean view, and a stone fireplace. There's also a Japanese-style cottage, **Wake Robin.** ◆ 36601 Hwy 1 (west of the Gualala River). 884.3303, 884.3335 ⅙

Restaurants/Clubs: Red   Hotels: Blue
Shops/♥ Outdoors: Green   Wineries/Sights: Black

Within St. Orres:

St. Orres Restaurant ★★★$$$ The inn's dramatic dining room is in one of the Russian-style towers, and has a soaring three-story ceiling. Tables are set with elegant flower arrangements and handsome dinnerware, and the service is attentive. In the kitchen, chef Rosemary Campiformio, who is also part-owner of the hotel, turns out inventive prix-fixe, three-course meals, and you can also order à la carte. Appetizers might include a sumptuous venison pâté, stilton cheese wrapped in phyllo, or a sea-urchin mousse. The menu changes daily, but Campiformio's selection of appealing entrées leaves most diners struggling to decide what to order; choices may vary from venison in a wild huckleberry and Zinfandel sauce to grilled quail marinated in tequila and garlic that's served with yam and green-onion pancakes. There's a very good all-California wine list, too. ◆ Eclectic ◆ Daily dinner. Reservations recommended

264 Mar Vista Cottages $ A dozen white-clapboard cottages are set at the edge of a redwood forest. Choose between one- or two-bedroom housekeeping cottages, each with a queen-size bed and a private bath, and some with additional double or twin-size beds. Several have fireplaces or outdoor decks. The eight-acre property also includes a picnic and barbecue area, a hot tub, and a path to the beach. ◆ 35101 Hwy 1 (just north of Anchor Bay). 884.3522

264 Whale Watch Inn by the Sea $$$$ This contemporary inn is set on two acres at the edge of the sea and offers 18 luxurious guest rooms in five separate buildings, all with ocean views, private baths, and oceanfront decks. Each features queen-size beds with down comforters; most have fireplaces, whirlpool baths or saunas, and skylights; some have kitchens. One of the most luxurious is the **Bath Suite,** which features hand-carved furniture, a fireplace, and a two-person whirlpool bath at the top of a spiral staircase with a view of the Pacific. A full breakfast is served in your room. ◆ 35100 Hwy 1 (just north of Anchor Bay). 884.3667, 800/WHALE.42 ⅙

Wildflowers of the Wine Country

The wine country encompasses a wide variety of terrain, from lush valley floors and stony hillside slopes to rocky coasts, riverbanks, and wetlands. An abundance of wildflowers are found in all of them, and their diversity ensures there's almost always a plant in bloom. Here are some of California's most popular wildflowers.

California Poppy—
Eschscholtzia californica

With its grayish-green foliage and golden orange cup-shaped blossoms, California's state flower is easy to recognize. It grows by the roadside and often carpets entire hillsides. In vineyards, the cheerful poppies are sometimes found growing at the feet of the vines. Season: February through November

California Rhododendron—*Rhododendron californicum* and **Pacific Rhododendron**—*Rhododendron macrophyllum*

These broad-leafed evergreen shrubs grow from 3 to 15 feet or more in height, blossoming in the springtime with large, lightly freckled rose flowers in big, showy clusters. Visit the **Kruse Rhododendron Reserve** (see page 151) on the Sonoma Coast to see this native flower in all its splendor. Season: April through June

Cobweb Thistle—*Cirsium occidentale*

This is one thistle that attracts a number of admirers, including butterflies, honeybees, and hummingbirds. The spiky plant, which grows up to two feet tall, has prickly leaves and tufted flowers ranging from crimson to light purple. Sand dunes are a favorite habitat, but it can also be found inland. Season: April through July

Douglas Iris—
Iris douglasiana

Named for David Douglas, a botanist who did extensive collecting in California in the 1830s, the Douglas iris comes in many shades, from cream and yellow to blue and delicate tones of lavender and mauve. In coastal redwood forests, the two-foot-tall plants can sometimes be found in large colonies, an entrancing sight when in bloom. Season: March through June

ILLUSTRATIONS BY PATRICIA KEELIN

Farewell-to-Spring—*Clarkia amoena*

This annual wildflower is found primarily in oak groves. It first blooms in June, heralding the end of spring, which was the inspiration for the name. It's also known as **Godetia** and **Summer's Darling**. The large, open blossoms are deep pink or lavender with a darker rose or crimson spot on each petal. Season: June through August

Larkspur—*Delphinium*

Many species of larkspur abound in Northern California and are easy to recognize, with their tall, slender stems covered with large blue to deep-purple blossoms. In profile, the blossoms resemble spurs, and, indeed, the Spanish name for this graceful flower is *espuela del caballero* (the horseman's spur). Some varieties are poisonous to livestock. Season: March through July

Lupine—*Lupinus*

This common wildflower derives its name from *lupus* (or wolf), because it was once considered destructive to the soil. Lupines are abundant and come in many sizes and colors, including several shades of blue, white, and yellow. One of the prettiest is called "sky lupine" because of its bright, clear color. Its rounded leaves grow in clusters of three, five, or seven, depending on the variety, and the delicate flowers grow in tiers off a central stem. Season: April through June

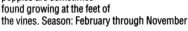

Queen Anne's Lace—*Daucus carota*

The showy blossoms of this common roadside wildflower are flat and arranged in clusters with a minuscule purple flower at the center. Seen up close, the blossom resembles a snowflake or a Victorian lace parasol, and along some roads, the wildflower is so abundant it forms a dazzling, lacy border. Season: May through September

Mendocino County/ Hopland-Ukiah Wine Road

From Cloverdale in the Russian River Valley, it's a short jaunt north on **Highway 101** to the tiny township of Hopland and to the dozen or so wineries scattered along the highway close to town and north toward Ukiah.

A rural, sparsely populated area, this part of Mendocino County has enjoyed a renaissance of wine making since the early 1970s. Hopland, the improbable center of it all, was a hop-growing region hit by an economic slump when the sales of hops (the aromatic dried flowers of the hop vine used to make beer) declined in the 1950s. The most visible sign of the town's newfound prosperity is the **Fetzer Vineyards** tasting room, a former high school turned into an attractive wine-tasting bar and shop featuring local products (it's the first building on the left as you drive through the three-block town). Several local wineries also have opened tasting rooms in Hopland. If you have the time, drive the back roads and visit such wineries as **McDowell Valley Vineyards, Hidden Cellars**, or tiny **Whaler Vineyards**, all set in a bucolic, rugged landscape. More wineries are strung along the highway all the way to Ukiah, the county seat. And north of **Lake Mendocino**, a few more remote, small wineries are tucked into the folds of the **Redwood Valley.**

In between visits to favorite wineries, it's easy to fit in some bicycling around the wine country or even some water sports on Lake Mendocino. From Hopland or Ukiah, you can drive over the mountains to **Clear Lake**, visiting such wineries as **Konocti** in **Kelseyville** on the **Mendocino** side of the lake. Depending on which route you take, it's a 30- to 40-minute drive one way. This part of Mendocino is also home to two of the few producers of pot-still brandies (made by the same process used in the Cognac region of France). **Jepson Vineyards** produces brandy and wine, and you may see the copper alembic (or distilling apparatus) when you visit, but, alas, you cannot taste the brandy there. The second producer is **Germain-Robin**, and while it's not open to the public, you may purchase **Germain-Robin** brandy at the **Fetzer Vineyards** tasting room in Hopland.

If you're visiting on a weekend, be sure to visit the **Fetzer Food & Wine Center at Valley Oaks**, a remarkable, 50-acre complex with a showcase organic garden devoted to the study of food and wine. In Ukiah, the **Grace Hudson Museum and Sun House** is a must-see. As for lodging, try the three-story, Victorian **Thatcher Inn** in Hopland or a bed-and-breakfast inn in Hopland or Ukiah. A little-known alternative is **Vichy Springs Resort** east of Ukiah, a historic hot-springs inn (they also bottle the naturally effervescent mineral water under the Vichy Springs label).

Good restaurants in the Hopland and Ukiah regions include **Il Vigneto Ristorante & Bar** for Italian cuisine, the **Bluebird Cafe** for hearty diner fare, or the **Mendocino Brewing Company** for casual pub fare and live music on Saturday nights. The wineries in this area are also close enough together for you to spend the morning visiting the tasting rooms in Hopland, plus a few more nearby wineries, and still have time to lunch in Boonville.

For information on the state parks in Mendocino County, call 937.5804; for camping reservations, call 800/444.7275; and for vacation home rentals, contact **Mendocino Coast Reservations** by writing to Box 1143, Mendocino, CA 95460, or call 937.5033 or 800/262.7801.

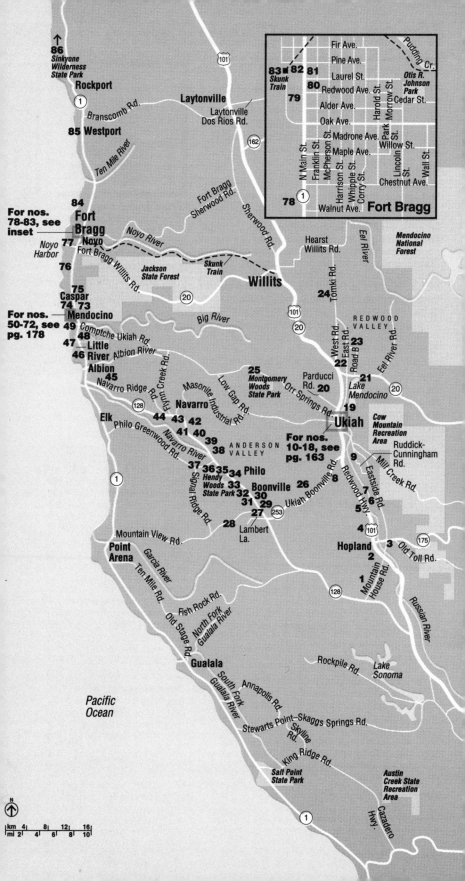

Fort Bragg (inset)

Fir Ave.
Pine Ave.
Laurel St.
83 82 81
Skunk
Train
80
79 Redwood Ave.
Alder Ave.
Oak Ave.
Madrone Ave.
Maple Ave.
N Main St.
Franklin St.
McPherson St.
Harrison St.
Whipple St.
Corry St.
Walnut Ave.
Chestnut Ave.
78
Pudding Cr.
Otis R. Johnson Park
Harold St.
Morrow St.
Park St.
Lincoln St.
Willow St.
Cedar St.
Wall St.
Fort Bragg

86 ↑ Sinkyone Wilderness State Park
Rockport
Branscomb Rd.
85 Westport
Ten Mile River

Laytonville
Laytonville Dos Rios Rd.
101
162

For nos. 78-83, see inset
84
Fort Bragg
77 Noyo
Noyo Harbor
76
75
Caspar
74 73
For nos. 50-72, see pg. 178
49
47 48
46 Little River
Albion
45

Noyo River
Fort Bragg Willits Rd.
Jackson State Forest
Skunk Train
Fort Bragg Sherwood Rd.
Sherwood Rd.
Hearst Willits Rd.
Willits
20
Big River
Comptche Ukiah Rd.
Albion River

Mendocino National Forest
Eel River
24
Tomki Rd.
REDWOOD VALLEY
West Rd.
East Rd.
23 Road B
22
21 Lake Mendocino
Eel River Rd.
20

Mendocino
Navarro Ridge Rd.
Flynn Creek Rd.
128
Elk
44 43 42
41 40
Navarro
39
38
37 36 35 34
Hendy Woods State Park 33
32
31 30
27 29
28
Lambert La.

Masonite Industrial Rd.
Low Gap Rd.
25 Montgomery Woods State Park
Orr Springs Rd.
Parducci Rd. 20
19
Ukiah
For nos. 10-18, see pg. 163
Philo
Boonville 26
Ukiah Boonville Rd.
253
ANDERSON VALLEY
Navarro River
Philo Greenwood Rd.
Signal Ridge Rd.

9
Cow Mountain Recreation Area
Ruddick-Cunningham Rd.
8
7
5 6
4
Hopland
2
3 Old Toll Rd.
175
Redwood Hwy.
Eastside Rd.
Mill Creek Rd.

Mountain View Rd.
Point Arena
Garcia River
Ten Mile Rd.
Fish Rock Rd.
Old Stage Rd.
North Fork Gualala River
Gualala
South Fork Gualala River
1 Mountain House Rd.
128
Russian River
Rockpile Rd.
Lake Sonoma
Annapolis Rd.
Stewarts Point–Skaggs Springs Rd.
Skyline Rd.
King Ridge Rd.
Salt Point State Park
Austin Creek State Recreation Area
Cazadero Hwy.
1

Pacific Ocean

N ↑
km 4 8 12 16
mi 2 4 6 8 10

Hopland

Just three blocks long, Hopland is billed as the gateway to the **Mendocino** wine country. It is surrounded by vineyards, with the majority of the valley's wineries strung out along **Highway 101** north of Hopland all the way to **Ukiah** and the **Redwood Valley** beyond. To make their products more easily accessible to visitors, several of the wineries have installed tasting rooms right in town. **Fetzer Vineyards** is the most prominent, but you'll also find **McDowell** and **Hidden Cellars,** plus a few antiques shops and the restored **Thatcher Inn.**

Before the entire **Sanel Valley** was granted to Fernando Féliz, Indians lived in the area around Hopland. Féliz had come from Pueblo San José south of San Francisco, and the town of **Sanel** grew up around his home in the valley. The township was established in 1859 and named after an Indian village that once occupied a nearby site on McDowell Creek. By the mid-1860s the surrounding area had become the prime producer of hops for the brewing industry, and in 1887 Sanel was renamed Hopland in honor of its best-selling crop.

Despite a setback during Prohibition, farmers continued to grow mainly hops until the 1950s, when the market diminished and it became more profitable for most of them to replant their fields with pear and prune orchards and grape vineyards. The town was a quiet backwater until **Fetzer Vineyards** opened their tasting-room complex in 1977, but even today you wouldn't exactly call Hopland a hopping town.

DUNCAN PEAK
Vineyards

Mendocino County
Cabernet Sauvignon 1988
Produced by Hubert Lenczowski

BOTTLED BY DUNCAN PEAK WINE COMPANY, UKIAH, CA
ALCOHOL 12.5 PERCENT BY VOLUME

1 Duncan Peak Vineyards This tiny vineyard makes just one wine: a Cabernet Sauvignon from grapes grown on a few hillside acres on the edge of Sanel Valley near Hopland. Owner Hubert Lenczowski produces only 500 cases of hand-crafted Cabernet each year. ♦ Tasting and tours by appointment only. 14500 Mountain House Rd (off Hwy 101). 744.1129

Restaurants/Clubs: Red   Hotels: Blue
Shops/ 🍸 Outdoors: Green   Wineries/Sights: Black

2 Milano Winery When wine maker Jim Milone founded this winery (pictured above) in 1977, he incorporated into the winery the old barnlike hop kiln his grandfather and father had built. The weathered redwood structure houses the tasting room, where you may sample Chardonnay, Cabernet Sauvignon, and Zinfandel. Also try the special late-harvest dessert wines, if there are still any left when you visit. Almost all of the winery's vintages are sold here. ♦ Tasting daily; tours by appointment only. 14594 Hwy 101 (near Mountain House Rd). 744.1396

Also at Milano Winery:

Private Reserve Cottage $$ Jim and Pat Milone offer a self-contained cottage for rent on the **Milano Winery** property. It stands alone just off the drive, but it's not really secluded. It has a small yard, a barbecue, and bicycles. Guests may also walk through the 64-acre vineyard.

3 Fetzer Food & Wine Center at Valley Oaks Since the dynamic Fetzer family opened this culinary research center in 1984, more than 50 acres have been developed, including a spectacular four-and-a-half-acre organic garden and an experimental organic vineyard. The garden is planted with more than 1,000 varieties of fruits, vegetables, herbs, and ornamental and edible flowers. The center also includes conference rooms and a state-of-the-art demonstration kitchen where weekend cooking classes are hosted. The culinary director is John Ash, who owns **John Ash & Co.,** a popular wine-country restaurant in Santa Rosa. Some classes are taught by Ash, others by a roster of celebrated guest chefs. ♦ Daily. 13601 Eastside Rd (at Hwy 175). 744.1250; fax 744.1439

4 Fetzer Vineyards
Though the Fetzer family winery is actually several miles north of Hopland in the Redwood Valley, they transformed the former downtown Hopland High School into the **Hopland Tasting Room,** a tasting center for Fetzer wines. The winery was founded in 1968 by the late Bernard Fetzer and

his wife, Kathleen; it is now owned by the Brown-Forman corporation. Paul Dolan, the president and former wine maker, has been with the winery since 1977. He introduced the excellent Fetzer Reserve wines in 1990; try the Fetzer Reserve Cabernet or the late-harvest Riesling. The Barrel Select Vintage wines are vinified vineyard by vineyard (meaning the grapes from different vineyards are not mixed), and they're selected by the barrel. The tasting area is set up at a bar at the end of a large room. Check the small wine library for bottles of Fetzer Reserve, older vintages, and special bottles such as double magnums. In 1992 the winery introduced its first wines made from organically grown grapes, including a Chardonnay and a Cabernet Sauvignon. You'll also find **Germain-Robin** brandy, picnic supplies, cookbooks, herb vinegars, virgin olive oils, and all sorts of local food products. A cooler holds chilled white wines, plus organic Chardonnay and Cabernet grape juice from **The Tinman** in the Anderson Valley. There's also a deck and a grassy area adjoining the tasting room where you may sit and enjoy a snack with a glass of wine. ♦ Tasting and sales daily. 13500 Hwy 101 (north of Hwy 175). 744.1737; fax 744.1439 &

Also at Fetzer Vineyards:

Made in Mendocino This cooperative gallery, featuring the work of 40 Mendocino artists and artisans, is staffed by the members themselves. A wide range of media is displayed here, from photographs and paintings of the Mendocino landscape to handwoven baskets, textiles, and hand-thrown pottery. You can find smaller gift items, too, such as jewelry crafted in silver, ceramic, and glass. ♦ Daily. 744.1300 &

5 John Carpenter's Hopland Antiques Inveterate browsers won't be able to resist poking around the cluttered rooms of this antiques shop. It has a little bit of everything —and more than a little bit of vintage and estate jewelry; antique fishing lures and reels; fine, old china; and cast-iron doorstops. ♦ Daily. 13456 Hwy 101 (north of Old Toll Rd). 744.1023

5 Hopland Superette & Liquor This modest, family-owned grocery and liquor store stocks basic picnic fare, chilled drinks, and local wines. ♦ Daily. 13400 Hwy 101 (north of Old Toll Rd). 744.1171 &

6 McDowell Valley Vineyards This small winery owned by the Keehn/Crawford families is a leader in Rhône-style wines. Vintners Richard and Karen Keehn built it in 1979. Part of their property had been planted to Syrah and Grenache grapes in the early 20th century, and these vines, perhaps the oldest in California, provide the grapes for many of their wines. Wine makers Bill Crawford and Kerry Damsky make a graceful Grenache

Rosé in the style of Provence's Tavel, an intense, concentrated Syrah from vines planted in 1919, a lower-priced Bistro Syrah from a blend of old and new vines, and a rich, perfumed Viognier made from difficult-to-grow white Rhône varietal grapes. The two generic white and red table wines are ideal for a casual picnic or barbecue. Tastings and sales are offered at the tasting room in downtown Hopland instead of at the winery, which is located on Highway 175 in the McDowell Valley. ♦ Tasting and sales daily. 13441 Hwy 101 (between Old Toll and Ukiah Boonville Rds). 744.1516; fax 744.1826 &

6 Thatcher Inn $$ This striking, many-gabled property first opened in 1890 as a rest stop for travelers heading by stage or by train from San Francisco to the Oregon border on the old Redwood Highway. At the time, the stagecoach horses were kept in an old barn behind the hotel and rooms were lit with kerosene lamps and candles. The drivers occupied the tiny rooms at the very top of the hotel, and Pomo Indians tended the vegetable gardens and livestock. Named for its former proprietor, W.W. Thatcher, the restored Victorian hotel offers 21 rooms with private baths, all appointed with original and reproduction antique furniture. The bridal suite features a queen-size bed dressed in pink satin and lace with a matching armoire and a large bay window draped in lace curtains; the spacious bathroom has a Victorian claw-foot tub with brass shower fittings. Among our other favorite suites are the **Ornbaum Room** (No. 12), which is located at the back of the hotel and overlooks the patio and pool, and the **Milone Room** (No. 15), which has a brass bed and a claw-foot bathtub tucked in a corner. The hallways of the hotel are lined with gilt-framed photos of old Hopland and local families. Downstairs, there's a lovely library room paneled in Philippine mahogany, just the place to enjoy a toddy from the hotel bar's wonderful collection of single-malt scotches, brandies, Cognacs, and Armagnacs. Be sure to try a taste of **Germain-Robin** or **Jepson**, both locally distilled, fine brandies. The hotel has lower mid-week rates and special weekday getaway packages that include accommodations, a bottle of sparkling wine, and breakfast and dinner in the hotel dining room. ♦ 13401 Hwy 101 (between Old Toll and Ukiah Boonville Rds). 744.1890

159

Within the Thatcher Inn:

Il Vigneto Ristorante & Bar ★★$$$
Chef Silvio Bruschi does his Florentine roots proud at this Northern Italian restaurant. At lunch you will find a selection of individual pizzas, including Bruschi's special Vigneto pizza made with tuna, tomatoes, mozzarella, green peppers, and onions; focaccia sandwiches on fresh-baked bread; calzones; and a few seafood and pasta dishes. Dinner offers more elaborate fare. Tuscan-style grilled salmon, homemade gnocchi in a fresh tomato-basil cream sauce, organic rabbit sauteéd with extra virgin olive oil, garlic, fresh tomatoes, and sage in a creamy white wine sauce, and a

Florentine-style charbroiled T-bone steak are all good choices. Save room for the sumptuous desserts—such as tiramisù, Italian chocolate tart, and cheesecake—which are all made from scratch. You can dine outside on the back patio, outfitted with ornate white Victorian garden furniture and shaded by an 800-year-old oak tree.

Bruschi also prepares breakfast daily for guests at the **Thatcher Inn,** featuring freshly squeezed orange juice, omelettes, and French toast. The most popular breakfast item is the hazelnut griddle cakes, served with real maple syrup. ♦ Italian ♦ M, W-Su breakfast, lunch, and dinner. 744.1074 ♿

Deciphering a Wine Label in Nine Easy Steps

1 This title is usually either the **brand name** or the name of the wine producer (some producers bottle wines under several different brand names).

2 The term **"estate bottled"** indicates that the wine was made entirely from grapes grown or supervised by the producer, and was created and bottled by the producer.

3 The **vintage** is the year that at least 95 percent of the grapes used to make the wine were grown and harvested. Not all wines have a vintage date, in which case the wine inside the bottle is a blend of wines from different vintages (a typical practice for making Champagne and Port). Wine without a vintage date is not necessarily an inferior wine.

4 When the grapes come from a special **vineyard** or section of a vineyard that consistently yields a parti-cularly high quality of grape, the producer will some-times, but not always, indicate that fact by placing the name of the vineyard on the label. By law, 95 percent of the grapes must come from the named vineyard.

5 The **appellation** (place of origin) specifies the geographic area where the grapes were grown. It may be as simple as "California," in which case 100 percent of the grapes must come from that state. For a county designation, 75 percent of the grapes must be from that county. To have a more specific viticultural appellation, such as "Stags Leap" or "Guenoc Valley," 85 percent of the grapes must come from the area indicated.

6 The wine type in California is most often the **grape variety,** such as Chardonnay, Merlot, or Zinfandel, and 75 percent of the grapes used to make the wine must be the stated varietal. If the wine is made from a blend of grapes, the label may bear a generic name, such as "Table Wine" or the more old-fashioned terms "Chablis" or "Burgundy," which were borrowed from wine regions in France and bear little resemblance to wines produced in those two regions.

7 What is listed on this section of the wine label varies from bottle to bottle, but generally it provides information about the wine **producer** and **bottler.** When this line says "produced and bottled by," the winery made the wine and watched over it until it was bottled, but a large percentage of the grapes were purchased from other vineyards. If it only says "bottled by," the winery probably bought the finished wines and blended them at their cellar before bottling. "Grown, produced, and bottled by" is essentially the same as "estate bottled."

8 This is the **trade name** and address of the wine bottler.

9 The **alcohol content** of the wine is listed here (plus or minus 1½ percent), and it may not exceed 14 percent for most wines. Dessert wines may not be more than 21 percent alcohol by volume.

The terms **"reserve," "special reserve,"** and **"private reserve"** may be added to a wine label by the producer to indicate a special wine, such as one that comes from a particular cask or that has been aged a little longer.

7 Mendocino Brewing Company ★$ When California changed its laws in the early 1980s to permit breweries to sell directly from attached taverns, Michael Laybourn, Norman Franks, and John Scahill—all avid home brewers—put their heads together and decided to open a brewery and brew pub in Hopland, the center of the old hops industry. After adding master brewer Don Barkeley and Michael Lovett to the partnership, they formed this company and opened the second brew pub in the nation since Prohibition.

Installed in the old-brick **Hop Vine Saloon Building,** just across from the **Thatcher Inn,** the brew pub is one of the prime attractions of Hopland. It's a casual place, something like a rustic English pub, with an outdoor beer garden shaded with a grape arbor and hop-vine trellis. The partners produce four brews, all made in the traditional manner with 100 percent malted barley, whole hops, pure yeast culture, and water. Peregrine is the lightest, an ale brewed with pale malt and Cascade hops, while medium-bodied Blue Heron Pale Ale has a slightly bitter finish. Black Hawk Stout is made from fully roasted black malt, and the most popular brew is the amber, full-bodied Red Tail Ale. This being a brew pub, it serves appetizers such as Buffalo wings and soft pretzels, plus burgers, BLTs, and other sandwiches, including a tofu-veggie sandwich. Local wines are also served, and the live music on Saturday nights—which runs the gamut from blues to country—has become a big drawing card. A shop at the back sells all sorts of beer paraphernalia: etched-glass mugs with the brewery's logo, baseball hats inscribed with the name of your favorite brew, Red Tail Ale T-shirts and sweatshirts, along with a nice, tall pint glass and nifty coasters. ♦ Pub ♦ Daily lunch and dinner. Tours by appointment only. 13351 Hwy 101 (between Old Toll and Ukiah Boonville Rds). 744.1361, 744.1015; fax 744.1910 ♿

"A Californian vineyard [has] nothing to remind you of the Rhine or Rhône, of the low Côte d'Or, or the infamous and scabby deserts of Champagne; but all is green, solitary, covert."

Robert Louis Stevenson,
The Silverado Squatters

7 The Cheesecake Lady Originally hailing from Philadelphia, the "Cheese-cake Lady" now bakes her goods in the large kitchen in the back of this shop in Hopland. Her wares can be sampled in restaurants and cafes throughout Northern California as well as here. In the morning, stop by for espresso drinks and her freshly baked croissants, Danish pastries, and bagels. You'll also find a slice of her superlative cheesecake uplifting any time of the day. She makes as many types of cheesecake as local vintners make of wine, but the hands-down favorite is her original sour-cream version made with a graham-cracker crust and topped with sour cream. The more adventurous might like to explore the version topped with white chocolate and toasted almonds. One of the best is the espresso cheesecake, which has a chocolate-cookie crust and a sour-cream topping. The ladies in the kitchen also whip up deep-chocolate tortes layered with butter creams and mousses. For the flower child at heart (and there are a lot of them 'round these parts), they bake carrot cakes. ♦ Daily. 13325 Hwy 101 (between Old Toll and Ukiah Boonville Rds). 744.1441; fax 744.1312 ♿

7 Bluebird Cafe ★★$ The menu says, "Quality food, big portions, reasonable prices," and this recently opened cafe lives up to that promise. With a 1950s-style decor (Formica tables and vinyl booths and chairs), it serves good, hearty food throughout the day. Breakfast features "Specialty Scrambles" (spicy Cajun eggs or vegetarian tofu served with home fries), omelettes, blueberry blintzes, and whole-wheat pancakes with blackberries. For lunch, choose from grilled chicken Caesar salad, burgers topped with mushrooms and cheese (or gardenburgers for vegetarians), and other sandwiches, while dinner offers steak, pizza, pasta, fresh fish, and roast beef with real mashed potatoes and gravy. The cafe also makes its own fresh juices, including pineapple-orange, fruit punch, and grape, plus old-fashioned milk shakes, sundaes, and banana splits. All orders are available for takeout. ♦ American ♦ Daily breakfast, lunch, and dinner. 14430 Hwy 101 (between Old Toll and Ukiah Boonville Rds). 744.1633 ♿

Ukiah/Redwood Valley

The Ukiah area was once part of the **Yokayo** land grant, which extended from the southern end of the **Ukiah Valley** to the northern end of the Redwood Valley and was ceded to Mexican militia captain Cayetano Juarez by his government in 1846. Some historians say John Parker was the area's first white settler; other accounts have Samuel Lowry staking out the first homestead in 1856 at what is now the corner of **Main** and **Perkins Streets.** An influx of settlers arrived within the next year or two, attracted by the climate and fertile soil. Grain was the first crop planted, followed by fruit trees, tobacco, grapes, and hops for the brewing industry. Hops soon became the major crop in the area and you may still see some of the old drying kilns in the countryside. The spelling of Yokayo (an Indian word meaning "deep valley") was soon changed to Ukiah. In just a few years the town emerged as the region's chief commercial center, and in 1859 it became the county seat. It has a small downtown, with many businesses strung along **State Street,** and a Victorian residential area. Of primary interest to most visitors is the **Grace Hudson Museum and Sun House** (see page 164).

8 Jepson Vineyards

When Chicago business-man Robert S. Jepson Jr. founded his winery just north of Hopland, he decided early on to specialize in just three products: Chardonnay, sparkling wine, and

JEPSON
VINEYARDS

brandy. The Chardonnay is barrel fermented and aged in small oak barrels; his Mendocino sparkling wine, made entirely with Chardonnay grapes, is produced by the *méthode champenoise* traditionally used in the Champagne region of France, where a blend of still wines is bottled with a measured amount of sugar and yeast to induce a second fermentation in the bottle. To distill the brandy, he acquired an alambic pot still, just like those used to produce the famous French brandies, and he distills his spirits from French Colombard, the same grape used in Cognac. You may taste everything but the brandy at the fieldstone-and-wood tasting room on the property; when the weather is warm they put tables outside. The Sauvignon Blanc, called "Château d'Alicia," is sold only here. Tours include the winery and, if requested, the copper alembic (but you might not see anything in operation because they distill only one month a year). ♦ Tasting and sales daily; tours by appointment only. 10400 Hwy 101 (2 miles north of Hopland), Ukiah. 468.8936; fax 468.0362 ♿

9 Hidden Cellars Winery

In 1981, Dennis Patton, a local farmer and avid home wine maker, decided to turn pro. With money borrowed from friends and a garage converted into a micro-winery in a hidden mountain canyon, he made his first award-winning wines. His production has grown by leaps and bounds, and he is now well known for his Sauvignon Blanc and rich, supple Zinfandels. He also makes Zinfandel, Chardonnay, Johannisberg Riesling, Sauvignon Blanc, and Alchemy (a blend of Sémillon and Sauvignon Blanc) from organically grown grapes. But the wine that always stops tasters in their tracks is the Chanson d'Or, a lush, apricot-and-honey-scented dessert wine made from a blend of Sémillon and Sauvignon Blanc. ♦ Tours by appointment only. 1500 Ruddick-Cunningham Rd (off Hwy 101), Ukiah. 462.0301; fax 462.8144

9 Whaler Vineyards

Russ and Annie Nyborg specialize in Zinfandel at their tiny winery on 35 acres near Ukiah. After almost 15 years, they're still fascinated with this intriguing grape, turning out Zinfandels in several different styles. It's fun to visit the weathered redwood barn that houses the winery, and in the small barrel-aging room you might hear how this family came to realize their dream of becoming vintners. The ship on the label is from the Viking Museum in Oslo, Norway. Norwegian-American Russ Nyborg works as a bar pilot, directing large ships into San Francisco's harbor, and his family shares his affinity for the sea. ♦ Tasting, sales, and tours by appointment only. 6200 Eastside Rd (off Hwy 101), Ukiah. 462.6355 ♿

10 Vichy Springs Resort

$$ Established in 1854, this mineral-springs resort and its famous mineral-water baths were named after Vichy Springs in France because the naturally effervescent waters surging forth from miles beneath the surface resemble those in Europe. The 700-acre property, now a California landmark, was well known in the 19th century, attracting the likes of Mark Twain, Robert Louis Stevenson, and Jack London. Teddy Roosevelt and pugilists John L. Sullivan and "Gentleman" Jim Corbett took to the waters here, too. The hot-springs resort's current

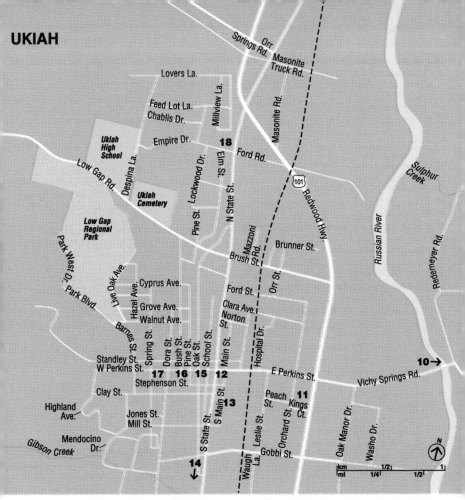

UKIAH

Orr Springs Rd.
Masonite Truck Rd.
Lovers La.
Feed Lot La.
Chablis Dr.
Millview La.
Masonite Rd.
Empire Dr.
18
Ford Rd.
Ukiah High School
Lockwood Dr.
Elm St.
Despina La.
Low Gap Rd.
Pine St.
Ukiah Cemetery
N State St.
101
Redwood Hwy.
Sulphur Creek
Low Gap Regional Park
Mazzoni Rd.
Brunner St.
Russian River
Park West Dr.
Park Blvd.
Brush St.
Orr St.
Redemeyer Rd.
Live Oak Ave.
Cyprus Ave.
Ford St.
Grove Ave.
Clara Ave.
Hazel Ave.
Walnut Ave.
Norton St.
Barnes St.
Spring St.
Dora St.
Bush St.
Pine St.
Oak St.
School St.
Main St.
Hospital Dr.
Standley St.
W Perkins St.
E Perkins St.
10→
17 16 15 12
Vichy Springs Rd.
Stephenson St.
Clay St.
Peach St.
11
Kings Ct.
Oak Manor Dr.
Washo Dr.
Highland Ave.
Jones St.
Mill St.
13
S State St.
S Main St.
Leslie St.
Orchard St.
Mendocino Dr.
Gibson Creek
14 ↓
Waugh La.
Gobbi St.
km 1/2 1
ml 1/4 1/2
N

proprietors, Gilbert and Marjorie Ashoff, have completely refurbished and reopened the inn for overnight guests and recreational activities, such as hiking, picnicking, and mountain biking.

You may stay in one of the guest rooms in the inn, which dates back to the 1860s, or rent one of the two cottages on the property—which were built in 1854 and are among the oldest existing buildings in Mendocino County. Or you may buy a pass and spend the day relaxing by the pool, soaking in the mineral-water tubs, or hiking up to the Old Cinnabar mine shaft or the fern-shrouded falls.

A dozen rooms are strung along a broad veranda; most have queen-size beds (one has twin beds). These pleasant, simply decorated rooms have natural wood floors, print coverlets, and throw rugs; each has a private bath and shower. The emphasis is on country retreat more than luxury. The blue cottage has a bedroom with a queen-size bed, a living-room area with a sofa bed and a fireplace, and a full kitchen. The larger, white cottage is furnished with a long, overstuffed couch, a wood-burning stove, and a beautiful 1930s-era gas stove. There's a large, shady porch in front and a barbecue. The resort has eight indoor and outdoor bathing tubs (in pairs, so you can chat with a friend), a therapeutic massage building, and a refurbished Olympic-size pool (also filled with mineral water). One- or one-and-a-half-hour Swedish massages or foot-reflexology massages are available by appointment. The Ashoffs also bottle the mineral water under the Vichy Springs label. ♦ 2605 Vichy Springs Rd (off Hwy 101), Ukiah. 462.9515; fax 462.9516 &

11 Ukiah Farmers' Market Shop for farm-fresh produce at this twice-weekly summer market at the **Orchard Shopping Center.** ♦ Tu 4-6:30PM, Sa 8AM-noon June-Oct. Orchard St (between Kings Ct and E Perkins St), Ukiah

12 Main Street Wine and Cheese A well-chosen selection of imported and domestic cheeses and local wines are carried in this shop on State Street (the name dates from the shop's former location on Main Street). Pick up assorted picnic fixings or order one of the generous sandwiches to go. ♦ M-Sa. 113 S State St (at E Perkins St), Ukiah. 462.0417 &

Restaurants/Clubs: Red   Hotels: Blue
Shops/♥ Outdoors: Green   Wineries/Sights: Black

13 Grace Hudson Museum and Sun House The Grace Hudson Museum (1986) and **Sun House** (1911), along with **Hudson-Carpenter Park,** occupy four-and-a-half landscaped acres in the middle of downtown Ukiah. Bring a picnic lunch and then visit the museum dedicated to artist Grace Hudson (1865-1937) and her husband, anthropologist Dr. John W. Hudson (1857-1936). Hudson was known for her portraits of the local Pomo Indians, and the museum has many of her graceful studies of Indian life. It includes a collection of Pomo art and artifacts of anthropological interest, many of them collected by the Hudsons. The museum also shows the work of local artists. The house next door, an arts-and-crafts-style bungalow built by architect/artist **George Wilcox,** is where the Hudsons lived and worked. It may only be visited in the company of a docent, but it's worth taking the 15- to 20-minute tour. Tours depart from the museum. A **California Historical Landmark,** the lovely redwood house is filled with the personal touches of the couple; Grace designed the lanterns, painted a folding screen with a Mendocino landscape, and designed the hooked rugs. Pomo baskets and other Indian artifacts reflect the Hudsons' fascination with California Indian culture. Grace's studio has been left just as it was, with her easel set up to paint a portrait in the north light. John, who was a physician as well as an anthropologist, devoted much of his life to studying and documenting native Indian cultures. ♦ Donation requested. Museum: W-Su (Sun House tours offered hourly from noon to 3PM). 431 S Main St (between Gobbi and E Perkins Sts), Ukiah. 462.3370

14 Moores' Flour Mill & Bakery Make a run into Ukiah for bread, flour, and other basics or pick up a deli sandwich made on fresh-baked bread at this unique shop. Through a window in the back, you can see the century-old mill wheel grinding out beautiful whole-grain flour. Try the whole wheat for baking bread, and you may also buy bulk bags of unbleached and specialty flour such as cornmeal, polenta, and rye. Even if you don't bake, pick up a bag of the buttermilk or buckwheat pancake mix—the best you'll ever taste. The store is also a mini-museum of old flour sacks with quaint logos. ♦ M-Sa. 1550 S State St (at Talmage Rd), Ukiah. 462.6550 ₺

15 Chamber of Commerce You'll get the scoop on restaurants, lodging, wineries, recreation, and other activities in Ukiah Valley here. ♦ M-F. 200 S School St (at W Perkins St), Ukiah. 462.4705

16 Sanford House Bed & Breakfast $ If Ukiah's motel row on State Street is not your style, there is an alternative: this gracious bed-and-breakfast inn set in a quiet residential neighborhood. The stately Queen Anne Victorian was built in 1904 as the home of Senator John Bunyon Sanford, a longtime California state legislator. Innkeepers Dorsey and Bob Manogue have five air-conditioned guest rooms, each with a private bath and decorated with antiques and custom fabrics and wallpapers. The Manogues serve a breakfast of freshly squeezed juice, fruit, homemade muffins and breads, omelettes or French toast, and coffee or tea in the dining room. ♦ 306 S Pine St (at Stephenson St), Ukiah. 462.1653

17 Held-Poage Memorial Home and Research Library To get a better sense of Mendocino County history, visit this research library housed in a Queen Anne Victorian (pictured on page 165), once the home of Mendocino County Superior Court Judge William D.L. Held and Ethel Poage Held. Dedicated to the collection of archival materials relating to the county's history, the library contains more than 5,000 volumes, with a wonderful collection of historical photographs, plus documents and maps. ♦ Tu, Th, Sa 1:30-4PM and by appointment. Mendocino County Historical Society, 603 W Perkins St (between Dora and Spring Sts), Ukiah. 462.6969

18 Discovery Inn $ This inexpensive motel provides lodging just one mile from downtown Ukiah. The 154 rooms with standard contemporary decor feature queen-size beds, cable TV, a stereo, and direct-dial phones. In the summer the swimming pool offers respite from the heat; there's also a Jacuzzi, whirlpool, and tennis court. If you plan to stay for a few days, ask about the rooms with kitchenettes or the executive suites. ♦ 1340 N State St (at Empire Dr), Ukiah. 462.8873; fax 462.1249 ₺

DUNNEWOOD

CALIFORNIA
Cabernet Sauvignon

VINTED & BOTTLED BY DUNNEWOOD VINEYARDS & WINERY
UKIAH, MENDOCINO COUNTY, CALIFORNIA • ALC 12.5% BY VOL.

19 Dunnewood Vineyards & Winery Sample Sauvignon Blanc, Chardonnay, Cabernet, Gamay Beaujolais, Zinfandel, and more at this winery's tasting bar in Ukiah. Wine maker George Phelan also produces Merlot and Pinot Noir. ♦ Daily. 2399 N State St (near Lake Mendocino Dr), Ukiah. 462.2987; fax 463.0323 ₺

1986
MENDOCINO COUNTY
CHARDONNAY
PREMIUM TABLE WINE

PRODUCED & BOTTLED BY PARDUCCI WINE CELLARS
UKIAH, MENDOCINO, CO., CA. B.W.C. #3632

20 Parducci Wine Cellars After first starting a winery in Cloverdale, Adolph Parducci moved north to Ukiah in 1931 to found this family winery in which four generations of Parduccis have now worked. The tasting room, a white, Spanish-style building, is just north of Ukiah, and offers the full gamut of moderately priced wines from this popular producer. The tasting-room complex also houses a small gift shop with wineglasses, decanters, wine buckets, and other related paraphernalia. In back there is a picnic area with tables and umbrellas on a sheltered patio. ♦ Tasting, sales, and tours daily. 501 Parducci Rd (off Hwy 101), Ukiah. 462.3828

21 Lake Mendocino Recreation Area Ten miles north of Ukiah, this recreational lake was created when the Army Corps of Engineers dammed the Russian River at the mouth of the Coyote Valley in 1958. The 1,822-acre lake, bordered by foothills, is a popular destination for boating, waterskiing, windsurfing, and swimming. The lake has two large boat launches and protected beaches for swimming, plus nearly 300 family campsites (available on a first-come, first-served basis), and a hundred picnic sites, each with tables and a barbecue pit. In season, there's lots of good fishing for striped bass, large- and smallmouth bass, crappie, bluegill, and catfish. Miles of hiking paths wind through the foothills surrounding the lake, which also includes 689 acres of protected wildlife habitat. ♦ Park entrances: off Hwy 101 at Calpella; off Hwy 20, east of 101; or on Lake Mendocino Dr, off N. State St, Ukiah. Recreation area office: 1160 Lake Mendocino Dr. 462.7581

Within the Lake Mendocino Recreation Area:
Visitor Center To learn more about Native American traditions and Lake Mendocino, visit this center located in the **Pomo Day-Use Area** at the north end of the lake. It was built by the Army Corps of Engineers in the shape of a ceremonial dance house. The exhibits, films, and programs provide information about local Indian ways. ♦ Free. W-Su Apr-Sept; Sa-Su Oct-Mar. 485.8285

Lake Mendocino Marina This privately owned marina offers ski boats, pedal boats, and fishing boats for rent, plus slip rentals for those who want to bring their own crafts. The store sells bait and tackle as well as marine and camping supplies. There's also a snack bar with burgers and sandwiches, and a picnic area with barbecues. ♦ Daily Apr-Oct. 485.8644

22 Weibel Champagne Vineyards Locals say the tasting room here resembles an upside-down Champagne glass. You decide while sampling one of the sparkling wines

Held-Poage Memorial Home and Research Library

Premier Grape Varieties of Northern California Wine Country

Cabernet Sauvignon

A transplant from Bordeaux, this grape has become California's most famous varietal. It yields medium- to full-bodied red wines that are rich in berry flavor and have a distinct herbaceousness. They may be tannic when young.

Chardonnay

California wine country's most widely planted grape produces medium- to full-bodied, dry white wines. Chardonnay ranges in taste from rich to delicate, and from fruity to oaky. The grape is also used to make sparkling wines.

Chenin Blanc

This grape creates delicate, light-bodied, and fruity wines. The straw-colored wines vary from dry to semisweet.

Merlot

A relative of Cabernet, although Merlot wines are softer, fruitier, and less tannic. The medium- to full-bodied wines have a pleasant bouquet reminiscent of cherries.

Pinot Noir

This grape is difficult to grow and convert into wine, but it produces complex, rich red wines with a silky texture. Fuller and softer than Cabernet; and light- to medium-bodied.

Riesling

A popular grape used for fruity white wines that range from dry to sweet and are light- to medium-bodied.

Sauvignon Blanc

The source of crisp white wines that vary in flavor from tart to fruity to slightly grassy. Light- to medium-bodied.

Zinfandel

Unique to California, this grape produces popular, dark, spicy, and fruity red wines and blush wines. Dry and medium- to full-bodied.

DRAWINGS BY PATRICIA KEELIN

from this longtime producer. This facility was founded in 1973, but the firm had already been making sparkling and other wines in Alameda before it moved north. The parking lot is set up for RVs, and guests are welcome to stay overnight in their campers. There is also a picnic area with tables and barbecue pits. ♦ Tasting and sales daily. 7051 N State St (at Hwys 101 and 20), Redwood Valley. 485.0321; fax 485.6710 &

23 Lolonis Winery Tryfon Lolonis emigrated to the Redwood Valley in 1915, and by 1920 he was already planting vineyards. Grapes from the original Zinfandel vines go into the wines his son Ulysses makes today. ♦ Tasting by appointment only. 2901 Road B (off Hwy 20), Redwood Valley. 485.8027

24 Frey Vineyards Owned by Marguerite Frey and her 12 children, this small winery on a 145-acre ranch was constructed bit by bit with salvaged timber from the old **Garret Winery** in Ukiah. The vineyards are cultivated organically, and wine maker Jonathan Frey makes only small amounts of several different varietals. Gewürztraminer, Chardonnay, Sauvignon Blanc, and a white table wine comprise the whites. Reds include Cabernet, Syrah, Petite Sirah, Zinfandel, and Pinot Noir. This is one of the few wineries in California that doesn't add sulfites. ♦ Tasting and tours by appointment only. 14000 Tomki Rd (off West Rd), Redwood Valley. 485.5177, 800/760.3739

"The first settlers arriving in Sonoma County found the valley floor covered with a growth of wild oats that could hide a man on horseback. We latecomers can only imagine that it must have been a beautiful sight."

Harvey J. Hansen,
Wild Oats in Eden: Sonoma in the 19th Century

"I feast on wine and bread and feasts they are."

Michelangelo

Bests

John Ash
Chef/Restaurant Owner, John Ash & Co., Santa Rosa

A day exploring **Salt Point State Park** on the **Sonoma Coast** near **Fort Ross.** It's an incredible convergence of several geologic formations, and the tide pools are fantastic.

A hike to the top of **Mount St. Helena** during a full moon or on Christmas morning.

Shopping at the Thursday-night farmers' market during the summer months in **Santa Rosa.**

Schmoozing at the wine auctions in **Napa** and **Sonoma.**

Bicycling through the **Alexander Valley.**

Mud baths at the **Golden Haven Hot Springs** in **Calistoga.**

Enzyme baths at **Osmosis** in **Freestone.**

Frank J. Prial
Wine Columnist, *The New York Times*

The breathtaking view of the **Mayacamas Mountains** through the archway at the **Robert Mondavi Winery** in **Oakville.**

The self-conducted tour of the stunning **Sterling Vineyards** winery near **Calistoga** (accessible only by tramway).

Any of the beautiful rooms at the tiny **Boonville Hotel** in the **Anderson Valley.**

Driving from **Napa** to **Sonoma** over the mountains via the **Oakville Grade** in a five-series BMW.

The Pacific at sunset from the candlelit dining room at the **Albion River Inn,** on the ocean cliffs just south of **Mendocino.**

Admiring **Napa Valley**'s blazing late-fall colors from **Philip Togni**'s vineyard high up on **Spring Mountain** while sipping his Sauvignon Blanc.

The serene beauty of architect **Michael Graves'** inner courtyard at the **Clos Pegase** winery near **Calistoga.**

The hiss of a propane burner and the sudden shadow of a multicolored, hot-air balloon floating majestically over the vineyards.

Lunch in the garden at **Tra Vigne** in **St. Helena** on an early-spring day, with a good Italian wine (just for a change of pace).

John Scharffenberger
President, Scharffenberger Cellars, Philo

Hendy Woods State Park near **Boonville**—the best stand of old-growth timber; an easy 30-minute hike.

David's at the Floodgate in **Navarro**—best food in the **Anderson Valley.**

Philo Pottery Inn—it's the best bed-and-breakfast in the Anderson Valley; quiet, comfortable, and friendly.

Anderson Valley

Just north of Cloverdale in Sonoma, take **Highway 128** west toward **Boonville** and the Anderson Valley for a tour of one of the most pleasurable wine roads in California. There's no four-lane superhighway here to carve up the landscape, just a fairly narrow country road that dips and turns with the topography, more or less following the course of the **Navarro River** through this ravishing 25-mile-long valley and then through the redwoods to the **Mendocino Coast.** It's an unforgettable drive, meandering past apple orchards and weathered farmsteads and then through the hamlets of **Philo** and **Navarro.** The wineries are all strung along the main route, so there's no getting lost on backcountry roads. There's also no reason to hurry; these tasting rooms stay open until 5PM or later, and it only takes a half hour at most to drive from one end of the valley to the other. The best company for the road is Philo's KZYX (90.7 FM), one of the smallest public radio stations in the country. It plays a mixed bag of great music: rock, jazz, classical, folk, and country.

The first stop is Boonville, where you can lodge at the comfortable **Boonville Hotel** (which also has one of the best restaurants in the region), and sample the Anderson Valley brew at the **Buckhorn Saloon.** The burg also has several secluded bed-and-breakfast inns and a historical museum in the little red schoolhouse at the north end of town.

Then come the wineries, renowned for crisp, dry whites, primarily Chardonnay, Riesling, and Gewürztraminer, all grapes that thrive in the cool growing conditions of the Anderson Valley. Pinot Noir does well here, too, but the valley is gaining world recognition for its sparkling wines, led by **Scharffenberger Cellars** and **Roederer Estate**, owned by the prestigious French Champagne house **Louis Roederer.** All of this means inviting wine tasting awaits you in this little valley. In fact, as you travel along this wine road sampling the local varieties, you may discover that you really *do* like dessert wines after all.

This valley was apple country long before vineyards ever appeared, and it remains a prime apple-growing region. Many of the farms have switched to commercial growing methods and added antique-apple varieties to their repertoire. September and October yield the freshest prime apples, but you'll find apple juice and other apple products year-round. **The Apple Farm** in Philo is a great source for organic cider and chutneys, while **The Tinman** offers tastings of apple and grape juices made from different varieties. And just down the road is an excellent produce stand, **Gowan's Oak Tree,** where you can find all of summer's bounty.

Every inch of this valley is gorgeous— the ideal plan is to stay at the **Boonville Hotel** or at one of the rustic bed-and-breakfast inns for a day or two before heading for the coast through 15 miles of redwoods and the **Navarro River Redwood State Park.** At the coast, you have your choice: Head south seven miles to **Elk,** or north to **Albion, Little River,** and **Mendocino.**

Boonville/Philo/Navarro

During the early years of this century, the Anderson Valley was still fairly remote, and few travelers made their way along the narrow country road to the tiny community of Boonville. To amuse themselves and totally mystify the rare stranger who did show up, the folks here developed an elaborate language of their own that they called "Boontling." Much of it is bawdy stuff—or at least what would have passed for bawdiness in those days. It's been the subject of scholarly study (you can pick up books about Boontling in town), and you can still see a few signs of it around (such as the name of the **Horn of Zeese Coffee Shop**). The **Boonville Hotel** and the **Buckhorn Saloon** across the street are the two main places to eat; the hotel and several bed-and-breakfast inns offer lodging. Be sure to pick up a copy of *The Anderson Valley Advertiser*, an eccentric local newspaper filled with passionate debate on a number of subjects. The tiny towns of Philo and Navarro are marked by just three or four buildings, with several wineries and other attractions set along the highway between them.

25 Montgomery Woods State Park There's a self-guided nature trail through groves of redwoods in this 700-acre park, as well as several picnic sites with tables. ♦ Day-use only. Orr Springs Rd (11 miles northwest of Ukiah), Orr Springs. Call Mendocino State Parks for information at 937.5804

26 Toll House $$ When you take Highway 253 over the mountains from Ukiah Valley, a few miles before Boonville and the Anderson Valley, you'll pass a farm-house on your right. Set on a 360-acre ranch, the 1912 house with its big front porch and backyard veranda is now a comfortable bed-and-breakfast inn.

Guests have the run of the ranch, which is home to two llamas and six sheep. Proprietors Barbara McGuiness and Betty Ingram will point out the best paths for hiking. The decor is blissfully free of knickknacks and Victoriana, with large, comfy sofas in the living room and a serene, pale color scheme. Upstairs are three pleasant, sunny rooms. A larger room at the back of the house is the most private, with its own entrance and deck. It also features a hand-crafted willow bed, an ornate hardwood armoire, a fireplace, and a deep Jacuzzi. If you really want to get away from it all, you may rent the owners' chalet in the midst of the inn's garden down by the Navarro River in Philo.

The chalet has its own kitchen, and guests are welcome to pick organic vegetables from the showplace garden. Any of the inn's guests may spend the afternoon at its mile-long, private beach. Breakfast at the inn includes

café au lait served in small bowls (just like the French serve it in the country), juice, freshly baked scones and other pastries, the inn's homemade preserves, a fruit plate, and perhaps poached eggs with sautéed chard and apple-smoked bacon. ♦ 15301 Hwy 253 (between Hwys 101 and 128), Boonville. 895.3630; fax 895.3632 ♿

27 Rookie-To Gallery This gallery, named after the Boontling term for "quail," features pottery, jewelry, textiles, and sculpture—primarily the work of local craftspeople. ♦ Daily June-Dec; M, W-Su Jan-May. 14300 Hwy 128 (near Lambert La), Boonville. 895.2204

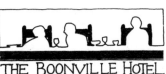

THE BOONVILLE HOTEL

27 Boonville Hotel $$ The eight simple but wonderfully stylish guest rooms upstairs at this historic hotel are a real surprise. Designed by owner John Schmitt, the decor is Shakerlike in its simplicity and thoughtfulness. The rooms are filled with beautifully crafted details, such as the marble star set into the bathroom tile, the hand-crafted steel shower-curtain rods, and the natural-wood Venetian blinds. One room even has handblown water glasses. When Schmitt took over the hotel in 1987, the upstairs was virtually gutted. Instead of going to furniture showrooms, he sought out a handful of local artisans, proposing that each create a bedroom set. One room has a geometric blonde-wood and ebony bed and matching armoire. Another features a whimsical four-poster metal bed made by local artist Steven Derwinski. The same room features pale, satiny wooden floors and an extra-large oval tub. The most spacious are the two suites with tall French doors opening onto a broad, second-floor balcony. The smaller but equally comfortable room **No. 4** gets the morning sun and has a queen-size bed and a shower. Come downstairs to the sunny dining room in the morning to enjoy a buffet continental breakfast (freshly squeezed juices, fruit, and warm, crumbly scones served with sweet country butter and homemade jams). Eat it there or take it onto the patio beside the garden. ♦ Hwy 128 (at Lambert La), Boonville. 895.2210

Also at the Boonville Hotel:

Boonville Hotel Restaurant & Bar ★★ $$$ John Schmitt learned to cook in his parents' popular Yountville restaurant, **The French Laundry** (which they have since sold). Here Schmitt and co-chef Melinda Warshaw focus on the vibrant flavors of Southwestern cooking with a little Italian and American regional tastes thrown in for good measure. The restaurant is eminently cheerful and fun to boot. Start with a home-made soup or one of the individual pizzas topped with pancetta (unsmoked Italian bacon), goat cheese, olives, and thyme, or maybe potato, garlic, rosemary, and Teleme cheese. The kitchen also boasts a great Caesar salad and a dynamite burger. Grilled items are excellent, too, such as the fresh fish served with an avocado-and-lime salsa or the Spencer steak (a little fattier—and tastier—than rib eye) served with grilled red onions and pasilla chili butter. Desserts are just as festive. Try the Mexican chocolate ice cream and cookies or the semolina pudding and berries.

The wine-and-beer bar is a lively place at night, a local hangout with good conversation, good music, and wines by the glass. Terrific espresso and sassy repartee from the staff make this the highlight of the Anderson Valley. ◆ Eclectic ◆ M, W-Su dinner. Reservations recommended ⅃

Boonville Farmers' Market
You will find organically grown produce and armloads of hollyhocks and roses at this local farmers' market. ◆ Sa 9AM-noon May-Oct

28 Faulkner County Park This 40-acre park off twisting Mountain View Road offers a quarter-mile-long nature trail through wild azaleas and redwood groves, plus several picnic areas, a few with barbecue pits. ◆ Day-use only. Mountain View Rd, 2 miles west of Boonville. 463.4267

29 Buckhorn Saloon/Anderson Valley Brewing Company ★$ Pub grub with California flair, including fresh fish, fish-and-chips, burgers, and porter-steamed sausages, is served at this funky saloon and local hangout. Forget about wine here and order one of the eight kinds of beer and ale on tap, all brewed downstairs at the brewing company. If you want to see how they make stout, ale, or porter, they give a brief tour in the late afternoons upon request (providing someone is available to take you). ◆ California/Pub ◆ Daily lunch and dinner July-Sept; M, Th-Su lunch and dinner Oct-June. 14081 Hwy 128 (at Mountain View Rd), Boonville. 895.2337 ⅃

29 Horn of Zeese Coffee Shop ★$ "Horn of zeese?" you might ask. That means "a cup of coffee" in the local Boonville lingo. And this is the place to get that quick caffeine fix. Eggs, biscuits and gravy, homemade soups, burgers, and other sandwiches are also served. Note the sign over the booth outside: "buckey walter" (otherwise known as a phone booth). ◆ Diner ◆ Daily breakfast and lunch. 14025 Hwy 128 (at Mountain View Rd), Boonville. 895.3525 ⅃

30 Boont Berry Farm Stop here for picnic fare (sandwiches, cold cuts, vegetarian dishes, etc.) and freshly baked goods, along with produce and berries. ◆ Daily. 13981 Hwy 128 (north of Mountain View Rd), Boonville. 895.3576

31 Anderson Valley Historical Society Museum One mile north of Boonville, look for the little red schoolhouse on the south side of the road. If the flag is flying out front, this homespun museum dedicated to the history of the valley is open. The one-room Conn Creek schoolhouse dates from 1891; the museum also includes a model sheep-shearing shed. Exhibits are set up to demonstrate different aspects of everyday life in the early days of the valley. Pieced together with donations from local families, the museum's collection includes old farming tools, everyday objects, and furniture. The Pomo Indian baskets and stone tools on display were all found in or around the Anderson Valley. ◆ Donation requested. F-Su. Hwy 128 (north of Mountain View Rd), Boonville. 895.3207

32 Anderson Creek Inn Bed and Breakfast $$ Set in the redwoods off Highway 128, this comfortable ranch-style inn has two creeks coursing through the 16-acre property, and three llamas and several sheep have the run of the place. Innkeepers Lee and Ed Lewis have five guest rooms, all with king-size beds, private baths, and a fresh, contemporary decor. All the rooms have views of meadows and redwoods, and three have fireplaces. A full gourmet breakfast is served, which includes homemade breads and organic juices. There's a swing on the 300-year-old oak tree out back, plus a two-person hammock, hot tub, and large pool. Borrow a bike and make the easy ride into town down the frontage road, past apple orchards and blackberry fields. ◆ 12050 Anderson Valley Wy (off Hwy 128), Boonville. 895.3091, 800/LLAMA.02; fax 895.2546 ⅃

32 The Tinman *The Wizard of Oz* was owner George Bergner's favorite book as a child, and so when it came time to name his apple-juice company, he dusted off the valiant Tinman character. Tinman signs along the road give you just enough time to make the turnoff for this wooden hut, which offers freshly pressed apple juices to taste at the bar. The store manager will start you off with Gravenstein, then move on to Macintosh, Golden, and Tasty (the last a blend of Jonathan, Pippin,

---

Restaurants/Clubs: Red   Hotels: Blue
Shops/ ▼ Outdoors: Green   Wineries/Sights: Black

and Spartan apples). Then she'll give you a taste of cider, warmed and spiced. (One of the best is a blend of Golden Delicious, Jonathan, and Pippin called Dorothy's.) The nonalcoholic Cabernet, Pinot Noir, and Chardonnay juices are good for lunch or brunch. If you liked the hot apple cider, ask for their recipe, which includes a stick of cinnamon, cloves, and a dash of nutmeg, allspice, and cardamom—but the real secret is the apple juice itself. Also look for the jams and vinegars from **Kozlowski Farms** in Sonoma. You may buy the juice by the bottle or the case, and they will ship anywhere in the US. ♦ Daily. Anderson Valley Wy (off Hwy 128), Boonville. 895.2759

33 Obester Winery This is the Anderson Valley outpost of Obester Winery, which started in 1977 in Half Moon Bay on the coast south of San Francisco. Ever since Grandpa Gemello taught Paul Obester

and his wife, Sandy, how to make wine in their garage, they haven't looked back. The Obesters traditionally con-centrated on white wines, but now they're focusing more on red wines and have planted Sangiovese, the grape used in Tuscany's top red wines and a relative newcomer to California. At the homey tasting room in a yellow 1923 house, sample the Chardonnay, Sauvignon Blanc, Mendocino County Riesling, Sangiovese, and Anderson Valley Gewürztraminer. Obester also makes a full-bodied Zinfandel and a Pinot Noir aged in small oak barrels, an Anderson Valley Sémillon, and a vintage red table wine, plus juices made from Gewürztraminer, Riesling, and Pinot Noir grapes, and organic apple juice from its Anderson Valley farm here. Stock up on the beautifully packaged herbal wine vinegars, mustards, salsa, and extra-virgin olive oil, and other gourmet food products. Chilled wines are available for a picnic in the gazebo. ♦ Tasting and sales daily; tours by appointment only. 9200 Hwy 128 (north of Mountain View Rd), Philo. 895.3814; fax 895.3951 &

33 Indian Creek County Park This is an easily accessible, lovely spot for a picnic along the creek. There are also self-guided nature walks among the coast redwoods. ♦ Hwy 128, 1 mile northwest of Boonville. 463.4267

33 Philo Pottery Inn $ Built entirely of heart redwood, this 1888 house, once an old stage-coach stop, makes a thoroughly appropriate and charming bed-and-breakfast inn. Inn-keeper Sue Chiverton has four guest rooms in the main house (two with private baths, two with shared), although the little one-room cottage with a wood-burning stove, detached private bath, and its own back porch is every-body's favorite. For breakfast Chiverton might

serve fresh melon, wholewheat buttermilk pancakes, chicken-and-apple sausages, and fresh blackberry muffins from the inn's own blackberry patch. The word "pottery" in the name of the inn comes from the original owners, who were potters and had a gallery on the premises. ♦ 8550 Hwy 128 (near Hendy Woods State Park), Philo. 895.3069

34 Scharffenberger Cellars Founded in 1981 by John Scharffenberger, this winery is affiliated with the French Champagne house Champagne Pommery. Scharffenberger was the Anderson Valley's pioneer in *méthode champenoise* wines (sparkling wines made in the traditional French way). Today he and wine maker Willis Tex Sawyer produce three cuvées: a toasty, beautifully balanced nonvintage Brut made from a blend of 54 percent Pinot Noir and 46 percent Chardonnay; a vintage Brut Rosé made primarily from Pinot Noir; and a subtly effervescent nonvintage Crémant. They also produce an elegant vintage Blanc de Blancs made entirely from Chardonnay. Made from a blend of grapes similar to that used in the nonvintage Brut, the Crémant was created for the White House to serve at the 1988 Moscow summit. Sample them all at the winery's tasting room in a remodeled farmhouse. The discrete winery building was designed by **Jacques Ullman** of Sausalito, who also designed the **Roederer Estate**. ♦ Tasting and sales daily; tours by appointment only. 8501 Hwy 128 (near Hendy Woods State Park), Philo. 895.2065; fax 895.2758 &

35 Gowan's Oak Tree Since the 1930s, the Gowan family has been selling their homegrown produce at this white clapboard roadside stand, one of the Anderson Valley's main attractions. Stop here for fresh-pressed cider and apples from their own orchards, which you will see as you drive up. They have peaches, plums, apricots, and whatever else is in season, such as cucumbers, green beans, incredibly fresh sweet corn, and vine-ripened tomatoes. In hot weather, they have apple and berry popsicles; in winter, hot spiced cider. And in a shady grove out back, there are picnic tables and a swing for kids, making this a great rest stop on the drive to the coast. ♦ Daily. 6600 Hwy 128, 2 miles west of Philo. 895.3353, 895.3225

36 Hendy Woods State Park From the highway, following a ridge to the south, a tall grove of enormous redwoods, so dark they almost look black against the sky, marks this 805-acre state park. **Gentle Giant Trail** leads visitors for a half mile through groves of redwoods harboring trees more than 1,000 years old and 270 feet tall. Bring a picnic to enjoy beside the Navarro River; there are several hiking paths and trails along the river (but no fishing is allowed). The park has 92 campsites suitable for tents, trailers, and RVs, and it has day-use facilities. ◆ Campgrounds must be reserved from mid-May to early October by calling 800/444.7275; the rest of the year they're available on a first-come, first-served basis. Entrance on Philo Greenwood Rd, a half mile west of Hwy 128. 895.3141

37 The Apple Farm Karen Schmitt, husband Tim Bates, and their children live right in the midst of the organic apple orchard where they grow about a dozen varieties of antique and heirloom apples. At harvest time (August through November), they have apples galore, but year-round you may stop by for their subtle, organic apple-cider vinegar, jams, jellies, and chutneys. They also make lovely dried-apple wreaths, and the bundled apple twigs are terrific for barbecues. ◆ By appointment only. 18501 Philo Greenwood Rd (at Signal Ridge Rd), Philo. 895.2333

38 Navarro Vineyards

This small, family-owned winery founded in 1974 specializes in premium white wines and Pinot Noir, made in both a traditional Burgundian style and a fresh, youthful style. It is best known for its classic dry Gewürztraminer, among the best in the state, but also try the elegant and complex Chardonnay Première Reserve and the excellent dessert wine, including a late-harvest White Riesling. The wine maker is Jim Klein. The tasting room here is quite small and tours are infrequent, but it's hard to find a friendlier welcome (owner Ted Bennett and his wife, Deborah Cahn, can sometimes be found in the tasting room pouring wines).

The winery's vintages are sold only at the winery and at a few selected restaurants; most are sold by mail order. Also note the bottled grape juice that comes in a wine bottle with the vineyard's handsome label. Outside the small wooden building is a redwood deck with brightly colored umbrellas overlooking a landscape of vineyards and rolling hills—a peaceful spot for a picnic. A few more tables are sheltered under an arbor shaded with grapevine leaves. ◆ Tasting and sales daily. 5601 Hwy 128 (north of Philo Greenwood Rd), Philo. 895.3686, 800/537.9463 ق

39 Greenwood Ridge Vineyards

The redwood building with a distinctive, tall roof (inside it resembles a wooden tepee) is surrounded by a vineyard originally planted in 1972. The winery gets its moniker from a ridge that was named for the Caleb Greenwood family who settled the area in the 1850s. By coincidence the current owner and wine maker is a graphic designer and wine aficionado named Allan Green, who came to the Anderson Valley in the early 1970s. He produces off-dry (semisweet) White Riesling and a sweet late-harvest White Riesling, along with Chardonnay, Cabernet, Pinot Noir, Merlot, Sauvignon Blanc, and a Zinfandel from the **Scherrer Vineyard** (planted in 1919) near Healdsburg in the Russian River Valley. Several picnic tables are set up by the pond, and visitors may stretch out on the lawn. Since 1983, the annual **California Wine Tasting Championships** have been held here the last weekend in July. Food, wine, live music, and sunshine are the components of this spirited event, in which novice tasters and experienced professionals alike try to identify a series of wines by varietal type. ◆ Tasting and sales daily. 5501 Hwy 128 (north of Philo Greenwood Rd), Philo. 895.2002 ق

40 Roederer Estate When the prestigious 200-year-old Champagne firm Roederer (maker of Cristal and Brut Premier) decided to establish a California estate in the late 1970s, Jean-Claude Rouzaud spent more than two years researching sites before choosing the Anderson Valley. With its long, cool growing season, the climate is remarkably similar to that of Champagne. Local residents are very happy with the winery's low-key design, which fits unassumingly into the hillside—the large state-of-the-art structure is built partially underground to better maintain the cellars' cool temperature. The estate's French wine maker, Dr. Michel Salgues, worked for seven years to develop the vineyards and hone his skills before releasing his first wine, the Anderson Valley Brut, in October 1988. Made from a blend of Pinot Noir and Chardonnay, it spends 20 to 24 months aging on the yeasts.

Tours of this first-class operation give a good overview of the complicated process of making sparkling wines by the traditional *méthode champenoise.* The tasting room, which features an antique French bistro bar topped with zinc, is furnished with comfortable banquettes and iron-and-tile tables. The 200-year-old terra-cotta tiles on the floor come from an old château in France. ◆ Tasting and sales daily; tours by appointment only. 4501 Hwy 128 (north of Philo Greenwood Rd), Philo. 895.2288; fax 895.2120 ق

41 Husch Vineyards Founded in 1971, this is the oldest winery in the Anderson Valley. In 1979 the Oswald family purchased it from the Husch family, and five members of this third-generation farming family are involved in the winery. The tasting room is a rustic redwood shack covered with climbing roses, and it is hosted by one of the friendliest and most knowledgeable staffs around. More than six people at the bar is a tight fit, but you may take your glass of wine out to the sundeck. Nearby picnic tables are set up under a vine-covered arbor.

The wines are all well made and offer some of the best values in Mendocino County. The whites range from a barrel-fermented, oak-aged Chardonnay and a dry Sauvignon Blanc to a dry, Alsatian-style Gewürztraminer and an off-dry Chenin Blanc. Reds include a good Pinot Noir and a firmly structured Cabernet (look for the North Field Select bottling). The grapes for the Pinot Noir, Gewürztraminer, and Chardonnay come from the winery's vineyards in the Anderson Valley, while the Sauvignon Blanc, Cabernet, and Chenin Blanc hail from its warmer Ukiah vineyards. After tasting the wines, guests are welcome to stroll through the vineyards. ♦ Tasting and sales daily. 4400 Hwy 128 (north of Philo Greenwood Rd), Philo. 895.3216; fax 895.2068 ♿

42 Christine Woods Winery After spending 20 years as a home wine maker, Vernon Rose decided to take the plunge in 1980 and move from Walnut Creek, east of San Francisco, to the 40-acre property he bought as a vacation site in 1966. With classes in wine making and viticulture at the University of California at Davis under his belt, he made his first commercial Chardonnay in 1982, and it won a gold medal at the Mendocino County Fair. He also makes Pinot Noir. The name comes from an early settlement called Christine in honor of Christine Gschwend, who was the first white child born in the Anderson Valley. Remnants of the old road to the settlement can still be seen on the property. ♦ Daily June-Sept; M, Th-Su Oct-May. 3155 Hwy 128 (north of Philo Greenwood Rd), Philo. 895.2115 ♿

42 Handley Cellars Milla Handley, great-great granddaughter of beer-brewer Henry Weinhard, studied enology at the University of California at Davis and worked at **Chateau St. Jean** before founding this winery in the basement of her home near Philo in 1982. (She and husband Rex McClellan have since moved into these larger quarters.) A rich, complex, barrel-aged Chardonnay is her best-known wine, but she also makes a fine Sauvignon Blanc from grapes grown on the Handley family's Dry Creek Valley vineyard in Sonoma, a spicy, off-dry Gewürztraminer, and a small amount of sparkling Brut, three parts Pinot Noir to one part Chardonnay, aged on the yeasts (*sur lie*) for 24 to 36 months. Her rosé, made from Pinot Noir grapes and a touch of Chardonnay, is an ideal picnic wine. Some wines, such as her Pinot Noir and late-harvest Riesling, are primarily available only at the winery. Sample them all at the sunny tasting room. Just outside the tasting room is a garden courtyard for picnics. ♦ Tasting and sales daily; tours by appointment only. 3151 Hwy 128 (north of Philo Greenwood Rd), Philo. 895.3876, 895.2190; fax 895.2603 ♿

43 David's at the Floodgate ★$$ This little roadside cafe in a blue-gray clapboard building with a peaked roof is an appealing spot for lunch or a casual dinner. Look for the neon "Eats" sign over the front door. Inside, there's a wood-burning stove, patchwork quilts on the walls, wood tables, and chairs painted in primary colors. Lunch includes homemade soups, a great BLT, a grilled buffalo burger on a bun, and a wonderful smoked duck-breast salad with apples, pecans, and gorgonzola cheese. Dinner features freshly made soups and delectable appetizers such as steamed mussels with wine or an artichoke served with roasted garlic mayonnaise. Each entrée comes with a green salad, fresh vegetables, and potatoes. Choose from a grilled center-cut pork chop or loin lamb chops with a Sicilian eggplant salad. Or how about Chinese smoked chicken breast glazed with plum sauce? They also offer one or two vegetarian entrées, which might include black-bean chili or vegetable lasagna. And for dessert there's Texas fudge pie, an irresistible raspberry-macaroon sundae, Anderson Valley pie (with in-season Anderson Valley fruit such as pears or apples), and more. The wine list features North Coast wines. ♦ California ♦ M, Th-Su lunch and dinner. Reservations required. Hwy 128 (near Flynn Creek Rd), Navarro. 895.3000 ♿

44 Navarro River Redwood State Park As you drive from Boonville or Philo past the last of the wineries and enter a thick redwood grove, you'll pass this state park on the left, a 12-mile corridor of redwoods extending from the river to a little north of the highway. In 1991 more than 600 acres of Navarro redwoods were added to the original 22-acre **Paul Dimmick State Park** to create this spacious recreation area, which offers visitors numerous activities, including swimming in the Navarro River, fishing for steelhead, hiking on many trails, and camping. The campground has 30 sites suitable for tents or RVs. The one primitive campground has a flush toilet and water in the summer (only a pit toilet is available in the winter) . ♦ Hwy 128, west of Navarro. 937.5804

Mendocino Coast

From the Anderson Valley wine country, it's only a 30- to 40-minute drive—every bit of it scenic—to the coast at **Albion**, where the **Navarro River** opens into the sea. Head north, and 10 minutes later you'll arrive at the area's prime attraction, the Victorian village of **Mendocino**. All along the **North Coast**, particularly south of Mendocino, are dramatic coves and secret, sheltered beaches inset with tiny seaside villages such as Albion, **Little River, Caspar,** and **Westport.** These hamlets were once the centers of the logging industry, which became a booming business after the Gold Rush increased San Francisco's population and created a demand for building materials.

With no superhighway straight to the coast, this area has remained relatively inaccessible; it's a three-and-a-half- to four-hour drive from San Francisco by way of **Highway 101** and **Highway 128** through the Anderson Valley. And the drive from the city up **Highway 1** is an even more arduous (though beautiful) trek, taking up to seven hours on the twisting, narrow road. So when people come to the Mendocino Coast, it's usually for more than a couple of days. The idea is to find a hideaway near the sea to indulge in relaxed, quiet pleasures—walking in the forests of **Van Damme State Park** or in one of the many coastal parks, or strolling along the headlands watching for seals and, from November through April, migrating whales. There are a few tourist-oriented diversions, such as the **Skunk Train** to **Willits** and some small museums with displays of local history, but most people end up doing little more than admiring the spectacular scenery.

Albion

Homesick for Britain, Captain William A. Richardson, former port captain of San Francisco and a large landholder on the Mendocino Coast, dubbed this coastal village Albion, the ancient name for Britain. Richardson also built the town's first sawmill in 1853, just where the **Albion River** meets the sea. Today, with clusters of wooden buildings clinging to the bluffs above the river, Albion is a charming seaside town popular with tourists. The section of town along **Highway 1** is lined with several good bed-and-breakfast places.

45 Fensalden Inn $$ Right off Highway 1 on Navarro Ridge Road, this bed-and-breakfast is set on 20 acres of land, with views of the ocean on the other side of the road. Originally built as a stagecoach stop in the 1860s, the structure now houses four guest rooms and a two-room suite with a fireplace. The property's water tower has been converted into two guest rooms, and a separate bungalow has been added that sleeps four and has a full kitchen. All accommodations have private baths. Guests may gather in the living room around the fire or the grand piano. And in the morning

Fensalden Inn

innkeepers Scott and Frances Brazil serve a full breakfast in the dining room. ♦ 33810 Navarro Ridge Rd (off Hwy 1, 7 miles south of Mendocino). 937.4042 ಓ

46 Albion River Inn $$$ A series of contemporary cottages strung across a dramatic piece of real estate overlooking the ocean comprise this popular Mendocino retreat. Each of the 20 rooms (complete with a private bath and fireplace) has a knockout view through the large windows or from the deck. Six of the rooms have Jacuzzis, and eight feature bathtubs built for two. The decor has been kept fairly plain, but the style is definitely more condo than rustic cottage. The room rates include a full breakfast that's served in the restaurant (see below). ♦ 3790 Hwy 1 (6 miles south of Mendocino). 937.1919, 800/479.7944 (in northern CA); fax 937.2604 ಓ

Within the Albion River Inn:

Albion River Inn Restaurant ★$$$ At the very end of the row of cottages is the inn's restaurant, a large, simply tailored room that boasts a spectacular view (especially at sunset) of the headlands and the sea beyond. Start with a fresh seafood chowder or a green salad, then try the grilled prawns or the grilled New York steak served with caramelized onions and mushrooms and either a black-pepper or a Dijon-mustard sauce. Specials might include grilled king salmon or roasted pork loin. There is also quite a good list of North Coast wines from hard-to-find producers such as **Dehlinger** and **Williams & Selyem.** ♦ Continental ♦ Daily dinner. Reservations recommended ಓ

Little River

Like many of the small cities up and down the coast, Little River was once a bustling logging and shipbuilding town. Now it's a quiet, charming hamlet dotted with quaint inns. It's certainly worth a visit, particularly for a stroll along the lush trails in **Van Damme State Park** and a boat ride through the **Big River** estuary.

47 Heritage House $$$ Dating from 1877, this New England–style lodge on a 37-acre estate is perhaps the best  known on the Mendocino Coast, and it offers privacy and outstanding ocean views from many of the 68 rooms and cottages. The inn includes a range of accommodations, from moderately priced rooms to large, costly suites and cottages. All are individually decorated with contemporary or antique furniture, and many have fireplaces. The cottages overlooking the cove are the most popular, and many are reserved several months in advance. ♦ Closed January to mid-February. 5200 Hwy 1 (south of Comptche Ukiah Rd). 937.5885, 800/235.5885 ಓ

Within Heritage House:

Heritage House Restaurant ★★$$$ Diners gather under the beautiful chandeliered ceiling to enjoy a meal prepared by chef Deagon Williams-Geney, who offers prix-fixe breakfast and dinner menus and an à la carte lunch menu. Breakfast dishes vary from honey-cinnamon waffles with Anderson Valley apple preserves to corned-beef hash with poached eggs, but there's always a morning buffet of juices, cereals, and fresh fruit. Dinner entrées, which change nightly, might include herb-marinated rack of lamb with grilled eggplant, seared breast of Sonoma duckling with Blue Lake green beans, or grilled Southern California white sea bass with cilantro pesto. At lunch, diners can pick from a small selection of salads, sandwiches, and a pasta dish. No smoking is allowed. ♦ Continental ♦ Daily breakfast, lunch, and dinner. Reservations recommended ಓ

47 Little River Market Here you'll find cheese, cold cuts, cold drinks, ice cream, and a collection of local wines, among other basic items. ♦ Daily. 7746 Hwy 1 (south of Comptche Ukiah Rd). 937.5133 ಓ

47 Little River Restaurant ★★$$$ Adjoining the post office is this very cozy spot, with no more than half-a-dozen tables and no view to speak of. The attraction is the well-prepared food and the pleasure of dining in an intimate and friendly setting. Start with baked brie wrapped in phyllo or prawns in a Champagne beurre-blanc sauce. Entrées, which come with garden soup, salad, and freshly baked breads, include poached salmon in a tarragon cream sauce, broiled quail in a hazelnut sauce, and roasted duck in a sauce made with apricot vermouth. The small dessert menu usually includes fresh fruit ices, caramel fudge walnut pie, and a chocolate amaretto mousse. ♦ Continental ♦ Dinner; closed Wednesday and Thursday July through November, Tuesday through Thursday from the last week of December through June. Reservations recommended. 7750 Hwy 1 (next to the post office). 937.4945 ಓ

48 Little River Airport This small airstrip accommodates private aircraft—and certainly a small plane is the fastest and most convenient way to get to Mendocino, if you can afford it. The airport also handles car rentals and chartered small planes. ♦ 43001 Little River Airport Rd (off Hwy 1). 937.5129

48 Victorian Farmhouse $$ Gingerbread scrolls and curlicues adorn this Victorian bed-and-breakfast inn that was originally built in 1877 as a residence. Innkeepers George and Carole Molnar have 10 guest rooms and a cottage. All have queen- or king-size beds, private baths, and either ocean or forest views. They are furnished with period antiques, and some have fireplaces. In the morning the Molnars will deliver breakfast to you if you'd rather enjoy it in the privacy of your room. ♦ 7001 Hwy 1 (south of Comptche Ukiah Rd). 937.0697, 800/264.4723

48 Little River Inn $$$ A white New England–style farmhouse (pictured below) built in the 1850s serves as the inn's office, while lodgings are spread out in bungalows and cottages throughout the hillside grounds. All of the 66 units have private baths and are furnished with country pine antiques or modern oak, and most have balconies overlooking the sea; a few have views of the **Little River Golf & Tennis Club** (see below) in back. The more expensive rooms also have fireplaces, and some have Jacuzzis, TV sets, and VCRs. ◆ 7751 Hwy 1 (across from the post office). 937.5942 ૬

At the Little River Inn:

Little River Inn Restaurant ★$$ The tables by the windows offer a glimpse of the ocean at this casual place for breakfast or dinner. Breakfast features hotcakes, egg dishes, and omelettes, while the dinner menu offers a dozen regular entrées along with daily specials. Everything is served with freshly made soup or salad, vegetables, rice or potatoes, and warm biscuits. Choose from the broiled swordfish fillet marinated in tequila and lime juice, the grilled prawns rolled in bread crumbs and chopped hazelnuts, or the charbroiled New York steak. Saturday night is prime-rib night. ◆ American ◆ Daily breakfast and dinner ૬

Little River Golf & Tennis Club This club features two championship tennis courts and a regulation nine-hole golf course with a driving range and putting green. Golf-cart rentals are available, and the pro shop can supply you with golf togs and equipment. ◆ Daily. 937.5667

48 Van Damme State Park This beautiful park covers 1,826 acres of dramatically diversified landscape. The visitors' center at the head of the park can give you trail maps and information; pick up some bird- or fern-finder guides to take on the hike along the lush **Fern Canyon Trail,** which is definitely worth a stroll and is also a great place for an early-morning jog. Another prime attraction is the **Pygmy Forest,** where the acidic, compacted soil has stunted cypresses and pines; some of the mature trees are only a foot tall. The park also has 74 very popular campsites suitable for tents or RVs; reserve ahead. Ten additional campsites can be reached only on foot. ◆ Fee per vehicle. Off Hwy 1 (3.5 miles south of the town of Mendocino). 937.5804, 800/444.7275 (for camping reservations)

48 Stevenswood Lodge $$ Tucked away on a private drive off Highway 1 and bordered on three sides by **Van Damme State Park,** this distinctive inn is a great place to get away from it all without sacrificing comfort (there's even concierge service). All ten of the guest rooms are equipped with private baths, wood-burning fireplaces, and honor bars (stocked with California wines, of course); nine also have separate sitting rooms. Owner Robert Zimmer has decorated the lodge with modern furnishings and tasteful artwork. Breakfast is served in the dining room. ◆ 8211 Hwy 1 (a quarter-mile north of the park entrance). 937.2810, 800/421.2810 ૬

48 Glendeven Inn $$ Isaiah Stevens first settled this two-acre property on the east side of Highway 1 in 1867; he built the New England–style farmhouse the same year. The handsomely renovated farmhouse, the restored hay barn, and a newer building make up the inn. There are 10 guest rooms and suites; some are larger than others, and they range in price from moderate to expensive. They're all furnished country-style, with a mix of antique and contemporary pieces, and all have private baths; the four suites also feature fireplaces. Innkeepers Jan and Janet deVries serve a continental breakfast (juice, fruit, homemade pastries, and coffee or tea) either

Little River Inn

in your room or in the main house, which features a large, attractive living room with a fireplace and a grand piano. ◆ 8221 Hwy 1 (south of Comptche Ukiah Rd). 937.0083, 800/822.4536; fax 937.6108

Within Glendeven Inn:

Gallery Glendeven This gallery features fine arts and crafts created by local artisans. ◆ M, W-Su. 937.3525 ⅍

48 Rachel's Inn $$ In the early 1980s Rachel Binah renovated an 1860s farmhouse and turned it into a pleasant bed-and-breakfast inn. Not only are all the rooms comfortable and quite private, but Binah turns out wonderful, generous breakfasts served family-style around a long wooden table. The main house has five guest rooms: three upstairs and a parlor suite and a secluded garden room with its own entrance downstairs. A former textile artist who is now active in the ocean sanctuary movement (fighting against offshore oil drilling), Binah has furnished the rooms in quiet colors and with some of her artwork. All rooms have queen-size beds and private baths; most feature views of the meadow and the Mendocino headlands. A contemporary barn beside the house is equipped with four large guest rooms and suites on three levels. They have most of the conveniences of a small, first-class hotel—all four have fireplaces, and the suites boast wet bars, refrigerators, private sitting rooms, and Murphy beds for extra guests and families.

Two great walks await just outside the inn: one down to the beach in front of **Van Damme State Park,** the other a long hike through the headlands, among pines and meadows where deer and other wildlife abound. Binah has placed bales of hay at the point where the path meets the sea, so guests can sit and watch the seals and sea lions below. ◆ Off Hwy 1 (2 miles south of the town of Mendocino). 937.0088 ⅍

Mendocino

This Victorian village, perched at the very edge of a high bluff overlooking the ocean and flanked on three sides by the wild sea, has captured the imagination of visitors from all over the world. A protected historical area with Cape Cod–style architecture, Mendocino resembles a New England village uprooted and relocated to this Pacific paradise. In the popular television series "Murder She Wrote," the fictional town of Cabot Cove, Maine, is actually Mendocino. Many of the town's old homes have been turned into bed-and-breakfast inns, restaurants, shops, and galleries. But the headlands, with their marvelous vistas of the sea, have remained unchanged.

Legend has it that Mendocino means "path to the sea," but the cape may actually have been named for the Spanish captain who discovered it in the 16th century, or perhaps for his ship. At any rate, the town's history began in 1852, when German immigrant William Kasten, apparently the sole survivor of a shipwreck off the coast, washed up on a nearby beach. With no rescue in sight, he built himself a cabin on the headlands and lived there for almost two years before a ship finally ventured into the bay. The sailors on that vessel noted the vast redwoods surrounding the cape, and Henry Meiggs, a lumberjack then working in Bodega Bay to the south in Sonoma County, organized a party of men to head up the coast to begin logging operations. In 1853, after much difficulty, they constructed a sawmill, and Mendocino (then known as the town of **Big River**) became a logging center.

By 1865 the fledgling metropolis had a population of 700, and a number of hotels and rooming houses had been built for the loggers. Most of the grander homes were built in the 1870s and 1880s for lumber barons and bankers. Mendocino remained a logging town until the 1930s, when economic depression shut down operations. In the 1950s, artists discovered the picturesque little town, and it became an artists' community much like Laguna Beach in Southern California and Carmel on the central coast.

49 Stanford Inn by the Sea $$$  Also known as **Big River Lodge,** this 26-unit inn stands on a bluff overlooking Big River and the ocean. In addition to great views from all the rooms, the large hillside estate features a greenhouse with an organic garden that provides produce to the very popular **Cafe Beaujolais** (see page 180) and other restaurants, as well as an Olympic-size pool, a spa, and a sauna. Rooms come with coffeemakers and all sorts of nice touches, including four-poster beds (queen- or king-size), fireplaces, and VCRs (plus a videotape library of classic and current movies). Innkeepers Joan and Jeff Stanford permit guests to bring well-behaved pets—in fact, a few llamas roam the property. A full buffet breakfast is served. ◆ Hwy 1 and Comptche Ukiah Rd. 937.5615, 800/331.8884; fax 937.0305 ⅍

Restaurants/Clubs: Red   Hotels: Blue

Shops/ ▼ Outdoors: Green   Wineries/Sights: Black

Also at the Stanford Inn by the Sea:

Catch a Canoe & Bicycles Too! Both guests and nonguests may rent kayaks or canoes to explore the Big River estuary, rated Class 1, meaning it's a gentle river suitable for the novice. It's still advisable, however, to get information on tides and river conditions before setting off. The office also rents mountain bicycles and can suggest various routes. ♦ Daily. 937.0273

50 Joshua Grindle Inn $$ Set on two acres overlooking the village, this inn (pictured above), originally built in 1870 by town banker Joshua Grindle, has faithful clients who come back year after year. The main house has five guest rooms; two more are in a rear cottage, and the water tower out back offers another three rooms. Much of the decor follows a nautical theme, with blue and white colors predomin-ating, and paintings of sailboats and ships are scattered about. All of the rooms have private baths, and some have wood-burning fireplaces. The **Nautical Room** is quite attractive, and comes complete with a queen-size bed, ship's table, and ocean view. The **Library Room** features a four-poster queen-size bed, a fire-place framed in original tiles, and a floor-to-ceiling bookcase. And the three rooms in the water tower, stacked one on top of the other, are charming. Innkeepers Arlene and Jim Moorehead serve a full breakfast on a 150-year-old pine harvest table in the kitchen. ♦ 44800 Little Lake Rd (off Hwy 1). 937.4143, 800/GRINDLE

51 Good Taste This is the best picnic supplier in town. Stop here for imported and domestic cheeses, cold cuts, and a bottle of North Coast wine. They also have condiments galore, from Mendocino mustard and special chutneys to locally made jams and jellies. Owners Ellen and Bob Bushansky also prepare great classic deli sandwiches, and when the weather is damp, a bowl of their house-made chili (vegetarian or regular) is ideal. Salads are more interesting than the usual deli fare; you might find tabbouleh (a Middle Eastern bulghur-wheat salad), a celery-root salad, or a well-made

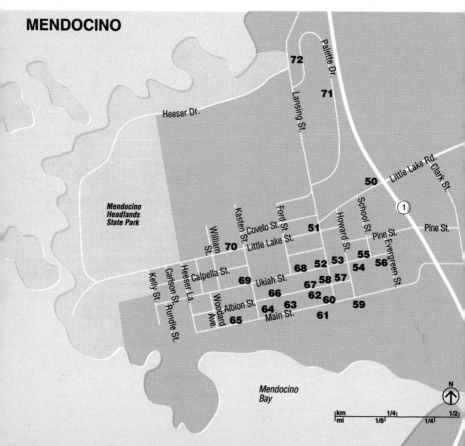

coleslaw. The store is also crammed with all sorts of gourmet gift items, wine accessories, and one of the best selections of local wines in town. Seating areas are provided inside as well as in the garden. ◆ Daily. 45050 Little Lake St (at Lansing St). 937.0104

52 Masonic Temple Now the Savings Bank of Mendocino County (established in 1903), this white wooden building with its single soaring steeple (pictured below) was built as the **Masons Lodge** in 1866 by Erik Albertson, the first Worshipful Master of Mendocino Lodge No. 179. Albertson also sculpted the statue of Time and the Maiden, standing atop the steeple, from a single redwood trunk.
◆ Lansing St (at Ukiah St)

Masonic Temple

REPRODUCED FROM A BLOCK PRINT BY EMMY LOU PACKARD

53 Mendocino Gold This shop features unusually nice jewelry, much of it contemporary and hand-crafted, plus Australian fire opals, colored stones, and a selection of wedding rings. ◆ Daily. 10483 Lansing St (between Ukiah and Little Lake Sts). 937.2018

53 Mendocino Chocolate Company Famous for their truffles, which they make in more than 20 flavors, this homey chocolate company also offers other specialties, including Mendocino toffee (a butter toffee dipped in light chocolate and rolled in toasted almonds) and Mendocino Breakers (chocolate caramels dipped in light chocolate, almonds, and white chocolate). They'll box special assortments and ship them for you, too.
◆ Daily. 10483 Lansing St (between Ukiah and Little Lake Sts). 937.1107

53 Mendocino Bakery & Cafe ★$$ Pizza by the slice, garlic and onion bialys, bagels, and an assortment of hefty pastries, muffins, and scones are made in-house at this cafe. Take your espresso or cappuccino outside on the deck. Early dinner is now served as well, with entreés ranging from lasagna to glazed chicken with polenta. ◆ Cafe ◆ Daily breakfast, lunch, and early dinner. 10483 Lansing St (between Ukiah and Little Lake Sts). 937.0836 &

53 Rainsong Shoes The emphasis here is on comfort and style, with good walking shoes, sneakers, dress shoes, and boots. The Aerosole shoes are good looking, comfortable, and moderately priced. The slippers shaped like little piggies or schnauzers just might tickle someone's fancy. The same company also has a clothing store just down the street (see page 182). ◆ Daily. 10483 Lansing St (between Ukiah and Little Lake Sts). 937.1710

53 Mendosa's Merchandise & Market This full-service market has plenty of picnic supplies. Choose from cheese, cold cuts, barbecued chicken, and Mendocino County wines, including chilled whites. The hardware division next door stocks fishing equipment, barbecues, picnic baskets, enameled camp cookware, and corkscrews. ◆ Daily. 10501 Lansing St (between Ukiah and Little Lake Sts). 937.5879; fax 937.0563 &

The pigments in wine are the same pigments that cause the red and blue colors in most fruits and flowers.

54 Whitegate Inn $$ This elegant white Victorian gem in the heart of the village offers six guest rooms with private baths (some boasting claw-foot tubs). There's also a one-bedroom cottage with a fireplace, living room, full modern kitchen, and private yard and deck. Antique crystal chandeliers, brass and iron beds, lace-edged sheets, and fireplaces add to the charm. Innkeepers Carol and George Bechtloff prepare a full country breakfast that might include caramel-apple French toast, muffins, fruit parfaits, juice, tea, and coffee; they also serve wine and hors d'oeuvres in the parlor in the evening. ♦ 499 Howard St (at Ukiah St). 937.4892, 800/531.7282

55 Sweetwater Gardens Here's the spot for indulging in a hot tub and sauna (there's even a large tub and sauna for groups). Swedish/Esalen massage and deep-tissue bodywork are available by appointment. The best deal is the "Rub-a-Dub" special: on Monday, Wednesday, and Friday you get a free soak in the hot tub with your massage. ♦ Daily. 955 Ukiah St (between Evergreen and Howard Sts). 937.4140

CAFE BEAUJOLAIS

56 Cafe Beaujolais ★★★$$ The author of two best-selling cookbooks, *Cafe Beaujolais* and *Morning Food,* owner/chef Margaret Fox is famous for the sumptuous country breakfasts she serves on weekends in this lovely Victorian. Highlights include the silver-dollar buttermilk pancakes with local blueberries and andouille sausage, buttermilk and cornmeal waffles (the best you'll ever taste!) with real maple syrup, and a Thai chicken and ginger-sausage omelette with goat cheese and peppers.

Simply decorated with beribboned wallpaper and antique chairs, this dining room is the perfect setting for Fox's down-home cooking. At lunch she features savory homemade soups, such as the Ukrainian beet soup or black-bean chili, along with individual pizzas baked in a wood-fired oven, a dynamite grilled hamburger made with naturally raised beef and topped with roasted pasilla peppers and goat cheese, and great salads. Be sure to save room for dessert, such as her famous *panforte di Mendocino* (a dense, nut-studded, Italian-style confection) and the deep-chocolate-mousse cake with strawberry sauce. At dinner, executive chef Chris Kump, Margaret's husband and the author of the cookbook *Evening Food,* takes over the stove, offering a menu of nouveau California dishes with Asian touches, including seared sea scallops with coconut milk and black chanterelle mushrooms, and a spicy smoked Thai beef salad. Also, try the roasted free-range chicken with pecan-and-brandied-prune stuffing or the rib eye steak Bordelaise (most of the meats and poultry come from local sources). Monday night features a "Beau Thai" prix-fixe menu of Thai dishes.

The garden around the house is surrounded with drought-tolerant shrubs, edible and decorative flowers, lots of herbs, and long-blooming antique roses that have been a labor of love for years. Call ahead to sign up for one of the monthly garden tours given by landscape designer Jaen Treesinger, followed by lunch at the cafe. ♦ Eclectic ♦ M, Th-F lunch and dinner; Sa-Su breakfast, lunch, and dinner. Reservations recommended. 961 Ukiah St (at Evergreen St). 937.5614 ↔

Also at Cafe Beaujolais:

The Brickery This wood-fired oven is Chris Kump's project, hand-built brick by brick and decorated with tiles he brought back from Provence after a visit to the French teacher and cookbook author Simone Beck. It sits in the middle of the garden and turns out wonderful breads. The breads change daily (from a repertoire of more than a dozen), and might include a Mendocino sourdough leavened with wild yeasts, a sourdough rye that includes a little Red Seal Ale, an Austrian sunflower bread, and a buckwheat bread with hazelnuts. ♦ Daily until the breads are sold out (usually about 1PM)

57 Mendocino Cafe ★$$ Blue tables and bright paintings set the sunny mood in this charming little cafe serving fresh, healthy fare. Brunch offers such items as *huevos rancheros,* a Thai scramble (eggs laced with stir-fried vegetables and rock shrimp), and cornmeal waffles. Lunch may include Thai burritos made with smoked meats and homemade Thai chili sauce, quesadillas with black beans, Greek salads with feta cheese and olives, or a series of well-made sandwiches such as tasty smoked chicken with garlic mayonnaise or Cajun-spiced sautéed snapper with tartar sauce. The dinner menu emphasizes fresh seafood, including blackened rockfish and steamed shellfish, along with pasta dishes from Italian and Asian traditions, barbecued ribs, and a decent steak. Sushi and sashimi are served on weekends. Vegetarian dishes are always on the menu, too. For dessert, try the fresh local blackberry pie or the nectarine-berry cobbler. They have a well-chosen list of beers and North Coast wines. In good weather, sit on the deck out back. ♦ Eclectic ♦ M-F lunch and dinner; Sa-Su brunch and dinner. 10451 Lansing St (at Albion St). 937.2422

> "A bottle of good wine, like a good act, shines ever in the retrospect."
>
> Robert Louis Stevenson

Thar She Blows: California Marine Mammals to Spot from the Coast

California Gray Whale—*Eschrictius robustus*

These large sea mammals range in length from 35 to 50 feet and can weigh anywhere from 20 to 40 tons. They are actually black; patches of barnacles and scars give their skin its gray appearance. Every year the whales make a great migration from their summer feeding grounds in the Arctic Sea all the way down to Baja California to breed. It takes them three months to travel each way (an astonishing 12,000-mile round trip), and they cruise at about four to five miles per hour, sometimes traveling 20 hours at a stretch. They head south from December through February and return to the north from March through April. As they pass by the Sonoma and Mendocino Coasts, they can be spotted from the headlands.

California Sea Lion—*Zalophus californianus*

The playful California sea lion, with its distinctive, sharp bark, can reach seven feet in length. The males weigh a hefty 700 to 900 pounds and the females range from 200 to 500 pounds. These sleek, whiskered marine mammals with a pronounced brow have a rich dark-brown coat; the females are a bit lighter in color. The sea lions' agile, rotatable flippers and their adaptability to training have made them a hit at circuses and aquatic shows. Sea lions are gregarious and curious, and will come right up to boats and skin divers to investigate.

Harbor Seal—*Phoca vitulina*

These pale silver-gray seals with dark spots and whiskers are generally four to six feet long and weigh 200 to 300 pounds. They belong to the family *phocidae,* which is characterized by the absence of ear flaps and by flippers that cannot rotate forward, making their movement on land awkward. Among the shiest of seals, they keep to themselves, basking on sandbars or offshore rocks at low tide. Much quieter than sea lions, they sometimes slap the water sharply with their flippers and vocalize in snorts and hisses.

Killer Whale—*Orcinus orca*

Also known as orcas, killer whales are members of the family *delphinidae,* and like other members of this group of cetaceans, they have a prominent dorsal fin. Easily recognized by their black-and-white markings, orcas are found most commonly from Monterey Bay north to the Aleutian Islands, and often travel in pods of five to 30 animals.

WILKES SPORT
THE WILKES BASHFORD COMPANY

58 Wilkes Sport Wilkes Bashford couldn't resist bringing part of his mini-retail empire to Mendocino when he bought a house on the coast in the early 1990s. This outpost of the exclusive San Francisco store carries casual clothing for men and women, plus a selection of home furnishings, including Mexican pottery, clever folding wicker tables, hand-blown glass, and hand-painted screens and tables designed by local artists. ♦ Daily. 10466 Lansing St (at Ukiah St). 937.1357; fax 937.0837 ♿

58 Deja-Vu The Mendocino Hat Co. Just what you need to keep your head warm on a foggy day. This shop stocks Stetsons, Akubra felt hats from Australia, rain hats, and owner Kat Henderson's original designs. ♦ Daily. 10464 Lansing St (at Ukiah St), Mendocino. 937.4120

58 Village Toy Store An electric train chugs along on its tracks in this old-fashioned toy shop owned by Bill and Susie Carr. Shelves are stuffed with high-quality toys, books, and games, as well as a great selection of kites. Brio trains and Breyer horses are among the most popular items. ♦ Daily. 10450 Lansing St (between Albion and Ukiah Sts). 937.4633 ♿

58 Mendocino Cookie Company This is the spot for very sweet, freshly baked cookies (including a dynamite double chocolate chip), scones, and muffins, plus espresso and coffee drinks to go. Fat-free goodies are available, too. ♦ Daily. 10450 Lansing St (between Albion and Ukiah Sts). 937.4843 ♿

Restaurants/Clubs: Red   **Hotels:** Blue
Shops/♦ Outdoors: Green   **Wineries/Sights:** Black

58 Tote Fête ★$ Choose from at least a dozen kinds of sandwiches, including homemade chicken salad, meat loaf, and turkey, avocado, and jack cheese. They also have pizza by the slice, their own rosemary-and-garlic focaccia bread, and an array of salads. Try to get here a little before the lunch hour—the place is tiny and the line of people waiting often spills through the door into the street. Bread for the sandwiches comes fresh from the oven in the **Tote Fête Bakery** (937.3140) around the corner on Albion Street, along with baked doughnuts, pastries, double chocolate cake by the slice, and other delectable treats. ♦ Takeout ♦ Breakfast, lunch, and early dinner. 10450 Lansing St (at Albion St). 937.3383 ♿

59 Mendocino Farmers' Market Fill a basket with fresh fruit, vegetables, flowers, or the makings of a picnic supper or lunch at this farmers' market held on Fridays in a parking lot during the summer and early fall. ♦ F noon-2PM May-Oct. Intersection of Howard and Main Sts

60 Rainsong Toasty Patagonia coats, sweaters, and designer clothing for men and women are sold in this tastefully decorated shop. ♦ Daily. 4500 Main St (entrance on Lansing St). 937.1720; fax 937.2531 ♿

61 Mendocino Headlands Ford House Visitors' Center and Museum This park, which encompasses the headlands in and around the town of Mendocino, uses a two-story 1857 residence, originally built for Bursley Ford, co-owner of one of the town's first sawmills, as a visitors' center. Stop here for information on Mendocino and for books on its history, nature, and wildlife, and on the sea. Tide tables, maps, field guides to tide pools and birds, and, of course, books on spotting whales are also available here. In fact, the house is a favorite observation point during the annual migration of the California gray whale. Pop in to see the large model of Mendocino circa 1890, created for the town's centennial by Leonard Peterson. A couple of rooms have exhibits on the logging and seafaring days of Mendocino. Outside, the park has picnic tables with views of the headlands. ♦ Daily. 735 Main St (on the headlands). 937.5397 ♿

62 Kelley House Museum The restored home of Mendocino pioneer William Kelley is now a museum that chronicles the cultural life and history of this seaside town. It is also the headquarters for Mendocino Historical Research, Inc., which operates the museum and has compiled impressive archives of historical photos and research material. The museum staff has done extensive work on the grounds, planting native California plants and old-fashioned flowers. ♦ Nominal admission. Daily June-Sept; M, F-Su Oct-May. 45007

Albion St (between Lansing and Kasten Sts). 937.5791 &

63 Bay View Cafe ★$$ Light casual fare is served almost all day here. Breakfast includes omelettes, pancakes, and French toast, and for lunch there's a short menu of sandwiches, burgers, fish-and-chips, and salads. Dinner is only a bit fancier, with pasta and steaks added to the list. The entrance is at the top of the water tower's stairs; the dining room has an outdoor deck and a great view of the ocean. ♦ American ♦ Daily breakfast, lunch, and dinner. 45040 Main St (between Lansing and Kasten Sts). 937.4197

63 Book Loft Look for the white picket fence on Main Street to find this cozy shop, where you can curl up with a book on a window seat with a view of the headlands or put on a headset and listen to music tapes. There's a good selection of local authors, as well as gardening and travel books, mysteries, and best-sellers, plus a smattering of used books. You can also reach the bookstore by following the brick path off Albion Street. ♦ Daily. 45050 Main St (between Lansing and Kasten Sts). 937.0890 &

63 Irish Shop A small house at the back of a brick walk features woolens and cottons from Ireland and Scotland. Look for natural cotton, crocheted or hand-knitted throws, tweed sport coats and caps, along with teatime necessities such as shortbread, imported jams, and teas. ♦ Daily. 45050 Main St (between Lansing and Kasten Sts). 937.3133 &

63 Highlight Gallery The works of local and regional artisans fill this large two-story gallery. Paintings, bronze and marble sculptures, ceramics, hand-turned and hand-carved wooden bowls made with exotic hardwoods, weaving, and other mediums are featured. Don't miss the beautiful jewelry boxes and the small collection of hand-crafted furniture exhibited upstairs. ♦ Daily. 45052 Main St (between Lansing and Kasten Sts). 937.3132

ESTABLISHED 1878

63 Mendocino Hotel & Garden Suites $$$ This 1878 false-front hotel sits on Main Street and has an unobstructed view of the sea. There are a number of buildings in back, including the 1852 **Heeser House** and an acre of gardens. The accommodations here cover a wide range of prices, from simple European-style rooms with shared baths (the hotel provides bathrobes) and twin or double beds to rooms with private baths, queen-size beds, and wood-burning stoves, deluxe rooms, and large suites. There are 51 units in all, most

decorated with Victorian antiques and each differentiated by its decor, the view, or by having a balcony or a garden. The most luxurious are the **Heeser Garden** suites, all with fireplaces, spacious modern bathrooms, and king- or queen-size beds, plus an extra sofa bed that's handy for families. ♦ 45080 Main St (between Lansing and Kasten Sts). 937.0511, 800/548.0513; fax 937.0513 &

Within the Mendocino Hotel & Garden Suites:

Mendocino Hotel Restaurant ★$$$ The chef here is Colleen Murphy, formerly head chef at the **Little River Inn Restaurant** (see page 176). The hotel actually has two restaurants: Breakfast and lunch are served in the informal garden room filled with plants, while dinner is served in the more formal Victorian dining room. Breakfast offers Belgian waffles with olallieberries (a distant relative to the blackberry), pecan pancakes with pear marmalade, omelettes, and other egg dishes. Lunch features moderately priced sandwiches, burgers, and salads. Dinner entrées include linguine tossed with a mix of seafood and a garlic-and–white wine sauce, roasted free-range chicken, loin of lamb with rosemary glaze, or grilled New York steak. For dessert, try the deep-dish olallieberry pie, served with homemade vanilla ice cream. That same ice cream goes into the sinfully rich sundae, which is topped with melted chocolate truffles and honey-roasted pecans. ♦ American ♦ Daily breakfast, lunch, and dinner &

63 Mendocino Ice Cream Company ★$ Winner of a gold medal at the California State Fair, this shop does a brisk business in ice-cream cones, scooping out more than two dozen of their homemade ice creams into regular or waffle cones. Try the Black Forest (chocolate, bing cherries, and chocolate chips) or the black walnut. Sundaes and shakes are also available, along with low-calorie ice cream (try cappuccino chocolate chunk or chocolate raspberry truffle). Eat at one of the wooden booths inside or take your cone out to enjoy as you stroll along Main Street. ♦ Ice cream ♦ Daily. 45090 Main St (between Lansing and Kasten Sts). 937.5884 &

63 Golden Goose The opulent beds on display will tempt all weary shoppers to plop themselves down here. This is a good place to buy featherbeds, duvets, down pillows, fine Austrian linens, or even an antique bed or armoire. ♦ Daily. 45094 Main St (between Kasten and Lansing Sts). 937.4655 &

"Wine is constant proof that God loves us and wants to see us happy."

Benjamin Franklin

63 The Courtyard Big blue bowls with high rims for mixing bread dough, as well as lovely pottery pie plates are for sale here. There are also spices, country crafts, and cookware. ♦ Daily. 45098 Main St (between Kasten and Lansing Sts). 937.0917 &

64 Gallery Bookshop This is where you can find the *New York Times,* the *San Francisco Chronicle,* and the *Wall Street Journal,* plus an intriguing mix of good reading (and not just the usual best-sellers). Founded in 1962, the bookstore is the oldest on the North Coast. The owners of this shop clearly love to read; they'll take special orders and are ready to advise on what's new or best in a number of subjects. **Bookwinkle's Children's Books,** which used to be down the street, has now merged with this store, giving it a top-notch children's books section. You also can find a good collection of books on the history of Mendocino and Northern California. ♦ Daily. Corner of Main and Kasten Sts. 937.BOOK &

65 Mendocino Art Center Showcase This gallery features the work of local artists in a wide variety of media and crafts. Shop here for handwoven shawls and mufflers, marbled silk scarves, hand-thrown dinnerware, ceramics, woodcuts, prints, and paintings. ♦ Daily. 560 Main St (between Kasten and Woodward Sts). 937.2829

65 Out of This World Big and little kids will have fun browsing through this space-age store, which features maps of the heavens and earth, star charts, and celestial music tapes. Several powerful telescopes are set up inside, so you can gaze out at the headlands and beyond. ♦ Daily. 45100 Main St (at Kasten St). 937.3335 &

65 Crossblends This tiny shop is crammed with everything to do with quilting—embossed paper quilts, wrapping paper in quilt patterns, patchwork greeting cards, books on quilting, and a collection of antique and contemporary patchwork quilts. ♦ Daily. 45156 Main St (between Kasten and Woodward Sts). 937.4201

65 The Collector Although it's not the same as gathering your own on the beach, all manner of seashells and rocks can be found here. The collection of items won't set the true connoisseur's heart afire, but you can find some beautiful shells to use as paperweights or to hold to your ear for a sound of the sea. ♦ Daily. 45160 Main St (between Kasten and Woodward Sts). 937.0888

65 Creative Hands of Mendocino Handmade gifts and clothing from a group of local artisans are sold here. Don't overlook the imaginatively made stuffed animals—from penguins to dragons—from the **Soup Factory** in Elk. ♦ Daily. 45170 Main St (between Kasten and Woodward Sts). 937.2914

65 Artists Co-op of Mendocino Eight local artists run this second-floor gallery that features landscape paintings. Their work covers a variety of media, including pastels, oils, watercolors, and acrylics. Every two months a well-known guest artist is showcased. ♦ Daily. 45270 Main St (between Kasten and Woodward Sts). 937.2217

65 Mendocino Jams & Preserves A small, blue cottage at the very end of Main Street houses Robert and Shay Forest's wide variety of tasty toppings. You may even stop by and sample all the jams and preserves the Forests make. The top-selling flavors are rhubarb marmalade, olallieberry, sour cherry, and apricot. They will pack up your purchases and ship them for you. Mail order is available, too. ♦ Daily May-Jan; M, F-Su Feb-Apr. 440 Main St (at Woodward St). 937.1037 &

66 Wind & Weather All the instruments to study and stay attuned to the weather are displayed in this converted water tower. Choose from barometers, thermometers, and chronometers, as well as special weather radios. They have all kinds of weather vanes, too, from the whimsical to the classical. Add your name to the mailing list to receive their annual catalog. ♦ Daily. 45080 Albion St (between Lansing and Kasten Sts). 937.0323

> "By making this wine vine known to the public, I have rendered my country as great a service as if I had enabled it to pay back the national debt."
>
> Thomas Jefferson

MacCALLUM HOUSE INN

66 MacCallum House $$ This ornate 1882 Victorian was built as a honeymoon haven for Daisy Kelley (daughter of lumber magnate William Kelley) and her husband, Alexander MacCallum. The inn, comprising the main house, carriage house, greenhouse, barn, and water tower, features 22 guest rooms. Most of the rooms in the main house have shared baths, while the more expensive—and larger—rooms have private facilities. All are furnished with period decor, including treasured antiques. The greenhouse has been turned into a rustic redwood cottage with skylights, a private bath, and a wood-burning stove, while the water tower offers one room on each of its three floors with ocean views, two queen-size beds, and a private bath. The fanciest accommodations are in the restored barn, which features an upstairs suite with a private deck. ♦ 45020 Albion St (between Lansing and Kasten Sts). 937.0289

Within the MacCallum House:

MacCallum House Restaurant ★★$$$ Under separate ownership, the restaurant on the first floor offers dinner in the formal dining room or in the more casual cafe and bar area. Start with one of the homemade soups such as seafood chowder or a potato-garlic soup swirled with parsley pesto. The emphasis here is on pasta dishes such as the feathery light spinach-and-ricotta gnocchi or the pappardelle (wide ribbon noodles) with braised rabbit sauce. Main courses might include half a free-range chicken, grilled Pacific king salmon, or lamb chops marinated in rosemary and garlic and served with mint pesto. For dessert, don't pass up the peach crisp or one of the homemade ice creams. The menu changes with the seasons. There is also a good selection of North Coast wines. ♦ Eclectic ♦ M-Tu, F-Su dinner; closed Jan-mid-Feb. Reservations recommended. 937.5763

The first member of the University of California faculty to teach viticulture was Professor Eugene Hilgard, who started instructing in 1880.

The tomb of King Tutankhamen (who died in 1352 BC) included 36 amphoras of wine meant to accompany his spirit on its journey to the afterlife.

---

67 Old Gold Furnished with Oriental carpets, palms, and orchids, this elegant shop specializes in antique jewelry and wedding rings. The store has some top-notch pieces, such as a ruby-and-diamond Victorian bracelet and a 1940s floral diamond-cluster brooch by Cartier (both made of 18K gold), as well as an English Victorian opal-and-diamond ring. It also carries contemporary pieces and a large selection of wedding rings. ♦ Daily. Albion and Lansing Sts. 937.5005

68 Corners of the Mouth You can't miss the old red **Baptist Church** (constructed in the late 1800s) that houses this natural food store. Stop in for organic produce, juices, bottled water, bulk items, or the vitamins you left at home. A wood-burning stove keeps the store extra warm. ♦ Daily. 45015 Ukiah St (between Lansing and Ford Sts). 937.5345; fax 937.2149 &

WILLIAM ZIMMER
GALLERY

69 William Zimmer Gallery Formerly **Gallery Fair,** this is the place for fine hand-crafted jewelry, paintings, and superb handmade furniture created by local and other North American artisans. Everything here is very special—and rather costly. For those looking for the perfect rocking chair, designer Robert Erickson will make one to your measurements. ♦ Daily. 45101 Ukiah St (at Kasten St). 937.5121 &

69 John Dougherty House $$ The severe facade of this hotel, built in 1867, belies its charming interior. There's a small living room with sofas in front of the fireplace and a large veranda with views of the town and the bay beyond. The **Captain's Room** upstairs has an even better view from its private balcony, and the sloping ceiling gives it a cozy feel. Like the **First Mate's Room,** it has a private bath and is decorated with pine antiques and a double-woven, blue-and-white bedspread. Innkeepers Marion and David Wells also offer a two-room suite with a wood-burning stove, a four-poster bed, and a veranda with a view. Another room with a four-poster bed is installed in the water tower; this one has a sitting room and a private bath. They also have two large garden cottages, each with sitting room, private bath, and veranda. ♦ 571 Ukiah St (between Kasten and William Sts). 937.5266

70 Mendocino Art Center In the 1950s, with its studios, summer study programs, and performing arts, this art center became a hub for artists of many types. Today the educational and recreational programs offered in painting, drawing, ceramics, woodworking, and textiles attract students from around the country. This is also the site of the **Helen Schoeni Theater,** home to the **Mendocino Theater Company.** ♦ Daily. 45200 Little Lake St (between Kasten and William Sts). 937.5818 &

71 Reed Manor $$$$ If you'd really rather be in a condominium than in rustic Mendocino, this bed-and-breakfast inn is located on a spectacular piece of real estate overlooking the town, and its guest rooms are furnished with all the conveniences of a big-city hotel— color TV sets (one room even has a second TV in the bathroom for viewing from the tub), VCRs, refrigerators, wet bars, telephones, and answering machines. The five huge rooms and suites boast glitzy French-style furniture, cedar-lined closets, and balconies; three have views of either the ocean or Mendocino (and telescopes are provided so you can get an even closer look at the scenery). For ultimate privacy, the makings of continental breakfast are stocked in each room. ♦ Palette Dr (off Lansing St). 937.5446 &

71 Hill House $$$ The television series "Murder She Wrote" has made this hilltop hostelry famous by using it as a regular setting. The inn has 44 guest rooms, most furnished with brass beds, reproductions of antiques, and lace curtains—all of which sound innocent enough, but the effect is just a bit dowdy. The views are quite good, though. Continental breakfast is served to guests each morning. ♦ 10701 Palette Dr (off Lansing St). 937.0554 &

The oldest grape seeds discovered came from the Republic of Georgia; carbon dating has revealed them to date from 7,000 to 5,000 B.C.

A French immigrant from Bordeaux by the apt name of Jean-Louis Vignes planted the first non-Mission grapes in California at his Los Angeles ranch in the mid-19th century.

The Sebastiani family of Sonoma has the largest collection of carved wine barrels in North America.

Restaurants/Clubs: Red   **Hotels:** Blue
Shops/ ♦ Outdoors: Green   **Wineries/Sights:** Black

Within the Hill House:

Hill House Restaurant ★$$$ The dining room offers wonderful ocean views, an elegant Victorian atmosphere with antique sideboards and oil paintings of 19th-century Mendocino, and a classic continental menu. It serves New York pepper steak and grilled center-cut pork chops, along with several pasta dishes, grilled fillet of salmon, and prawns flamed in brandy. A more casual menu is available in the more casual **Spencer Lounge**: soups, salads, pasta, and sandwiches. Breakfast features straight-forward egg dishes, omelettes, Belgian waffles, and homemade corn beef hash. ♦ Continental ♦ Daily lunch and dinner &

AGATE COVE INN BED & BREAKFAST

72 Agate Cove Inn Bed & Breakfast $$ Scott and Betsy Buckwald moved up the coast from Southern California to run this secluded inn overlooking Agate Cove. The hillside property, with an extensive flower garden of old-fashioned varieties, has cottages scattered around the grounds; all but one have a fireplace and a private deck where you can settle in to watch the ocean. Most of the 10 rooms have four-poster or canopy beds, an attractive country decor, private baths, and TV sets. There is also a breakfast room at the inn with an old wood-burning stove and a spectacular view of the sea. Breakfast is a cheerful, sociable affair, with Betsy cooking omelettes, eggs Benedict, or French toast along with sausages and ham. ♦ 11201 Lansing St (at Heeser Dr). 937.0551

73 Russian Gulch State Park This park includes acres of redwood groves, spectacular ocean views, and 12 miles of hiking trails, including a path along the headlands where visitors encounter an ocean blowhole (a hole in the rocks from which water emerges with tremendous force, resembling a whale's spout). There are entrancing views of the village of Mendocino along the path, and some trails head inland to meet the enormous **Jackson State Forest** to the east. The park has specially marked trails for horseback riding and bicycling. There are also 30 campsites, plus a small camp for equestrians. ♦ Fee per vehicle. Hwy 1 (2 miles north of Mendocino). 937.5804

74 Caspar Pass through this quiet town, with its white, steepled church, and a scattering of old cottages and farmhouses, and it's hard to imagine that this was once the site of one of the busiest lumber mills along the Mendocino Coast. So much lumber was produced here, in fact, that the Caspar Lumber Company, which closed in 1955, ran its own fleet of ships to sail it down to San Francisco.

75 Jug Handle State Reserve This park is home to the five-mile **Ecological Staircase Trail,** a hike through a series of hundred-foot-high terraces that were cut out of the landscape by waves eons ago. Each "step" is 100,000 years older than the next, and at the end of the trail you'll find the **Pygmy Forest,** with dwarfed cypress and pine trees. Pick up a brochure at the ranger's headquarters before setting off to explore. ♦ Hwy 1, 1 mile north of Caspar

Fort Bragg

Founded as a military outpost to supervise the Mendocino Indian Reservation, Fort Bragg, six miles north of Mendocino, later became an important logging and fishing town and the largest city along the Mendocino Coast. It's a working-class town and has little of Mendocino's carefully preserved charms, except for the row of restored buildings and historic facades located where **Highway 1** turns into **Main Street.** Otherwise you'll just see rows of motels, gas stations, and stores. Fort Bragg is, however, home of the **Skunk Train,** a narrow-gauge engine that departs from the refurbished **California Western Railroad Station** twice a day for the trip to **Willitts,** 40 miles to the east.

76 Mendocino Coast Botanical Gardens It took retired nurseryman Ernest Schoefer 16 years to clear the 47 acres he bought on a bluff overlooking the ocean at Fort Bragg. He purchased the property in the 1960s to create a showcase botanical garden, making the trails and planting rhododendrons and other flowering plants. Spring is the best time to visit, when the rhododendrons and roses are in full bloom. Major plant collections here include heathers, fuchsias, succulents, ivies, and camellias, so there is always something of interest to look at. In all, the garden is home to hundreds of varieties of native and cultivated plants. You can follow a trail into the headlands, where it's possible to see the gray whales on their annual migration. If you want to make an afternoon of it, there is a shady picnic area. The gardens are owned by the nonprofit Mendocino Coast Recreation and Park District and are supported by admission fees, sales of plants, and a volunteer staff. The gift shop sells garden-related items and works by local artists. ♦ Admission. 18220 Hwy 1 (south of Fort Bragg Willits Rd). 964.4352 &

77 Noyo Harbor This working fishing village at the mouth of the Noyo River at the south end of Fort Bragg is a good spot to watch boats enter and leave the tiny harbor. A public boat-launching ramp and a sandy beach are beneath the highway. It's fun to go down to look around, maybe stopping for fish and chips or smoked salmon. Every Fourth of July, Noyo Harbor is the site of what's billed as the world's largest salmon barbecue. ♦ Off Hwy 1 (Harbor Dr exit)

Also at Noyo Harbor:

Misty II Charters Sportfishing and whale-watching expeditions are offered here. ♦ Daily by reservation. 964.7161

Lady Irma II More sportfishing and whale watching expeditions are offered by this charter service. ♦ Daily by reservation. 964.3854

Eureka Fishery ★$ Order fish-and-chips to enjoy on the outdoor deck with a view of the harbor and the boats. Or buy fresh fish for the barbecue or smoked salmon for a picnic at this fresh seafood market. Takeout is available, too. ♦ Seafood ♦ Fish-and-chips stand: M-Tu lunch; W-Su lunch and early dinner. Market: daily. 32410 N Harbor Dr (off Hwy 1). 964.1600 &

78 Georgia Pacific Nursery Look for the greenhouses and nursery on the left as you drive into town. When operating at full capacity, this working nursery contains two million coastal redwood and Douglas fir trees. Visitors can learn about reforestation management and today's lumber business on self-guided tours. The site also includes nature trails with trees labeled with identification plaques. Picnic tables are also available. ♦ M-F Jan-Nov. N Main St (on the west side of the street near Walnut Ave). 964.5651

79 Guest House Museum The home of Charles Russell Johnson, founder of the Union Lumber Company, has been turned into a museum filled with photos, artifacts, and memorabilia from Fort Bragg's days as a logging and lumber center. ♦ Nominal admission. W-Su Apr-Oct. 343 N Main St (west side of the street between Alder and Redwood Aves). No phone

80 Egghead Restaurant ★$ This tiny storefront cafe offers more than 40 types of omelettes, in addition to pancakes, eggs Benedict, and other breakfast dishes, along with freshly squeezed orange juice and espresso drinks. For lunch, there are salads, sandwiches, and half-pound burgers. ♦ Cafe ♦ Daily breakfast and lunch. 326 N Main St (between Redwood and Laurel Sts). 964.5005 &

80 Carol Hall's Hot Pepper Jelly Company
Try Hall's line of hot pepper jellies, which come in four varieties, along with a half-dozen jams, two chutneys, two mustards, a garden salsa, and all sorts of dressings and condiments, plus coffee beans from **Thanksgiving Coffee,** the celebrated local roaster. ♦ Daily. 330 N Main St (between Redwood and Laurel Sts). 961.1422 &

80 Fort Bragg-Mendocino Coast Chamber of Commerce This storefront office offers good advice on what to see and do along the North Coast. ♦ M-Sa. 332 N Main St (between Redwood and Laurel Sts). 961.6300, 800/726.2780 &

81 Round Man's Smoke House For fans of smoked meats and poultry, it's hog heaven here. At the counter, owners Marilynn Thorpe and Stephen Rasmussen turn out smoked chinook salmon and albacore, plus some terrific peppered salmon jerky. For picnics, consider the small specialty hams, boned and lean, or the smoked chicken breast, both fully cooked and ready to eat. They also have a corned beef brisket. All of their smoked products are vacuum-packed for a shelf life of six to eight weeks. Mail order is also available. ♦ Daily. 137 Laurel St (between Franklin and N Main Sts). 964.5954, 800/545.2935; fax 964.5438 &

81 The Restaurant ★$$ Just around the corner from **Round Man's Smoke House** (see entry above) is this savvy eatery, where you can get a sandwich made with **Round Man's** smoked turkey breast, avocado, and fontina cheese, or a burger and salad. Somebody in the kitchen must be Italian, because they offer a typical Tuscan dessert—a glass of *vin santo* (an amber dessert wine) with biscotti. At dinner, the creative cooks turn out Mediterranean fare

along with a few Asian-style dishes. It's a welcome respite from the crowds in Mendocino. Live jazz is featured on Friday and Saturday night. ♦ Eclectic ♦ M-Tu, Sa dinner; Th-F lunch and dinner; Su brunch and dinner. 418 N Main St (between Laurel St and Pine Ave). 964.9800 &

81 North Coast Brewing Company ★$$ A handsome cream-colored building trimmed in green houses this local brew pub. Belly up to the bar for a glass of Scrimshaw, a Pilsner-style beer; Old No. 38, a dry stout; or the firm's best-known brew, Red Seal Ale, a copper-red pale ale. You can eat light or hearty, choosing from a menu of sophisticated pub grub. Try the Texas-style Championship Chili (made without beans), the Cajun black beans and "dirty" rice, or the half-pound burgers served with fries. The mixed grill of prawns, chicken, and spicy sausage, served with black beans and rice, is great, as are the grilled local salmon and one-and-a-half-pound slab of spareribs slathered in the pub's own barbecue sauce. For dessert, there's Mendocino Mud Cake, a fudgy confection topped with whipped cream, or a fruit cobbler. ♦ Pub ♦ Tu-Sa lunch and dinner. 444 N Main St (at Pine Ave). 964.BREW &

82 Fort Bragg Farmers' Market Everyone from backyard growers to high-school agriculture students to farmers sets up shop in front of **City Hall** to hawk fruits, vegetables, and flowers. The market is run by **Main Street,** a state program that revitalizes and preserves historic downtown areas. They draw the crowds with their produce (almost all organically grown), which is sold just hours after being picked. ♦ W 3:30-5:30PM May-Oct. N Main and Laurel Sts. 961.0360

83 Skunk Train Named for the noxious fumes the early gas engines gave off, this narrow-gauge railroad has been making the run from Fort Bragg to Willits since 1911. Step up to the spiffy restored **California Western Railroad Station** in downtown Fort Bragg to get tickets for the six- to seven-hour round-trip ride through 40 miles of redwood forest and mountain passes. On the way, the train crosses 31 bridges and trestles. Less avid rail fans may sign up for a half-day trip, traveling only to Northspur and back. Refreshments, such as hot dogs and cold drinks, are available at **Willits Station,** and restaurants are within walking distance.

♦ Day trips are daily except Thanksgiving, Christmas, and New Year's Day. Half-day trips are daily in the summer; Saturday and Sunday only in the winter. Reservations recommended. Foot of Laurel St. 964.6371 &

84 MacKerricher Beach State Park Just north of Fort Bragg lies this state park blessed with one of the longest stretches of sandy beach in California. Picnic among the dunes or explore the miles of trails by foot or bike. From November through April, follow the wooden boardwalk to the whale-watching platform. Two of the most popular activities here are marveling at the tidepools along the coast and observing the seals from the rocks. The park includes 143 sites for camping. ♦ Off Hwy 1, 3 miles north of Fort Bragg. 937.5804

85 Westport Fifteen miles north of Fort Bragg is the coastal town of Westport, with its rich heritage of New England–style architecture left over from the days when this was the largest seaport between San Francisco and Eureka. Once the railroad from Fort Bragg to Willits was completed in 1911, the seaport lost its importance. Now it's better known as the gateway to Mendocino's Lost Coast, the wild stretch of seashore north of Westport where Highway 1 turns inland. The only access to the coast is a dirt road that travels 21 miles into the **Sinkyone Wilderness State Park** (see below). ♦ Along Hwy 1, 15 miles north of Fort Bragg

86 Sinkyone Wilderness State Park This 1,576-acre park on the Lost Coast is rugged country, unspoiled and unsettled, with unforgettable ocean views, secret beaches, and secluded campsites. Inside the park are two dozen back-country campsites, which can be reached only by foot. Camping in vehicles is permitted only at **Usal Beach**, at the southern end of the park. The primitive campsites all have a picnic table and barbecue pit. For more details contact the park ranger at the visitors' center in a turn-of-the-century house at **Needle Rock**. ♦ 50 miles north of Fort Bragg via Hwy 1 and County Rd 431. 986.7711

Bests

Margaret Fox, Chris Kump, Tricia Priano
Cafe Beaujolais, Mendocino

An early-morning jog or walk along **10-Mile Beach,** north of **Fort Bragg.**

A canoe trip up **Big River** in **Mendocino.**

The **Mendocino Coast Botanical Gardens** in Fort Bragg.

Steelhead fishing.

Ocean kayaking.

A picnic on the headlands in Mendocino.

Riding the **Skunk Train** from Fort Bragg to **Northspur.**

A walk to the waterfalls in **Russian Gulch State Park.**

A trip to any of the rhododendron nurseries in Fort Bragg at the end of April or May.

Wine tasting along **Highway 128** from **Boonville** to the coast.

A hike up the ecological staircase at **Jug Handle State Park** in **Caspar.**

Madeleine Kamman
Director, School for American Chefs, Beringer Vineyards, St. Helena

Sunset on the **Silverado Trail** in **Napa Valley.**

Picking grapes for the vintage at **Schramsberg Vineyards** in **Calistoga.**

A massage in Calistoga.

Dinner at **Terra** in **St. Helena.**

Lunch on the terrace of **Domaine Chandon** in **Yountville.**

Chamber music concerts in the cellars at **S. Anderson Vineyards** in St. Helena.

New Year's Eve at **Meadowood Resort** in St. Helena.

Touring the art galleries of Napa Valley.

Helen M. Turley
Wine Maker

An hour's massage by Frank Hughes, owner of **Nance's Hot Springs** in **Calistoga**—the ultimate in pain-and-tension relief.

Lunching at **River's End** in **Jenner**—completely undiscovered original food with an emphasis on just-caught fish.

Climbing **Mount St. Helena**. On a clear day you can see the ocean and the snow-topped Sierra.

Jack Cakebread
Wine Maker/Owner, Cakebread Cellars, Rutherford

Early morning (sunrise) in **Napa Valley.**

A walk through the vineyards tasting the grapes.

A balloon ride over Napa Valley.

A quiet lunch with my wife on our patio.

My "commute" to work—a two-mile walk through the vineyard.

Quiet feeding of our sheep, piglets, and ducks each day.

Winter days with spectacular clouds and rain in front of the fireplace.

The hectic pace of harvest—the thrill after all is done.

Meeting people from all over the world.

Entertaining (lunch and dinner) guests from many walks of life.

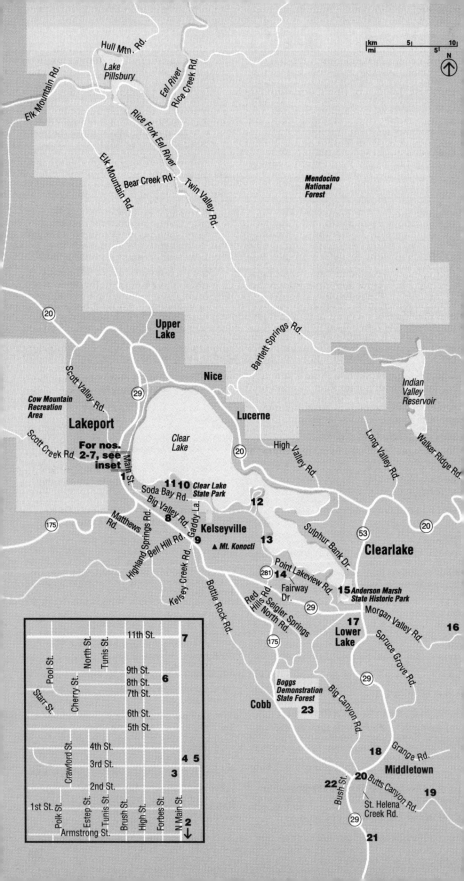

For nos. 2-7, see inset

km 5 10
mi 5
N

Hull Mtn. Rd.

Lake Pillsbury

Eel River

Rice Creek Rd.

Elk Mountain Rd.

Rice Fork Eel River

Bear Creek Rd.

Elk Mountain Rd.

Twin Valley Rd.

Mendocino National Forest

20

Upper Lake

Bartlett Springs Rd.

Nice

Scott Valley Rd.

29

Cow Mountain Recreation Area

Lakeport

Scott Creek Rd.

Clear Lake

Lucerne

20

High Valley Rd.

Long Valley Rd.

Indian Valley Reservoir

Walker Ridge Rd.

Main St.

1

11 10

Clear Lake State Park

12

Soda Bay Rd.

Big Valley Rd.

8

175

Matthews Rd.

Highland Springs Rd.

Bell Hill Rd.

Gaddy La.

9

Kelseyville

▲ Mt. Konocti

13

Sulphur Bank Dr.

53

20

Clearlake

Kelsey Creek Rd.

Point Lakeview Rd.

281

14

Fairway Dr.

29

15

Anderson Marsh State Historic Park

Bottle Rock Rd.

Red Rd.

Seigler Springs Hills Rd.

Hills North Rd.

Morgan Valley Rd.

17

Lower Lake

16

Spruce Grove Rd.

175

29

Boggs Demonstration State Forest

23

Cobb

Big Canyon Rd.

18

Grange Rd.

Middletown

22

Bush St.

20

Butts Canyon Rd.

19

29

St. Helena Creek Rd.

21

11th St.

7

North St.

Tunis St.

Pool St.

9th St.

8th St.

6

7th St.

Cherry St.

Starr St.

6th St.

5th St.

Crawford St.

4th St.

3rd St.

4 5

2nd St.

3

1st St.

Polk St.

Estep St.

Tunis St.

Brush St.

High St.

Forbes St.

N Main St.

2
↓

Armstrong St.

Lake County

Due north of Napa County and east of Mendocino County, Lake County is dominated by **Clear Lake,** California's largest natural lake and the county's main tourist attraction. With no big cities and only a sprinkling of towns, most on the shores of the lake, this region offers the great outdoors in a wine-country setting. The feeling around here is small-town and rural, comfortable and unpretentious. Asking a question will spark a conversation—on wine, weather, or the state of the country. Even more refreshing, you won't find busloads of tourists crowding you at the tasting bar or fanatical connoisseurs bent on putting yet another notch in their wine-tasting belts. It's hard to get too stressed-out or competitive about visiting wineries here because there are just a handful—a couple lie on the **Kelseyville/Lakeport** side of the lake (and only **Konocti Winery** can be visited), and a few more are located at the southern end of the lake near **Middletown** and the **Napa** border.

But there's plenty to do besides winery-hopping. Winery visits in Lake County could fit easily into a day of golfing, boating, or hiking among the redwoods. Summer events in Lakeport include the Lakeport Revival, a June festival of classic cars, motorcycles, and boats; the Lake County Rodeo at the county fairgrounds in July; and the Lake County Fair held in late August and early September. Lake County is also the site of **Anderson Marsh**, a large wetlands nature preserve rich in Indian history and wildlife habitats. Clear Lake's great fishing (lots of bass, catfish, and crappie) is one of the county's biggest draws. So catch that fish and pop that cork. This could be the life.

While there are only a handful of wineries now, this is not a new region for wine. Grapes were planted as early as the 1870s in Lake County, and just after the turn of the century, when people flocked to the lakeside resorts, the county boasted 36 wineries. Then, just like today in Napa Valley and Sonoma Valley, the rich and famous were getting involved in wine making. The celebrated British actress Lillie Langtry bought an estate in **Guenoc Valley** in the 1880s and brought a wine maker over from Bordeaux to make her wines. Before things really got going, though, Prohibition closed the wineries, and farmers had to turn to other crops. It's only been a few decades since the vineyards were replanted with grapevines, but in that short time, Lake County has reestablished itself as an up-and-coming wine region. Its production is still very small, however, accounting for less than five percent of the total wine grapes grown on the North Coast.

One way to visit Lake County wineries is to make a day trip, starting from **Guenoc Winery** in Middletown and following the lake to Kelseyville and Lakeport. (Unfortunately **Kendall-Jackson** no longer offers wine tasting at its Lakeport vineyards, though you can still visit its tasting room in Healdsburg.) If you decide to stay overnight to take in the sights, resorts along the shores of Clear Lake offer a wide variety of lodging, from the luxurious **Konocti Harbor Resort and Spa** to several moderate and inexpensive family resorts.

---

1 **Lake County Visitor Information Center** The dynamic, interested staff has the low-down on everything about Clear Lake and its surroundings. The center also has a great view of the lake from the parking lot. ♦ M-Sa June-Sept; Tu-F Oct-May. 875 Lakeport Blvd (off Hwy 29), Lakeport. 263.9544, 800/LAKESIDE; fax 263.9564 ₺

2 **Lakeport Chamber of Commerce** This office will provide you with information on Lakeport and Lake County lodging, restaurants, activities, and events. ♦ M-F. 290 S Main St (at Martin St), Lakeport. 263.5092; fax 263.5104

3 **Lake County Museum** Housed in the **Old Courthouse,** a stately 1870 Georgian building that was the county seat until 1958, this museum has a wonderful collection of local Indian artifacts, including intricate Pomo baskets, arrowheads, tools, and polychrome baskets adorned with feathers. Historical photos provide a glimpse of how the lake and town looked in the days of steamships and old spas. Upstairs the displays change and may include collections of old clocks, gems, and musical instruments. The museum also houses a research library and a genealogy

library. ♦ Donation requested. W-Sa. 255 N Main St (between Second and Third Sts), Lakeport. 263.4555

4 Bicycle Rack This full-service shop sells and repairs bicycles. The owners, Brian and Norma Aldeghi, also rent mountain bikes and single-speed bikes by the half or full day. No tours are available. ♦ M-Sa. 350 N Main St (at Third St), Lakeport. 263.1200 ♿

5 Park Place ★★$ Partners Nancy Zabel and Barbara Morris had just the right idea when they put together this popular cafe. A garden at a friend's farm supplies the vegetables, herbs, and greens—all picked fresh every morning. The menu concentrates on light fare, including soups, salads, sandwiches, and a few special daily entrées. You can eat inside at one of the booths or take your food outside onto a deck with a view of the lake. None of the food here is ordinary. The soups are all prepared with homemade stocks, such as the fresh mushroom soup with thyme and cream and Nancy's Italian vegetable soup (everybody's favorite), which is chock-full of seasonal vegetables. They also make their own pasta and top it with an array of homemade sauces. There's always a New York steak on the menu, as well as fresh fish, such as grilled sea bass with ginger butter. For dessert, don't hesitate to order the blackberry sorbet (the blackberries are from their own patch). Best of all, they serve throughout the afternoon, so you can stop by whenever your body cries out for food after a spell of wine tasting. ♦ Eclectic ♦ Daily lunch and dinner. 50 Third St (at N Main St), Lakeport. 263.0444; fax 263.4837 ♿

5 Park Place to Go ★★$ If you're planning to spend the day at the lake, order a gourmet picnic to go from this new eatery run by **Park Place** owners Nancy Zabel and Barbara Morris. The menu changes daily but might include Mediterranean pasta salad and grilled chicken sandwiches on freshly baked baguettes. Beer and wine are also available. ♦ Eclectic ♦ Daily lunch and early dinner May-Sept; M-F lunch and early dinner Oct-Apr. 54 Third St (at N Main St), Lakeport. 263.1033 ♿

5 On the Waterfront Rentals of jet skis, pedal boats, ski boats, water skis, patio boats (which accommodate up to 14 people), and fishing boats are available here. ♦ Daily. 60 Third St (at N Main St), Lakeport. 263.6789; fax 263.6353 ♿

6 Forbestown Inn $$ Just a block from the lake, this bed-and-breakfast dates from 1863, when Lakeport was still called Forbestown (in honor of early settler William Forbes). Furnished with oak antiques, the inn has just four guest rooms, and all but one share a bath. The largest is the **Bartlett Suite,** with a king-size bed and a private sitting area. The **Sayre Room** features a queen-size bed and a private bath with a Victorian claw-foot tub; like the **Henry McGee Room,** it adjoins the library. On the grounds are lots of trees and a secluded garden with a large pool and hot tub. Innkeepers Jack and Nancy Dunne thoughtfully offer their full country breakfasts at two different times; not only that, they ask what you'd like to eat the night before. Choose from omelettes with bacon, ham, or sausage on the side; eggs Benedict, which Nancy serves with homemade hollandaise sauce; or Jack's sourdough Belgian waffles. They also offer afternoon tea with desserts and wine and cheese, and have bicycles available for guests who want to ride into town or along the lakeshore. ♦ 825 Forbes St (between Eighth and Ninth Sts), Lakeport. 263.7858; fax 263.7878

7 Skylark Motel $ Reserve early for this moderately priced lakefront motel with 45 comfortable, conventionally decorated units. Accommodations include poolside rooms, housekeeping cottages with one or two bedrooms (rented by the day, week, or month), and fancier suites (some with kitchens) in a one-story building with lake views and patios. It also has a boat-launching ramp and dock. ♦ 1120 N Main St (at 11th St), Lakeport. 263.6151; fax 263.7733 ♿

8 Konocti Winery Situated in a former walnut orchard a little north of Kelseyville, this winery may lack a bit in ambience, but it makes up for it with well-made, attractively priced wines. It was started in 1979 by a group of small Lake County grape growers who mostly focused on red varietals. Since white wines were particularly strong on the market at that time, they developed blush wines first, but lately they've been concentrating on premium varietals. Wine maker John Clews produces Fumé Blanc, Riesling, and Chardonnay, along with Merlot, Cabernet Sauvignon, Sémillon, and Cabernet Franc. Guests are welcome to use the large lawn and shaded picnic area, as well as to inspect the small demonstration vineyard. ♦ Tasting and sales daily. Hwy 29 (at Thomas Dr), Kelseyville. 279.8861; fax 279.9633 ♿

9 Holdenried Farms This attractive country gift shop is stocked with collectibles, snowy linens, candles, handmade pottery, and baskets stuffed with samplings of wine, dried pears, kiwis, honey, wild rice, walnuts, and other goodies. Owner Marilyn Holdenried, a fifth-generation Lake County farmer, grows Bartlett pears and wine grapes. ◆ M-Sa. 3930 Main St (between Second and Third Sts), Kelseyville. 279.9022 &

10 Clear Lake State Park Each year thousands of people visit this spectacular park at Soda Bay on the southwest shores of beautiful Clear Lake, the largest natural lake in California. The park covers a diverse terrain, from 1,400-foot elevations all the way down to lake level. There are four developed campsites, plus numerous picnic sites and several miles of hiking trails. The three-mile **Dorn Trail,** rated moderately strenuous, winds through forests of oak and chapparal to emerge now and then in fields of wildflowers; the easy quarter-mile, self-guided **Indian Nature Trail** is designed to show visitors a sample of the local tribes' in-depth knowledge of native plants. The picnic area along the east side of Cole Creek has tables and barbecues, and, if you're lucky, you might catch a crappie, catfish, or largemouth bass to cook for lunch. (The Department of Fish and Game periodically restocks the lake, so the fishing is usually very good.) Indigenous fish include blackfish, Sacramento perch, and tule perch. The park also has a fine swimming beach and a boat launch. Stop at the visitors' center (west of the boat-ramp parking lot) for more detailed information about lake resources and activities. A large aquarium will introduce you to some of the fish that live in Clear Lake. ◆ Fee per vehicle. Entrance to the park is via Soda Bay Rd, north of Kelseyville. 279.4293

Within Clear Lake State Park:

Cole Creek Campground Set in the shade of oaks and cottonwoods next to an open meadow, this campground is very popular during the hot summer months. The 26 individual campsites are flat, suitable for tents and RVs (up to 24 feet long). ◆ Call up to eight weeks in advance to make reservations. 800/444.7275

Kelsey Creek Campground This camp- ground has 53 sites, as well as two sites for people with disabilities, and most of the campsites have a view of the lake. Each will accommodate a tent or RV (up to 35 feet long). Reserve early for this campground area; spaces go quickly. ◆ Call up to eight weeks in advance to make reservations. 800/444.7275

Within Kelsey Creek Campground:

Lakeside Premium This site has 10 camp- ing spots right on the shoreline that accom- modate tents and RVs (up to 21 feet long). Campers may even pull their boats onto the beach. ◆ The campground fills up quickly, so call up to eight weeks in advance to make reservations

Lower and Upper Bayview Campground Located in a shady grove of oaks and buckeyes, this campground features some

sites with good views of the lake. It is also quite close to the swimming beach. Each of the 56 sites has a flat area for a tent; several spots can accommodate trailers and RVs (up to 21 feet long). Shower facilities are located at the entrance to the **Upper Bayview Campground.** Call up to eight weeks in advance to make reservations. 800/444.7275

11 Oak Barrel ★★★$$ Fresh seafood is the specialty of Brian and Marcie Cline's popular restaurant located a few miles from downtown Kelseyville. Cozy touches include a fireplace, knotty pine walls, and antique tables and chairs (some for sale). Brian, the chef, prepares a dynamite rendition of Cajun-style blackened fish, which might be swordfish, shark, or ahi tuna depending on the catch of the day. Steaks cut to order, lamb, and chicken are also always on the menu, and soup and salad come with every entrée. The Sunday night seafood buffet is not to be missed, from oysters and mussels on the appetizer table and fresh salmon pâté to a 25-item salad bar and such entrées as fresh seafood creole and Louisiana-style prawns that you peel yourself. And don't leave without trying Marcie's Lake County Pear Cake (the recipe has appeared in *Bon Appétit* magazine). ◆ Seafood ◆ W-Su dinner. 6445 Soda Bay Rd (off Gaddy La), Kelseyville. 279.0101 &

12 Buckingham Golf and Country Club This nine-hole golf course sits at the foot of the inactive volcano Mount Konocti. The golf course and clubhouse restaurant are open to the public. ◆ Daily. 2855 E Lake Dr (off Soda Bay Rd), Kelseyville. 279.4863

13 Konocti Harbor Resort $$$ The fanciest place to stay in these parts is at the 250-unit resort at the foot of Mount Konocti on the shores of Clear Lake. All the rooms, suites, apartments, and cottages come equipped with phones, cable TV, and air- conditioning. And even in the lowest price range,  some rooms have views. Deluxe apartments feature king-size beds (or two double beds), a sofa bed in the living room, a kitchen, and a large balcony; every four units share a barbecue. The most secluded accommo- dations are the **Haven Apartments,** which have two double beds and a full kitchen. The beach cottages, set on a large lawn that leads down to the lake, are the most popular. If decor is important to you, consider the fancier apartment suites that are furnished with whitewashed pine.

The staff will arrange for fishing, boating, waterskiing, and other sports, or even services at their multimillion-dollar **Dancing Springs Health and Fitness Spa** (see page 194).

The tennis complex (with eight regulation courts) overlooks the lake, and a pro is on hand to teach you the basics or help you brush up on your backhand. Two championship swimming pools ensure that it's never too crowded to swim, and there are a couple of wading pools for children. The resort also provides a playground, a recreation center for teenagers, and a miniature golf course. There's a fully equipped marina with boat rentals, a boat-launch ramp and hoist, a fueling station, and a bait-and-tackle shop. Guests also get preferred starting times at any of the local golf courses. The resort sponsors concerts year-round (everything from country music to classic rock) and offers special room rates for concertgoers. ◆ 8727 Soda Bay Rd (off Hwy 29), Kelseyville. 279.4281, 800/862.4930; fax 279.8575 ᚛

Also at Konocti Harbor Resort:

Konocti Princess During the summer months this 64-foot, Mississippi-style paddleboat sails out of the **Konocti Harbor Resort**'s marina for a two-hour tour of Clear Lake. The boat is a double-decker with room for a hundred passengers, and as it moves along at a stately pace, the captain will point out the sights. ◆ Tours: Th-Su July-Sept

Dancing Springs Health and Fitness Spa This spa offers a number of half- and full-day packages at very affordable prices (that is, compared with the luxury resorts in Napa and Sonoma). You can sign up for massages, facials, or even an herbal body wrap, or forgo all that and head straight for the spa's steam room, sauna, and whirlpool. Day-use privileges include exercise classes, workouts in the fitness room, and use of the lap pool (a small fee is charged both for hotel guests and outsiders). You can also get your hair done and your legs waxed, and for true hedonists, the spa offers an almond-mint body scrub and a special honey-mango or seaweed bubble bath. ◆ Daily. Reservations recommended for massages, facials, and spa packages. ᚛

Konocti Landing Restaurant ★★$$$ Every Sunday year-round, the resort's formal dining room offers an impressive Champagne brunch buffet featuring a choice of entrées ranging from eggs Benedict to chicken Kiev, as well as waffles, made-to-order omelettes, salads, and seafood. In addition, the restaurant serves dinner on Saturdays and Sundays in summer (except when the resort is hosting a concert). The menu features hearty preparations of steaks, seafood, and pasta dishes. ◆ Continental ◆ Sa dinner, Su brunch and dinner Memorial Day through Labor Day; Su brunch the rest of the year. Reservations recommended. ᚛

Mallard's Cafe ★$$ You'll find typical breakfast fare and burgers, sandwiches, pasta specials, and much more on this cafe's varied menus. On Friday and Saturday evenings, a seafood and prime rib buffet is offered. ◆ Continental ◆ Daily breakfast, lunch, and dinner. ᚛

14 Clear Lake Riviera Golf Course This is another nine-hole golf course at the base of Mount Konocti. It's also open to the public, and there's a restaurant here that serves Sunday brunch and dinner Wednesday through Saturday. ◆ Daily. 10200 Fairway Dr (off Soda Bay Rd), Kelseyville. 277.7129

15 Anderson Marsh State Historic Park A state park since 1983, this site is rich in Indian artifacts and wildlife. It was inhabited by Native Americans for more than 10,000 years. Located at the southern end of Clear Lake, the park includes more than 50 percent of the lake's remaining wetlands. A paradise for bird-watchers, the marsh counts numerous American bald eagles among its feathered residents. More than 151 species have been identified in the park, including herons, marsh wrens, mallard ducks, and great egrets.

The best way to observe the marsh's wildlife is by boat, which you can rent nearby (call **Garner's Resort,** 994.6267, or **Shaw's Shady Acres,** 994.2236). You can also hike through the 170-acre **McVicar Preserve,** which is run by the **Redbud Audubon Society.** The **Audubon Society** hosts a nature walk on the first Saturday of every month at 9AM, but you can take the hike on your own and finish at the picnic tables at the end of the trail. ◆ The official schedule is Friday through Sunday year-round, but the park is accessible the rest of the week as well. During off hours, park across from the entrance. On Hwy 53 between Lower Lake and Clearlake. 994.0688

16 Homestake Mining Company's McLaughlin Mine A few times a month during the tourist season, the Homestake Mining Company offers tours of one of the largest working gold mines in the country. The interesting one-and-a-half-hour tour demonstrates how the mine extracts one ounce of gold from seven tons of ore. ◆ Tours are scheduled May through October; for more information, call the Lake County Visitor Information Center in Lakeport (see page 191). Reservations required. Morgan Valley Rd (off Hwy 29)

17 Wildhurst Vineyards Wine maker Kathy Redman produces Merlot, Zinfandel, Chardonnay, Sauvignon Blanc, Pinot Noir, and an award-winning Matillaba (a blend of Sémillon and Sauvignon Blanc) at this winery located a mile south of Lower Lake. ◆ Tasting, sales, and tours daily. 11171 Hwy 29 (just north of Spruce Grove Rd). 994.6525, 800/595.WINE; fax 279.1913 ᚛

17 Lower Lake Historical Schoolhouse & Museum This Lake County museum opened in 1994 in the restored **Lower Lake Grammar School,** which was built in 1877 and is now a state historic site. Inside are a reconstructed classroom from the late 1800s to early 1900s, an extensive geological display donated by the Homestake Mining Company, a scale model of the dam on Cache Creek, and collections from pioneer families. ♦ W-Sa. 16435 Main St, Lower Lake. 995.3565 ♿

18 Crazy Creek Gliders and Skydivers With its 4,200-foot grass strip, the **Middletown Glider Port** is home to this company's experienced glider pilots. You can sign up for a ride high above the Lake County landscape or take gliding lessons. For those who own their own gliders, they'll tow your plane aloft. And for the particularly adventurous (or insane!), there's also the **Crazy Creek Skydiving School.** ♦ Daily. Hwy 29 (southwest of Grange Rd), Middletown. 987.9112; fax 987.2494

Guenoc

19 Guenoc Vineyards Estate and Winery Six miles east of downtown Middletown lies this large estate, once owned by British actress Lillie Langtry, who bought the property in the 1880s as a country retreat. She thought she'd try her hand at running a vineyard and imported a wine maker from Bordeaux to help her, but Prohibition intervened before they could get the experiment off the ground. When the current owners, Bob and Orville Magoon, bought the 23,000-acre estate and built their well-equipped winery in 1982, they decided to feature Lillie's portrait on their labels. There's a view of the vineyards and Langtry's Victorian house from the winery and tasting room. Hoist a glass of the Cabernet to her memory and vision. The winery also produces Sauvignon Blanc, three Chardonnays, two Meritage reds, a Petite Sirah, a Port, and several other wines. ♦ Tasting, sales, and tours M, Th-Su. 21000 Butts Canyon Rd (off Hwy 29), Middletown. 987.2385; fax 987.9351 ♿

20 Channing Rudd Cellars This very small winery started out in founder Channing Rudd's home in Alameda (near Oakland) in 1976. A graphic designer with a love of good wine, Rudd designed his own label and moved up to Lake County in 1982 to produce Chardonnay, Cabernet Sauvignon, Cabernet Franc, and Merlot. ♦ Tasting and sales by appointment only. 21960 St. Helena Creek Rd (at Hwy 29 and Butts Canyon Rd), Middletown. 987.2209

21 Horne Winery The first winery you'll encounter on the drive north on Highway 20 from Napa Valley, it is owned by the Horne family, who have been grape growers since the 1970s. Now, they offer their wines to the public at their tasting room just south of Middletown. The winery focuses on Sauvignon Blanc and Chardonnay. ♦ Tasting and sales M, Th-Su. 22000 Hwy 29 (near Rancharia Rd), Middletown. 987.3743, 987.3503

22 Lake County Visitor Information Center This small branch of the main office in Lakeport is open only a few days a week in the summer. Volunteers provide information about Lake County, Clear Lake, and their surroundings—including, of course, Lake County wineries. ♦ M, Th-Su mid-May to mid-Sept. 21337 Bush St (off Hwy 29), Middletown. 987.0707

23 Boggs Demonstration State Forest The purpose of this park is to demonstrate forest-management practices; ask the forest manager for a tour if you're interested. Otherwise just enjoy the groves of pine and fir trees on this ridgetop site on Boggs Mountain. The forest has miles of trails for hiking, horseback riding, and mountain biking. There are 14 primitive campsites (which are currently in poor condition) with tables and fire rings; you can park near the campsites. The campground is operated on a first-come, first-served basis. ♦ Hwy 175, 1 mile north of the tiny town of Cobb, at the State Fire Station sign. 928.4378

History of the Wine Country

Native American tribes lived in this fertile California paradise for thousands of years, thriving off the bounty of the land by hunting, fishing, and gathering. Many tribes shared the area, including the Miwok, Wappo, Pomo, Yuki, and Wintun.

1542 After repeated attempts by Spaniards Hernán Cortés and Viceroy Antonio de Mendoza to explore the coast north of Mexico, Juan Rodríguez Cabrillo first sights Alta (upper) California.

1579 Englishman Sir Francis Drake and his ship, *The Golden Hind,* find safe harbor at Drake's Bay near Point Reyes in Marin County.

1603 Mexican explorer Sebastián Vizcaíno sets off from Acapulco to explore the coast of Northern California and changes many of California's old Spanish place-names along the coast.

1775 Spanish explorer Juan Francisco de la Bodega y Cuadro discovers the bay that now bears his name (**Bodega Bay,** about an hour-and-a-half north of San Francisco).

1776 The **San Francisco Mission and Presidio** is founded.

1808 Russian fur traders explore Bodega Bay.

1811 The Russians build **Fort Ross** on the coast just north of the **Russian River,** and hunt for sea otters.

1821 California becomes a far-flung province of independent Mexico.

1822 The Russians build the **Fort Ross Chapel** with hand-hewn redwood.

1823 The first recorded expedition into **Napa County** is made when Padre José Altimira scouts sites for his northernmost California missions. He selects **Sonoma** and founds **Mission San Francisco Solano de Sonoma,** bringing Mission grapes with him to plant in the fertile valley.

1834 General Mariano Guadalupe Vallejo secularizes the mission and establishes a presidio in Sonoma; one year later, he surveys the site of the Sonoma plaza.

1836 George C. Yount, a pioneer from North Carolina, receives the **Rancho Caymus** land grant: 12,000 acres in the heart of what is now **Napa Valley** and the town of **Yountville.**

1841 Cyrus Alexander is given a 120-acre land-holding in the Russian River region that is eventually named after him (**Alexander Valley**).

1843 The impoverished English surgeon Edward Turner Bale marries General Vallejo's niece and receives the **Rancho Carne Humana** land grant, encompassing the whole northern Napa Valley.

1846 The Bear Flag Revolt in Sonoma. General Vallejo is imprisoned and an independent California Republic is proclaimed; 25 days later, the US steps in to halt the rebellion, and the American flag flies over Sonoma.

1847 While tracking bear, hunter William B. Hackett discovers geysers in the **Russian River Valley** and describes his find as "the gates of the inferno."

1848 Gold is discovered at Sutter's Mill in the foot-hills of the Sierra Nevada, heralding the Gold Rush.

1850 California gains its statehood.

1852 German immigrant William Kasten, lone survivor of a shipwreck off the Pacific coast, is washed ashore and builds a cabin in the area now known as **Mendocino.**

1857 After tasting General Vallejo's wines, Agoston Haraszthy realizes the potential of wine making in the region and soon founds **Buena Vista,** California's oldest winery.

1857 Lieutenant Horatio Gates Gibson is ordered to establish a military post on the Mendocino Indian reservation; the site of that military post is now the city of **Fort Bragg.**

1858 Millionaire Samuel Brannan purchases a tract of land in Napa Valley to establish a hot-springs resort and plant a vineyard. Ten years later he establishes the town of **Calistoga.**

1861 Governor Downey commissions Agoston Haraszthy to go to Europe and bring back cuttings of European grape varieties. Haraszthy returns from his venture with 100,000 cuttings of 300 varieties.

1864 The first formal vintage celebration in California history is held at Agoston Haraszthy's Pompeian-style villa near Sonoma; the guests of honor are General and Mrs. Mariano Guadalupe Vallejo.

1869 The transcontinental railroad is completed and California wines are shipped to the Midwest and the East Coast.

1871 Prospector Charles Evans excavates the **Petrified Forest** near Calistoga, and is thereafter known as "Petrified Charlie."

1874 A destructive root louse called "phylloxera" begins to attack Sonoma vineyards planted with European vines and eventually destroys much of California's vineyards before it is discovered that vines can be grafted onto native American rootstock resistant to the pest.

1876 Frederick Beringer establishes the **Beringer** winery in **St. Helena.**

1878 Luther Burbank moves from Massachusetts and begins his horticultural experiments in **Santa Rosa.**

1880 Robert Louis Stevenson and his bride, Fanny, spend their honeymoon in a deserted miner's cabin on the slopes of **Mount St. Helena,** an experience the author memorializes in his book *The Silverado Squatters.*

1888 British actress Lillie Langtry purchases an estate in the **Guenoc Valley** and hires a wine maker from Bordeaux to start a winery.

1895 Samuele Sebastiani arrives in the US from Tuscany and makes his first wine, a Zinfandel, a few years later.

1906 The Great San Francisco Earthquake hits; the epicenter is near Santa Rosa.

1909 Author Jack London settles permanently at his **Glen Ellen** estate, **Beauty Ranch.**

1919 National Prohibition is voted into law and hundreds of wineries close throughout California.

1933 Prohibition is repealed, but only a handful of wineries that produce sacramental wines or wines for medicinal uses are still in operation.

1935 The University of California at Berkeley Department of Viticulture and Enology, the leading research and training institute in wine making and viticulture, moves to the University of California at Davis.

1937 The completion of the Golden Gate Bridge opens a new era of business and travel between San Francisco and the North Coast.

1938 André Tchelistcheff, wine consultant extraordinaire, arrives in California from Europe.

1943 Newspaperman Frank Bartholomew buys and reopens the old **Buena Vista Winery,** which had closed after the 1906 earthquake.

1950s A handful of abandoned wineries are acquired, mostly by outsiders moving to the wine country from San Francisco.

1956 James D. Zellerbach, former owner of **Hanzell Vineyards** in Sonoma, decides to try aging his wines in *barriques* (French oak barrels from Burgundy), creating a trend among local vintners.

1964 Jack and Jamie Davies buy the **Schramsberg** winery near Calistoga.

1966 Robert Mondavi builds his winery in **Oakville,** ushering in a new wine-making era in Napa Valley.

1968 Americans now drink more dry table wine than dessert wine.

1975 The French Champagne house of **Moët-Chandon** builds its Napa Valley winery, **Domaine Chandon.**

1976 The famous Paris tasting, organized by Paris wine merchant Steven Spurrier, changes the world's preconceptions that California produces inferior wines; a blind tasting of Chardonnay and Cabernet Sauvignon is conducted with an expert panel of French tasters and results in top honors for two Napa Valley wines: the 1973 Château Montelena Chardonnay and the 1973 Stag's Leap Wine Cellars Cabernet Sauvignon.

1979 The first vintage of **Opus One** is launched. The brainchild of Robert Mondavi and Baron Philippe de Rothschild of **Mouton-Rothschild, Opus One** becomes the inspiration for a number of Bordeaux-style wines to come.

1980s Foreign investment in the California wine country increases. Producers from Europe enter into joint ventures with American vintners or establish their own California-based wineries.

1991 Attempting to balance the state's budget, California legislators increase the excise tax on wine production from one cent to 20 cents per gallon (still much lower than the US average of 70 cents). To the consumer this equals about a 10-cent increase per bottle.

1995 One of the worst winter rainstorms of the century hits Napa, Sonoma, Mendocino, and Lake Counties in late March. The deluge of rain floods hundreds of acres of vineyards and pounds the delicate leaf buds on many grapevines. However, because the vines are not yet in bloom, the damage is not extensive.

Wine Glossary

acidity: Refers to a wine's tartness. Acidity comes from a grape's natural acids and keeps wine from spoiling during the fermentation and aging processes.

aerate: To allow a wine to breathe (come in contact with air) by decanting. You can also aerate a wine by swirling it around in a glass, which releases aroma.

age-worthy: Describes a wine that has the potential to age. Not all wines are suited for aging. What determines age-worthiness is the varietal, the vintage, the style of vinification, and the balance of tannins, acids, and fruit in the wine.

aging cellar: Where wines in a cask or bottle are aged. Traditionally, the cellar or cave was underground or tunneled into a hillside, where a steady, cool temperature was naturally maintained. Today it can be any structure that is dark and has temperature control that's suitable for aging wine.

appellation: The geographic region a wine's grapes are grown in. To be classified by state, such as "California," 100 percent of the grapes used for the wine must come from that state. For a county designation, such as "Sonoma County," a minimum of 75 percent of the grapes must come from that area. And for a more specific American Viticultural Area (AVA) designation, such as "Guenoc Valley" or "Anderson Valley," at least 85 percent is required.

aroma: The fragrance of a wine (it's redolent of the grape from which it was made). It can be sensed through smelling and tasting.

barrel fermented: When wine has been fermented in small oak barrels, instead of the usual stainless-steel tanks. The technique requires more wine-making skill, but results in a wine with a more complex flavor.

barrique: The name for a type of wooden barrel used in the Bordeaux region of France. Made of oak, the small barrel holds 225 gallons of wine and is widely used by California wine makers, particularly for aging Chardonnay, Cabernet Sauvignon, Merlot, and Pinot Noir.

Blanc de Blancs: White wine, particularly a sparkling wine, made from white grapes. The term originated in the Champagne region of France to distinguish more delicate Champagnes from those made with both white and red grapes.

Blanc de Noirs: White wine made from "black" or dark grapes (i.e., red grapes). In Champagne, France, where the term originated, it refers almost exclusively to Pinot Noir. The color of the grapes resides in the skins; if the juice is separated immediately from the skins, the juice will remain clear. In California, Blanc de Noirs also refers to so-called blush wines, such as White Zinfandel or White Cabernet, which are tinged with color.

blend: A wine created from several grape varietals (e.g., a Cabernet Sauvignon and Merlot blend or a Sémillon and Sauvignon Blanc blend). A wine can also be a blend of wines from different vintages.

blind tasting: When a group of wine "tasters" meets to compare a selection of wines. The participants know which wines are featured in the tasting, but they don't know in what order the wines are being poured into their glasses. In a **double-blind tasting,** the wines as well as the order of the pouring are unknown. In both situations, the wines are usually disguised in plain brown paper bags until their identities are revealed at the end. This is done so the tasters' ratings and comments will not be influenced by the label or by any previous knowledge of the wine producer.

blush wine: The term used in California to describe the pale rose-colored wines made from red grape varieties including Zinfandel, Cabernet Sauvignon, or Pinot Noir. (See **Blanc de Noirs.**)

body: The way a wine feels on your tongue. Body may range from thin and light to full and heavy. Heaviness results from a wine's solids (sugars, glycerine, and pigments).

Bordeaux-style: See **meritage.**

botrytis or Botrytis cinerea: A beneficial mold known as noble rot (or, in French, *pourriture noble*) that creates tiny pinpricks on the grapeskin. As the liquid content of the grape evaporates, the sugar content becomes increasingly concentrated, so much so that when the grapes are crushed and the wine is fermented, not all of the sugar is transformed into alcohol. A certain amount of residual sugar remains, creating a dessert wine, such as late-harvest Riesling.

bouquet: The fragrance or scent of a wine that develops from the aging process. It tastes and smells more pronounced in a bottle of mature wine.

Brut: This French term for very dry Champagne is widely used in classifying sparkling wines throughout the world. Champagnes range from sweet to very dry. (See "Wine Varieties" on page 133.)

cask: A large wooden container, usually oak, built much like an oversized barrel with oval or round heads joined by curved staves. Casks are generally used to age or store wines. Sometimes the face of the barrel is ornately carved.

cave: The French word for cellar. Also refers to the tunnels hollowed out of hillsides used as aging cellars.

cellar: Where wines are made, stored, and aged. It may also refer to the act of storing wine while it ages.

crush: The period immediately after the harvest when the grapes are shipped to the winery, crushed, and made into wine; it's also another term for the grape harvest itself.

current release: The most recent vintage on the market. For white wines it is usually the previous year, but for red it can be two or more years earlier, depending on how long a producer ages each wine before releasing it to the marketplace.

cuvée: A French term that denotes a particular lot or blend of wine. It can be wine from a special barrel, such as **Stag's Leap Wine Cellars'** famous Cask 23 Cabernet Sauvignon, or a special blend that has a higher proportion of grapes from an especially good vineyard or from a particular variety.

decanting: The process of pouring wine from the bottle into another container. This is only necessary if the wine has sediment on the bottom.

dessert wine: Sweet wines, such as a late-harvest Riesling or Gewürztraminer, that are served with dessert or as dessert.

dry wine: Wines that lack sweetness; generally those with less than 0.5 percent residual sugar.

enology: The art and science of wine production. This field covers every aspect of producing wine, from the harvest and pressing of the grapes to the fermentation, aging, and bottling of the wine. An enologist is professionally trained in this science.

estate wines: Wines made from grapes grown by or supervised by the winery estate instead of grapes bought by the estate on the open market. The idea is that if the wine maker has control over the quality of the grapes, and all goes well, the quality of the wine should be consistent from year to year.

fermentation: The segment of wine production in which the sugar in grape juice is turned into alcohol by the enzymes in yeast.

fining: The process of clarifying wine by adding such ingredients as clay, raw egg whites, or gelatin. These products drag the wine's suspended particles to the bottom of the tank.

French oak: When a winery boasts that a particular wine has been aged in French oak, this refers to the barrels (or *barriques*) and the wood they are made from. Currently, a French oak barrel costs more than $600; the barrel imparts an oaky flavor to the wine for only a few years, so it can be quite an investment. After a few years have passed the barrels are called "neutral."

generic wines: These wines do not come from one specific grape variety. The wine's name, such as Chablis or Burgundy, reflects that it's a general type of wine. A generic wine is different from a *varietal* or *proprietary* wine.

horizontal tasting: A tasting in which all the wines come from the same year or vintage. Participants rank the wines and try to distinguish the characteristics of the wines of that particular year.

jug wine: Inexpensive wines that are typically sold in jugs; they are of a lower quality than bottled wines. They are usually generic, but sometimes they may be a varietal wine.

late-harvest: Wines made from extremely ripe grapes and/or grapes affected with *Botrytis cinerea.*

lees: The sediment young wines develop in a barrel or tank as a result of fermentation or aging. When the wine is transferred to another container or "racked," which happens several times before it is bottled, the lees remain behind. Sometimes a wine is deliberately left "on the lees" for a period of time in order to develop a more complex flavor.

library wines: Wines that come from the winery's "library" of older vintages. These are sometimes offered for tasting, so that visitors can get a sense of how wines evolve as they age, and many are sold only at the winery.

magnum: A large bottle that holds the equivalent of two regular bottles of wine. Often preferred by connoisseurs because the wine ages more slowly in the larger bottle, resulting in the development of more complex flavors.

meritage: The name used for Bordeaux-style blends of California wines in which the predominant grape is below the 75 percent minimum required to bear a varietal label, yet the quality of the wine is such that calling it mere "table wine" would be a disservice. To honor these top-notch blends of Cabernet Sauvignon, Merlot, Cabernet Franc, and other varieties for reds, or Sauvignon Blanc and Sémillon for whites, the term *meritage,* combining the words merit and heritage, was coined. (The word was chosen in a national contest that attracted more than 6,000 participants and was won by Neil Edgar of Newark, California.)

méthode champenoise: The traditional method of making sparkling wine in the Champagne area of France in which a special cuvée (or blend) is bottled, and a precise amount of sugar and yeast is added to induce a second fermentation inside the bottle, thereby trapping the bubbles that are a by-product of the fermentation process.

microclimate: Refers to a vineyard's particular combination of soil, angle of exposure to the sun, slope, altitude, weather, temperature, and other factors, all of which influence the quality of the grapes.

nonvintage: Describes a wine that bears no particular vintage date. For example, many Brut Champagnes or sparkling wines are nonvintage, because they are actually a blend of wines from more than one year. The fact that a wine has no vintage does not necessarily mean that it is of inferior quality.

nose: The scent of a wine as determined by smelling alone. This is different from *aroma* and *bouquet,* which can still be sensed after tasting.

old vines: Grapevines that are typically more than 50 years old and are prized for the quality of grapes they produce. Old vines are less vigorous and produce fewer grapes, but they have a more concentrated flavor.

phylloxera: The plant louse that ravaged the world's vineyards in the late-19th century. The pesky insect actually comes from America's East Coast (where the native grapevines were resistant to its attack) and was accidentally introduced to Europe in 1860 when it arrived in the roots of vine cuttings exported for experimental purposes. It was not until most of the vineyards of Europe and later Russia, South Africa, Australia, New Zealand, and California (where European varietals had been planted) had been destroyed that scientists came up with a solution: grafting European grape varieties onto disease-resistant American rootstock. This is still the practice today, although it doesn't completely eliminate the problem. In the early 1990s, many California vineyards were faced with yet another phylloxera threat, forcing some Napa and Sonoma wineries to replant their vineyards.

press: The wine-making apparatus that recovers the juice after the grapes have been crushed, and later recovers the wine after the fermented must (pulp, seeds, and skins) has been discarded.

proprietary: A winery's exclusive right to the brand name created for its own use. Examples include Trefethen's **Eschol Red** and **Opus One,** created by the **Mouton-Rothschild** and **Robert Mondavi** collaboration.

rack: The process of clarifying wine by transferring it from one storage container to another.

reserve or private reserve: This term has no legal definition in California and is often used to denote a producer's top-flight wines. A reserve may be a special blend or may come from a special vineyard; in some cases the term is used to designate wines that are aged longer than a regular bottling before release.

residual sugar: The grape sugar that is unfermented in a wine.

rootstock: The stem and root of a non-fruit-producing grapevine to which wine-grape varieties are grafted. Growers choose a rootstock according to its level of pest-resistance (see **phylloxera**) and other qualities that will benefit the grafted grapevine.

second or secondary label: In addition to a premium line, many wineries produce a second line of wines under a different label. These may be less expensive wines or wines made in a different style.

single vineyard: Designates a wine made from grapes grown in one particular plot.

sparkling wine: A wine that has gone through a second fermentation, resulting in bubbles.

sweet wine: Wine that generally has at least one percent residual sugar. Sweetness becomes noticeable at about 0.5 percent residual sugar.

tannin: This compound is what makes your mouth pucker when tasting a red wine and is the cause of a wine's astringency. Tannins come from grape skins, seeds, and stems.

varietal: A wine called by the name of the specific grape used to make it, such as Cabernet Sauvignon or Chardonnay. In California, a varietal must include at least 75 percent of the named grape.

vertical tasting: Tasters compare different vintages from one estate to understand how the wines age and how consistently the estate performs under varying conditions.

vinification: The conversion of fruit juice into wine through the fermentation process.

vintage: The year the grapes were picked and the wine was produced. Champagne and sparkling wines are often nonvintage wines—that is, they are made from a blend of wines from different years.

vintner: One who takes part in the process of making wine.

viticulture: The cultivation of grapes for wine production.

wine maker: See **vintner.**

Index

200

Index

Restaurants

Only restaurants with star ratings are listed below. All restaurants are listed alphabetically in the main (preceding) index. Always call in advance to ensure a restaurant has not closed, changed its hours, or booked its tables for a private party. The restaurant price ratings are based on the average cost of an entrée for one person, excluding tax and tip.

★★★★ An Extraordinary Experience
★★★ Excellent
★★ Very Good
★ Good

$$$$ Big Bucks ($30 and up)
$$$ Expensive ($20–$30)
$$ Reasonable ($15–$20)
$ The Price Is Right (less than $15)

Hotels

The hotels listed below are grouped according to their price ratings; they are also listed in the main index. The hotel price ratings reflect the base price of a standard room for two people for one night during the peak season.

$$$$ Big Bucks ($200 and up)
$$$ Expensive ($150–$200)
$$ Reasonable ($100–$150)
$ The Price Is Right (less than $100)